# THE
# RENOVATION
# BOOK

# THE RENOVATION BOOK

## A Manual for Self-Reliance in the Home

### DAN BROWNE

**MCGRAW-HILL BOOK COMPANY**

New York    San Francisco    St. Louis    Toronto

ALSO BY DAN BROWNE:
*The Housebuilding Book*

Book design by Stan Drate

123456789MUBP79876

Library of Congress Cataloging in Publication Data

Browne, Dan.
    The Renovation Book.

    Includes index.
    1.   Dwellings—Remodeling—Amateurs' manuals.
I.   Title.
TH4816.B76        643'.7        75-25987
ISBN 0-07-008488-2

# Acknowledgments to:

Michael Porter, who took all the pictures.
Harold and Mathew Klosty, Klosty Hardware Co.
Emmy and Bruce.
Michael, Richard, Don, Yen, Joe, and Norman, who
helped do the work.

*For Joshua and Lila*

# CONTENTS

# Contents

**3** **Plumbing**

**4** **Renovation Carpentry**

## Flooring

## Masonry

# Contents

**7**

## Kitchen Cabinets and Counters

**8**

## Finishes

# INTRODUCTION

The purpose of this book is to enable the reader to do electrical, plumbing, and other building trades work in his or her own apartment or home by demonstrating how I do the identical work professionally.

A good part of the material is based upon my recent renovation of a 4000-square-foot Manhattan apartment, but I have also drawn from a great many other renovations and more than 100 new custom houses I have built. I have personally done all the work discussed many times, and my techniques have evolved out of this firsthand experience.

I have always made the transmission of my skills to inexperienced people working with me an integral part of every job; this has taught me the specific difficulties people new to the work are likely to have. I have also had additional on-the-job training as a result of running a building school in San Francisco where, during the course of two years, 125 students and I built two new houses and performed dozens of renovations on a commercially competitive basis. I have anticipated difficulties by using techniques designed to eliminate the "skill" from "skilled" operations wherever possible, a trend that exists in the construction industry as a whole. I have also focused on the actual working process so that mere information isn't all the reader has to work with in this book, but also a thorough and detailed demonstration of how each particular undertaking is successfully accomplished from start to finish.

Each chapter is devoted to a particular building trade and composed of those items one is most likely to encounter in the course of a renovation or repair of a malfunction. Before work is begun on any particular job, read the entire pertinent chapter to obtain general information which may have been omitted from the segment relating specifically to that job to avoid repetitiveness.

None of the work presented is beyond the capacity of an inexperienced man or woman, a conviction I have arrived at on the basis of results over many years. If this book helps toward self-reliance by enabling anyone to do his or her own "skilled" work, its purpose will have been achieved.

# DEMOLITION

**1**

## Removing Debris

Before any demolition is begun in the interior of a house or apartment, arrangements to remove the debris must be made. On major jobs, a container is usually rented and placed at the street curb near the front door, but for an individual it may be more economical to lease a dump truck or arrange with the owner of one to remove the unwanted material. In an apartment, one can often make a deal with the superintendent of the building to dispose of the rubble, particularly if it has been placed in easily removable cardboard boxes. (Rubble is heavy; these boxes shouldn't be larger than 3 feet on any side or they will be hard to handle and may break.)

Keep in mind that the rubble of a demolished wall will be one cubic foot for every square foot of wall removed.

As demolition proceeds, the debris will accumulate rapidly. It should not be allowed to reach the point where it impedes work or creates a hazardous condition. A wheelbarrow and pointed shovel will be useful tools in handling the rubble. (Later, the same wheelbarrow can be used for mixing and moving masonry material.) A wheelbarrow costs under $50 and will pay for itself in labor saved even if the amount of work contemplated is not extensive.

Since the debris resulting from interior demolition is mainly masonry, a hat and work gloves as well as a filter mask should be worn. The mask will substantially reduce the amount of plaster dust inhaled. Prompt removal of debris will further reduce the inhalation health hazard and increase work efficiency.

## Structural Considerations

A wall was removed to enlarge the kitchen and provide space for an island counter (a counter accessible on all four sides) and appliances. Before its demolition I had to consider whether the wall served a structural function. Was it holding up the ceiling or a wall above it, and would anything collapse as a result of its removal?

Kitchen after demolition

Floor joist supported by brick side wall

Kitchen after renovation

Except for tenements, most apartment buildings have interior "curtain" walls which divide space but have no structural significance. They are usually erected after the framework and exterior walls have been completed, and when they are removed, the structure of the building is not affected.

This is also true in townhouses where wooden joists (structural members that support the floors) extend from one exterior brick wall to another and are supported by these walls. Interior walls therefore very often serve no structural function. Occasionally, a townhouse may have had an addition built in the back yard. The original rear wall will then appear as an interior wall but in fact will be a "bearing" wall and must be treated as such. Since renovation work in urban and suburban areas rarely involves alterations of bearing walls, our discussion will be limited to interior-wall demolition.

Electrical Considerations

Parents and teachers caution children about the dangers of electricity and instill a fear of it. This is, of course, legitimate, but the fear continues into adulthood, and a great many people shy away from any physical contact with electricity. Unfortunately, we live in an environment in which electricity plays a large part. Here and throughout this book, whenever I deal with electricity it is with an awareness of the fears most people have and the lack of practical experience that has resulted.

I have done every electrical operation described here many times. Not one is dangerous. Nevertheless, the work should be done with concentration and none of the precautions skipped.

I have taught wiring to many people and have built up an inventory of mistakes inexperienced people are likely to make. "My way" of doing electrical work is to eliminate all possibility of

Tester in live outlet

"shocks" and other unpleasantness. My purpose is to enable totally inexperienced people to cope with their electrical needs in a totally safe manner.

Before demolition is begun, it is necessary to locate and cut off all current to live electrical positions in the wall to be removed. The device in the photo is an electrical tester that can be bought in any hardware store for a couple of dollars. It is used to determine whether electrical current is present in wires, receptacles (outlets), fixtures, etc. It consists of a light bulb in an insulated sheath and two wires called "leads." Insulation has been stripped from the ends of the leads to expose the copper wires, and these ends are placed inside a receptacle (outlet) in the same way one would plug in an appliance. If the bulb lights, the receptacle is said to be "live" or "hot." To remove current from this receptacle and any other live electrical positions in the wall to be demolished, we must first locate the "main."

The two mains shown in the photographs are typical in older structures. The main is a metal box into which electricity is fed into the apartment or house and through which it is distributed and controlled. In an apartment it will most often be located in the kitchen; in a house it will be in the basement or another readily accessible area. In newer installations, the main will contain

Typical apartment main

Typical apartment main

"breakers" instead of fuses which perform the same function. These breakers may be thought of as switches and they have the advantage of being reusable when they are tripped by a short or by overloading. A breaker is reset after the cause of the tripping has been removed by simply pushing it fully to the Off position, then flipping it back to the On position. Whatever the size of the main and whether it contains fuses or breakers, it always serves the same function and is dealt with in the same way. It is from here that the current to all electrical installations is cut off.

I place the leads of the tester into a receptacle in the wall to be demolished. If the light bulbs goes on, I know the outlet is hot. A helper standing at the main then partially unscrews the first fuse and continues down the line of fuses in sequence until the tester light goes out. The end of each fuse makes contact with copper at the back of the fuse holder and as it is unscrewed, a gap is created and the contact broken. When the tester light goes out I

3

call to the helper that this has occurred. He then turns the fuse clockwise until the light goes on, to double-check that we have located the correct fuse. *He then unscrews the fuse completely.* This is an added precaution to make sure that this particular fuse controls the outlet that I have been testing. Also, if the fuse is only partially unscrewed, an accidental movement may cause it to make contact again. Removing the fuse completely eliminates this possibility.

This fuse may control only this one outlet or it may—and probably does—control other outlets and light fixtures, not necessarily all in the same room. All the outlets and lights controlled by the fuse are said to be on the same "circuit," and removing the fuse will cut off the current to all of them.

In the wall to be demolished there may also be a "junction" box. This is a metal box, usually round or hexagonal, rarely larger than 4 inches in diameter, covered by a blank plate. Behind the plate,

Junction box, cover plate on

which is removed by unfastening the two machine screws which go through it, are various wires which have been joined together.

After the cover plate has been removed, *all* power in the apartment must be cut off. If the main is the type previously shown, the two cylindrical fuses can be removed and all the power in the apartment will be cut off. If the main has a main switch, all power can be cut off by simply moving the switch to the Off position. Otherwise *all* the fuses in the main must be unscrewed.

With all the power cut off, the wires in the junction box can be separated in safety. I separate them either by unscrewing the Bakelite caps (called wire nuts or solderless connectors) or by cutting away the tape over the ends of the wires. I then restore power to the junction box by rescrewing the fuses in the main, replacing the cartridge fuses, or placing the main switch in the On position.

The ends of all the wires in the junction box will have had their insulation removed. I place one lead of the tester against the end of a wire and the other lead against the metal box. If the wire is hot, the bulb of the tester will light. My helper now unscrews fuses as if I were testing a receptacle and removes the fuse through which power to that line is being delivered.

The only other electrical position that may be in the wall to be demolished is a switch. If it controls an operative light, the fuse that governs it can be removed without the use of the tester, since the fuse controlling the light controls the switch.

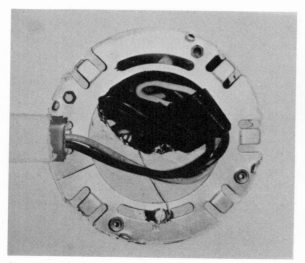

Same junction box, cover plate off

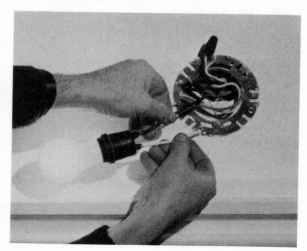

Testing for hot wires in junction box, one tester lead on wire, other on metal plate

If the switch is not controlling an operative light, I shut off *all* the power, remove the two screws on the switch cover, and remove two additional screws that become visible after the plate is removed. These two screws lie at the top and bottom of the switch and hold it to the metal box in the wall. I pull out the switch and *make sure that there is no contact* between the metal box and the ends of the wires attached to the two large screws on the switch. I then put the power back on.

I place one lead of the tester against the large screw on the side of the switch, to which the end of a wire has been attached. I place the other lead against the metal box. If the wire is live the bulb will light. I remove the fuse that controls it. If the tester doesn't light up, I repeat the procedure on the second wire, attached to the second switch terminal. If the tester bulb again doesn't light, no power is being delivered to the switch.

*Remember, before any demolition is begun, check all electrical positions in the wall to be demolished and remove the fuses in the main that control them.*

## Removing Plumbing

Two sinks, back to back, are on opposite sides of the wall to be demolished. They are supplied by hot and cold water pipes and a drain pipe that carries away the waste. (There is also a vent, but that doesn't concern us at this point.)

Water to the sinks is controlled by valves, one for the hot and another for the cold. In newer installations these valves are directly below each sink or fixture, which makes replacement and maintenance more convenient.

In older buildings such as the one we are dealing with (built in 1904), this is rare. Very often the valve which controls the flow of water to one fixture also controls water to other fixtures and its location will lie at a convenient place between the two. Sometimes it will be in a closet (in old apartments closets are favorite locations for valves) or in a bathroom, and most often only the handle will be visible. The usual practice is to run the cold water riser (the pipe which rises through the building, most often in a straight line, with a valve on each floor) against an exterior wall. The pipe itself will be hidden by plaster while part of the valve is exposed.

The hot water riser usually runs inside a curtain wall and is wrapped with insulation. By convention it is always placed to the left of the fixture, whether sink, shower, tub, or basin.

In every instance the valves needed to shut off the water to any fixture will be located in the apartment.

Cold water main valve on riser

The cold water valve in the photo is located in the kitchen at the exterior wall. The hot water valve is a foot off the floor, part of it embedded in the wall to be demolished.

I open both taps of both sinks and turn both valves clockwise as far as they will go until water stops coming through the faucet.

To remove the sinks, I first loosen a large nut which lies under each sink below the strainer. I do this with a tool called a channel-lock pliers. This separates the sink from the waste line.

Channel-lock pliers on slip nut to separate waste line from sink

A channel-lock pliers is an essential tool for plumbing work. It is light, widely adjustable, and convenient for placement in tight positions.

I next detach the water lines from the sink. If there is a union in the pipes directly under the sink, it is simplest to unscrew the nut of these fittings. Turn the nut counterclockwise until it has cleared the threads of the male part of the union. (When threads are on the outside of the pipe the end is called male, when insde the pipe, female.) All fittings, unless otherwise stated, are loosened by turning counterclockwise and tightened by turning clockwise.

Union, together and apart

If there are no unions, I free the water lines by detaching nuts directly under the ends of the faucet.

These nuts are less accessible than unions but if there are no unions in the water lines, they are the second choice. When they are unscrewed, the sink is detached.

The weight of the sink is carried by a special piece of cast iron mounted on the wall with heavy screws. It is called a hanger bar. ("Backing" wood is usually embedded in the wall to hold the screws.) With the water lines and drain disconnected, the sink is lifted by one person at each end until the prongs on the back of the sink are raised out of the slots in the hanger bar.

For convenience in working, I remove most of the old pipe from the water lines and drain, then stuff paper into the remaining drain openings to prevent debris from clogging them.

The water lines in this apartment are brass, not to be confused with "yellow" brass, a much less durable material easily distinguished by its yellow color. These pipes and their brass fittings, though

seventy years old, are in excellent condition and although plumbing codes in some areas forbid the use of old material in new work, I reuse them since they are equal or superior to anything I can buy today. (They are also valuable as scrap.)

The drain is made of 2-inch galvanized steel pipe. (All pipe sizes are the interior measurement of the pipe. Tubing is designated by its exterior measurement.) The galvanized pipe is worthless.

I remove this pipe with a tool known as a Stilson wrench.

A pipe extremely difficult to turn is referred to as frozen. This 2-inch drain is frozen. I first place a scrap of pipe over the handle of the wrench in order to lengthen it and increase leverage. I then stand on the end and bounce my weight on the extension pipe. This is often enough to free the pipe, but in this case I do not succeed. A propane torch then becomes necessary.

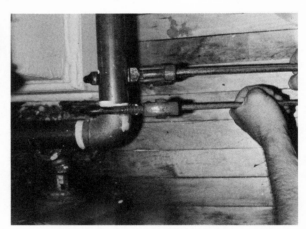

24-inch Stilson wrench on 2-inch drain

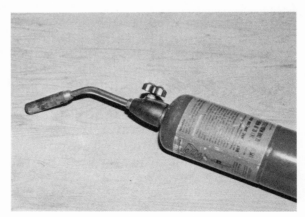

Propane torch

**6**

This propane torch is sold in hardware stores and costs under $8. I direct the flame against the drain pipe and the fitting into which it is screwed. Since the fitting is heavier than the pipe, it expands more slowly. This difference creates a looseness and facilitates turning. (Two minutes of heating is necessary.)

## Removing a Door

I place the swinging door in a fully open position on either side of the wall. This exposes two screws in a metal plate that attach the plate to the floor on the pivot side of the door. I remove the screws with a Yankee screwdriver.

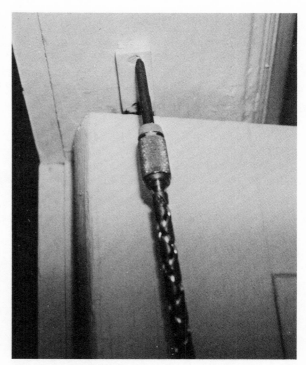

Removing top of swinging-door hardware

Removing screws from lower half of swinging-door hardware

Since screws will often have to be removed or installed during the course of the renovation, this expensive screwdriver is well worth its cost. The bit is removed by pulling back the cylinder immediately behind it with the left hand while pulling the bit forward with the right. Several sizes of ordinary and Phillips-head bits are available for use with the screwdriver.

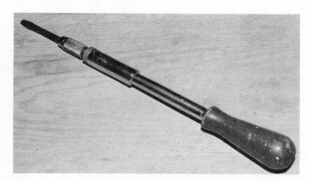

Yankee screwdriver

I swing the door around to the opposite side of the wall and remove the remaining two screws. I slide the bottom of the door toward me. At the top of the door is another metal plate with a protruding pin that fits into a hole which has been drilled into the top of the door. As I slide the door away, it is lowered out of the hole and freed. I will use this door and hardware elsewhere. I place them in a large closet that serves as a general storage area for the material from the demolition which I intend using later.

7

## Removing Door Frames

This door frame is wooden. Ordinarily I don't save frames because of the amount of time required to remove them in reusable condition. However, it is difficult to duplicate the special designs of trim used in old apartments and in this case I save the pieces.

The frame consists of nine pieces. The smooth vertical ones which are as wide as the thickness of the wall are called jambs. The smooth top piece is called the head. On each side of the wall are three pieces which lie flat against the wall. They are called casing or trim.

The tool in my hand is a flat bar and is essential for many operations. I place its tip at the joint between the jamb and side casing, then hammer it

Flat bar

into this joint and pry away from the wall. I have started an inch or so above the floor. At this point the casing is held with a finishing (small-headed) nail and will come away easily for for an inch or so. I raise the flat bar another few inches and pry again. At the bottom, the casing will move out a bit more and I proceed in this way until I have loosened all the nails that hold it to the jamb.

On the thick side of the casing farthest from the jamb there are additional finishing nails which have been driven into the wall. I start at the bottom, hammering the end of the flat bar into the joint between the back of the casing and the wall. Very often this joint is hard to locate since it is covered by numerous coats of paint, but the paint will crack quickly, defining the joint. I proceed up the casing in this manner until all the nails on one side are loose. For greater leverage, I now place a block of wood in the opening I have made between the jamb and casing and pry against it with the flat bar. The tip of the flat bar is against the back of the casing and the back of the bar is against the wood scrap. In this way the casing is not marred during the prying. This will also free the casing completely. I repeat the process to remove the remaining five pieces of casing.

To avoid stepping on the nails in the trim, I remove them immediately if the trim is to be reused. If not, I flatten the nails against the casing.

Once the casing has been removed a gap will appear between the back of the frame and the wall in which additional finishing nails will be visible. These tie the frame to the wall. I place the V at the end of the flat bar against these nails and whack it with a hammer. This will shear the nails and permit the entire frame to be removed from the opening in one piece. (A new frame and trim would cost about $25.)

## Removing Baseboards

At the bottom of the wall, running along its entire length, is the baseboard. In older structures the baseboard is made of three pieces of wood. The largest is a flat 1 x 6 which has been nailed to the wall or to a smaller piece of wood embedded in it called a "ground." The ground is used as a thickness reference during plastering and also serves as backing for the baseboard. On the top edge of the flat 1 x 6 a rounded-over smaller piece is nailed to hide the irregularities of the masonry wall and to prevent the top of the 1 x 6 from becoming a dust-catcher. A third piece is nailed over the joint between the bottom of the 1 x 6 and the floor. This piece is commonly 3/4-inch quarter round and serves to hide the gaps between an uneven floor and the bottom of the 1 x 6. It also makes sweeping easier.

It is not worth trying to save the baseboard unless it has been milled into an unusual shape difficult to duplicate or is a "naturally" finished hardwood that might later be needed elsewhere. If the baseboard is to be saved, the same technique that was used to remove the door frame will serve. If it isn't to be saved, I insert blocks against the wall for increased leverage with the flat bar.

## Removing Masonry

With the current and water off, the door and frame removed, and the baseboard removed, only the masonry wall remains standing, and this is now ready to come down.

The pictured drill is the same type used in filling stations to remove or tighten nuts on a wheel. It has a lateral hammering action in addition to the boring action of an ordinary drill. (Another type which works equally well has a forward hammering action similar to that of the jackhammers used to cut paving on streets.) The bit has a carbide steel tip, which is much harder than ordinary steel and retains its sharpness much longer. The usual wood-boring bit will become hopelessly dull after boring a hole or two in masonry. A carbide bit in an ordinary drill will usually spin without making a hole as it encounters the harder interior core of the

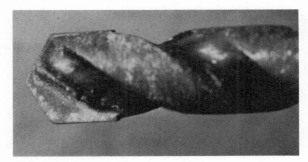
Carbide tip of bit

Structural tile core of wall

wall, and this spinning action will dull the bit very quickly. With the impact drill and carbide bit I can bore through a masonry wall almost as quickly as an ordinary bit in an ordinary drill bores through wood.

The interior core of this wall is made of 4-inch structural clay tile. On top of this is a 3/4-inch layer composed of a mixture of gypsum plaster and sand. On top of this is another layer, roughly 1/8-inch thick, made of a mixture of gypsum plaster and slaked lime. This arrangement is typical in older structures although gypsum block is often used instead of the structural tile.

All masonry walls have little lateral strength until weight is placed on them. The strongest part of a wall is at the very bottom, since this is where most weight is concentrated. I therefore begin at the very top and drill a series of holes a couple of inches apart to approximate the circumference of a circle a foot or so in diameter. I then strike blows on a diagonal with a 2-pound hammer to remove the masonry material between the holes. (It is best to strike a masonry wall on a diagonal since when one hits it head-on one encounters the greatest resistance.)

Impact drill and carbide bit

9

Once this pilot hole has been made, I nail two 8-foot 2 x 4s together. I hold my left hand about three feet up from the bottom, cup my right hand over the end, and use the 4 x 4 as a battering ram. I aim at an angle 3 or 4 inches away from the circumference of the pilot hole. I enlarge the hole in this manner and continue to work outward and downward.

This wall is 14 feet long, 9 feet 6 inches high and 5-3/4 inches thick. It takes three-quarters of an hour to demolish it completely using the technique I have described. It takes more than a day to put the rubble in boxes and, with the wheelbarrow, cart it into the back hallway where the superintendent picks it up.

Several other walls are removed in the same manner, completing the alteration part of the demolition. I am now ready to begin removing renovative material. It is important to do this now since the unwanted material will interfere with the installation of new material.

## Removing Flaking Wall and Ceiling Paint

Flaking paint is best removed by sliding a spackling knife behind the flake and over the plaster until all loose material has been eliminated. There will usually be more loose paint adjacent to the hanging flake; this must also be removed since the new paint will not "glue" the loose portions back to the plaster.

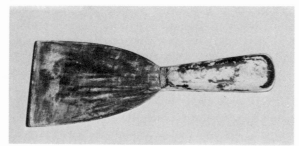

3-inch spackling knife

## Eliminating Cracks and Bulges in Masonry Walls

The pictured crack is common in masonry walls and occurs when a portion of the covering has separated from the scratch coat or the core of clay tile behind it. A mixture of gypsum plaster and sand

Crack in second coat of plaster

Hook scraper and plasterer's hatchet

3/4 inch thick is applied in two coats. The first coat, which lies against the core of the wall, is 3/8 inch thick and has been scored with horizontal indentions for better adhesion of the second coat. (In newer construction, Structolite, a type of gypsum, has for the most part replaced both coats.) The crack may also extend partially into the scratch coat, though this is less usual.

The hook scraper is regularly used as a flooring tool but works well in cleaning out cracks prior to filling them. I insert the corner of the blade into the crack, press, and pull it down along the crack's center. I go to the depth of the crack, which is usually down to the scratch coat. I widen the crack until all loose material has been removed. I do this only when the crack *bulges*, an indication that the masonry has loosened from its bond.

When there is no bulge at the crack or loose masonry behind it, I score the surface of the crack into a V with the hook scraper, going to a depth no greater than 3/16 inch or whatever depth results after making one pass with light pressure.

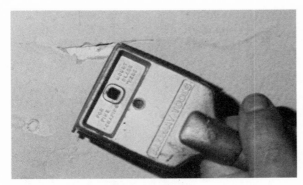

Hook scraper enlarging hair crack

Wood lath and plaster on wood-core wall

In most townhouses, tenements, brownstones, and many old wooden structures, the core of the interior walls and ceilings is wood. Slats of rough wood with 3/8-inch gaps between them are then nailed on top of the core. These slats are called "lath." When the scratch coat is applied to the lath, a portion is pushed through the gaps and sags on the back of the lath to form keys that hold the scratch coat to the lath. The brown coat and final film of plaster and lime are then applied to the scratch coat and the keys hold all three.

At times, particularly on ceilings with wood lath, a portion of the masonry covering will bulge without cracking. This is dangerous since it means that the entire area has pulled loose from the lath although the masonry covering is still bonded to itself. The weight of the sagging area places stress on the surrounding keys. More keys are broken and the sagging area enlarges, creating even greater stress. A larger area of the ceiling may suddenly fall as a result. Any bulge should therefore be removed immediately whether or not there are cracks.

A few blows with the plasterer's hatchet at the center of the bulge will remove the loose masonry.

The periphery of the area should now be examined and all portions removed where the keys are broken and the scratch coat has separated from the lath. One has to be prepared for an unpleasant surprise since it is quite possible that a good part of the ceiling will have to be removed even though the original bulge seemed only a foot or so in diameter.

Where the top of the baseboard meets the wall there is often a multitude of gaps and cracks. The material around these cracks frequently consists of spackle and dried paint. Spackle is a plaster product with a "retarder" to lengthen the time of its workability. Its advantage is easy handling and it is a favorite with painters, who use it to fill baseboard gaps. Its disadvantage is that it cracks easily and has no adhesive quality when placed against wood. It looks good for a short while after it has been applied but begins to crack and separate after a few months. I use the hook scraper to remove the paint and old spackle along the joint. This same problem occurs at the joints of the casing and wall and the casing, jambs, and head in doorways. I deal with it in the same manner.

Another familiar sight is paint flaking and powdering on windows and window frames. Here again the hook scraper laid flat on the material to be removed works well. This should be complemented with a spinner sander.

These two tools may look very similar, but they should not be confused. The first is a sanding tool, manufactured for that purpose, which works very

Spinner sander and drill with sanding attachment

**11**

well. The second is an ordinary drill with a mandril attachment that works very poorly. The ordinary drill revolves 2250 times per minute at maximum speed. This is an adequate speed for boring holes in wood but is far too slow for efficient sanding.

The Miller's Falls spinner sander turns at a speed of 3600 rpm, which is much more effective for sanding, while its 3/8 horsepower permits it to retain most of its speed *while sanding is being done*. With this tool it takes about ten or fifteen minutes to sand away most of the paint on a window and expose bare wood. Around the muntins (pieces of wood that divide the sash, the movable part of the window), I use the hook scraper to remove paint in places I cannot reach with the sander.

## Removing Tile and Linoleum

Vinyl asbestos tile laid directly on the oak floor of the living room is to be removed. The Mastic holding it is nonwaterproof (costing about a third of the price of waterproof Mastic). All the tiles are easily removed by sliding the end of the flat bar under them and lifting. Some of the dried Mastic adheres to the wooden floor. No effort is made to remove the Mastic at this time. An initial rough sanding while redoing the floors will remove it easily.

The linoleum over the kitchen floor was properly installed with a felt underlayment held by waterproof Mastic. (The usual practice is first to install underlayment, which may be heavy tar paper, composition sheets, Masonite, plywood, etc., which reduces the variations in the board floor and provides a smooth surface for the final covering material.) The job of removing properly laid linoleum or tile is neither quick nor easy. It is best to begin where an edge of the linoleum is accessible. In this case it is where the wall had formerly been. The flat bar is laid under the linoleum, jabbed forward, and lifted. This rips away pieces of linoleum. Although the Mastic is waterproof, the area worked on is kept wet with water, which makes the removal process a bit easier. Gasoline works even better as a solvent to loosen the Mastic, but I do not recommend its use because of the fumes and the danger of fire. The most expensive, quickest, and easiest way to remove linoleum (or tile) where good Mastic has been used is to put 20-grit open-coat sandpaper on

the flooring machine and sand it all away. One can combine both methods, using the flat bar first to remove the easiest portions, then using the floor sander and returning to the flat bar when looser patches are encountered.

## Removing Cabinets

We decide not to save any of the wood from the pictured cabinets since the job of dismantling the cabinets and reassembling them elsewhere is far too expensive. I begin by inserting the flat bar between each hinge of each cabinet door and the stile to which it is attached. (Stiles are the horizontal and vertical stationary surface members of the cabinet.) I pull the bar outward, which rips the screws from the stile and frees the door.

Old kitchen cabinets

I next remove the trim around the top by driving the flat bar between the trim and the stile behind it, then pulling toward me.

This exposes a slight gap between the top edge of the stile and the ceiling. Behind the stile there is usually a cleat fastened to the ceiling into which the cabinet frame has been anchored. I drive the flat bar between this cleat and the ceiling and pull downward, working on the outer side of the cabinet away from the intersecting wall. A couple of pulls will usually cause this end of the cabinet to sag. I place a 2 x 4 on edge in the gap between the partially lowered cabinet and the ceiling and jerk downward. The entire upper cabinet comes free.

I remove the lower half of the cabinet in a similar fashion.

In older structures the usual practice was to install the kitchen cabinets before the walls were plastered. The plaster on intersecting walls was then butted to the cabinets. When I removed these cabinets, I found bare block of the side curtain wall against which they had been resting set back several inches from the line of the wall in the kitchen.

I mention this now because, while it is relatively easy to destroy and demolish an area, building and refinishing it to blend into its surroundings is time-consuming. This fact should be kept in mind before ripping anything out, especially when the items are old kitchen cabinets. Many of these, despite their appearance, can be restored much more easily than imagined and often consist of beautifully aged wood put together in a highly professional way. (One should avoid using paint remover, which is expensive, time-consuming, and messy, and use instead a combination of "burning"

and light sanding to restore the cabinets—see page 233.)

(Similar considerations should be taken in relation to doors. Those which are hung on exterior walls or lead to public areas will most always be sheathed in metal. However, interior doors and frames are very often wood and can readily be restored and finished. These "naturally" finished doors require little maintenance and justify the initial expense by eliminating the necessity of frequent painting and cleaning.)

The final step in the demolition stage is to go through each room and closet and to remove all unwanted miscellaneous items such as carpets, drapery hardware, broken toilet seats, unnecessary pipes, and any other items that may have accumulated.

# WIRING

## 2

In practice, at this point, helpers begin preparing walls and ceilings for painting, "roughing in" the plumbing and wiring, setting up to build kitchen cabinets, and a variety of other jobs. For the sake of continuity, I will not follow the actual sequence of work but will instead complete each item that is started. Generally I first do those things which create the greatest mess so that as the job proceeds I will have less and less disarray; when the "finishing" work begins, it will not have to be redone because working nearby has marred it.

## Installing a New Outlet

In the master bedroom, the owners discover that the sole wall outlet is located where they intend to place their bed. Having previously experienced the inconvenience of moving their bed each time they wanted to plug something in, they want this outlet moved to a more convenient position.

I insert the leads of the tester into the outlet and the light bulb goes on.

A helper at the main unscrews the first fuse and calls out "yes" to me. The light bulb still shines and

I call back "no." He tightens the fuse, unscrews the second, and calls out "yes" again. The tester's bulb still shines and I call back "no." We continue this way until he unscrews a fuse and the bulb goes out. I call out "yes." He screws the fuse back and the tester light goes on again. I yell "yes." He then unscrews the fuse completely and removes it.

I now know that no electricity is coming to the outlet and that I may work on it without fear of shocks or shorts.

The plate that covers the gem box and part of the receptacle is taken off by removing the screw in its center. If the plate doesn't come away, paint has probably caused it to stick to the wall. I slip my screwdriver behind the plate and twist to free it.

Two machine screws are now exposed, one at the top and one at the bottom of the receptacle. Both go through horizontal slots that are wider than the shanks of the screws. This allows the receptacle to be shifted to the center of the box to be properly covered by the plate. The heads of the screws are larger than the slots and secure it to the box. I remove these two long machine screws and pull out the receptacle.

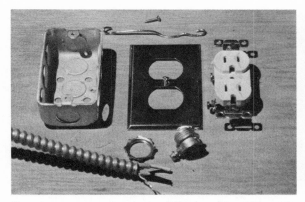

Gem box, cover, receptacle, BX connector, BX cable, receptacle grounding wire

Receptacle removed from box, screwdriver loosening terminal screw to detach wire

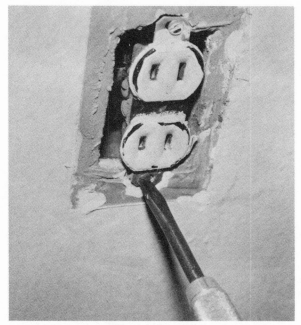

Receptacle with cover plate removed, screwdriver at one of the two screws holding receptacle to box

The receptacle extends for 5 inches or so and is held by two wires (in some cases four) the ends of which are attached to screws (called "terminals") on each side of the receptacle.

On one side the terminals are brass-colored. On the opposite side they are aluminum-colored. The insulation over the wires attached to them is also colored. Most often, it will be black or white. *The black or "hot" wire is always attached to the brass-colored terminal. The white wire (the ground or neutral wire) is always attached to the aluminum-colored terminal.*

When the insulation is dirty and its color hard to identify, I scrape away a bit more insulation at the end of the wire. If this still doesn't reveal the color, a rarity, I make the assumption (usually safe) that the wire attached to the aluminum-colored terminal is white and the other black.

Sometimes one wire is white and the other red, yellow, or blue, etc. By convention and code, the coloring of wires is fixed. *The neutral wire is always white. The hot wire may be any color other than white or green.* (Green is reserved for grounding wire, which is not to be confused with the white neutral wire which—as noted above—is also sometimes referred to as the ground wire.) Almost always, however, in old construction, only a white and a black wire are in the box, or two white and two black.

I loosen the terminal screws on the receptacle and slip out the looped wires, freeing the receptacle.

I take a new gem box and trace its outline on the wall where I intend to install the new outlet. Using the impact drill and carbide bit in conjunction with cold chisels, I remove masonry material within the outline to a depth of at least 2 inches. I want the outer edges of the box to lie flush with the wall or be slightly indented. No special effort is made to make the perimeter of the hole for the new gem box exact since the area around it will later be filled with plaster of Paris.

(It is mandatory to contain the ends of all wires in either metal or plastic boxes. This provides protection against accidental shocks or shorts.)

I draw a line on the wall between the old gem box and the cutout for the new one. I bore a series of

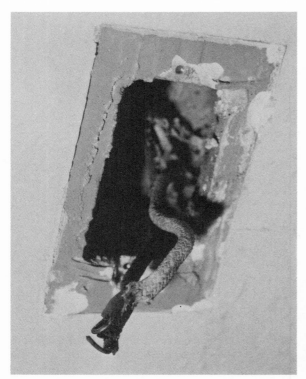

Receptacle removed, one black and one white wire remaining

Several cold chisels

inch-deep holes with the impact drill along this line, spacing the holes an inch or so apart. I remove the masonry between the holes using the impact drill held at a flat angle or by using a cold chisel.

Along the sides of the old and new gem boxes are indented circles called "knockouts." The metal has been stamped and partially cut to facilitate removal. There are several knockouts; I have chosen one on the side of the new box that will face the old box and through which I intend to bring the new wire. I tap the tip of a screwdriver against the circle toward the inside of the new box. This causes the circle of metal to break partially. I grip the circle with pliers, raise and lower it quickly a few times, and break it off. Similarly, I remove a knockout from the old box.

Knockout in box being removed

Channel cut in plaster for BX cable

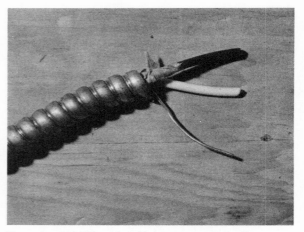

Two-wire #12 BX cable with bare grounding wire

The pictured wire is flexible armored cable commonly called BX. A flexible metal shield protects the wires through which the current will travel. The wires themselves are copper with insulation around and between them. There are two, one white and the other black.

(There is also a third wire which is much thinner, aluminum-colored, with no insulation. This is a grounding wire which can be ignored for the time being.)

Electrical-wire sizes are designated by numbers. As the number increases, the diameter of the wire decreases. For ordinary outlets a #14 wire is used, although I use heavier #12 wire. This is slightly more expensive but provides less resistance to the current and is more economical in the long run. (In some areas, such as New York, #12 wire is mandatory for ordinary light circuits.) BX is the optimum type of cable to use when the wire is to be buried in the wall.

I fold the BX wire about 8 inches from an end and cause the metal sheath to break. (If this is difficult, I can cut through the metal sheath carefully with a hacksaw, avoiding the wire inside.) I twist the wire counterclockwise at the break to unravel a bit of the armor. I then snip the metal with wire-cutting pliers and slip off the 8 inches or so of metal sheathing.

Sharp edges are left at the end of the armor and, to protect the wires from being accidentally cut, I insert a plastic bushing between the outside of the wires and the inside of the armor.

To secure the BX to the boxes, a device known as a BX connector is used. The connector may come built into the box or be purchased separately.

I am using the separate connector. I fold back the noninsulated grounding wire and slip the male half of the connector over the two remaining wires to the point where the armor has been cut. I wind the aluminum-colored noninsulated grounding wire

BX folded to break armor

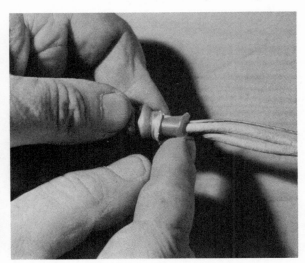

Plastic bushing being inserted between wires and armor

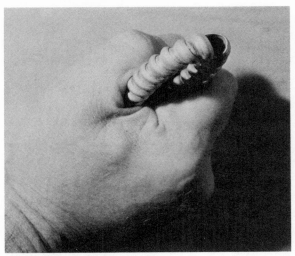

Wire-cutting pliers completing cut of broken armor

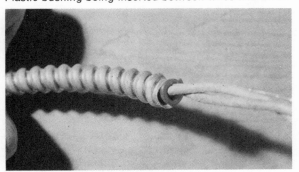

Plastic bushing in place

**17**

BX connector, apart and assembled

Grounding wire attached to BX connector screw

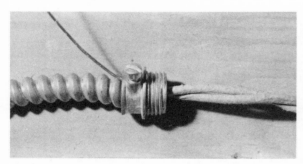

Grounding wire pulled back, male half of connector on cable

Locknut half of connector tightened inside box

Gem box with side mounting bracket

around the machine screw on the connector and tighten the screw. This also wedges the machine screw against the outside of the BX and secures the two. I insert the threaded end through the knockout hole into the box and screw on the locknut half of the connector from inside the box. I tighten the locknut by driving it clockwise, placing a screwdriver against the notches along its circumference and hitting it with a hammer. I now have 8 inches or so of white and black wire extending from the box.

I cut the BX 8 inches longer than the distance between the old and new box. I remove 8 inches of armor and attach the newly cut end to the new box in the same way I attached the other end.

The new box (shown in the photo) has a side mounting bracket ordinarily used when the core of the wall is wood. It can also be used in this instance. There are predrilled holes in the bracket. I drive two #6 common (large-headed) nails through these holes and into the mortar joints of the brick to attach the new box temporarily. I also use small wooden wedges to position and hold the box in the opening. Once the area between the outside of the box and the wall has been refilled with plaster, the plaster alone will hold the box in place.

The tool on page 19 is a wire stripper; its purpose is to remove insulation from wires. Along its jaws are numbers that correspond to wire sizes. I insert about 7/8 inch of the white and black wire in the hole numbered 12, close the jaws, turn the strippers, and pull. Completing the ends where the new box is located, I strip 5/8 inch from the ends at the old box in the same manner.

#12 wire in #12 hole of wire strippers

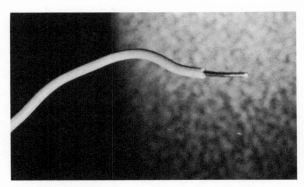

Stripped end of wire

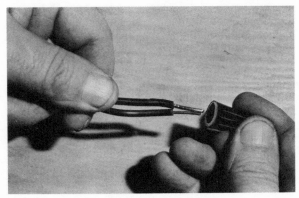

Two #12 wires in position with solderless connector to join them

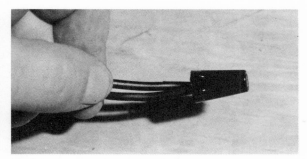

Wires joined with solderless connector (wire nut)

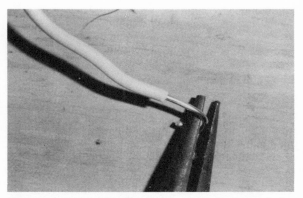

Needle-nosed pliers forming loop at stripped end of wire

If I intend to attach the end of a wire to a terminal, stripping 7/8 inch of insulation is optimum. If I intend to attach ends of wires to each other, 5/8 inch is optimum. The purpose of the shorter amount is to keep any portion of the stripped wire from extending below the wire nut or solderless connector—another safety precaution.

In the old box I place the old and new white wires together as shown in the photo and screw the wire nut over their ends. I place the black wires together in the same way and screw a wire nut over them also.

Wire nuts are manufactured in a variety of sizes. In this instance, since I am joining two #12 wires, I use a wire nut for two #12 wires.

I bend the wires accordion-style and push them back into the old box.

At the new box I form a loop out of the stripped ends of the white and black wires with needle-nosed pliers. I loosen the *aluminum*-colored terminal screw on the side of the receptacle and place the loop in the *white*-colored wire under it. The direction of the loop is clockwise, so that when I tighten the screw the loop will not open.

**19**

# The Renovation Book

Aluminum-colored terminal for white wire attachment

Brass-colored terminal for black wire attachment

I form a loop in the *black* wire and attach it to the *brass*-colored terminal.

The receptacle is a duplex type, which means that it has two places to receive plugs. It has two aluminum-colored terminals on one side and two brass-colored ones on the other. (If I wish to add still another outlet, I would use these additional terminals.) Both positions in the receptacle will receive current even though two of the terminals have no wires attached to them, since both positions are connected by a brass strip along the side.

I bend the wires accordion-style and push the receptacle into the box. At the bottom and top of the receptacle there is a metal extension with two oblong holes. At the top and bottom of the gem box there are also two holes with interior threads. I align the holes in the receptacle with those of the box and tighten the receptacle to the box with the two long machine screws provided with the receptacle. I shift the receptacle as needed while I am tightening it *so that neither the ends of the wires nor the terminals are touching the box.* (As an

Attaching receptacle to box with two machine screws

added precaution I can wrap electrician's tape around the receptacle and over the stripped wires and terminals before tightening.)

I now screw back the fuse into the main and use the tester to make sure that the new outlet operates.

The BX is lying loosely in the channel cut in the wall. To secure it I drive case-hardened nails at an angle above and below the cable to hold it temporarily. Here again, if the nails are driven into the mortar joints the operation will be much easier.

I mix a fistful of plaster of Paris and water, fill the channel, and cover the BX. I do the same around the boxes.

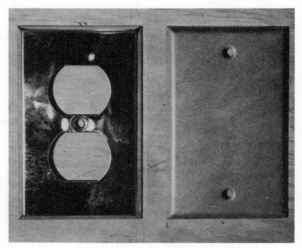

Duplex receptacle and blank cover plates

Because the plaster will harden in a few minutes, I mix only a small amount each time. I insert it with a 3-inch spackling knife, laying in the plaster with the knife parallel to the channel, then turning the knife at a right angle to smooth and level the plaster with the adjoining surfaces.

The duplex cover has a single screw hole in its center which corresponds to a threaded hole in the receptacle. The blank cover I will fasten over the old box has two holes which correspond to the two threaded holes in the gem box. I fasten both covers and the installation is complete.

The price an electrical contractor in New York City would charge for doing the work described is around $55. The cost of materials is under $5. (In general, the cost of electrical materials is very low compared to that of labor.)

The amount of description of the process of installing a new outlet may create the impression that it is a long, involved operation. But the actual "electrical" work took less than fifteen minutes and was done by a totally inexperienced helper after I had explained in specific terms what was to be done.

The total amount of electrical work that was done in this apartment was the equivalent of completely wiring three new houses, yet it took only about ten days.

## Installing Wire Mold or Surface Raceways

Wiring in new construction is almost always buried in walls, between floors, in the basement, and the like. In existing structures it is more economical to run wires along the exposed surfaces than to chop into walls or ceilings to hide them. The wires themselves are protected by a choice of devices, one of which—surface raceways—is more commonly called wire mold. This is a two-part metal container that lies on the surface of floors, walls, or ceilings and inside of which one places the needed wires.

There are many kinds of wire mold. The one in the photo is a snap-on type. The cover or cap (the larger half which has been primed with paint) snaps over the smaller half or base which is first attached to the surface of the wall, ceiling, or floor. Wire mold is available in many sizes. This one is 1/2 inch wide and is appropriate for two #12 wires. If it is

Wire-mold base, cap, and cap snapped on over base

necessary to use more wires inside the mold, larger sizes will have to be used. Wherever wire mold is sold a chart will specify the size of wire mold that corresponds to the maximum number and size of the wires it should contain.

In the inner half of the mold are small plastic devices through which the wire may be threaded and which hold the wire inside the mold during installation.

## Installing a Ceiling Light and Switch with Wire Mold

When a door to a room is opened there should be a switch on the knob side of the door inside that room that will illuminate it. Switches are most often located adjacent to the casing at a height of about four feet. The switch need not control a ceiling light, but when it is flipped a light somewhere in the room should go on. I am now going to install such a switch.

Switch on mounting plate and box cover

Special switches are manufactured for use with wire mold. Photo on p. 21 shows a switch factory-connected to a mounting plate, with a box cover and two screws for attaching it over the switch assembly. The mounting plate has two pre-drilled holes in diagonal corners. I attach the mounting plate and switch to the wall by driving lath nails through these holes. (Lath nails are thin-shanked, large-headed, and are usually colored blue.) The lath nails should be smooth-shanked rather than annular (ringed) since these hold better in plaster.

If the lath nails do not hold the mounting plate securely, I bore holes in the plaster behind the predrilled holes in the plate, insert a plastic shield, and use screws to fasten the plate. If no shields are available, I place wooden dowels or wedge wooden kitchen matches (after removing the heads) into the holes and then use wood screws. Generally, however, smooth-shanked lath nails will be adequate.

Removing duplex cover plate

Fixture-mounting plate and box

The flat round plate has four predrilled holes, and I mount it on the ceiling where I intend to hang the light fixture. (The procedure is the same if the light fixture is to be hung on a wall.) Lath nails won't do here since the weight of the fixture will tend to pull them loose. I use plastic shields or securely wedged dowels and screws to attach the flat round plate to the ceiling.

I must now provide current for the light. If I intended this power for a washing machine or anything else with a high wattage, I would proceed in another way. However, a light bulb is a hundred watts or so and an ordinary circuit will take a dozen light bulbs or their equivalent. I therefore select an already existing outlet which is closest to either the

Machine screws at top and bottom of receptacle

light or switch I intend to install. In this case it is an outlet located about eight feet from the new switch. I "plug" in the tester, and after trying various fuses my helper completely unscrews the fuse that controls the electricity to it. I then remove the cover.

I remove the two machine screws at the top and bottom of the receptacle.

I loosen the terminal screws and remove the receptacle. I now have two wires coming out of the

Two wires out of gem box

Old and new white wires attached to aluminum-colored terminals

Wire-mold mounting plate over old box

gem box recessed in the wall, one white and one black.

The rectangular mounting plate has an interior cutout the same size as the box recessed in the wall that held the receptacle. It has predrilled holes in the corners. Using lath nails I attach the plate to the wall over the box.

The box which will fit over the attached plate has indentions on all sides that are similar to knockouts in that they have been partially cut for easy removal.

The inner knockout is for the 1/2-inch wire mold I am using, the outer for 1-inch. I choose the 1/2-inch knockout that will be closest to the switch I am installing and remove it by bending it up and down sharply while holding the tip with pliers.

Removing 1/2-inch knockout from wire-mold box

Sometimes the knockouts are defectively stamped. When this occurs, the large knockout will come out with the smaller unless the cut in the smaller is first deepened with a hacksaw.

The mounting plate over the old gem box has two raised circular pieces of brass located in diagonal corners which have interior threads. The box has two holes in corresponding positions. I attach the box to the mounting plate with two machine screws. (All necessary screws are provided with purchased boxes, outlets, switches, etc.)

The receptacle has two aluminum and two brass terminals on each side. I attach the old white wire to an aluminum-colored terminal and the old black wire to a brass-colored terminal and leave the receptacle for the time being.

Box being attached to mounting plate with machine screws in diagonal corners

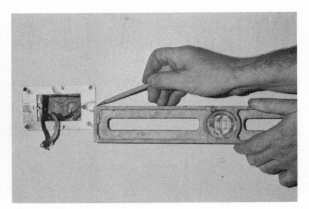

Using level to establish horizontal line from tab of mounting plate

Attaching new receptacle to wire-mold box

Right-angle base at intersection of lines

Spring clip to hold base

I am now ready to mark the path of the wire mold between receptacle and switch and from the switch to the fixture mounting plate attached to the ceiling.

The receptacle is 14 inches off the floor. The switch is 4 feet off the floor. The lateral distance between the two is somewhat under 8 feet. Using a 4-foot carpenter's level, I draw a horizontal line centered on the knockout of the box where the old receptacle had been. I extend this line past 8 feet. With the same level, I draw a vertical line down from the switch box so that it intersects the horizontal line. The wire mold will follow the path of these lines.

Where the two lines intersect I nail a flat wire mold right-angle piece that lies centered over the intersecting lines.

Along the perimeter of the mounting plates are raised rectangular tabs. A spring-clip device is provided with the wire mold for holding the end of the mold in the box.

I take a length of inner wire mold and place one end into the clip and through the knockout.

On the flat side of the wire-mold base are pre-drilled holes spaced every foot. I center the holes over the horizontal line I have marked and attach it to the wall with lath nails. Since the head of the hammer is greater than the 1/2-inch width of the mold, I complete driving the nails with a nail set. (A common nail can be substituted for the nail set.)

Wire mold is sold in 4-foot lengths. After installing the first length along the horizontal line, it is less than 4 feet to the right-angle base where I will

Spring clip inserted under tab of mounting plate

Nail set to complete driving lath nail to attach base to wall

Base under right-angle tab

I mark the second length at the point where the first length ends. I snip the raised sides of the mold with wire-cutting pliers at the mark, then bend the mold back and forth sharply until it breaks. I file the ragged edges along the break as a precaution against later damaging the wire.

In a similar fashion I mark, cut, and install the length of wire mold that runs between the right-angle piece and the raised tab on the switch-mounting plate. It isn't necessary to use the spring clip here to hold the mold since the tab will fit over the mold.

I am now ready to install the inner half of the wire mold between the switch-mounting plate and the fixture-mounting plate attached to the ceiling.

Wire-cutting pliers cutting sides of base

Base under tab of switch-mounting plate

be changing direction. I therefore have to cut the length to fit. I place an end of the second length so that it lies under the raised tab on the right-angle base.

Base bent for right-angle joint between wall and ceiling

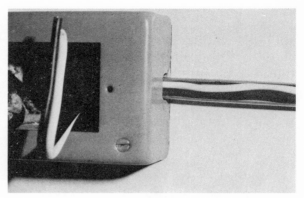

Box attached, new wires in new box

New #12 wires, one white and one black laid in base and over plate

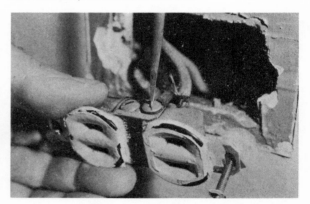

Old and new black wires attached to brass-colored terminals, old and new white wires attached to aluminum-colored terminals on opposite side of receptacle

I mark a path and continue up the wall from the switch, installing the inner mold in the manner already described. At the top of the wall, I snip the sides of the mold and bend it so that I can continue it along the ceiling.

I extend the wire mold to the ceiling fixture-mounting plate the same as if I were continuing along the wall.

I am now ready to insert the wires and make the connections.

The photograph shows two separate wires, one covered with black insulation and the other with white.

I slip the ends of both wires through the knock-out of the box I installed over the old outlet. I want about 8 inches of wire to extend out of the box. I strip 7/8 inch of insulation from the ends by placing the wire in the strippers at the #12 hole, turning, and pulling.

The receptacle left earlier has two remaining unused terminals, one aluminum-colored and one brass-colored. I make loops and attach the black wire to the brass-colored terminal and the white wire to the aluminum-colored terminal.

I bend the wires accordion-style and push the receptacle against the box. I attach the receptacle to the box with two machine screws that go through the oblong holes at each end and into the threaded holes in the box.

I attach the duplex cover plate with a machine screw which goes through the hole in the center of the cover plate and into the threaded hole in the center of the receptacle.

I now lay the white and black wires side by side in the mold. (If necessary, I can use the plastic devices inside the mold. They are slipped out, the wire threaded through their two holes, then they are slipped back into the mold. Ordinarily, wedging the

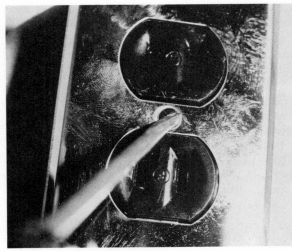

Duplex cover being attached

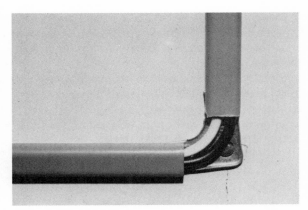

Cover snapped on top of base

Wires bent around right-angle base

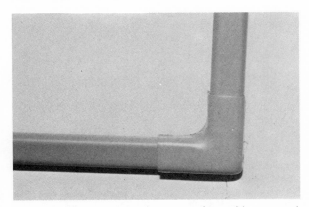

Right-angle cover snapped on over wire-mold cover and right-angle base

wires against one another will keep them inside the mold.) When I have inserted more than 4 feet of wire, I lay the outer half of the mold on the inner and snap it on by striking it with my palm.

I bend the wires to go around the flat right-angle piece.

I continue to insert the black and white wire into the base until I reach the switch. I cut and install a length of the outer half of the wire mold between the flat right-angle piece and the switch.

I place a right-angle cover over the right-angle base and snap it on.

I fold the black wire on the mounting plate and around the switch so that it extends an inch or so beyond the bottom terminal. I remove 7/8 inch of insulation from the end, make a loop, and attach the end to the terminal.

Black wire cut, end attached to lower terminal of switch, black wire attached to upper terminal and continued to fixture box

I strip 7/8 inch of insulation from the outgoing black wire, attach it to the upper terminal, wind it on the mounting plate and around the switch, and continue into the mold above the switch. *I do not cut the white wire.* I continue to lay the white wire in the inner half of the wire mold as if the switch weren't there.

## The Renovation Book

*The white wire is never attached to a switch.*

I remove the appropriate knockouts in the box cover of the switch and attach it with the screws provided.

I continue to insert both wires in the wire mold until I reach the round ceiling plate. I then cut them so that 8 inches or so extend beyond the plate. I snap on the outer half of the wire mold.

At the joint made between the wall and ceiling, after I have installed the outer half of the mold, I snap on an interior elbow.

I attach a ceiling box to the mounting plate with two machine screws that go through the predrilled holes in the box and into two raised circular brass pieces on the mounting plate that have interior threads.

I strip 5/8 inch of insulation from the white and black wire that extends 8 inches from the box.

I cut a piece of black wire 8 inches long, strip one end 7/8 inch and the other 5/8 inch. I do the same with an 8-inch length of white wire.

I attach the 7/8-inch end of the black wire to the brass-colored terminal on the back of the fixture. I attach the 7/8-inch end of the white wire to the aluminum-colored terminal.

I join the black wire from the fixture to the black wire coming out of the ceiling box with a wire nut. I do the same with the white wires.

White wire continuous through switch box

Box cover being attached to mounting plate and over switch

28

Internal elbow cover

Porcelain fixture unassembled, back view

External elbow cover

White wire attached to aluminum-colored terminal, black wire to brass-colored terminal

Porcelain nut to hold assembly, installed at front of fixture

Porcelain fixture assembled, front view

I bend the wires accordion-style and lay the fixture against the ceiling box. On each side of the fixture are predrilled holes that correspond to threaded holes in the box. I attach the two with the machine screws provided. These screws carry the weight of the fixture. The box to which it is attached

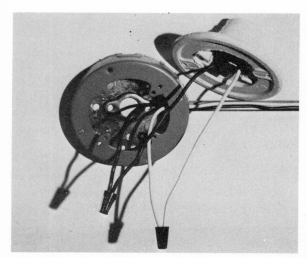

Wires of same color joined with wire nuts

Porcelain fixture attached to fixture box with two machine screws along circumference

is carried by the previously installed screws attached to the mounting plate, which in turn is attached to the ceiling. *The weight of the fixture is not carried by the wires.*

I place the fuse back and the installation is complete.

## Mounting a Series of Suspended Light Fixtures Controlled by One Switch

The owner found these light fixtures in a junk shop. They cost $7 each. They were formerly used in a factory and, like a great number of highly usable items, were collecting dust. The parts necessary to install the fixtures weren't available with them and were bought in a local hardware store at a very nominal cost.

Ceiling light installed, five more of same in series

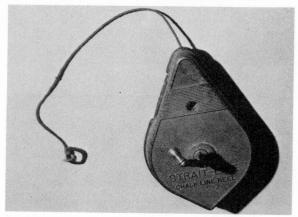

Chalk line

When a number of light fixtures are to be installed, six in this instance, the first step is to mark the location of the fixtures and the path of the wire mold between them. This is done with a ruler and chalk line.

This tool is simply a string wound on a spindle held in a case containing powdered chalk (usually blue for easier visibility). I will use it first to mark the kitchen ceiling.

From both ends of a wall parallel to the planned fixture line, I measure out and make equidistant marks on the ceiling that correspond to that planned line. I hold one end of the chalk line on one mark and a helper does the same at the other mark. I stretch the chalk line taut, pull it downward a foot, and release it. This deposits a blue line on the ceiling which corresponds to the position the fixtures will occupy. Since I am installing two parallel rows of fixtures, I pop a second chalk line that corresponds to the position the second row of fixtures will occupy. In order for each fixture in both rows to be equidistant along the parallel lines, I measure outward from the nearest wall which lies at a right angle and place marks along each of the parallel lines, which are also equidistant. I now pop chalk lines between the equidistant marks on each of the parallel lines. The intersection of the chalk lines marks the center of each fixture. The lines themselves serve as a reference for the path of the wire mold.

I install the round metal fixture-mounting plates over the intersections of the chalk lines in the manner described in the previous segment. I position the plate so that the rectangular tabs on its circumference are centered over the chalk lines.

I remove the half-inch knockouts from each fixture box where wire mold will enter and leave each box. I attach all the boxes to the mounting plates with machine screws.

I now install the wire-mold base between all of the boxes in the manner described in the previous segment.

I install a black and white wire inside the wire-mold base from the switch to the first box and cut the wires so that 8 inches extend from the box. I now install a black and white wire from the first box to the second box and also cut it so that 8 inches extend from each box. I continue in this manner to all boxes but the last. In all boxes but this last one I have four wires, two white and two black. In the last box, I have only two, one white and one black. This is the box farthest from the power source.

I cut the outer halves of the wire mold to the needed lengths and snap them on.

To minimize the glare from the light bulb, I decide to place the bottom of each fixture at a height of 6 feet 4 inches from the floor—which also reduces the chance of people walking into them.

Continuously threaded 3/8-inch nipple

The continuously threaded nipple shown in the photo is a necessary component for mounting the fixture and will protect the wires that will be run inside of it. I must now cut it to a length which will result in a 6-foot-4-inch height for the fixture and I calculate the length of the nipple in the following manner.

The ceiling height is 9 feet 6 inches. The box extends 1-1/2 inches below the ceiling. The fixture shade is 12-inch. I add 1-1/2 inches, 12 inches, and 6 feet 4 inches, giving a total of 7 feet 5-1/2 inches. I subtract this from 9 feet 6 inches, which leaves 24-1/2 inches as the length needed for the nipple. I mark this length on the nipple and thread a nut onto the nipple until it lies above the mark where I will cut. I use a hacksaw to cut the nipple, then unscrew the nut.

In cutting the nipple, the threads may become damaged, and unscrewing the nut over them will straighten the threads should this have occurred.

#18 light wire

The pictured wire contains two wires separated from each other by insulation. They are #18 wires and are of more than sufficient size for carrying current from the #12 wires in the box to the light. I draw this wire through the nipple and cut it so that 8 inches or so extends beyond each end.

I thread a nut onto the nipple for a distance of about 14 inches.

I slip the pictured fixture cover over the nipple and slide it to the nut. See photo on next page.

Brass canopy on top of shade with nuts, shade omitted

Pull-chain socket disassembled

Light wires attached to socket terminals, shade omitted

I slip the shade over the nipple to the cover.

I slip the washer over the nipple, slide it to the shade, then screw the nut up to the washer. This assembly holds the shade to the nipple. By raising or lowering the nuts, the shade can be positioned upward or downward as desired.

This is an ordinary pull-chain socket. It comes apart by twisting counterclockwise. The projection at the top has interior threads; I screw this projection onto the nipple.

I slit the outer insulation of the #18 wire, separate the two wires within it, and strip 7/8 inch of insulation from each. When the light socket is in half, two terminals are exposed and I attach a wire to each—the black wire to the brass-colored terminal and the white wire to the aluminum-colored terminal. I assemble the light socket with a clockwise turn.

At the other end of the nipple, I thread a nut 1/2 inch or so, then place the pictured round plate with a hole in its center against the nut. I screw on a second nut and tighten the plate between the two nuts so that the plate lies slightly below the end of the nipple.

Socket screwed on continuously threaded nipple and locked with set screw

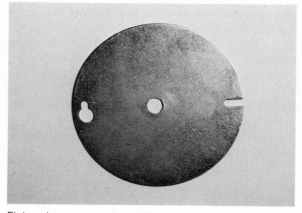

Fixture-box cover plate with 3/8-inch-diameter center hole

Cover plate held on nipple with nuts on both sides

This plate also has two predrilled holes whose position corresponds to the predrilled threaded holes in the fixture-mounting box.

I slit the outer insulation of the #18 wire, separate the wire in it, and remove 5/8 inch of insulation from each end.

I remove 5/8 inch of insulation from the ends of the two black and two white wires in the box. I place the ends of the two white #12 wires together with the end of the white #18 wire and join all three together with a wire nut that is appropriate for two #12 and one #18 wire. I do the same with the two #12 black wires and the remaining black #18 wire.

I attach the round plate to the box with two machine screws.

Plate attached to ceiling box with two machine screws through holes along circumference

Here again, the wires do not carry the weight of the fixture.

All the remaining fixtures are installed in exactly the same manner. (In the last one, of course, where only two wires are present, the #18 wire will be attached with a wire nut appropriate for a #12 and a #18 wire.)

All the lights will go on in this arrangement only when the switch is in the On position and all the pull chains are also in the On position. A pull chain in the Off position will shut the light of its own particular bulb without affecting any of the others.

## Installing Two Switches That Control One Light

The purpose of having two switches that control one light is to enable the user to put on or shut off that light from two different locations, such as the top and bottom of a flight of stairs or each end of a hallway. The installation is called "three-way."

Long hallway, typical location for a three-way switch at each end

I mount switch boxes on the walls at the two positions from which I will control the ceiling light. I locate them about four feet above the floor and in the hallway opposite the hinged side of the door. I mount a ceiling fixture box where I intend to hang the fixture. I run either BX, thinwall conduit, or wire mold between both switch boxes and the ceiling box.

From the power source (which may be any convenient outlet), I run a black and white wire into the ceiling box, first using the tester to make sure that the fuse which controls the outlet has been unscrewed. Later, when I am ready to attach the light fixture, I will install an 8-inch piece of white wire on the aluminum-colored fixture terminal and join the other end to the incoming white wire in the ceiling box with a wire nut. This is all that will be done with the white wire, and for the rest of this segment it will not enter into any of the work.

Three-way switch, two terminals on one side, one on opposite side

I will need two of these three-way switches, one that will be installed in each of the previously mounted boxes. There are three terminals, two on one side, one on the other. The screw of the single terminal on one side is a deeper-colored brass than the two on the other side. There is also the word *common* stamped beside it. This is the terminal to which the hot wire from the power source will be attached. *The black wire which I have brought to the ceiling box will be continued to this terminal.*

Since there are two switches and each has this common terminal, I may attach the hot black wire to either.

From the ceiling box to each of the switch boxes I run black, red, and blue #14 wires.

At one of the boxes, I attach the blue wire to the upper terminal and attach the red wire to the lower terminal on the same side. I attach the black wire to the single terminal on the opposite side.

The other end of this black wire is extending 8 inches from the ceiling box and is as yet unattached.

At the second switch box, I attach the blue wire to the upper terminal and, on the same side, attach the red wire to the lower terminal.

I attach the black wire in the second switch box to the single terminal on the opposite side, also stamped *common*. I attach both switches to their respective boxes with machine screws and put the switch covers on.

In the ceiling box, I join the ends of the two blue wires together with a wire nut. I do the same with red wires.

I now have three black unattached wires remaining in the ceiling box. One has come from the power source; the other two run to each switch and are connected to the common terminal of each.

I join the black wire from the power source with either of the remaining two black wires with a wire nut.

I am now left with one black unattached wire and the white wire from the power source.

I cut two 8-inch lengths of wire, one black and one white. I strip 7/8 inch of insulation from an end of each and attach these ends to each of the two terminals on the back of the fixture, the black wire to the brass-colored terminal and the white to the aluminum-colored terminal.

I strip 5/8 inch of insulation from each of the other ends of the 8-inch wires. I attach the black wire to the remaining black wire in the ceiling box with a wire nut. I attach the white wire to the end of the white wire from the power source.

Two three-way switches completely wired. Wire lengths have been shortened and boxes omitted for easier wire identification, but in practice boxes are mandatory

I mount the fixture to the ceiling box by placing the two machine screws provided through the holes at the circumference of the fixture and into the threaded holes in the ceiling box. The installation is complete.

## Installing Light Fixtures That Lack Circumference Mounting Screws

A great many light fixtures are manufactured without predrilled holes along their circumference that correspond to the threaded holes in the fixture-mounting box. However, all standard fixtures have an alternate method of attachment suitable for use with all standard fixture-mounting boxes.

The metal fixture strap that is shown in the lower left photo is attached to the box with a machine screw at either end. The hole in the center has interior threads and a nipple is screwed into it. The fixture will have a hole in its center which is placed over the nipple. The fixture is then held to the nipple with a cap.

An alternative to the strap arrangement is to purchase a fixture box with a threaded fixture stud in its center. A hickey, a device with outer and inner threads, is attached to the stud and then a nipple is screwed into the hickey. The fixture is then placed in position and held with a cap.

The mounting plate used in conjunction with wire mold has a built-in threaded fixture stud at its center which will take a nipple directly or a reducing hickey and a smaller-diameter nipple.

Various ceiling light fixtures

Fixture stud, hickey, and nipple attached to fixture-mounting plate

Fixture box, strap, and threaded nipple for installing center-mounted ceiling fixtures

Wire-mold mounting plate with optional fixture stud for center-mounted light fixtures

Fixture stud attached to plate with nut on rear

## General Information on Wiring

Before proceeding to actual installation, it is useful to understand a few basic facts about electricity.

Electricity is generally accepted to be a stream of electrons, those negatively charged particles which orbit around the positively charged nucleus of the atom.

Three terms are widely used in connection with this stream of electrons: volts, amperes, and watts.

*Volts* is the measurement of the electrical pressure—the force of the stream. The greater the voltage, the greater the pressure.

*Amperes* is the measurement of the amount of electricity. While voltage tells the pressure, it does not indicate the amount. The pressure of water in a pipe doesn't indicate the amount of water in it, and this parallel holds true for electricity.

*Watts* is the measurement of electricity being used. It is calculated by the formula: watts = volts × amperes.

A *kilowatt* is 1000 watts.

A *kilowatt hour* is 1000 watts used for one hour. The kilowatt hour (kwh) is the unit by which electricity is metered and sold.

A *circuit* is one or more positions for electrical use provided by a wire (conductor) from the main.

An ordinary circuit will carry 110 to 120 volts. It will be conducted through a #14 wire with a maximum of 15 amperes. Theoretically there will there-fore be 120 x 15 or 1800 watts available. To guard against exceeding this capacity, a fuse rated at 15 amperes is installed in the main. As electricity is used, the wire's resistance to its flow creates heat, which increases as more electricity is used. In actual practice, enough heat will be created to blow a fuse rated at 15 amps when 12 or 13 amps are present. Since the voltage is often 110 and the limit of a 15-amp fuse is 12 amps, 110 x 12 = 1320 watts. This means that for an ordinary circuit which uses a #14 wire fused at 15 amps, the practical limit is around 1300 watts. To anticipate further occasional drops in voltage and other factors which influence the wattage, *a maximum of 1200 watts should be projected for an ordinary circuit.*

The following list is the wattage that might be expected from various 120-volt appliances:

Room air conditioner. . . . . . . . . . . . . .1200
Dishwasher . . . . . . . . . . . . . . . . . . . . .1100
Washing machine . . . . . . . . . . . . . . . .1200
Dry or steam iron. . . . . . . . . . . . . . . .1000

The wattage of an appliance is usually stated on an attached metal tag.

From the wattages listed it is clear that using a room air conditioner would bring an ordinary circuit close to its maximum capacity. Any additional factor such as a drop in voltage would overload the circuit.

A large number of people, particularly those who live in apartments, encounter this situation regularly. They have plugged their air conditioner into a 15-amp circuit which has several other outlets and lights on it consuming electricity. The result is well known and hardware stores do a thriving business selling replacement fuses.

Some people replace the 15-amp fuse in the main with a 20-amp or even a 30-amp fuse. This is hazardous, since the #14 wire of that circuit is designed to carry a maximum of 15 amps. When the amperage exceeds this and the higher-rated fuse doesn't blow, the wire heats up. The heat created is sufficient to ignite an electrical fire.

The use of a 20-amp fuse with a room air conditioner is in fact correct, but *it must be accompanied by the use of #12 wire.* With such an arrangement a theoretical capacity of 2400 watts and a practical capacity of 1800 to 1900 watts is achieved. Since a fairly heavy room air conditioner will consume 1200 watts, a more than safe margin exists.

Neutral terminal bar; screwdriver is on incoming white wire from power source

Apartment main, screwdriver at one of four screws holding cover

## Installing New Wiring for a 120-Volt Air Conditioner

I install a mounting plate and box for wire mold in the same manner as described on pp. 00–00. Its location is near the air conditioner and convenient for plugging it in.

I remove the cover of the main by unscrewing the screw in each of the corners.

On the left side, a white, a red, and a black wire enter the box through a knockout at the rear. These wires are significantly larger than any other and are *the incoming power source*.

Near the top of the box is a metal bar with a horizontal series of aluminum-colored screws. These are neutral terminals. A larger screw at the end of a short metal projection is at the center. The incoming white wire is attached to this terminal.

Screwdriver on incoming black wire from power source

Screwdriver on incoming red wire from power source

There are two vertical lines of fuse holders. Parallel to them are vertical lines of screws, or terminals, located directly beside each fuse holder.

The second screw up from the bottom on each side has a metal device with a cutout containing another screw that clamps onto the incoming red wire on one side and the incoming black wire on the other. This clamp arrangement is used for attaching the ends of heavier wires since it would be difficult and cumbersome to loop them as is done with lighter wires.

The red and black wires each carry 120 volts from the power source in the basement. In the basement, the other ends of the red and black wires are similarly attached in a box which has a main switch. (The apartment number is usually painted on the cover of the box.) The white wire goes continuously through the box and is not attached to the switch. The three wires then go through a meter and are

connected to the utility company lines under the street.

When clamped as shown in the photo, electricity is entering the apartment main. This can be verified by placing one lead of the tester on the exposed end of the wire and the other lead against the box. (The lead must be touching bare metal for the test.) The bulb will light if power is on.

Each circuit supplied with 120 volts in the apartment will carry one white wire that will be attached to any of the unused screw terminals along the horizontal bar where the incoming white wire has been attached. A black wire will be attached to any unused terminal screw beside any of the fuses *before* the fuse is installed.

The white and black wires are brought through a knockout in the main and these two wires provide current for the 120-volt circuit.

The apartment main is recessed into the wall and the knockouts lie within the wall. (This particular main, as in most apartments, does not have a main fuse or breaker that will cut off all power in the box. Later, when the rest of the work is completed and only the attachment of wires in the main remains, *I will cut off power to the main from the switch in the basement.*)

The flexible armor below, called "greenfield," is BX without wire in it. I chop a channel in the wall beside the main until I can remove a knockout along its side that lies in the direction I will be taking to the new air-conditioner plate and box. I hacksaw the greenfield to a length that will travel in a shallow arc till it emerges from the wall. I install the male end of a BX connector on each end of the

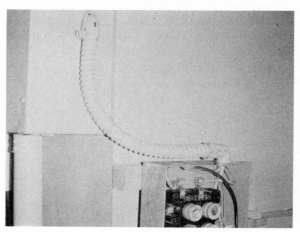

Greenfield

greenfield. I slip one end through the knockout in the main and tighten with a locknut.

I remove the knockout in the back and center of a wire-mold mounting plate, insert the other end of the greenfield through the plate, and fasten with a locknut. I then attach the plate to the wall beside the main and attach a wire-mold box to the plate.

I install wire mold to the new air-conditioner mounting plate and box in the same manner as previously described.

I feed a #12 white and black wire through the greenfield into the main until I have enough wire in the main to reach an unused terminal for the white wire and an unused terminal for the black.

I lay the white and black wire continuously in the wire mold until 8 inches or so of each extends from the wire-mold box near the air conditioner.

The pictured receptacle has, in addition to the two usual slots, a third for grounding purposes. It also has an additional green hexagonal screw. I ground the receptacle by stripping a piece of #12 wire, attach one end to the hexagonal screw and the other end to a screw at the back of the box. (Gem boxes now have a small threaded hole at the back for this purpose. If the hole isn't threaded, you may insert any small sheet-metal screw through any of the factory-drilled holes.)

I attach the black wire to the brass-colored terminal and the white wire to the aluminum-colored terminal. I fasten the receptacle to the box and mount the cover plate.

*I turn the power to the main off in the basement by flipping the main switch to the Off position.* I check with the tester to make sure that the power to the apartment main is off.

I strip 7/8 inch of insulation from the end of the white wire and attach it to any unused screw terminal on the horizontal bar near the top. (All these terminals are aluminum-colored.)

I strip 7/8 inch of insulation from the end of the black wire and attach it to the screw terminal beside any unused fuse holder. The fuse is not yet in place.

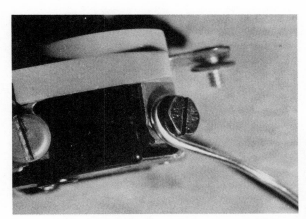

One end of bare wire attached to green terminal on receptacle for grounding

Other end of bare wire attached to screw at back of box

Typical switch located in basement to cut off power to apartment

Switch with cover removed

I turn the power back on from the basement.

I install a blank cover over the wire-mold box beside the apartment main.

I screw a 20-amp fuse into the fuse holder beside the black wire I have just installed and replace the main cover.

The air conditioner is now on its own line, which has a 20-amp fuse coupled with a #12 wire that has a practical capacity of about 1900 watts. This is adequate for even the larger 12-amp air conditioners.

## Installing an Appliance Outlet When No Circuits Are Available

When electrical use was initially being projected for an older structure, the installations were invariably minimal and are almost always inadequate today. In an older apartment one rarely finds that there is room for an additional circuit in the main. Nevertheless, 60 amps or more may be delivered to the main despite the fact that all of its possible circuits are in use. (If, as in many installations, only 30 amps is being brought in and only two circuits are present, not much can be done without bringing additional power into the apartment. I discuss this on pp. 48–52. However, if 60 amps or more is present,

the following procedure for installing a new appliance outlet will usually work.

*I turn off the power to the apartment main with the cutoff switch in the basement.*

I remove the cover of the apartment main. Centered on the bottom of the box is a knockout, which I remove.

The small box under the main will become an additional power source for two circuits, though I will be using only one. It is called a sub-feed and can be purchased at any electrical supply store.

I remove a knockout at the back and top of the sub-feed box.

I remove a small portion of wall directly under the knockout hole in the main and at the place I plan to connect it to the knockout hole I have made at the back of the sub-feed box.

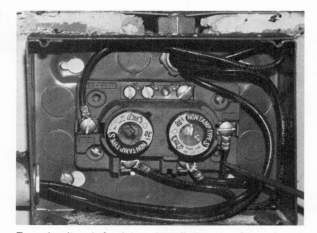

Two-circuit sub-feed box installed on surface of wall directly below apartment main

Elbow linking main to sub-feed box

I place a threaded end of the pictured elbow through the hole at the bottom of the main and attach it with a locknut.

I place the other end of the elbow into the hole at the back of the sub-feed box and secure it with another locknut.

I attach the sub-feed box to the wall with screws and plastic shields which I have lagged in the wall. (There are predrilled holes in the back of the sub-feed box for this purpose.)

I insert a #12 white wire through the elbow until I have enough length in the main to attach the end to an unused aluminum-colored terminal along the horizontal bar near the top. (It is rare not to find an unused neutral terminal even when all circuits are in use. If all terminals are in use, I place the end of the white wire adjacent to the large incoming white wire and use the screw directly over it to tighten the two.)

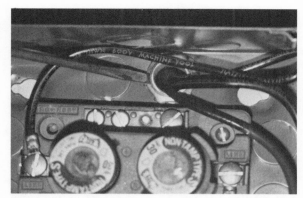

Screwdriver at wires entering sub-feed box from main through elbow

Screwdriver at one of two screws used to attach box to wall; screws enter plastic shields lagged in wall

Screwdriver on black wire from main attached to *line* terminal

I cut the other end of this same white wire in the sub-feed box and attach it to the large aluminum-colored screw terminal along the horizontal bar at the top.

I loosen the screw which holds the incoming black wire at the second terminal up from the bottom. I insert a black wire from the sub-feed into the main and attach the end of the black wire beside the incoming black wire in the cutout, then tighten the screw down on both.

I cut and attach the other end of the black wire to a brass-colored terminal screw on the outer side of

the sub-feed box. *Line* is stamped directly under this terminal. (There is another terminal marked *line* on the opposite side of the box. Either terminal may be used.)

I remove a knockout from the side of the sub-feed box closest to where I intend placing the new appliance outlet. This hole will be larger than the 1/2-inch wire mold I intend to use; to cover this hole, I use wire-mold reducers and adapters.

I attach the adapter to the sub-feed box with a threaded nipple and locknut, then install the wire mold and outlet as previously described.

Wire-mold adapter, round end for round knockout hole of sub-feed box, other end for wire-mold shape

Screwdriver on outgoing black wire attached to *load* terminal at side of fuse holder

I lay black and white #12 wires in the mold and attach their ends to the receptacle, attach the receptacle to the wire-mold box, and install the cover plate.

I cut the other ends of the two wires in the sub-feed box and attach the white wire to either of the two smaller aluminum-colored terminal screws adjacent to the large white screw to which I have attached the incoming white wire.

On the side where I have attached the black wire to the line terminal is a fuse holder. Directly beside it is a terminal screw, and I attach the end of the outgoing black wire to this terminal.

I place a 20-amp fuse in the fuse holder, put the cover of the sub-feed box on with the two machine screws provided, replace the cover on the main, and turn the power on in the basement. The installation is complete.

In this arrangement I have not increased the total capacity of the electrical system. If 60 amps were coming into the apartment, there are still only 60 amps. However, I am drawing power for the new circuit directly from the incoming power source rather than from an existing circuit with other demands already on it. Only the air conditioner is on this line, and the chances of the 20-amp fuse

blowing in this arrangement have been radically reduced. (The operation and longevity of the air conditioner will also be substantially improved.)

## Installing a 240-Volt Appliance Outlet

Many appliances—such as electric stoves, hot-water heaters, heavy-duty wall heaters, and air conditioners—operate on 240 volts. As a rule, these appliances are better made, more efficient, and relatively cheaper to run than 120-volt appliances, although their initial cost is higher.

Earlier in this chapter the formula of watts = volts × amperes was given. Using 240 volts with 30 amperes, 7200 watts is available at the 240-volt outlet. The size of the appropriate wire would be #10. (This could use a fuse rated at 35 amps if ordinary rubber-sheathed wire is used to give the 30-amp fuse added insurance against blowing.)

All new electric installations have two hot and one neutral wire entering the main. A good many old installations have been partially updated, and even in old apartments the three-wire installation is often present. When it is, 240 volts is available. It is these three wires used together that provide the 240 volts.

(In some systems, the white wire has been omitted in the 240-volt circuit and only the two "hot" wires are used.)

As part of the 240-volt installation, a 240-volt receptacle must be used. It has three terminals rather than two. This should not be confused with the added terminal for grounding on 120-volt receptacles (the green hexagonal screw), or the four-terminal 120-volt receptacle where two terminals are used to bring in the power and the other two to continue the power to another point on the same circuit.

To provide the needed wiring for a 240-volt circuit, a choice of systems is available. With existent walls, one may use BX, wire mold, or conduit. When a new curtain wall is being constructed, the use of flexible nonmetallic cable may be feasible. I will discuss each system before demonstrating the installation I actually undertook.

When the wiring is to be buried in an existing wall or ceiling, three-wire BX is optimum for a 240-volt installation. (The method of doing this is the same as was detailed earlier.)

Typical 240-volt outlet

Thinwall connector and coupling

Thinwall conduit in conduit bender

When hiding the wiring is not a factor, wire mold on the surface of walls, floors, or ceilings offers a viable alternative. However, remember that the size of the wire and the number of wires will determine the size of the wire mold. In this particular installation I will be using three #10 wires and the wire mold will be 1 inch wide rather than the 1/2-inch mold I used with two #12 wires.

Conduit is yet another material widely used to protect wires.

Rigid conduit is available in the same sizes as water pipe; it is cut and threaded in the same way and employs similar fittings. It was widely used in large old structures, a practice that continues into the present. It has little application in renovations or new-house construction.

Thinwall conduit is cheaper than wire mold and quicker to install, but is more obtrusive. As its name implies, its walls are too thin to permit threading, and special fittings must be used.

The pictured threadless connector is used to secure conduit to a box and the coupling is used to join two lengths. (Thinwall conduit is sold in 10-foot lengths.)

Thinwall ell and cover plate

Thinwall conduit

Thinwall conduit is easily shaped to go around obstructions by means of a conduit bender.

To attain a smooth bend, a series of smaller bends is formed until the desired one is achieved. The bend should not exceed 90 degrees since it will be difficult to pull wires through the conduit if the angle is larger. If more than one 90-degree bend is necessary, an ell fitting is employed as shown on the photo.

The plate on the ell is removable and will aid in pulling the wires through the conduit.

Thinwall conduit in tubing cutter

Wires connected to loop at end of electrician's snake

To cut conduit, I position it as pictured between the rollers and cutting disc at the desired length, tighten gently by turning the knob, then turning and tightening around the conduit.

After the cut, I place the triangular piece of metal attached to the cutter inside the conduit and rotate to *remove the burrs*. The insulation over the wires is easily nicked, and removing the burrs is essential to avoid damaging the insulation. If an exposed wire makes contact with the conduit it will cause a short.

At the beginning of this chapter I stated that the ends of all wires must be contained within a plastic or metal box. (I prefer metal boxes because of their greater strength.) Switches and outlets must also be contained within boxes. Fixtures must be attached to boxes. Wires which are simply joined together and do not go directly to a switch, outlet, or fixture must also be contained within a junction box. An ordinary circuit may contain as many as ten of these boxes along the path of its wires from the main, and at each of them the wires from the main must be cut and spliced. The normal procedure in installing a circuit is first to mount all the appropriate boxes in the desired locations, install conduit between them, and then pull the required wires through the conduit.

After the boxes and conduit are installed, the needed wires are pulled through the conduit with the aid of "fishtape" or a "snake."

The snake is a thin flexible wire with a loop formed at one end. It is inserted at the first box from the main and pushed through until the loop emerges into the main. For the sake of brevity, I intend to pull two #12 wires through the conduit from the main to the first box along the circuit. I wind the two wires in and around the loop as shown in the photo, then pull the tape and wires until the wires emerge into the box. I cut the wires and leave 8 inches extending from the box.

I now go to the second box along the path of the circuit and push the snake through the conduit until it comes out of the first box. I attach the ends of the two wires to the loop, pull them through to the second box, and cut them so that 8 inches extend from the box. In this same way, I install wires in the conduit throughout the circuit.

With the plate from the ell removed, I use the opening to insert the snake and pull wires through to that point. I then proceed to the next ell or box along the line, insert the snake, and continue pulling the wires. If there were two or more 90-degree bends without ells, this would be very difficult or impossible to do. As a rule of thumb, I do not make more than four quarter bends in the conduit between boxes or ells.

In many instances during an alteration a curtain wall whose skeleton is wood or metal will be erected. In either case, the simplest, easiest, and cheapest method of electrical installation utilizes flexible nonmetallic cable. This is commonly called Romex. It is available in all sizes; its wires are separated from one another by insulation and all are enclosed by an outer covering of additional insulation. Since it is flexible, it is easily routed to wherever it is needed. It is connected to boxes through connectors in a manner similar to that for BX.

Practically all new suburban wiring is done with this material. In many cities codes are being altered to permit its use, while in others it is not yet approved. (This should be checked with your local building department.)

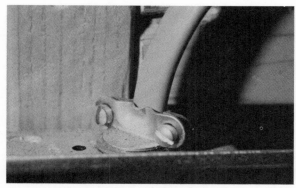

Flexible nonmetallic cable attached to box through knockout with flexible cable connector

Single screw holding cover of 240-volt outlet

#14 two-wire flexible nonmetallic cable with bare grounding wire

The cable is run through holes drilled in the center of studs, joists, and the like, or may run through open spaces (bays) between such structural members. It is held by a strap or staple every 4-1/2 feet and also secured within 12 inches of every box.

Some electrical codes require the use of a grounding wire (not to be confused with white wire) with nonmetallic cable. This wire inside the cable is bare. It is attached as was the grounding wire pictured earlier—from the green hexagonal screw to a screw at the back of the box.

By using the grounding wire, the system is continuously grounded, reducing the danger of shock should exposed metal accidentally become charged with electricity.

Since the electrical work I am doing is in an apartment, I choose to use wire mold for the installation despite its greater cost since it is far less obtrusive than thinwall conduit.

Cover removed, installation complete, screwdriver at three incoming wires, one black, one red and one white

I fasten the mounting plate and attach the 240-volt receptacle to the wall in a location that is convenient for plugging in the air conditioner or other 240-volt appliance. I drive lath nails through the predrilled holes in the mounting plate or use a combination of plastic shields and screws.

I intend to run three #10 wires from the main to the outlet; 1-inch wire mold is appropriate for this.

I install the inner half of the 1-inch wire mold between the main and outlet box in exactly the same manner as the previously described installation of 1/2-inch wire mold in which two #12 wires were placed. (See p. 21.)

Incoming black wire attached to upper terminal

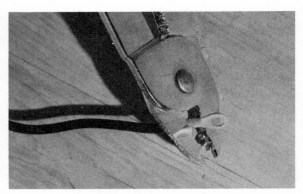

Front of wire strippers, also crimping tool to attach solderless terminals to bare wire ends

Incoming red wire attached to upper terminal on opposite side, white wire attached to lower neutral terminal between upper terminals

Solderless terminal attached

I insert three separate #10 wires in the mold; one black, one red, and one white. These wires are braided rather than solid and are more flexible.

At the main I leave a foot or so of each wire for connections. I leave 8-inches or so at the receptacle. At the receptacle I strip away 7/8 inch of insulation from the *white* wire. I loosen the bottom terminal screw. The prong here is vertical. I place the stripped white wire between the flat plates and tighten the screw.

Two slanted prongs lie above and on each side of the lower vertical prong. I strip the end of the red wire and attach it to either of these two terminals. I strip the end of the black wire and attach it to the upper remaining terminal. I place the cover over the outlet with a single machine screw.

*I shut off power to the apartment main by switching off in the basement the main switch that controls power to the apartment.*

I wind the white wire so that it lies around the side of the main and doesn't interfere or make

contact with any terminals. I bring its end to an unused aluminum-colored terminal on the horizontal bar near the top. I strip 1/2 inch of insulation from the end of the white wire.

The #10 wire is braided and thick and doesn't lend itself to the formation of the connecting loops used with thinner solid wire. To connect the wire to the terminal screw a device called a solderless terminal is used. An end is slipped over the bare wire. The front of the wire strippers are clamped over it. This crimps the device and fastens it to the end of the wire. At the other end of the device is a hole. The screw is placed through the hole and tightened.

I bend the *red wire* so that it lies around the side of the main. I strip 7/8 inch from its end and attach it to the same terminal as the incoming red wire from the power source. (This is the largest red wire in the main and is connected to the second terminal up from the bottom.) Directly beside this terminal is a fuse holder and I place a 30-amp fuse in it.

I bend and lay the black wire around the inside of the box so that it is out of the way of any terminals. I strip 7/8 inch of insulation from its end and attach it to the same terminal as the incoming black wire from the power source. Its location is on the right side of the box, the second terminal up from the bottom along the vertical line of fuses and terminals. I place a 30-amp fuse in the fuse holder beside the terminal.

I install the wire-mold cover, place the cover of the main back on, turn the power on in the basement, and the 240-volt installation is complete.

I have assumed that all the circuits in the main were in use. This is of course not always true. When unused circuits are available, the red wire, instead of being attached to the same terminal as the incoming red wire from the power source, is attached to any of the unused terminals along the same side. The black wire is attached to any of the unused terminals on the side of the incoming black wire from the power source. 30-amp fuses are then placed beside the attached terminals.

The installation I have described will take as much as 50 amps, since the black and red wires are each fused separately for 30 amps erecting a theoretical limit of 60 amps and a practical one of 50.

## Split-Circuit Wiring

The variety and volume of electrical appliances continue to grow. Many, particularly those used in the kitchen, have relatively high wattages. When two or more of these appliances are used simultaneously, a circuit may become overloaded.

Modern wiring methods anticipate this situation and provide a solution in split-circuit wiring.

In split-circuit wiring each half of a receptacle is placed on a separate circuit. Two appliances plugged into the same duplex receptacle thus receive their power from separate sources and do not overload either of the circuits.

### Installing a Split-Circuit Outlet

I install a mounting plate for a wire-mold box in the location that I want the receptacle. (Again, I use lath nails or plastic shields and screws.) I remove the appropriate knockout from the wire-mold box, then mount the box on the plate, placing two machine screws through the predrilled holes and into the

threaded holes in the mounting plate. I install the inner half of a 5/8-inch wire mold (the appropriate size for three #12 wires) between the box and the main. I remove the cover of the main and a knockout on the side facing the new box, then place three #12 wires (one red, one black, one white) inside the mold. I allow a foot of each wire to extend beyond the main, and 8 inches beyond the new box for the new outlet.

I shut off the power to the main, either at the apartment main if it is equipped with a main switch or main fuses or in the basement at the switch and box which has the apartment marked on its cover. (I verify that the power in the apartment is off by placing one lead of the tester against the terminal of the red or black wire and the other lead against bare metal of the box.)

Screwdriver breaking fin that connects both brass-colored terminals

Between the two brass-colored terminals of the receptacle is a strip of copper called a fin. This connects both terminals so that when a wire is attached to one, power is automatically brought to the other. To place each half of the duplex receptacle on a different circuit, the fin is first broken. I raise it with a screwdriver placed in the slot, then twist it with pliers, thereby severing the link between the two terminals.

I strip 7/8 inch of insulation from the red wire in the receptacle box, form a loop, and attach it to either of the two brass-colored terminals. I attach the black wire in the same way to the remaining brass-colored terminal. I attach the white wire to the aluminum-colored terminal on the opposite side of the receptacle.

I cut a piece of wire to a length of 8 inches and strip off all the insulation. I attach one end to the green screw terminal on the receptacle and the other end to a sheet metal screw, which I screw into any unused hole at the back of the box. I want the bare wire to be secure against the metal.

I fold the excess wire accordion-style and attach the receptacle to the box with two machine screws. I put on the cover plate with a machine screw that enters the threaded hole in the center of the receptacle.

In the main, I strip 7/8 inch of insulation from the red wire and attach it to any unused terminal beside any empty fuse holder. I do the same with the black wire, attaching it to any unused terminal beside any empty fuse holder. I strip 7/8 inch from the end of the white wire and attach it to any unused terminal on the neutral bar.

I place a 20-amp fuse inside the fuse holder beside the terminal to which I have attached the black wire and another 20-amp fuse in the fuse holder where I have attached the red wire. (These connections needn't be made on opposite sides of

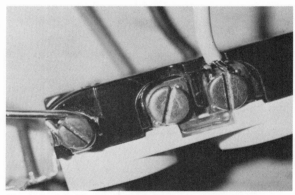

Single white wire and bare grounding wire attached

Opposite side of same receptacle, fin broken, red and black wires each attached to brass-colored terminals

the vertical row of fuses. Any unused terminals are appropriate.)

I put back the cover of the main, turn the power on, and the installation is complete.

The receptacle I have installed has a U-shaped hole in addition to the two rectangular holes. This is for use with three-pronged plugs, where the third prong is for grounding purposes. When this third prong is placed into the receptacle, a connection is made to the green screw and then to the attached bare wire, which in turn is held against the metal box. This provides protection against accidental shocks by grounding the receptacle to the metal box. (Conversely, if the bare wire is not connected to the green screw and box, the third prong serves no protective purpose.)

## Installing Supplementary Power into an Apartment

Many apartments, particularly those in townhouses, have only 30 amps coming into their main—usually divided into two circuits. (Many entire houses in San Francisco and elsewhere also have only 30 amps.) One circuit will serve the refrigerator and perhaps one outlet in the kitchen while the rest of the apartment will be served by the other. A sub-feed box may be installed in the manner detailed earlier (p. 40) to provide a couple of additional circuits, but since the 30-amp capacity is not increased, the basic problem of inadequate supply remains. The result is that tenants use electrical appliances individually, and when two or more are used at the same time, fuses blow. The proper solution when only 30 amps are coming into the apartment is a new and larger service. A minimum of 100 amps is now required for new houses. Newly renovated apartments in townhouses will usually have a three-wire service of #10 wire, each of the hot legs fused at 30 amps for a total of 60. The size of the service will of course depend on the anticipated usage, but in no case should it be less.

Providing a new service in a building is beyond the scope of this book, not because doing it is beyond the capacity of the ordinary owner or tenant, but because the permission to do the work must be secured from the landlord, the building department, and the utility company—all three are necessary. The utility company will not make the initial hookup unless the work is done by a licensed electrician. This situation is slowly changing, so that much of the work which was formerly within the province of licensed electricians can now be done by the owners of houses and apartments if those persons demonstrate to the building department their capability of doing the work.

At present the cost of electrical work has risen to a point where a line from the main to an adjoining room and the installation of an appliance outlet can cost as much as $150 (New York City). The materials cost is under $10 and the time required to do it less than an hour. Not only is it proper for tenants to do "skilled" work in their own apartments or houses as long as they do the work properly, inflation has made it a necessity for a great many people.

In many apartment buildings, landlords have acknowledged inadequate electrical power, and have run in new power lines. Often, however, the lines have *not* been brought into each individual apartment. The cost of doing this has fallen to the tenant, and in many buildings that have this supplemental power, the owner has yet to make it available. Where, however, these lines are installed and available, a tenant can use the following procedures to tap and use them to increase amperage.

The favorite place for running new power lines in apartment buildings is up through the back hallway. The photograph shows a typical installation.

To provide additional power for an apartment by tapping these lines, I first cut off the power to them in the basement. These lines are run through an appropriately fused switch box which has been marked to identify them. I turn the switch handle on the box to the Off position.

Same main with cover removed

Supplemental main in back hallway

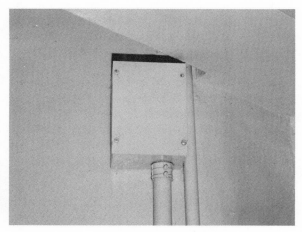

Typical junction box located in back hallway

Same junction box with cover removed

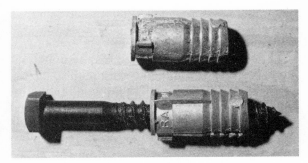

Lag shield and lag screw in shield

I remove the screws in the corners of the junction box in the back hallway and take off its cover. The junction box contains no receptacles or the like, but is simply a safe container for wires whose ends are joined and from which power may be provided simultaneously in several directions. Such boxes are made in various sizes. The size depends on the thickness and number of wires they contain. The electrical codes define what size is required, and in the electrical supply house where the junction box is purchased a specific box for the specific size and number of wires can be obtained.

I mount an auxiliary main box on a pillar in the back hallway with lag screws and lead shields inserted into the concrete.

These lead shields expand a great deal more than the plastic shields used with smaller boxes, and when coupled with lag screws, make a much sturdier attachment.

I remove the knockout at the top of the auxiliary main box and at the side of the junction box.

This auxiliary main is rated at 60 amps and has ten available circuits. A #10 wire is the appropriate

(two 30-amp lines) size to carry this amperage. I will be bringing three #10 copper wires from the junction box to the auxiliary main. This is a distance of only 3 feet or so. Nevertheless, I will have to protect these three wires. I could use conduit, but because I will be making several turns over a small distance I prefer to use flexible greenfield.

For three #10 wires, 1-inch diameter greenfield is permissible but I use instead 1-1/4 inch-diameter greenfield to facilitate pulling the wires through, since a #10 wire, in spite of being braided, is still fairly stiff.

I remove the 1-1/4 inch knockout in the junction box and one in the auxiliary main. I select the two that are closest to each other.

I cut a length of greenfield the distance between the two knockouts, attach 1-1/4 inch connectors to each end, and fasten them with locknuts to the junction box and auxiliary main.

I push a snake through the knockout in the auxiliary main, through the greenfield, and into the junction box. I attach white, black, and red #10 wires to the loop at the end of the snake and pull the three wires into the auxiliary main. I leave a foot or so of each wire extending from the auxiliary main.

I cut the three wires in the junction box so that a foot or so of each extends from it.

I strip 7/8 inch of insulation from the end of the red wire in the auxiliary main and attach it to the large terminal at the bottom of either of the two vertical rows of fuse holders. I attach the black wire to the terminal at the bottom of the other vertical row of fuse holders. I attach the white wire to the large aluminum-colored terminal on the horizontal bar at the top.

I strip 3 inches of insulation from the ends of the red, black, and white #10 wires in the junction box.

Red wire coming from junction box attached to terminal at bottom of fuse row

Wires crossed

Wires braided prior to soldering

(These are the wires I have pulled through the greenfield.) I strip 3 inches of insulation from the ends of the three wires coming from the basement. I cross the red wire from the auxiliary main with the red wire coming from the basement, then wind them around each other for half a dozen turns.

I now join the two red wires more securely by soldering them together with rosin-core solder. (Acid flux should be avoided.) I wrap the soldered splices with plastic tape to a thickness at least equal to the insulation I have removed.

I splice the two remaining white wires in the junction box together in the same way, also the two black wires. I now have three joints in the junction box where each colored wire going to the auxiliary main has been spliced to its matching counterpart coming from the basement.

The auxiliary main is now capable of providing ten new circuits.

To install one such circuit, I would first have to decide whether to use conduit, wire mold, BX, or flexible nonmetallic cable.

If the installation is in a suburban house and the interior core of the walls is hollow (stud construction), I would use flexible nonmetallic cable, since it is the cheapest and easiest to use.

If the installation is in a city structure and the walls are solid masonry, I would use BX if the wiring is to be buried.

If the installation is in an urban or suburban area and the wiring is to be exposed, I would use wire mold if a neat final appearance is desired. I would use conduit if relative neatness is not a factor.

If I choose wire mold or conduit, the first step would be to mount appropriate boxes in the desired locations, then install the inner half of wire mold or the conduit between the auxiliary main and each installed box.

If I choose nonmetallic cable or BX, the first step would be to recess appropriate boxes in walls or ceilings in the desired locations, then provide a path in the walls or ceilings for the cable which would later be covered.

A typical 120-volt circuit would employ a white and black #12 wire and a corresponding 20-amp fuse. With either wire mold or conduit, the separate identical wires are used and either pulled through the conduit with a snake or placed into the inner half of the wire mold. If flexible nonmetallic cable or BX is used, two-wire #12 is purchased.

A circuit composed of #12 wires and fused at 20-amps will have a practical capacity of around 1900 watts. I total the wattage likely to be used on this circuit and limit the number of receptacles and lights so that the maximum probable wattage at any given time does not exceed 1400 watts.

After installing all the wires in all the boxes and attaching them to receptacles, light fixtures and switches, I shut off the power to the auxiliary main from the basement switch. I attach the white wire to any of the aluminum-colored terminal screws beside the large terminal screw where I have attached the incoming white wire from the power source (in this case the junction box in the back hallway). I attach the black wire to any of the brass-colored terminal screws beside the vertical row of fuse holders on the side where I have attached the black wire from the junction box. I install a 20-amp fuse in the fuse holder, turn the power on in the basement, and the circuit is available for use.

If I wish to install a 240-volt circuit and desire a capacity of, say, 50 amps, I would use #10 wire, attach the white and black wires as described in the paragraph above, and attach the third red wire to any unused brass-colored terminal beside an empty fuse holder. This connection is made on the same side as the connection of the incoming red wire from the junction box. A second 30-amp fuse is screwed into the fuse holder beside this terminal. The red, black, and white wires provide 240 volts after being connected to their respective terminals in a 240-volt receptacle.

## Electrical Boxes

The following photographs show some of the more widely used kinds of electrical boxes.

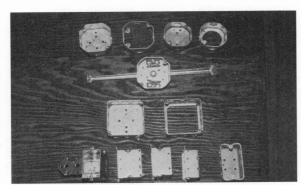

Various electrical boxes

The following photographs show some of the box covers used in conjunction with the above boxes.

Various covers

## Wire Sizes

The table below lists the proper size of the wire to use with various amperages.

| AMPERAGE | SIZE OF WIRE |
|---|---|
| 15 | 14 |
| 20 | 12 |
| 25–30 | 10 |
| 35–40 | 8 |
| 45–50 | 6 |
| 60–70 | 4 |
| 80–90 | 3 |
| 100 | 2 |
| 150 | 0 |
| 200 | 000 |

# PLUMBING

**3**

## Types of Pipe, Fittings, and Tools

The bulk of present-day plumbing work is done with copper pipe and tubing and various copper fittings. Polyvinyl chloride pipe and fittings (''pvc'') have also come into use but are still of minor importance in dwellings and are prohibited in many areas. Economical galvanized steel pipes and fittings, formerly in widespread use, are no longer employed today, except for the cheapest homes, for water lines, because scale, a combination of rust and impurities in water, accumulates inside the pipes and becomes a prime cause of blockage.

The most durable piping is brass. It is also the most expensive and enjoys the highest cost of installation since it takes much longer to install than copper. Its use has been mandatory in many urban areas, but this situation is rapidly changing. Brass is a viable alternative in renovations when the amount of pipe needed is relatively small.

The pipe vise is on a collapsible stand and serves to hold the pipe while it is being worked on. (The table of the stand has grooves for bending conduit as an added feature. When so used, the stand is held rigid by means of a pipe wedged between the silver-colored screw bolt and the ceiling.)

The pipe cutter has two wheels and a cutting disc. After the pipe has been marked at the desired length, the cutting disc is tightened against the mark by turning the handle clockwise. The pipe cutter is then rotated clockwise around the pipe while the handle is simultaneously tightened. A cut is easily made in less than a minute.

Pipe vise and stand holding 1/2-inch brass pipe

Pipe cutter

Pipe cutter in position to cut pipe

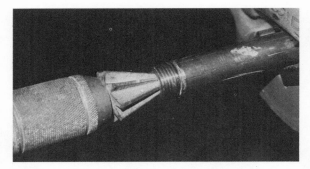

Reamer cleaning out burrs from inside cut pipe

When the cut has been completed, the inside of the pipe will have burrs or ragged edges. These collect foreign material in the water and should be removed from the pipe by placing a reamer bit tight inside the pipe and turning it a few times.

The pipe threader is composed of two parts: the handle, with a ring that contains a ratchet device and a silver-colored knob, and the die. The die has three sets of serrated teeth which cut into the pipe to make threads. The silver-colored knob is raised, then the die is slipped into the ring at the end of the arm. The knob is on a spring and will fall to secure the die.

Dies are available in various sizes for use with pipe of corresponding size. The pipe threader in the photo will take all of them up to 1-1/2 inches in diameter.

1/2-inch and 3/4-inch dies, guide-hole side

Die holder and ratchet

Inserting die into holder

Die inside holder, 3/4-inch die

Threading 1/2-inch pipe

Placing guide hole over pipe

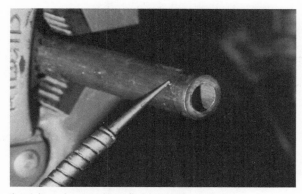

Applying pipe-cutting oil prior to threading

To cut threads into a pipe, I tighten the pipe in the vise leaving 8-inches or so extending beyond the jaws. If I am to thread 1/2-inch pipe, I place the 1/2-inch die into the pipe threader. I then squirt pipe-cutting oil over the area to be threaded. Use of this special oil is essential, since the serrated teeth of the die will soon become deformed and dull if the cut is made without it.

As shown in the photo, I place the die over the pipe through the hole at the end opposite the serrated cutters. This hole serves as a guide to align the cutting teeth with the pipe. The teeth lie around the circumference of the pipe. I hold the die tight against the pipe by pushing the palm of my hand forward against the die housing while turning the pipe-threader arm clockwise. Because of the ratchet device, the teeth will continue in a complete circle even though I move the arm only a short distance. (This is a helpful convenience since it would be awkward to move the arm in a complete circle.) Once the threading has begun—this becomes obvious by the increased force needed to turn the arm and the sliver of brass that begins to form as the teeth remove it—I place both hands on the arm and raise and lower it for a couple of feet until the threading is complete. The total length of the threads along the pipe should not be more than 1 inch or less than 5/8 inch. The length of the threads can be determined by glancing at the pipe and teeth. When the pipe is 1/4 inch or so from the end of the teeth, threading should be stopped. I wipe the cutting oil from the threads with a heavy rag before removing the pipe from the vise.

The brass cut from the pipe will accumulate around the teeth and should be removed often before it becomes wedged. This waste is sharp and should be removed with a rag or gloves.

These dies will only cut threads on the outside of a pipe to make a "male" end. (When the thread is inside it is referred to as "female.") There are other tools to thread the inside, but I will not be using them, nor will most plumbing jobs require them.

The threads made by the cutter are standard and will fit any of the fittings purchased in a hardware store or plumbing supply house.

When pipe is being screwed into a fitting or vice versa it is essential that it *not* be done too quickly. Friction will cause the joint to heat up if the assembly is done too rapidly, and cooling will create very small leaks. It is also a good practice to limit the penetration of the pipe into the fitting for a distance of 1/2 inch. This is the optimum amount for a good threaded joint. There is no necessity to keep tightening the joint beyond this amount since it will not prevent leaks and only increases the likelihood of creating them.

Where pipes are joined together by a fitting, it is essential that the pipe and fitting be properly seated first in order to align the threads of each. This is by no means automatic, and the placement of a fitting with interior threads on a pipe with exterior threads must be done with care. The first few turns of the fitting *should not require any force*. This is the best means of determining that the threads are aligned. They must go together *easily* during the first few turns. In general, the larger the diameter of the pipe, the more difficult the initial alignment. Very often, an initial counterclockwise turn before tightening clockwise will help seat the two ends properly.

Brass pipe may be bought by the linear foot or in standard 10-foot lengths. A plumbing supply house will add a surcharge if less than a standard length is bought since they will have to cut the pipe. This can add up quickly and should be avoided. The same holds true for threading. It is always substantially cheaper to buy standard lengths and cut and thread pipes yourself.

A great many fittings are manufactured, each designed to fulfill a specific need. Following are some of the more widely used brass pipe fittings and the purpose each serves:

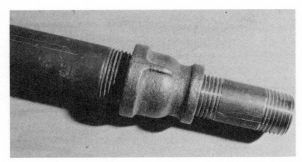

Reducing coupling, 3/4–1/2-inch, to join two pipes in a straight line, one with 3/4-inch diameter and the other 1/2-inch diameter

90-degree elbow, ell, for joining two pipes and changing direction 90 degrees

Street elbow, for joining two pipes while changing direction 90 degrees, has male and female end

Coupling, for joining two pipes in a straight line

45-degree elbow, joins two pipes and changes direction 45 degrees

Union, apart, joins male ends of already installed pipe in a straight line

Cap to close off male end of pipe

Union tightened

Reducing bushing, 2–1-1/2-inches, in 2-inch ell and 1-1/2-inch short nipple

Tee, joins two pipes in a straight line and provides a female opening at 90 degrees to the line

Stilson wrench

Close, short, and long nipple for providing additional length

Two Stilson wrenches; one holds installed pipe and fittings from moving while new pipe or fittings are being installed

To assemble fittings and pipes, channel-lock pliers and Stilson wrenches are used. The larger Stilson wrench on p. 57 has a 24-inch handle. Its jaws will open widely enough to grip the largest-diameter pipe likely to be used and its handle is long enough to provide the needed leverage. The smaller one has a 16-inch handle. Quite often I will need to use them together, one to hold a pipe or fitting stationary while I tighten or loosen another piece of pipe or fitting.

## Roughing In (General Information)

Plumbing work is divided into two stages: in the first, known as "roughing in," water lines and drains are brought to appropriate locations for later hookup to fixtures and appliances. In the second, the fixtures and appliances are themselves installed and connected to the water supply and drains.

Washing machine and gas dryer

Small and large sink, dishwasher

This is how the kitchen will appear after the plumbing is completed. There are two sinks, a dishwasher, a washing machine, a gas dryer, and a gas stove. Installing these fixtures and appliances and making them operational is what the remainder of this chapter demonstrates.

At the completion of the demolition described in Chapter 1, the hot and cold water lines, their valves and the drain were left standing as shown in the photographs. (There is also a sink vent which is not pictured.) This minimum amount of plumbing will be present in any apartment or house and is the point where we begin.

Gas stove

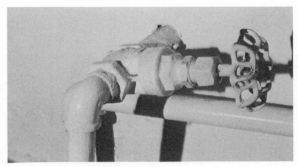

3/4-inch main cold water valve

3/4-inch main hot water valve and new 1/2-inch hot water valve

Old 2-inch drain

## Roughing In Risers and Reducing Pipe

A riser is a water pipe which runs vertically through a building and which has a valve at each apartment to control the flow of hot and cold water to that apartment. The diameter of the riser will vary with each particular structure, but its hot and cold water valves will invariably be 3/4 inch in diameter. While this size valve is fine for supplying water to the apartment, it is unnecessarily large for carrying water to the fixtures and appliances within the kitchen. In a proper economy move, the first thing I do is to thread a 3/4-to-1/2-inch reducing bushing into the outlet side of both the hot and cold water valves.

This reducing fitting changes the apartment's standard valve from 3/4 inch to 1/2 inch and from this point on I will use 1/2-inch pipes and fittings throughout.

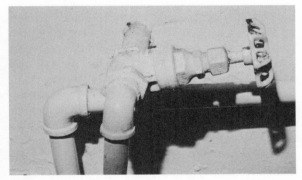

Reducing bushing, 3/4–1/2-inch in main cold water valve, street ell and nipple

The outlet side of the valve (there is only one opening, since the other opening is already connected to the hot and cold water risers) has a 3/4-inch female end. The reducing bushing has a 3/4-inch male end and a 1/2-inch female opening in the center.

Before tightening the reducing bushing into the female opening of the valve, I wrap the male end with a material called plumber's tape. This is made of plastic 1/2 inch wide. Its purpose is to prevent leaks in a male–female threaded joint and it is widely used as a substitute for the pipe dope which used to be brushed onto the threads prior to tightening. (It is more reliable than pipe dope, less messy, and more expensive.) To apply the plumber's tape, I hold an end on the threads, pull to tighten, wrap it one turn over the threads, cut it, then depress it into the threads with my finger. I put the tape on in a clockwise direction to prevent its loosening when I tighten the fitting.

## Roughing In a Cold Water Line

When the curtain wall between the kitchen and pantry was removed, a channel 5-1/2 inches wide and 2-1/2 inches deep was left in the floor. Since this channel will later be covered with flooring, it provides a convenient place to locate the cold water pipe.

The bushing I installed in the cold water valve is 1 foot or so up from the floor with its opening parallel to the channel.

The nearest fixture to it will be the small sink. The faucet that will later be installed in this sink will have the cold water tap on the right (this is standard). If the cabinet for the sink is not yet installed, I mark the rough location of the cold water faucet on the floor. (If the cabinet is in place, I place the mark on the back of the cabinet.) I now want to run the cold water line from the bushing in the valve to the "rough" location for the cold water tap. I do *not* want to bring the cold water line all the way up to the projected end of the faucet, only 6 inches or so up off the floor and in line with it. (During the second stage of the plumbing, after the sink has been fastened to the counter, I will make this relatively short connection.)

Street ell

The pictured fitting is a 1/2-inch street elbow (ell). One end is male, the other female. It changes direction 90 degrees. I am using this particular fitting since the bushing in the water valve is female. I also want a change in direction from horizontal to vertical so that I can proceed down to the channel.

I place plumber's tape over the male end of the street ell and screw it into the bushing so that the female end of the street ell faces down. (I will be using plumber's tape at every joint hereafter and will omit mentioning it.)

I now want to come down from the street ell to the channel, change from a vertical to a horizontal direction, then proceed along the channel to the

Valve, 3/4–1/2-inch bushing, street ell, nipple, ell, and pipe for descending to and continuing along channel in floor

rough position of the cold water side of the faucet. To do this, I will use a nipple (pipe less than 12 inches long threaded at each end is referred to as a nipple) and a 90-degree ell.

To situate the bottom of the ell at the bottom of the channel, I will have to cut the nipple between the street ell and the 90-degree ell to an exact length. To determine what that length is, I first measure the distance between the street ell and the bottom of the channel. It is 10 inches. The vertical distance of the 90-degree ell is 1-5/8 inches. (There are two types of ell, long and short sweep. This is a long-sweep elbow.) I subtract the vertical length of the ell, always 1-5/8 inches, from 10 inches leaving 8-3/8 inches. Since each end of the nipple will be screwed 1/2 inch into a fitting, I will need a nipple 1 inch longer, or 9-3/8 inches. (This is standard procedure; I will be using it throughout in order to determine the length of pipe needed between fittings.)

I cut 1/2-inch pipe to a length of 9-3/8 inches and thread each end. While it is still in the vise, I attach the 90-degree ell. (All ells are 90 degrees unless stated otherwise.)

The easiest place to assemble pipe and fittings is in the vise, and I do this wherever possible.

I now attach the nipple and ell to the street ell, making sure to leave the female end of the 90-degree ell parallel to the channel and in the direction I am taking to the small sink. In making the attachment, I hold one Stilson wrench on the street ell to keep it from changing position while tightening with another Stilson wrench on the nipple.

At this point, using a folding ruler, a chalk line, and a drawing provided by the architect, I lay out the positions of the cabinets, the appliances, and the sinks in the island.

Small self-rimming stainless steel sink

At the rear of this stainless-steel sink are two holes through which the faucet ends will go, later to be attached to the hot and cold water lines. The distance between the holes is 4 inches, measured from their centers. I measure the distance between the 90-degree ell at the end of the piping installed so far and the projected location of center of the right-side sink hole. (The actual hole is not in place as yet since I have not installed the sink. I locate its position from the architect's drawing.) This distance is 43-1/2 inches.

I now want to cut a length of pipe that will lie at the bottom of the channel in the floor. One end will be screwed into the 90-degree ell. The other end will receive a fitting the center of which will be in line with the center of the projected cold water tap. Since I intend to continue the cold water line to the other fixtures and appliances while leaving a connection for the sink's cold water tap, I use a fitting called a tee.

This fitting joins two pipes without changing their direction while providing an outlet for a third pipe that enters the tee at a 90-degree angle.

The distance between one inlet of the tee and the center of its outlet which changes 90 degrees in direction is 1 inch. This means I must deduct 1 inch from the distance of 43-1/2 inches I originally measured for the channel pipe. However, since the

pipe I am going to cut will be threaded into the 90-degree ell and the tee for 1/2 inch, I must also add 1 inch to its length. The 1-inch length of the tee cancels out the 1 inch which must be added to the length of the pipe. I therefore cut a length of pipe to 43-1/2 inches, thread each end, and attach the 1/2-inch tee while it is still in the vise. I screw the remaining end into the ell on the installed piping and tighten it so that the center of the tee faces up. The remaining outlet continues in the original direction.

I have not yet anchored the pipes to the floor so they can easily be raised to permit attachment, then lowered back into the channel.

The center outlet of the tee is in line with the projected center of the cold water tap. (No attempt should be made at this point to have the alignment exact.)

I attach a 6-inch nipple to the center outlet of the tee (any length between 6 and 12 inches can be used). I then attach an ell to the nipple, then another 6-inch nipple to that.

Tee, 6-inch nipple, ell, and 6-inch nipple for cold water supply to sink

The last nipple is still in line with the cold water tap. It comes through the projected location of the back of the cabinet and lies in a horizontal plane. I cover the end of the nipple with a cap.

(I will temporarily cap the ends of all water lines. After completion of the roughing, I will open the hot and cold water valves to determine if there are any leaks.)

The still unused outlet of the tee is within the area of the island. It is no longer necessary to keep the piping below the finished floor level, an awkward place for assembly. I therefore screw a street ell

Space behind washer and dryer where rough plumbing is located

Pipe strap for securing pipe

into the tee so that its outlet faces up, continue with a 6-inch nipple and then an ell with its outlet facing the direction I intend to go. This brings the pipe off the floor and continues its direction toward the larger sink.

On one side of the island are the dryer and washing machine, their backs facing inward. The second sink and dishwasher are on the opposite side of the island and their backs also face inward. Between the two sets of backs is a void of 12 inches. In this open area between the backs of the washer and dryer and the second sink and dishwasher, I construct a 2-x-4 skeletal wall 34 inches high (see page 201 for details).

Using the same techniques for measuring, cutting, threading, and assembling pipe and fittings, I continue the 1/2-inch cold water line at a height of about 8 inches and place a tee with its center outlet in line with the center of the projected position of the cold water tap of the second sink. I install an 8-inch nipple (again, the length may be anywhere between 6 and 12 inches) into the center outlet of the tee. The nipple brings me inside the projected back of the cabinet in which the second sink will be installed. It is in a horizontal position roughly 8 inches off the floor. I cap the nipple.

I nail the strap in the photo to the skeletal wall and over the pipe to secure it. (Two here are sufficient.)

I continue the cold water line from the remaining outlet of the tee to roughly the center of the projected position of the back of the washing machine, install an elbow with its outlet facing up, then attach a 6-inch nipple and cap it.

I have now brought the 1/2-inch cold water line from the 3/4-inch valve of the cold water riser to both sinks and the washing machine. I have ended the cold water line at each with capped nipples at convenient locations for their later connection to the faucets and to the inlet line from the washing machine.

## Roughing In a Hot Water Line

The hot water riser was located inside the curtain wall that was removed. The 3/4-inch valve pictured earlier is the original installation.

I discover a leak, a slow dribble out of the outlet side of the valve. To repair it, it would be necessary to shut off the hot water in the riser, which would affect all the apartments on the line. To avoid this inconvenience, I instead install a 3/4-1/2-inch reducing bushing in the female outlet of the valve, then connect a 2-inch nipple and a new 1/2-inch valve to it. I close the new 1/2-inch valve and open the old 3/4-inch valve completely. The old valve now acts as a coupling, and the new valve keeps the hot water from leaking. (This new valve happens to be located in the projected position of the cabinet under the small sink and will therefore be convenient for any future repairs or maintenance.)

In the same manner as the cold water line, I run the hot water line to the left side (hot water side) of the projected position of the faucet of the small sink. I end it with a capped nipple that lies at the same height as the cold water nipple and 4 inches away as measured from center to center.

I continue the hot water line to the second sink. Here the faucet ends are 9 inches apart as measured from center to center and I leave the capped nipple at that width from the cold water nipple. Both are 8 inches or so off the floor. Both enter the projected back of the cabinet that will hold the second and larger sink.

I continue the hot water line to the projected location of the back of the dishwasher. On the end of the pipe, I attach the center outlet of a tee. I tighten the tee so that one of its remaining outlets faces the dishwasher and the other the washing machine. I install 4-inch nipples and caps into each of the outlets.

(I have already installed a 1/2-inch hot water valve below the small sink, which is readily accessible. I will also install hot and cold water valves at the large sink and the washing machine as well as a hot water valve at the dishwasher when I am ready to attach the fixtures. This will enable the owners to shut off the water to any one of the sinks or appliances without interfering with the operation of any of the others. The dishwasher has only a hot water supply and therefore only one valve.)

For the two sinks, I now have hot and cold water pipes ending with horizontally capped nipples extending through the projected backs of the cabinets. They are 4 inches apart at the small sink and 9 inches at the large sink. I have hot and cold water pipes ending with capped nipples 4 inches or so apart for the washing machine. (These may end with the nipple either horizontal or vertical, anywhere from 6 to 12 inches off the floor.) I have a horizontal capped nipple at the end of the hot water line at the back of the projected location of the dishwasher.

With the ends of all the hot and cold water lines capped, I turn on the cold water main valve. This is the original 3/4-inch valve. I turn on the hot water main valve. This is the new 1/2-inch valve I have installed beside the old 3/4-inch valve attached to the hot water riser.

There are half a dozen minute leaks caused by joints being assembled too rapidly, as mentioned earlier. I correct these by removing the fittings and the old tape, winding new tape over the threads, and leisurely reconnecting the pipes. There are no more leaks.

## Roughing In Gas Pipe

We decide to shift the gas stove to the opposite side of the kitchen; piping for it must be routed from its former position to the new location. The first step is to shut off the supply of gas to the stove. This can be done from either of two positions—or both, as a greater precaution.

In ordinary installations, a gas valve will be located in the pipe behind the stove. A quarter turn from the open position will shut it off. (Another quarter turn will open it.) The other gas valve (see the illustration on p. 64) is located at the meter in the kitchen. (In newer installations, it is located in the basement.) The valve is shut when its arm is at a right angle to the gas pipe.

Gas valve at meter

The fact that no gas is coming through to the stove can be verified by opening a gas cock on the stove after the valves are shut and listening for escaping gas. Smaller amounts of escaping gas can be checked by placing a soapy solution over an aperture or fitting and noting whether bubbles form in the solution.

*After shutting both valves off*, the stove is disconnected by loosening the nut on the flexible connection attached to the incoming gas piping.

The material I will use for roughing the gas line is 3/4-inch black steel pipe and fittings.

Neither stove nor gas dryer is as yet actually in position, since their presence would clutter the working area. However, I have measured and marked their locations as given on the architect's drawing and noted where each of the gas inlets is positioned. (I used the same procedure with the sinks and other appliances.)

I replace the 1/2-inch die in the pipe threader with a 3/4-inch die and begin to install the gas pipe in the channel in the floor left by the demolished wall, where the water pipes have been laid. The techniques of measuring, cutting, threading, and assembling are exactly those used for water pipes with these few exceptions:

1. At connections, I sparingly spread pipe compound on the threads instead of using plumber's tape.

2. I do not bend the pipe to cause a change in direction but use a 22-1/2-degree ell.

3. I install a tee in the line to bring the gas supply to both the gas dryer and stove. *I keep the middle outlet up.* (In water-pipe installations the tee may be positioned in any direction. With gas, the takeoff from the tee should be either from the sides or up, *not down.*)

4. I *do not* use unions, bushings, or swing joints (a combination of fittings). These are more subject to leaks than other fittings.

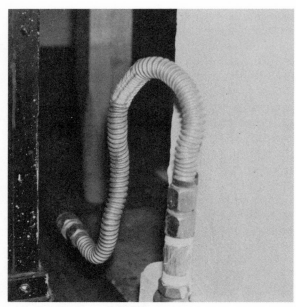

Flexible gas pipe connected to stove

I begin at the old gas valve in the former location of the stove and install 3/4-inch black steel pipe down to the channel in the floor. I install a tee where the void at the back of the fixtures and appliances intersects the channel in the floor. I continue one line to the gas dryer, which I terminate with a gas valve and nipple. It is roughly centered at the back of the dryer and about a foot off the floor. I continue from the remaining outlet of the tee to the opposite wall of the kitchen, where I come up from the channel with an ell, a 12-inch nipple, another new gas valve, and a short nipple.

I close the newly installed gas valves at the dryer and stove, then open the valves at the meter and the former location of the stove. I spread soapy water (or detergent solution) over *all of the joints in the newly installed gas lines.* If there are any leaks, bubbles will form in the solution. There are none. This is not unusual, since gas is delivered at relatively low pressure and, if one observes the precautions described, leaks will be rare.

After the floors have been finished, I will position the stove and attach the flexible pipe to the nipple at one end and the supply pipe of the stove at the other end. Flexible pipe is mandatory in New York City and many other areas. Its purpose is to prevent any fitting in the gas pipe from rupturing or springing a leak when a stove or dryer is moved for

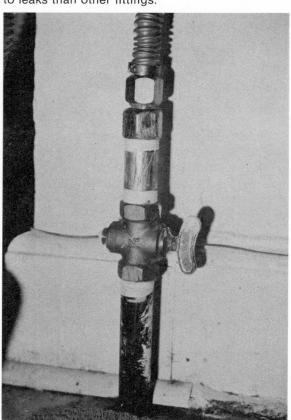

Gas supply pipe coming up from floor channel, new gas valve, nipple, flexible pipe, and nuts

cleaning or maintenance. It permits movement of the appliance without creating any stress on the rigid fittings. (It should be used whether codes require it or not.)

## Roughing In Drains

The pictured 2-inch galvanized steel pipe remained after the demolition. It is part of the building's waste-removal system and was installed at the time the building was constructed.

Old 2-inch drain pipe and fittings

By gravity, it will carry the waste produced in the kitchen to a house drain in the basement. From there the waste will continue through the drain to the house sewer line, where it will go under the street and into the city sewer system.

When waste water enters the drain it displaces air. If the displaced air has no means of exit from the system, it will cause blockage and no drainage action will occur. In addition, the noxious gases produced in the waste removal system must be provided with an exit. Drainage systems are therefore equipped with pipes called vents that permit displaced air and gases to exit. Vent pipes, connected to the drainage system, continue upward through the roof, releasing the displaced air and noxious gases into the atmosphere. The venting system is installed along with the original plumbing, of which it is an essential and integral part. All buildings under a hundred years old will be in compliance with the codes governing vents so that, as in this instance, they will already be in place, requiring no further work.

The bulk of kitchen waste carried to the drain will be water originating at both sinks, the dishwasher,

and the washing machine. To carry the waste from its sources to the 2-inch drain, I will be using 1-1/2-inch galvanized steel pipe. While 1-1/4-inch pipe could be used, the amount of pipe length needed here is rather small, and I prefer to use the larger diameter since its additional cost will be negligible.

My first step is to install a 2-to-1-1/2-inch reducing bushing into the 2-inch ell left at the drain line. This permits the balance of the pipe and fittings for the roughing to be 1-1/2 inches.

I will be running the 1-1/2-inch pipe first to the smaller sink, then to the second, larger sink, and then onward to the washing machine. I will *not* continue with the 1-1/2-inch pipe to the dishwasher since the waste from it will be handled in another way, detailed later in this chapter.

The path of the drain pipe lies in the void between the backs of the appliances and sinks. I will install a 1-1/2-inch tee in the drain line so that its center outlet is in line with the projected center of the first sink. I will use the side outlet to continue the 1-1/2-inch drain to the second sink and install another tee so that its center outlet also corresponds roughly to the projected center of the second sink. I will again use the side outlet of the tee to continue roughly to the back and center of the washing machine.

Measuring, cutting, and threading the 1-1/2-inch pipe is done with the same tools and in the same manner as with brass pipe detailed earlier. (Of course a 1-1/2-inch die must be used in the threader.)

1-1/2-inch drain tee behind cabinet back

1-1/2-inch galvanized nipple from tee

At the first sink, I install an 8-inch nipple into the center outlet of the tee so that it emerges horizontally between the hot and cold water lines already in place under the projected location of the sink. I center it between the water lines, which places it roughly at the projected center of the sink. I locate it 8 inches off the floor, but a few inches up or down will not make any difference. I do exactly the same at the second sink.

### Roughing In a Washing Machine Drain

From the side outlet of the tee in the drain line behind the second sink, I install a length of 1-1/2-inch pipe which ends at roughly the center and back of the washing machine. While this length of pipe is still in the vise, I screw an ell on an end. I want the outlet of the ell to face up after I tighten the pipe to the tee.

1-1/2-inch ell and drain pipe for washing-machine drain

I mark a scrap of 1 x 2 at 34-1/2 inches. I stand the stick beside the ell and measure the distance from the ell to the mark on the stick. I cut a length of 1-1/2-inch pipe to the measured length, thread *one* end only, and screw it into the ell for 1/2 inch. The top of this pipe is unthreaded and 34 inches off the floor.

### Additional Information on Roughing In Drains

I mentioned earlier in this chapter that in order to join a pipe and fitting it is sometimes useful initially to turn the pipe or fitting counterclockwise to seat it properly before turning clockwise to tighten. This is particularly true with larger-diameter drain pipes, and added care should be taken to align the pipe and fitting before tightening. Only *slight* resistance should be felt during the first few tightening turns. If any significant amount of resistance is felt, the threads of the pipe and fitting are not aligned. The initial tightening can be done with the fingertips. If the fitting or pipe must be gripped with the hands to make the initial tightening turns, chances are that the threads have not yet been aligned. If tightening is attempted in spite of misalignment, the threads of each are likely to be damaged. Occasionally, even misaligned threads will "attach" a fitting to a pipe, but the joint will always leak.

As each new piece of pipe or fitting is installed I want to prevent the pipe and fittings previously installed from moving. I place the smaller Stilson wrench on the already-installed pipe or fitting and apply counterclockwise pressure as needed. Simultaneously, I turn the new pipe or fitting clockwise. When the counterclockwise pressure is equal to the clockwise pressure it will prevent the installed piping from moving. The equilibrium is best achieved by *leisurely* building up the pressure needed for tightening.

### Installing a Kitchen Sink in a Countertop

The pictured installation is by far the most widespread in use today. The sink is made of stainless steel and is "self-rimming," which means that it has a rim built into it to facilitate installation. (A device known as a Houdee ring must be used when

Large kitchen sink

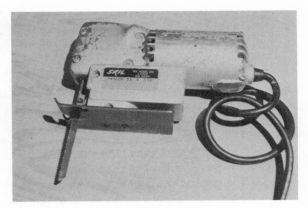

Sabre saw

installing ceramic or porcelain sinks.) However, the procedure for installing stainless-steel, ceramic, and porcelain sinks is very nearly the same.

After the cabinets have been built (see page 194), I place the stainless-steel sink upside down on the counter. (This is the large sink.) I measure the location of the waste pipe, transfer this measurement to the counter, then shift the sink so that its drainage hole is aligned above the waste pipe.

This particular counter is 30 inches deep; the standard width is usually about 25-1/2 inches, but the countertop material came in a 30-inch width and the owners preferred it. For convenience' sake, it is better to place a sink nearer the front of the counter than the back. However, it should not be placed closer than 1 inch to the back of the horizontal piece of wood directly under the counter (the stile) or it will interfere with the installation of the sink.

With the hole in the center of the sink aligned with the waste pipe under the counter and the forward edge of the sink located at least 1 inch away from the back of the stile, I use a carpenter's framing square to align the sink (still upside down). I place the arm of the framing square against the forward edge of the counter and the tongue against the side of the sink. I shift the sink so that its side lies against the tongue while the center hole in the sink is still aligned with the waste pipe under the counter. I trace the outline of the sink on the countertop with a pencil. I remove the sink and draw a parallel outline 3/8 inch inside the first.

The countertop is Corion, a solid plastic material, and I use a 1/2-inch carbide-tipped bit to bore a hole through it. The circumference of the hole lies on the inside of the smaller outline and at the pencil line. *No part of this hole extends beyond the smaller outline.*

The pictured sabre saw (also called a jig saw) is an excellent tool for cutting along the smaller outline.

It is manufactured by the Skil Company and is much better than other models in that its body is also its handle. This places the user closer to the work and also makes for greater maneuverability. A rough hollow-ground blade should be used on the Corion. (If the counter were 3/4-inch plywood and Formica, a medium hollow-ground blade would be used.)

Before I begin to cut the outline, I place two vertical scraps of 2 x 4 between the bottom of the cabinet and the bottom of the Corion I intend to cut. These "legs" should be placed within the outline but out of the path of the saw. They are *necessary* since Corion is heavy and will break before all the cutting has been completed unless propped.

I insert the blade of the sabre saw in the hole and (keeping the table of the saw *flat* on the counter) saw along the inner outline so that the pencil mark barely remains. I do this *without* pushing the blade heavily into the cut, using only light pressure to create forward movement. In variable-speed saws, maximum rpm is most effective.

Once I have removed the sawed portion of Corion, I place the sink into the cutout and move it around to see whether it binds anywhere. I also make sure that the lip around the sink lies flat on the counter. There should be a little play, but no part of the sink cutout should be visible.

I form plumber's putty into 1/4-inch-thick strands by rolling it between my palms. I lay it in a continuous line between the cutout and the larger outline first drawn. I place the sink in the cutout with its lip on the putty, position it so that its rim lies on the first outline marked, then press down moderately.

The sink is attached to the countertop by the pictured clips. Three are used on each of the sink's long sides, two on each of the short.

A hook on one side of each clip is attached to a bar which extends down from the bottom of the sink. The machine screw is then tightened against the underside of the countertop. As the sink is being pulled down to the countertop, excess putty, which is later removed, will be squeezed out. The sink may also shift a bit; before tightening any screw completely, repositioning the sink along the original outline may be necessary.

Sink retaining clip

Sink retaining clip attached under sink

## Completing the Sink Waste

The pictured device, an S trap, permits the free flow of the sink waste while simultaneously preventing noxious sewer gases in the rest of the waste system from entering the kitchen by rising up through the

1-1/2–1-1/4-inch trap

sink drain. This is accomplished by a body of water that is trapped in the lower U-shaped portion and forms a seal between the piping behind the trap and the piping in front of it. It is available in a variety of sizes. The one I am using has one female end 1-1/2 inches in diameter corresponding to the diameter of the waste pipe. The other end has a female opening 1-1/4 inches in diameter. Its overall length is 6 inches.

I unscrew the nipple in the waste line that goes through the back of the cabinet and into a tee. I now want to install a length of 1-1/2-inch pipe together with the trap so that the 1-1/4-inch end of the trap will be directly under the hole in the sink when tightened. (The 1-1/4-inch end will also be facing up.)

There are many ways to do this. The simplest is to place the trap directly under the center sink hole, then measure the distance from the 1-1/2-inch trap opening to the back of the cabinet. To this measurement I add the distance from the back of the cabinet to the front of the tee. I add 1 inch to this total, which allows for the 1/2-inch losses of length when I screw one end of the pipe into the tee and the other end into the trap. I cut 1-1/2-inch pipe to a length equal to the sum of the three measurements, thread each end, and assemble the pipe and trap in the vise. I then install the other end of the pipe in the tee and leave the 1-1/4-inch outlet of the trap facing up.

It is now time for me to make provisions for the waste from the dishwasher.

A dishwasher tee has 1-1/4-inch outlets at each end along with nuts. Its center outlet has an exterior dimension that corresponds to the 1/2-inch interior dimension of the rubber-hose drain of the dishwasher.

Dishwasher tee

Dishwasher tee and tail pipe combined

Basket strainer unassembled

I attach the dishwasher tee to the 1-1/4-inch outlet of the trap with one of the nuts provided. The upper end of the tee has a remaining 1-1/4-inch outlet and nut.

This type of strainer is common to all modern kitchen sinks. The waste hole of the sink has an indented ring around its circumference. The flange around the stationary part of the basket strainer will be seated on this indention. However, before I

Flared end of tail pipe, plastic washer, and slip nut for attachment to strainer end

install the strainer, I want to cut and attach another piece called a tail pipe.

The pictured tail pipe will go from the bottom of the stationary part of the basket strainer, penetrating 1 inch into the outlet of the dishwasher tee. To determine the length of tail pipe needed, I insert the stationary strainer into the waste hole, measure the distance between the bottom of the strainer and the 1-1/4-inch outlet of the dishwasher tee and add 1 inch. I cut the tail pipe to length with a hacksaw, removing the unwanted portion from the end of the tail pipe that is *not* flared. I ream the burrs away from the cut tail pipe, then install the basket strainer and tail pipe as follows.

I place strips of plumber's putty on the circular indention around the waste hole of the sink. Two nuts are supplied with the strainer. I remove them and place the stationary part of the strainer in the hole. I install the larger nut on the threads of the strainer that lie directly beneath the underside of the sink. I do not yet tighten the nut.

I slip the smaller nut over the tail pipe and slide it up to the flanged end. I place the plastic washer (supplied with the tail pipe) on the flange and tighten the nut to the threads at the very bottom of the strainer.

I slip the nut provided with the dishwasher tee up on the other end of the tail pipe and place a rubber washer over the tail pipe and under the nut. I raise the strainer and attached tail pipe and insert the end of the tail pipe into the dishwasher tee 1-1/4-inch outlet.

I now tighten the large nut directly below the strainer on the underside of the sink. It has raised pieces along the circumference similar to the lock-nuts used with BX connectors and can be tightened with a screwdriver and hammer in a similar fashion.

Tightening nut that attaches strainer to sink

Smaller lower nut for attaching tail pipe to strainer end

I have already tightened the upper part of the tail pipe to the lowest end of the strainer.

I tighten the lower part of the tail pipe to the upper part of the dishwasher tee with the nut and washer provided.

I remove the excess putty squeezed out around the strainer circumference.

At the very bottom of the trap is a clean-out plug. It should be unscrewed; I wrap pipe tape around its threads, then retighten it. (Presumably this plug shouldn't leak even without tape or pipe dope, but it leaks often enough to require the precaution.)

This completes the waste line for the large sink. Connecting the waste line between the smaller sink and the roughed in piping is done in the same manner.

## Installing Copper Sink Pipe and Fittings

After installing the waste lines to both sinks, I am ready to connect the hot and cold water lines, which were left capped below the sinks. I have a choice of using either copper tubing or brass pipe. I will use copper for the small sink and brass for the

4-inch faucet and nuts

large. (Either installation is perfectly acceptable. I use both for the purposes of teaching.)

I begin by closing the main hot and cold water valves and removing the caps from the lines.

Above is a special faucet for the smaller sink. It has continuously threaded pipe extending from its hot and cold water taps as shown in the photo. These are 4 inches apart as measured from center to center. Two holes, also 4 inches from center to center, are located at the back of the sink. Two sets of nuts are provided with the faucet. These fit the threaded ends extending from the taps. I place the faucet on the sink so that both threaded pipes go through the holes and extend below the sink. I mark the outline of the faucet on top of the sink, remove the faucet, put plumber's putty 1/4-inch thick along the inside of the outline, then set the faucet back in place.

I attach the faucet to the sink by screwing the thinner of the nuts provided to the hot and cold threaded pipe ends, tightening them against the underside of the sink. These are locknuts and can be distinguished from the other nuts provided by the fact that they have only one set of threads. (The other nuts have two.) After tightening the faucet, I remove the excess putty that has squeezed out along the outline of the faucet on top of the sink.

On the underside of the sink I now have the continuously threaded pipe ends of the faucet. 28 inches or so below them I have the hot and cold water brass nipples installed during the roughing. I am now ready to install copper tubing between the threaded ends of the faucet and the nipples.

This installation requires, however, some preliminary discussion; first relating to values and second to copper tubing.

Locknut attaches faucet to sink

1/2-inch copper tubing

Tubing in bender

As I noted earlier in the chapter, I would ordinarily install water valves in these two new copper lines so that, for example, if a leak developed in the faucet and a worn washer had to be replaced, I could shut off the water to the sink and not affect the supply to any other point. However I have decided not to do this here since the main hot water valve lies in the cabinet under the small sink and the main cold water valve is a few feet away. The owners will therefore be able to shut off the water to the small sink easily.

By convention, the hot water tap is located on the left side of the faucet and the cold water tap on the right. However, during roughing, I installed the cold water supply on the left and the hot water supply on the right. This was not an error. The main cold water valve was located at the left of the sink and it was more economical to rough in the cold water supply on the left and plan on switching it later with tubing rather than originally to add brass pipe and fittings and rough it in on the right. The hot water main valve was located on the right side of the sink and, for the same reason, I roughed it in on the right.

The pictured 1/2-inch copper tubing is the material I will use to connect the hot and cold faucet ends with the hot and cold brass supply lines. It is fairly malleable and small changes in direction can be made in it by manual bending. For larger bends it is best to use a tubing bender.

Both the faucet ends and the nipples in the supply lines have male ends. However, the special nuts which are supplied with the faucet have two sets of threads. The inner one corresponds to the size of the threads on the faucet ends. The outer threads of the nut correspond to the threads on a standard 1/2-inch male end. At the faucet end of the tubing I will therefore want a male fitting. At the other end of the tubing I will want a female nut to attach to the supply nipple.

There are three satisfactory methods of attaching fittings to tubing. I will discuss each before undertaking the actual connection.

One of these methods, called flaring, requires the use of the tool on p. 72. (Its cost is under $6.) The copper tubing is clamped in an appropriate hole, leaving 1/8 inch or so extending beyond. Each of the holes in the flaring tool has stamped beside it the size of the tubing to be inserted in that hole.

Flaring tool

Flared end of tubing

1/2-inch tubing in 1/2-inch hole of flaring tool

Flare at rear of nut

The hole on the top of the tool is beveled back; the flaring is done from that direction. The hole on the underside of the tool does not have a beveled end. To install the tubing in the 1/2-inch hole, I loosen the threaded bolts at both ends, insert the tubing, and tighten the bolts.

I clamp the second half of the flaring tool over the tubing as shown in the photo. I center the tapered point over the center of the tubing. To spread the end of the tubing into the desired washerlike flare shape, the end of the tubing must be round. If the end of the tubing is not round, the chances of

Nut, ferrule, and tubing

End of tubing being flared

producing a satisfactory flare are dim. I insert an appropriate-sized dowel into any tubing end that is not round and, by turning and pressing forward, bring the tubing back to its original shape. Once it has been made round, I turn the arm above the pointed flaring device clockwise until the end of the tubing is folded back into a circle.

The flared end of the tubing acts as a washer.

When the nut is tightened against the male end of the supply nipple (or any male end), the flare (serving as a washer) will create a watertight connection.

A second method of attaching fittings to copper tubing is through the use of pressure fittings.

Pressure fittings are composed of two parts, a ferrule and the threaded fitting for use with it. When using pressure fittings, it is *essential that the tubing be round*. The ferrule is positioned over the tubing so that half of it extends beyond the tubing's end. A nut is then slipped against the ferrule and tightened to the threaded brass nipple (or any 1/2-inch male end). To achieve a leakproof joint, it is *essential that the tubing and ferrule be aligned with the piece to which it is being attached.*

If alignment is not made before the nut is tightened, the ferrule will be squeezed out from the back of the nut and the joint will leak. The ferrule will become visible as it emerges between the tubing and hole of the nut. When this happens, no amount of tightening will stop the joint from leaking.

Sweat fitting, 1/2-inch, one end to receive tubing for soldering, other end threaded to receive 1/2-inch pipe and fittings

Nut, tubing, and ferrule in position for attachment

End of tubing cleaned before soldering

Sweat tee on tubing

Fitting on tubing

Once alignment is achieved, the nut is first hand-tightened, then wrench-tightened for another two or three turns. If a leak develops after the water has been turned on, the nut is tightened further until the leak stops.

A third method of attaching fitting to tubing is soldering.

Special fittings are manufactured appropriate for soldering. The pictured fitting is a "sweat" tee (all fittings to be soldered are referred to as sweat fittings). Sweat fittings are available in the same variety as standard fittings.

Sweat fittings have what are known as "shoulders"—slightly larger-diameter ends that allow the tubing to slide into them for a predetermined distance. The diameter of the fitting then

decreases slightly, enough to prevent the tubing from continuing into the fitting beyond this predesigned distance. Before soldering, I *shine the tubing by rubbing it with emery cloth.* The inside of the fitting is also cleaned. I then insert the tubing into the fitting as far as it will go.

I place the fitting and tubing I want to solder together in a vise or, if there is none, on a table with the fitting at least 6 inches over the table's edge so that the flame of the torch will not ignite anything.

I light the torch and direct the flame *at the fitting.* For the solder to adhere properly to the fitting and tubing, both must be heated to about the same temperature. Since the fitting is heavier than the tubing, it will require more heat. If the flame is directed only at the tubing or at the tubing and fitting simultaneously, the tubing will become hot-

Flame of torch directed at fitting

Acid-core solder applied to joint

Paste applied over heated joint to be soldered

Soldered joint after wiping

*I place an inch or so of solder on the joint. If the solder begins to run freely around the joint, I know that the copper is at the right temperature. The heat required to melt the solder must come from the copper and not the flame.*

The flux causes the solder melted by the heat of the copper to run around the joint. Capillary action will draw the solder into the space between the outside of the tubing and the inside of the fitting and make a satisfactory joint.

As soon as I apply the solder, I wipe the joint with a damp rag. This removes the excess flux, cleans the solder, and hastens its solidification.

The joint should be shiny with no black specks in the silver colored solder. If the tubing and fitting were not adequately cleaned or if any impurity in the joint obstructed the flow of the solder, dark specks will be visible in the shiny joint and a leak will probably result.

If an impurity has created a leak, the joint must be reheated, dismantled, cleaned, and resoldered.

Any of the three methods described will be satisfactory for attaching fittings to copper tubing. In some circumstances, such as joining two lengths of copper tubing together with a coupling, sweat-

ter than the fitting. By directing the flame only at the fitting, heat is transferred to the tubing and both achieve similar temperatures.

As the fitting is heated it will begin to change color. This should not take more than thirty seconds. I then brush a liquid material called flux over the joint. Its purpose is to cause the solder to flow.

When the flux makes contact with the heated copper it begins to boil. It decreases the temperature of the copper. I therefore direct the flame at the fitting for a brief interval to bring up the temperature of the copper.

I am now ready to apply solder to the joint.

The solder used should contain at least 30 percent tin, preferably more. Like flux, there are many types and brands available; any that is appropriate for soldering copper will be satisfactory.

Tubing in cutter

ing the joint would be most appropriate. On the other hand, if a connection is being made to the hot water inlet of a dishwasher, the use of heat may damage a nearby valve and flaring or using a pressure fitting would be more appropriate. I personally use the flaring method whenever possible since I have had the least number of leaks with it.

The copper tubing is cut with the tool pictured, a tubing cutter. Its operation is similar to a pipe cutter. The desired length is marked on the tubing. The tubing is then inserted between the rollers and the cutting disc with the disc on the mark. The knob handle is turned clockwise to press the cutting disc against the tubing. The cutter is then rotated around the tubing while the operator simultaneously tightens the disc as it cuts into the tubing. After the cut is made, the triangular piece of metal attached to the cutter is inserted into the tubing and rotated to remove the burrs.

This concludes the preliminary discussion on copper tubing. We are now ready to make the hot and cold water-line connections beneath the small sink.

## Installing Copper Tubing

I shape the copper tubing manually so that it extends from the cold water supply nipple on my left to the faucet end on my right. The bends are shallow and I need not use the bending tool discussed earlier. The supply nipple is in a horizontal plane and I continue the horizontal plane in the tubing for a couple of inches before starting the first bend.

The faucet end is in a vertical plane and I continue the vertical plane for a couple of inches at the

other end of the tubing. I mark the vertical end of the tubing where it meets the faucet end. I cut the tubing at the mark.

I insert a nut for flaring over the tubing at each end. I fasten the tubing in the hole marked 1/2 inch on the flaring tool. I flare each end of the tubing as described earlier. I attach one end to the supply nipple and the other to the faucet end.

I turn on the cold water valve. If there are any leaks, I tighten the nuts further. If a leak doesn't stop, the flare has probably not been properly made. I detach the tubing and nuts and examine the flare. It should be uniform in width and occupy almost all the area between the hole and interior thread of the nut. If both these conditions are not met, I cut off the flare with the tubing cutter and make a new flare.

I attach the hot water line from the supply nipple to the faucet end in exactly the same manner and test the connection.

The installation of the small sink is complete.

## Installing Brass Sink Pipe, Valves, and Fittings

The kitchen sink is a single bowl measuring 32 x 18 inches. It is stainless steel and uses standard faucets. At the center rear are three holes; a fourth is several inches to the right.

The pictured faucet ends will go through the outermost of the three holes and the center fitting through the middle one. Flexible tubing with a spray nozzle at one end will be installed in the hole farthest to the right. At the end of the flexible tubing is a small-diameter nut which corresponds in size to the male fitting at the bottom and center of the faucet. The supply connection for the spray hose

Standard faucet, locknuts, and nuts

will be made there. (It is similar to a garden hose fitting and simply screwed on.)

I begin the installation by temporarily attaching the faucet to the sink. I do this by inserting the faucet ends into the holes in the sink and hand-tightening the locknuts over the threaded faucet ends until they are tight against the underside of the sink. There will be a small amount of faucet movement before permanent tightening, allowing me to shift its position later for better alignment with the pipes coming up to it. Unlike tubing which is bent to alter direction, brass pipe is rigid and any factor which allows small changes in direction should be utilized.

The hot and cold water lines have been brought from the void behind the cabinets into the cabinet area with 8-inch nipples screwed into tees. They are roughly 8 inches up from the floor. They lie in a horizontal plane.

Ell at back of cabinet, nipple coming through plywood back into cabinet

The faucet ends are about 34 inches off the floor and lie in a vertical plane. In continuing the pipe from the nipples to the faucet ends I will have to alter direction by 90 degrees. I will also have to align the hot and cold water pipes with the faucet ends to connect them. Aligning the pipe requires simultaneous alignment both laterally and in depth. I will also be installing a valve in both the hot and cold water lines. I proceed as follows.

I cut a straight piece of 1 x 2 an inch or so longer than the distance between the cabinet floor and the cold water faucet end. I place the upper end of the 1 x 2 against the cold water faucet end at the point on its circumference that is farthest from the back of the cabinet. The thin side of the 1 x 2 is against the faucet end. I place a carpenter's level against

the opposite side of the 1 x 2 and shift the bottom end until the bubble in the level indicates that the 1 x 2 is plumb (vertical). I mark the cabinet floor to indicate where the bottom of the 1 x 2 should be placed to obtain verticality when the upper end is against the faucet end. (I will be moving the 1 x 2 from time to time, and with the mark, I needn't waste time replumbing it.)

After shutting off the water, I remove the cold water nipple from the tee. With the 1 x 2 in a plumb position, I measure the distance between the tee and the 1 x 2. (The nearest side of the 1 x 2 represents the outermost distance of the faucet end.) This is 13 inches. I intend to install a pipe with a street ell at one end into the tee. Since each end of the pipe will be screwed in for a depth of 1/2 inch, I must add 1 inch to my original 13-inch measurement. The street ell attached to the end of the pipe has a horizontal distance of 1-5/8 inches, so I must

1/2-inch brass pipe and street ell

subtract this amount from the total. The length of the pipe will therefore be 12-3/8 inches and I cut and thread a 1/2-inch pipe to that length. While the pipe is still in the vise, I attach the street ell to one end, then install the entire assembly into the tee.

I must now align the street ell laterally with the faucet end. Since I installed the line during roughing with a measurement taken from the plan, the lateral alignment is fairly close. (If the street ell is more than 1 inch either to the left or right of the faucet end, this will have to be corrected before I reach the faucet end. I will detail how this is done following this segment.)

I have chosen a street ell fitting since it changes direction 90 degrees from horizontal to vertical and also provides me with a male end into which I can now attach a water valve.

I now measure the distance between the outlet side of the water valve and the threaded faucet end. I add 1/2 inch to this measurement, and cut and thread 1/2-inch brass pipe equal to it. (The lower end will be screwed into the valve and 1/2 inch lost. The upper end will lie against the faucet end.)

I install the threaded pipe from the valve to the faucet end. I loosen the locknuts and shift the faucet if need be to make the alignment. (Although brass pipe is rigid, there is some give in the fittings and a little leeway can be obtained.)

I trace the outline of the faucet housing, which lies on top of the sink. I remove the locknuts and faucet. I form 1/4-inch-thick strands of plumber's putty and lay them around the inside of the outline. I put the faucet back on top of the putty and tighten the locknuts securely.

I thread the second nut provided with the faucet onto the faucet end. This nut has an interior set of threads that corresponds in size to the diameter of the threaded faucet end. The outer threads of the nut correspond in diameter to the 1/2-inch pipe. I attach the end of the 1/2-inch pipe to the end of the faucet by screwing the nut to the pipe end.

I complete the hot water line from the nipple to the faucet end in the same manner as the cold water line.

I insert the female fitting at the end of the flexible hose through the remaining hole at the right of the faucet. I screw the female fitting to the male fitting located at the center and bottom of the faucet. (This is under the sink.)

I remove the excess putty around the faucet housing squeezed out when the locknuts were secured.

This completes the installation. When the valves are open, the sink is operational.

Lateral alignment with two ells and nipple

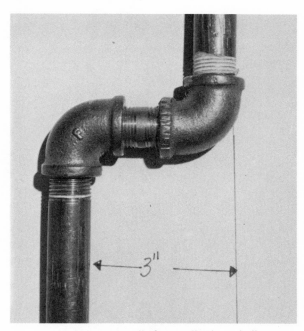
Shorter nipple between ells for smaller lateral alignment

## Alignment of Brass Sink Pipe

If for any reason the water lines have been placed more than 1 inch to the left or right of the faucet ends, alignment can be obtained in a variety of ways. The choice will depend on the how great the lateral misalignment is.

If the lateral distance between the supply nipple and the faucet end is 3 inches or greater, the use of two ells and a nipple of appropriate length is simplest. Once the lateral difference has been elim-

inated, alignment in depth is obtained in the same manner as described earlier.

If the lateral distance between the supply nipple and the faucet end is between 1 and 3 inches, the use of two 45 ells is simplest.

The photos show two arrangements used to align the supply nipple and faucet end laterally. In the

**77**

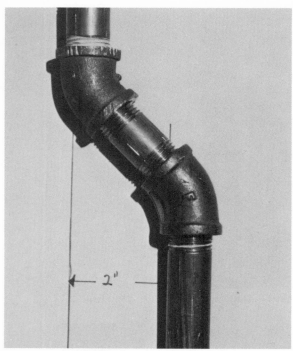

Shorter lateral alignment with two 45-degree ells and nipple

Shortest lateral alignment with nipple and two 45-degree ells in partial vertical position

first, the 45 ell is installed in a horizontal plane to the supply nipple, then followed by a 2-inch nipple and a second 45 ell that lies in the opposite horizontal plane of the first. In this arrangement the initial direction of the supply nipple is maintained while the lateral alignment is made. Using a 2-inch nipple and two 45 ells, lateral alignment can be obtained when the distance involved is 2 inches plus or minus 1/8 inch.

If the lateral misalignment is 2-1/2 inches or so, a 2-1/2-inch nipple is substituted for the 2-inch nipple; conversely, when the lateral misalignment is 1-1/2 inches or so, a 1-1/2-inch nipple is used.

When the lateral misalignment is 1-3/8 inches or less but still too large to be overcome by shifting the faucets, even a close nipple will be too long. In such cases the 45 ells are raised into a partial vertical position. The greater the verticality of the ells, the less lateral distance will be covered.

A similar change in lateral distance may be obtained by using a 90-degree ell, a nipple, and a 45 ell as shown in the photo.

Ell, nipple, and 45-degree ell to obtain lateral alignment of waste line

No matter which method is chosen, the lateral distance between the incoming supply nipple and faucet end will have to be determined.

This may be done by placing the 1 x 2 used in the previous segment against the *side* of the faucet end and marking its position on the cabinet floor. The arm of a framing square is then laid against the back of the cabinet with the tongue at the mark on the cabinet floor. A line is then drawn along the tongue; this line corresponds to the outermost part of the faucet end. The side of a level is laid against the outermost side of the supply nipple (the same side used on the faucet end) and is then brought into plumb by shifting the bottom of the level while keeping the upper portion against the nipple. A mark is made on the cabinet floor that corresponds to the side of the supply nipple. The arm of the framing square is then laid against the back of the cabinet while the tongue lies at the mark. A line is drawn along the side of the tongue. The distance between the parallel lines on the cabinet floor is the lateral distance between the supply nipple and faucet end.

After this distance has been determined, the necessary fittings and nipples should be assembled in the vise, where the greatest accuracy is obtained.

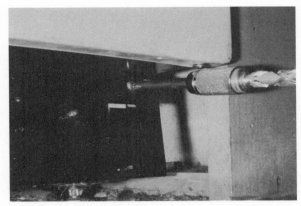

Dishwasher kick being removed, one screw at each end

Dishwasher at end of cabinets and adjacent to sink

## Installing a Dishwasher

The appliance in the photo was originally portable and had been used by its owners in their previous apartment. It took several hours to convert it to stationary use. Like any dishwasher, it requires two plumbing connections, a hot water supply line and a line to remove the waste.

The recessed part of the machine at the floor, the "kick," consists of two pieces of metal held at a right angle by Phillips-head sheetmetal screws at each end. To remove the kick, two other screws that attach the kick to the frame must be removed.

When the kick has been removed, the end of a threaded male fitting should become visible near the center of the machine and a few inches from its front. It is 3/8-inch. Since there is only one of these fittings there should be no confusion. This is the hot water inlet into the dishwasher. It faces downward.

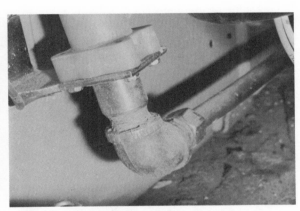

Kick removed, male fitting on dishwasher for hot water inlet, ell, nipple, flared tubing and nut—tubing continues to back of dishwasher

I slip a flaring nut onto one end of a length of 3/8-inch tubing, then flare the end of the tubing. Since the fitting on the dishwasher faces downward, I form a right-angle bend in the tubing by shaping it manually in a progressive series of shallow bends until I have obtained 90 degrees. I need this bend since the fitting faces downward and I want to continue the tubing toward the back of the machine and the 1/2-inch hot water supply nipple I installed during the roughing. I hand-tighten the flared end of the tubing and nut to the male fitting.

I extend the tubing to the rear of the dishwasher. It is approximately 4 inches above the floor.

I install a water valve and a 2-inch nipple on the 8-inch hot water supply nipple. The valve will allow the owner to shut off the hot water to the dishwasher without affecting the hot water supply to any other appliance or fixture.

The tubing is roughly 4 inches off the floor and lies in a horizontal plane as it emerges from the back of the machine. The 2-inch nipple I have just installed is also in a horizontal plane and roughly 8 inches off the floor. It is also about 4 inches from the back of the machine. To connect the tubing to the 2-inch nipple, I will have to make a right-angle turn in the tubing at the back of the machine, continue the tubing in an upward direction for 4 inches, then form another right-angle turn to return the tubing to a horizontal plane so that it can continue to the 2-inch nipple.

I make the first change in direction at the back of the machine by manually shaping the tubing. I now want to continue upward for 4 inches or so and make another right-angle turn. The 4-inch distance between bends is too short to allow the tubing to be bent without crimping. I therefore cut the tubing 3-1/2 inches above the bottom of the machine and solder a sweat ell fitting to the tubing.

The sweat ell fitting increases the height of the tubing 1/2 inch and its outlet side is now at the same height as the 2-inch nipple.

To complete the connection, I slip a 3/8–1/2-inch reducing nut on the end of a short piece of 3/8-inch tubing and flare the nut end. I hand-tighten it to the nipple and mark the tubing 1/2 inch longer than the distance to the outlet of the sweat ell. I cut the tubing at this mark and insert the end into the sweat ell. I solder the tubing to the sweat ell and tighten the nut to the nipple.

Each end of the installed 3/8-inch tubing is flared, and a nut has been used to attach each end to the dishwasher inlet fitting and the supply nipple. To prevent leaks it is essential that the tubing be aligned with the fitting before the connection is made. The alignment needn't be continuous but the tubing should be straight and aligned with the fitting for at least 1 inch behind each nut.

## Installing the Dishwasher Waste

When a dishwasher is purchased, a 1/2-inch-diameter hose is provided. This is the waste line, one end of which is already attached to the machine.

I bore a hole through the side of the cabinet that adjoins the dishwasher. (In standard installations, this cabinet will contain the sink.) The hole should be toward the back, where it will not interfere with storage inside the cabinet. I run the unattached end of the waste hose through the hole.

I cut the hose with a knife about 3 inches inside the cabinet.

A U-shaped piece of copper tubing is supplied with the dishwasher. Its purpose is to prevent waste

Tubing to back of dishwasher, bent 90 degrees, sweat-ell fitting soldered to end, tubing continued with flared end and nut making connection to hot water supply nipple

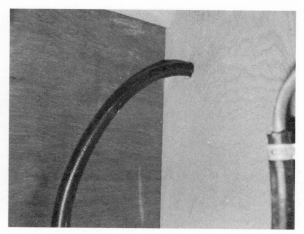

Dishwasher waste hose coming through hole at rear top corner of cabinet

Copper U in hose with ends clamped

Dishwasher secured to underside edge of 1 × 3 stile

from backing up into the machine. I insert an end of the U-shaped tubing into the waste hose attached to the dishwasher. I insert the other end into the piece of waste hose I have cut off.

To secure the U-shaped copper tubing to the waste hose, I tighten the pictured clamps over the hose with the U-shaped tubing passing through it. (Clamps come in a variety of sizes—the smallest will be big enough for these connections since they expand to fit 1 inch.) Using a strap and wood

screws, I mount the U-shaped tubing on the side of the cabinet with the uppermost portion of the U against the bottom of the countertop.

I attach the remaining end of the waste hose to the center outlet of the dishwasher tee previously installed in the sink waste line and use a clamp to secure it.

I now replace the previously removed kick.

At the front top of the machine (above the door) are two metal tabs with predrilled holes. I attach the dishwasher to the cabinet framework by placing wood screws through the predrilled holes and into the underside of the horizontal stile directly above them. (If the machine requires maintenance and has to be moved from underneath the counter, these two screws and the flared fittings at either end of the 3/8-inch tubing will have to be removed first.)

This completes the installation of the dishwasher.

## Installing the Washing Machine

In doing the rough plumbing, I have already brought the hot and cold water lines to the back of the washing machine, leaving nipples. I have also brought in the waste line, leaving a 1-1/2-inch pipe with an unthreaded end 34 inches above the floor.

I attach water valves and 2-inch nipples to the previously installed supply nipples. Again the purpose of the valves is to allow the owners to shut off water to the washing machine without affecting the supply anywhere else.

The washing machine comes equipped with hot and cold water hoses. (Each is marked.) One end of each hose is already attached to the machine. The other end has a fitting very similar to the fitting at

Hose end clamped to dishwasher tee

Hot and cold water hoses of washing machine attached to hot and cold supply nipples from valves

Lower end of washing machine waste pipe

Upper end of waste line, U-shaped waste hose inserted

the end of a garden hose. I screw the hot water hose to the hot water supply nipple using this fitting at the end of the hose and do the same with the cold water hose. (I make certain that a rubber

washer is in each hose fitting before connecting it.)

The washing machine also comes equipped with a waste hose, one end of which is already attached to the machine. The other end has an inverted U shape. The open end of the U is simply placed inside the unthreaded end of the 1-1/2-inch pipe 34 inches off the floor.

The hoses are long enough to permit pulling the machine forward several feet for maintenance work. If more room is needed, the water valves are shut off, the hoses disconnected, and the waste line hose lifted out of the waste pipe.

## Installing the Gas Dryer

The gas supply to the dryer has already been roughed in and the flexible hose we brought to the dryer's projected location is now connected to the nipple built into the machine by simply tightening the nut to it.

Gas dryers must also be vented so that their exhaust heat and gases will be channeled to the exterior of the building.

In a typical installation, the dryer will have its back to a wall. Near the top of the back of the dryer will be a pipelike projection 4 inches in diameter. This is the exhaust of the dryer. Ordinarily a duct or stovepipe is connected to the exhaust and routed through the wall to the roof or an exterior of the building. When this is impractical, a nearby window is used. Since this dryer is positioned at an island,

4-inch flexible pipe attached to exhaust on back of gas dryer

the exhaust will have to run across the floor space at some point to reach the building's exterior. However, 4 inches is too large a diameter to conveniently install in the floor and cover. As an alternative I could run the exhaust pipe to the ceiling, across to an exterior wall, then down and out through a window. This would be too obtrusive.

To solve the problem, I use the 4-inch flexible hose in the arrangement shown in the photo. One end is attached to the dryer's exhaust by means of a plastic clamp. A storage place under the sink is then set aside to house the hose when not in use. When the machine is to be used, the hose will be taken out of the cabinet and inserted into a 4-inch-diameter hole that I cut in a board fitted to the bottom of the window opening.

Removing screw holding handle of kitchen faucet

Other end of exhaust hose vented to street

In this arrangement a circle of 1/4-inch-thick plexiglass 4-1/2 inches in diameter is also cut. It is attached to the board by a single screw through a 1/8-inch hole bored in the plexiglass. When the dryer is being used, the circle of plexiglass is simply swiveled out of the way and the flexible exhaust inserted into the hole in the board. It is swiveled back to cover the hole in the board when the dryer is idle.

Handle removed, removing nut holding tap assembly

## Fixing a Leaky Faucet

Almost always, a leaking faucet will consist of either water dripping from the spigot when the tap is shut or water exuding from the nut below the faucet handle when the tap is open.

When water is leaking through the spigot, the first step is to shut off both the hot and cold water valves that control its flow. In newer installations these valves will usually be located directly under

Removing screw at bottom of assembly that holds washer

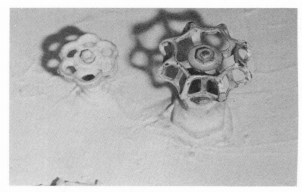

Hot and cold water valves located in closet

the fixture, in older installations in a nearby closet or in the room where the sink is located. The cold water valve will usually be along an exterior wall and the hot water valve at an interior wall. Quite often only the handle or a small portion of the rest of the valve will be visible.

The leak may be coming from either the hot or cold water tap or both. It's a good practice to assume that both are causing the leak since the fault will most often be a worn washer, and if one washer is gone the other will not be far behind.

I remove the handles of the faucets by removing the screw that lies at the top center of each handle. Some newer faucets have a plastic cap over this screw, which is removed by slipping the tip of a knife between the cap's circumference and the metal housing beside it, then lifting. The screw on older faucets may be located on the side of each spindle (the round length of metal directly below each handle).

When these screws are removed, each handle can be raised and taken off. Directly below each handle is a nut through which the spindle continues farther down. When each nut is removed, the faucet assembly can be lifted out of the faucet housing. At its end is a rubber washer which is held in place by a brass machine screw which goes through a center hole in the washer and threads into a threaded hole at the end of the tap assembly. This screw is removed together with the old washer; a new washer is then put in its place and the brass screw put back so that the new washer is snugly seated—not so tight that it deforms the rubber washer nor so loose that the washer isn't stationary. Hardware stores carry these screws and washers (the washers come in a variety of sizes, the

screws are standard). Replacing this washer will eliminate leaks 90 percent of the time.

A second kind of leak occurs only when the tap is opened. Water appears between the spindle and the hole in the nut through which the spindle continues inward; such leaks result from a distortion or reduction in the amount of "packing" around the nut. As a tap is opened or closed, its spindle rubs against this packing. Typical packing is a threadlike material impregnated with graphite which eventually, after long use, wears away. When the tap is turned off, the washer at the end prevents water from coming through despite the inadequate packing, but when the tap is turned on, the leak appears.

When the nut below the handle is removed, the packing should become visible. (Sometimes hardly any packing will remain since even a small amount will prevent leakage.) The old packing is removed. New packing (purchased in a hardware store) is then wound around the spindle and the interior threaded portion which holds the nut. Three or four turns around the spindle are sufficient. When the nut is tightened, it will push down the packing, compress it, and create a new seal between the circumference of the spindle and the inside of the stationary housing.

Either of the two leaks described can be repaired in less than five minutes and the materials cost under a dollar. A screwdriver and channel-lock pliers are the only tools needed.

## How to Unclog a Sink Drain

A slowly draining sink or basin is ordinarily caused by solid matter accumulated in the waste pipe *beyond* the trap. More specifically, the blockage will be located at the fitting in the wall to which the waste line is attached. (This is very often a tee.)

The pictured drain cleaner is commonly called a snake and costs less than $7. I use it as follows.

I place a bucket under the trap of the sink or basin. At the bottom of the trap is a clean-out plug which I unscrew, thereby emptying the water in the trap. I loosen the winged set screw at the aperture through which the coiled flexible snake emerges. I insert the end of the snake into the clean-out hole and push the snake into the waste line and toward the wall as far as it will go. I rotate the knob on the housing, which causes the snake to rotate within

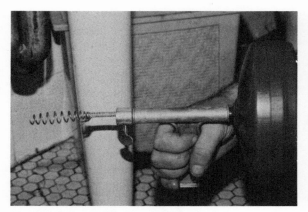

Drain-cleaning tool or plumber's snake

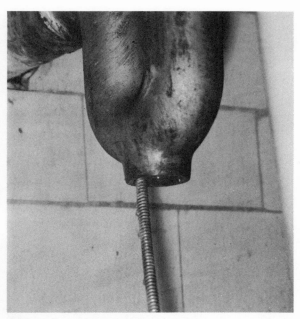

Snake end inserted through clean-out hole and pushed toward wall

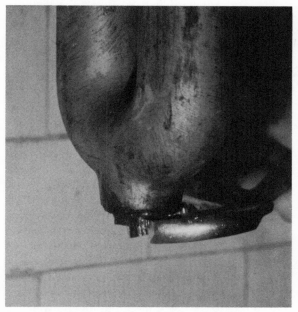

Removing clean-out plug at bottom of trap

the pipe. I pull the snake back out through the clean-out hole. Ordinarily the solid matter which has been causing the clogging will be enmeshed in the tip of the snake. I remove the material and reinsert the snake if need be to remove additional material.

When the snake has caught solid material, resistance will be felt as the snake is tugged backward. When resistance is no longer felt there is probably no more accumulation of solid matter.

This simple procedure, which takes only a few minutes, will unclog drains in most instances.

Occasionally, particularly in kitchen-sink drains, blockage may be caused by fat congealed in the tail pipe or trap or by solid material that has passed through the strainer. The trap is cleaned simply by removing the material with a finger. Material in the tail pipe is removed with the snake.

After removing the material that has caused the clogging, I wrap the threads of the clean-out plug with six turns of a threadlike material called lamp wick. This acts as a washer when the clean-out plug is screwed back and prevents leakage.

There are a large number of chemical products which purport to clean drains. In my opinion, all of them are a waste of time and money in that they ordinarily do not unclog drains except in very rare and special circumstances. Moreover, anything they accomplish can be done just as well by removing the trap clean-out plug and clearing the obstruction with a snake. A snake is inexpensive and simple to use, and it will avoid the need to call a plumber after use of commercial products has failed to produce results.

## Fixing Leaks in the Toilet Water Tank

Very often with tank-type toilets water will be heard running even when the toilet is not in use. The cause of this is usually the improper functioning of a device that should be cutting off the supply of water when the tank has been refilled. When a toilet

Float and tank ball or flapper inside toilet tank

Handle and trip lever

Lift wire and trip lever connection

is flushed—that is, when the handle on the outside of the tank is turned—it lifts a rubber or plastic object (called a tank ball) from an opening, which allows the water in the tank to flow into the toilet bowl. As the water in the tank lowers, a large round brass or plastic ball (called a float) drops. The float (which actually floats on top of the tank water) is connected by a rod to an intake valve, and when the float is low in the tank, it opens the inlet valve, letting water from the supply line stream into the tank.

The tank ball which is raised by turning the handle has a guide and bracket attached to it, and when the water level goes down, the tank ball descends until it is seated in the opening that leads to the bowl. Quite often, even in new installations, the tank ball does not seat itself properly in this opening and water escapes into the bowl. This causes the float to lower, which opens the intake valve slightly, and new water enters the tank continuously to replace the water that is leaking onto the bowl.

The leak can be stopped immediately by lifting off the tank cover and seating the tank ball properly into the opening. However, the next time the toilet is flushed, chances are that the tank ball will seat itself improperly again and the problem will recur.

There can be a number of reasons the tank ball doesn't seat itself properly. A common cause is that a guide which extends from the top to the tank ball through a guide bracket has been bent causing erratic motion of the tank ball as it descends. The guide is a thin, solid piece of alloy and is easily bent. I don't try to straighten it; I simply buy a new one. The piece is called a lift wire and costs less than a quarter. It has a thread at its end which is screwed into the top of the tank ball after first having been threaded through both the connecting rod that goes to the handle and the guide bracket which keeps it aligned during its vertical movement.

If the lift wire appears straight and is not the cause of the leak, I flush the tank and check the guide bracket as the lift wire moves inside it. Foreign material may have collected in the guide holes of the bracket, causing the lift wire to be deflected. To clear the holes, I pump the lift wire rapidly so that it strikes the sides of the guide holes, dislodging the accumulated foreign matter.

If the lift wire is straight and the guide-bracket holes are clear, I note whether the guide-bracket arm is horizontal. It may be loose on the refill tube to which it is connected. This will shift the guide holes out of perpendicular and cause the tank ball to descend at an angle rather than vertically. I correct this by tightening the bracket clamp. Occasionally, the screws which hold the clamp are frozen and I must wind a copper wire around the refill tube and the guide bracket to secure the bracket in a horizontal position.

If none of these steps offers a solution, I then examine the connecting rod that goes from the lift wire to the tripping mechanism behind the flushing handle outside the tank. If bent (and thereby shortened) it will raise the lift wire at an angle and will also pull on the lift wire while it is descending and prevent the tank ball from seating properly. If the connecting rod is bent, it can be easily straightened manually.

The sound of running water will also be heard if the float is too high in the tank. It shuts off the water supply only after the water level is above the refill tube, and since the water will drain continuously into the tube, the intake valve will remain slightly open. To correct this, I bend the arm of the rod that connects the float to the intake valve so that the float will shut off the valve completely just before the water level reaches the height of the refill tube.

If the water continues to run, I check the tank ball and the opening to the bowl. The tank ball may have become deformed (in which case a new one must be substituted) or the ball and opening may have foreign material attached to them which prevents the ball from sitting snugly.

If none of these solutions works, and as a last alternative, I substitute a new guide bracket, lift

wire, and tank ball. However, installing them may still not stop the leaking since the design of this type of system is faulty and has outlived its usefulness.

Occasionally, the tank handle is turned and nothing happens. This failure occurs when the connecting rod at the top of the lift wire has come loose from the end of the connecting rod which goes to the handle. The end of the flush handle connecting rod has three holes. I reinsert the end of the lift wire into one of these holes and make certain that I have chosen one that does not deflect the lift wire from a vertical position while it is in motion.

## Repairing a Flush Valve

A great many old and new toilets are equipped with the pictured flush or diaphragm valve which acts as a substitute for a tank. It is a superior arrangement and malfunctions occur less frequently than with tanks. However, they do occur and are evidenced either by water leaking into the bowl or failing to enter the bowl when the handle is moved. This may be caused by a worn washer, worn diaphragm, or a clogged by-pass.

Removing outer cover of valve

New flappers and stems

Outer cover off, inner cover

I shut off the water to the toilet and remove the outside cover by turning the nut-shaped extension on its top. I lift off the inside cover directly below. This exposes a round disc in the center (auxiliary valve) with a metal extension and I lift it out. I can now clean the by-pass by running a wire through the opening.

If the valve is the type that has a rubber valve seat, I lift out the washer around the center hole and unscrew the ring which holds the rubber valve seat. I also lift out the diaphragm below it. I clean off the bed on which the valve seat rests and replace both valve seat and diaphragm if they are worn. The diaphragm must be installed in its original position: the cup side down and the copper gasket on the upper side.

## Unclogging Toilets

When an obstruction in a toilet cannot be removed with a snake, the toilet will have to be removed temporarily to get at the cause of the blockage. Diapers and other such bulky material are frequently the cause.

The cold water supply to the tank or flush valve is first shut off. The tank is then emptied by siphoning off the water in it.

I disconnect the toilet from the tank by removing the large nut at the end of the pipe at the rear of the bowl. This is the pipe which delivers water from the tank to the toilet.

On each side of the base of the bowl are holes through which bolts emerge. Sometimes these bolts are covered with ceramic caps and attached with plaster. They will have to be broken to get at the nuts.

Loosening one of two nuts which hold toilet to floor

I unscrew each nut. The toilet bowl can now be raised and removed.

The cause of the blockage will now usually be apparent. If it is not, the snake can be inserted into the hole to remove the obstruction. The hole is 4 inches in diameter and anything that would cause a blockage is not likely to have traveled very far in the waste line.

To put the toilet back, I first place the pictured wax ring around the hole. I then lay a 1/4-inch band of plumber's putty on the floor around the perimeter of the base of the bowl. I put the toilet in its former position and retighten it to the bolts. Care must be exercised not to tighten the nuts excessively since the bowl is ceramic and will crack.

I replace the washer in the nut removed from the supply pipe to the bowl and tighten.

4-inch drain hole after toilet has been removed

Wax ring placed around hole before toilet is put back

## Refinishing Kitchen and Bathroom Fixtures

With long use, the surfaces of sinks, basins, bathtubs, etc., become worn and porous. The best solution is to replace the worn fixture. The fixture will be surprisingly cheap, although the same cannot be said for the labor charged to install it. However, if one is prepared to do the work, replacing the fixture is the first choice.

An alternative to replacing the worn fixture is to resurface it with epoxy paint. The new epoxy surface will not be as durable as the original finish, but it will be fairly long-lasting and will not require scouring to keep clean. Epoxy paint can be used on all fixtures except the toilet bowl, where the constant presence of water destroys the finish rather quickly. With ordinary use, the refinished fixture will remain in decent condition for about a year.

# RENOVATION CARPENTRY

4

In this chapter I will be discussing basic carpentry procedures and materials, the erection of skeletal walls to be covered with lath, sheetrock, and plasterboard; installing door frames, doors, locks, trim; and mounting a variety of objects on masonry ceilings and walls. I will also detail the repair of windows, doors, locks, and wooden furniture. This is work a carpenter will be called upon to perform during a renovation.

## Lumber

Lumber, the most widely used construction material, is sold by the board foot, which is the equivalent of a 1 x 12 a foot long. A 2 x 6 a foot long equals a board foot, while a 2 x 4 a foot long (a linear foot) equals 2/3 of a board foot. At this writing, construction lumber—that is, lumber used for skeletal structures which are later covered—costs about 24 cents a board foot.

The source of construction lumber is a northwestern evergreen, the Douglas fir. Other significant sources include hemlock fir and, to a smaller extent, spruce. Minor sources used regionally are redwood and a variety of southern pines.

Construction lumber is milled into standard lengths that begin at 8 feet and continue in multiples of 2 feet to a length of 24 feet. There is also a stud (continuous vertical member of a wall) precut to a standard length of 7 feet 8 inches for use with standard 8-foot ceilings. Longer lengths are available from special lumber yards but are many times more expensive.

Standard thicknesses are 2, 3, 4, and 6 inches.

Standard widths begin at 2, 3, and 4 inches, then continue in multiples of 2 inches to a width of 12 inches.

These dimensions are used for pricing purposes only. A 2 x 6 piece of lumber is actually only 1-1/2 inches thick and 5-1/2 inches wide. This variance between actual and descriptive size is traditional.

The skeletal structure of a townhouse wall built around the turn of the century has 2 x 4 members which measure 2-1/4 inches by 4-1/4 inches. This lumber was not planed and is furry. Had it been planed or "dressed," it would have measured 2 inches by 4 inches. In later years dressed 2 x 4s had an actual measurement of 1-5/8 inches by 3-5/8 inches. Several years ago the dimensions were

90

changed once again to their present configuration: a 2 x 4 is now actually 1-1/2 inches by 3-1/2 inches.

## Bringing Lumber into an Apartment

I bring all long lengths of lumber up to the apartment by removing the trapdoor in the ceiling of the elevator and stacking the lumber through the opening. I take care to see that the upper ends are not hitting the elevator cables or the well walls. In most elevators the trapdoor in the ceiling can be moved aside by simply lifting it out of the way.

The elevator I am using, as most will be, is too small to accommodate the standard 4-by-8-foot sheets of plywood and sheetrock that I need. To get them upstairs, I station the elevator in the basement, open the first-floor elevator door (the super has a special key to do this), and stack the sheets on *top* of the elevator. I then bring the elevator to the sixth floor, open the elevator door on the seventh (where the apartment is located), and remove the material from there.

If a great deal of material is to be brought into the apartment or if for any reason the above method isn't feasible, I can, as an alternative, bring it in through a window facing the street. When I purchase the materials, I arrange to have the lumber yard send a truck equipped with a telescopic boom, so that I can bring the materials in through the window opening. First, however, I must remove both sashes of the window to be used. I remove the lower sash by first removing the stops—the vertical strips of wood located immediately in front of the lower sash and toward the interior of the apartment. The stops are attached to the window frame with finishing nails or screws. When they are removed, the lower sash is free to swing into the room. Along each side of the sash is a groove with a hole at its bottom where the end of the chain is secured to the sash. I unhook the ends of the chains on each side and the sash is free.

Directly behind the lower sash and toward the exterior of the frame are two narrow strips of wood. They are press-fitted into a groove in the frame and are removed by inserting a screwdriver at the top end and prying back. When these two stops (which also act as guides) are removed, the upper sash is free to swing into the room and the chains may be unhooked as with the lower sash.

If the apartment is located on a floor too high for a boom to reach and bringing material to it on top of the elevator isn't feasible, I would arrange for a rigging company to deliver the materials. This will be more economical than purchasing or leasing the needed equipment.

## Basic Woodworking Procedures

### Tools

The cliché about buying only good tools is true, but to this must be added that these must be tools that will actually be used. There is little use, for example, in owning a wide variety of manual planes or an expensive miter box and backsaw since the occasion to employ these tools is rare.

I will detail the tools I use as I demonstrate the work they perform. I have no vested interest in the particular brands mentioned and recommend them only because they have given me good service over long periods. Other manufacturers may produce tools as good or better, but I caution the reader about a huge number of woodworking tools which do not accomplish what their manufacturers assert they will and cause relatively simple jobs to become laborious.

### Measuring and Marking

Whenever possible, I avoid using rulers by simply placing the wood to be cut in the position it will be installed and marking it. This eliminates a step and reduces the chances of error. However, where measurement and marking are necessary, I proceed as follows.

I use a Lufkin 100-foot white-faced tape for measuring distances longer than 16 feet. It has a metal extension at its end that pivots and holds the tape so that it may be unwound and used by one person. When rewinding the tape, I slide it between the middle and index fingers of my left hand to remove dirt that would otherwise enter the case.

For lengths shorter than 16 feet, I use a 16-foot Lufkin power-lock tape.

When a tape measure cannot be hooked onto an end, I use a 6-foot Lufkin folding ruler with a brass extension. I also use the ruler for measuring short distances up from the floor and down from the ceiling or laterally. The extension is convenient for

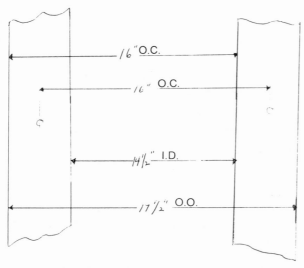

Standard measurements

measuring the inside distance between two fixed pieces.

To mark a piece of wood, I extend the appropriate ruler along the side closest to me, place a mark about 1/4 inch long opposite the desired length, then turn the mark to the left or right to indicate the piece that will *not* be used. When cutting material less than 12 inches wide it is not necessary to extend the mark across the width of the board with a square.

For distances such as that between two walls, I use two long 1 x 2s. I extend an end of each to each wall and mark the point at which the opposite end of one reaches along the second piece. This is particularly convenient when installing moldings or determining the distance between floors and ceilings.

Carpenter's pencils are best for marking because they can be sharpened to a flat line and retain enough strength not to break easily.

Several marking conventions used throughout the country are shown in the photo. The lines with arrow tips at their ends indicate the two points between which the measurement is being made. The number indicates the measured distance and is located anywhere along the arrow lines.

The abbreviation "o.c." means "on center." It signifies the distance between two pieces when measured from the center of one to the center of the other. The "o.c." measurement has to do with structural requirements—in practice it is awkward

to measure pieces by their centers. The same result is obtained when the measuring is done from the side of one piece to the corresponding side of the second piece, a universal practice.

The abbreviation "o.o." means from "outside to outside" of two pieces.

The abbreviation "i.d." means "inside diameter," but it rarely relates to circles and has come to mean the distance between two pieces when the measurement is between their inner sides.

The line inside the circle indicates the midpoint or center.

The apostrophe mark (') indicates feet. The quote mark (") indicates inches.

When a mark is made on a piece of wood to indicate where another piece of wood is to be installed, in order to avoid confusion about which side of the mark to install the second piece, an X is placed beside the mark for later reference. When the piece is installed, it is positioned at the mark and on the X. This convention is used throughout carpentry.

## Sawing

For cutting wood less than 1-1/2 inches thick, I use a 6-1/2-inch (blade diameter) Skil heavy-duty portable electric power saw.

For cutting wood 1-1/2 inches or thicker, I use an 8-1/4-inch Skil heavy-duty portable electric power saw.

Several manufacturers offer more expensive worm-driven saws that are mechanically superior to these two but I find them unbalanced, heavy, and clumsy, which obliges me to use both hands on the saw while making most cuts. For me this rules out worm-drive saws since I use my left hand for other purposes while making cuts.

The cheap models of all manufacturers should be avoided since the trigger and bushings will go bad with any extended use. All saws are sold with adequate maintenance instructions and blade recommendations.

For rough work, I use a 28-tooth carbide-tipped blade in the 8-1/4-inch Skil saw. The teeth of this blade are made of carbide steel and stay sharper many times longer than the chrome or other alloys used in ordinary blades. They are resharpened by grinding rather than filing. Carbide steel is brittle and will chip if struck against other metal; therefore care must be taken since it will cost several dollars to replace a damaged tooth or one that has been knocked loose. Despite this drawback and its significantly greater initial cost, the long life of the carbide-steel blade makes it purchase worthwhile.

For fine work, I use a plywood blade in the 6-1/2-inch Skil saw. When it becomes dull, I throw the blade away, since its numerous teeth would take too long to resharpen.

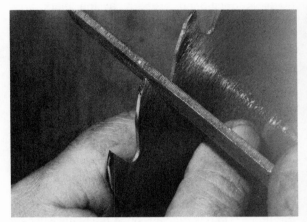

Mill bastard file on vertical side of tooth

For wood less than 1-1/2 inches thick, I use a combination blade in the 6-1/2-inch Skil saw. When the blade is dull, I resharpen by filing along the original angle at the top and side of each tooth.

Except for ripping (cutting lengthwise with the grain) or cross-cutting material wider than 12 inches, I always use a protractor in conjunction with either saw.

The protractor has a long stationary arm which lies across the board that is to be cut. The short arm is adjustable from 0 to 45 degrees, left or right, and the degrees are marked on a semicircular scale. A wing nut on the short arm locks and unlocks the protractor. The end of the wing nut has a point which serves as the indicator on the scale. The short arm lies along the far side of the board when the protractor is in use.

When cutting (cutting always means cross-cutting as opposed to ripping) a board at a right angle, I first set the protractor at 0 degrees. (When first purchasing a protractor and intermittently after that, it's a good idea to check its accuracy by first drawing a line across a board with a framing square, then placing the protractor set at 0 degrees along this line to determine whether the protractor

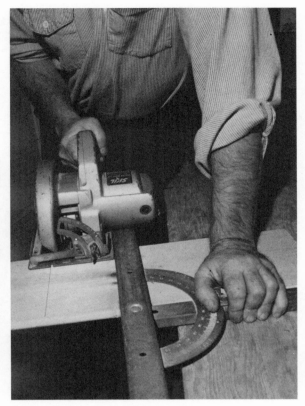

Saw, protractor on board to be cut

does in fact produce a right angle. If it doesn't, I shift its position until it does and scratch a mark on the scale indicating the adjusted position.) With the long and short arm forming a right angle, I place the protractor on the board, short arm against the far side, long arm across the width.

I maintain the short arm against the far side of the board by pressing it toward me. I place the table of the power saw on the board. The left side of the table lies against the long arm of the protractor, as pictured. The blade is back from the wood so that it can *rotate freely*.

When the power saw is started the blade should be permitted to develop maximum rpm before cutting is actually begun. (The required interval is very brief, a second or so.) This permits the motor to develop its full power and places a minimum strain upon it. Another important reason for this is that if the blade is held against the wood when starting, it will often jam and cause a short. It may also buck violently backward toward the operator, causing injury.

I press the trigger and start the saw. To properly place the blade along the mark I have made, I shift the protractor and saw *in unison* and very lightly nick the edge of the wood to see where the blade is actually cutting. I want to position the blade so that the kerf (the thickness of the blade and resulting gap) will lie on the piece of wood that will *not* be used. If any minor adjustment is necessary, I pull the saw back slightly and shift it in unison with the protractor. *I do not shift the saw and protractor laterally while the blade is nicking the wood.*

With the blade aligned and spinning freely, I use light forward pressure to push the saw ahead through the wood while sliding the base along the side of the long arm of the protractor. Since the long arm is at a right angle to the board and I am making a parallel cut, the cut will also be at a right angle.

As I approach the end of the cut, I increase my forward pressure so that I will complete the cut before the weight of the partially cut piece causes it to tear away and damage the rest of the piece.

When a power saw is rotating freely the sound it produces is a high-pitched whine. As a cut is begun, the blade rotates less quickly and the pitch lowers but the characteristic whine will remain. The whine will be replaced by a flatter-pitched sound as greater stress is placed upon the motor and as the blade turns at slower speeds. The optimum speed at which to make a cut is *the most rapid possible without placing undue stress on the motor*, a condition that can be identified easily by marked differences in sound.

During all cuts, the blade encounters resistance from the wood and heats up. If the cut is being made too slowly, more heat is created and has a longer time to build up. The heat created tends to warp the blade and the warped blade creates and encounters greater resistance. The resulting excessive heat builds up even more rapidly and creates even greater warpage. This condition is further aggravated because the greater heat causes the resin in the wood to caramelize on the blade, causing greater friction and reducing the sharpness of the teeth.

If this circle isn't broken, a new blade can be "worn out" in less than half an hour of cutting. (I once discussed this with a helper who said that he was forced to cut very slowly since there was so much smoke it was difficult to see what he was doing!)

When one first begins to cut with a power saw it is natural to use it slowly in the course of familiarization. Unless a protractor is being used, the operator is also trying to follow a squared line across the board, and this is a slow business. However, with the use of a protractor, there is no need to watch the blade or the line. As long as the side of the table slides along the side of the protractor, a right-angle cut will always be made, and if the blade is positioned properly at the mark *prior* to the cut, the exact desired length will always be obtained. The actual time of cutting can therefore be speeded up without any loss of accuracy.

If smoke appears while making a cut, stop immediately; you may be using a dull blade, cutting far too slowly (or both), or there may be an excessive amount of resin caramelized on the blade. The smoke may also be due to excessive heat on the motor insulation. This has an acrid odor and, if the saw is sniffed at the rear ventilating grill, can be readily identified. If none of these seems to be causing the smoke, check the blade with a wet forefinger. Do this quickly, since the blade will heat up enough to fry an egg. If the blade isn't excessively hot, there is probably an unusually large amount of resin in the particular piece of wood, and the cut can be continued.

Since the blade of a portable saw rotates counterclockwise, the cut is made from the bottom of a board upward through it. This leaves a smoother surface on the underside of the cut. (The reverse is true with a table saw.) It is therefore good practice to measure and mark the side that will be hidden and place this side up when the cut is being made with the portable saw.

Most cutting is done with the board to be cut placed directly on two horses. The portion to be cut off should be *free to fall beyond the horses*. If this isn't practical, as when a long board is being cut in half, another board should first be placed on the horses immediately beneath the board to be cut. At the bottom and left of the saw handle is a wing nut that, when loosened, permits the saw's table to be raised or lowered. The blade should be adjusted via the table so that it will cut 1/8 inch deeper than the thickness of the board to be cut.

(To establish the depth of the blade, raise the guard, place the blade against the side of the board to be cut, then raise or lower the table so that the teeth of the blade extend 1/8 inch below the board.) The cut can then be made safely. This will leave a 1/8-inch-deep cut on the bottom board's top surface, not so deep that it cannot be used later. I use the same board over and over again for this purpose.

When this safety procedure isn't followed and a long board is laid directly on horses and cut without another board underneath, the following will happen: the cut being made between the horses will begin in the normal way, but as it continues the board will begin to sag into an inverted V at the cut, the top of the V pinching the blade. This will cause the saw rapidly and unexpectedly to buck back with violence since it is now running on maximum power which is transferred into the bucking action. This can lead to serious injury.

I have never had an accident with a power saw but have seen a carpenter cutting a board as described. The saw bucked so quickly that the guard over the blade did not have time to drop and the man's thigh was ripped open.

The power saw is nevertheless a *safe tool* when the simple operating procedures described are followed. It is also a powerful tool which demands attention when in use.

When cutting material such as a 4-by-8-foot sheet of plywood, I first place four 2 x 4s on the floor a foot or so apart and parallel to each other. I then place the plywood sheet on the 2 x 4s. I pop a chalk line between marks on each side where I intend cutting the sheet. (A chalk line is a spool of string inside a chalk-filled case. It is stretched taut across the sheet between the measured marks, raised a few inches, then allowed to snap down, creating a line with its residue. The type with a clip at the end of its string is preferable since it enables one person to handle it alone.)

If I am making a cut that is parallel to the 2 x 4s under the sheet, I shift any 2 x 4 that lies in the path of the cut. When the cut is to be across the 2 x 4s, this isn't necessary.

I set the blade of the saw to cut about 1/8 inch deeper than the thickness of the plywood. I place the blade at the chalk line. Each tooth is flared in an opposite direction. During the cut the teeth will remove the width of the flare; 3/16 inch is common. I therefore position the blade so that this 3/16 inch will enter the piece I don't intend to use.

At the front end of the saw table is a U-shaped

slot that corresponds roughly to the position of the blade. When the blade is where I want it at the chalk line, I note the position of the slot in relation to the chalk line and maintain that same relative position throughout the cut—I will be watching the slot and chalk line, *not the blade.*

I begin my cut from a crouch, avoiding kneeling on the sheet. I should be able to maintain this same position across the entire sheet since it is on the floor and will support my weight. (It *is* the floor for me during the cut.) The cut portions of the plywood are being supported by 2 x 4s under them and will not bounce about or pinch the blade, and I am always at the cut in a comfortable position without having to reach far or contort my body. (If you really want to appreciate this 2 x 4 technique, try cutting a sheet of plywood placed on horses.)

While I am cutting, I am pinching the left front corner of the saw's table with my left index finger and thumb. My index finger is also pressed down against the plywood. This helps stabilize the blade

Table of saw being pinched for lateral stability during long cut

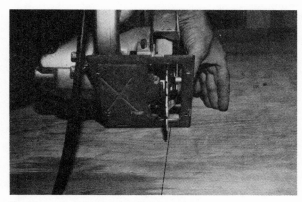

Position of saw prior to plunge cut

in its forward path and makes it easier to avoid drifting from the chalk line. Since the handle is much farther back from where the cutting is being done, control from there is more difficult. Even slight corrective movements at the handle result in overcompensating ones at the blade.

In the course of work there will be times when it is necessary to begin a cut within a sheet rather than the usual entrance from the perimeter. This is accomplished by a plunge cut. Having raised the guard with my left hand, I start the saw in the pictured position as is shown on page 95, with the blade away from the plywood, then lower it into the plywood until the table is flat on the sheet. I then continue the cut as described earlier.

Using side of index finger against edge of board as guide during ripping

## Nailing

For a long time I paid no attention to the type of hammer I used for nailing or the way I swung it. This came to an end when I was nailing oak flooring with a 20-ounce hammer that had a solid steel shaft with a rubber-grip handle. In the same room a man I had recently hired was laying three pieces of flooring for every one of mine. I knew that I possessed average speed but I never realized how slow that could be, and I was both puzzled and embarrassed. Later I was to study his swing, but in the moment I noticed only that he was using a 2-pound hammer with an ordinary wooden handle and an oversized claw head. I asked to use it. The greater weight and size made an extraordinary difference in power and accuracy and left me with the feeling that I had

Two-pound hammer and grip

previously been tapping nails with a toy. I offered to buy the hammer and he laughingly gave it to me. I still have that hammer and use it for all nailing.

To use a hammer, I grip the *end* of its handle. My thumb goes completely around and rests on my index finger. If the handle is gripped too hard, undue strain is placed on the wrist and forearm. Gripped too loosely, it will slide in the palm, causing blisters. The force used to grip the handle is only that necessary to keep the handle from sliding when a nail is struck.

A common error is to place the thumb on the handle to guide the head. The thumb cannot provide an adequate means of control and will cause the head to rock to the side inaccurately. To compensate for this incorrect grip and diminished control, the user must shorten his swing to an ineffectual tapping.

Another common error occurs when the wrist is used to guide the hammer and provide force for the blow. I use my wrist only to raise the hammer at the beginning of the swing. The wrist is located at the pivot point of the swing, at the center of an arc, and it can only deliver a minimum of force. The wrist is also a relatively weak joint, and using it as a source of power will tire one quickly.

Once the hammer has been started upward, no further strain should be felt by either wrist or forearm. In the beginning, power in the swing should be provided by the shoulder; later, when practice has created the facility, it should come from the back—which is its best source. It is useful to regard the wrist, arm, and shoulder as an extension of the hammer and the back as its source of power.

At the top of the swing the hammer head should be slightly behind the shoulder. As the hammer is brought down on the nail, effectiveness is increased by adding the weight of the body to the force delivered by the back.

If nailing is done incorrectly, it will take seven or eight blows to sink a tenpenny nail and the wrist and forearm will tire in less than half an hour. Using the 2-pound hammer and a correct swing, two or three blows will drive the same nail and I can nail all day without tiring. (I have average strength.)

The nail is started with a light tap which embeds it in the wood deeply enough to keep it from falling. Once this is achieved, the left hand should immediately be removed from the nailing area and placed in the nail apron for another nail. The presence of the left hand has become gratuitous.

When nailing two pieces of wood together, it is a good practice to start the nails into one piece alone and drive them down until they are almost through it before placing the pieces together. This makes it easier to nail one piece to the other by eliminating most of the bouncing between pieces which would otherwise occur.

It is also good practice to nail through an already-installed piece into one that isn't installed yet. It is much easier to position a new piece accurately if a nail is being driven through one already in place.

Nails hold most poorly when driven absolutely straight through one piece into another. It is not only unnecessary to strive for straightness, but absolute straightness should be avoided. Consequently, angled nailing is desirable.

One particularly useful type of angled nailing is called toenailing. It is frequently used during framing (assembling skeletal structures). To toenail, I

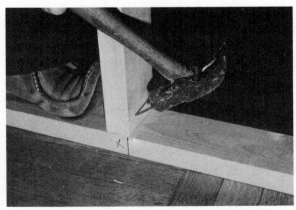

Toenailing with shoe on opposite side against bottom for backing

start the nail in about an inch up from the end of the piece to be attached and at about a 60-degree angle and then drive the nail down until its head is partially embedded.

A common problem created by toenailing is that the vertical piece bounces around before the end of the nail has entered the stationary horizontal piece and stabilized it. One way to reduce this bounce is to lay the vertical piece flat on the floor and drive the nail at a 60-degree angle until it is almost through, then position the piece and complete the nailing. This is time-consuming and should be used as a means of familiarization with toenailing rather than as a regular practice. With practice, one can eliminate most of the movement by positioning one foot against the opposite side of the vertical piece to be nailed.

If the angle of the nail is too steep, it will often cause the wood to splinter. If the angle is too shallow, the vertical piece will not only bounce excessively, but when driven through it, the nail's tip will also simply slide along the top of the horizontal piece without entering it, and no fastening will occur. I know of no way to avoid either of these pitfalls without trial and error through practice.

The best type of nail apron I have found is also the simplest—a canvas one with two large pockets in front and a string which is tied around the waist. When stooping or crouching to nail, I turn the apron so that its pockets are along my left hip, giving easier access to the nails than if the pockets were in front.

I don't suppose there's an adult who hasn't nailed something at one time or another and in the course of doing so adopted his or her own "technique." If the technique I have described is adopted, one must be prepared for a period of discomfort and mishit nails, but perseverance will pay off with greatly increased effectiveness.

## Curtain Walls

In cities and suburban areas, interior walls of structures used to be constructed with structural clay tile, gypsum, or concrete blocks covered with a masonry finish.

In townhouses and tenements these walls had a wooden interior skeleton to which strips of wood (lath) were nailed and then covered with a masonry

Top portion of typical interior wall framing

Structural clay-tile core of masonry interior wall

Wood lath nailed to wood studs with plaster on lath

finish. The wood lath was later replaced with a metal mesh (lath) since it was more fire-retardant and the masonry finish adhered to it better. More recently, the wooden skeleton has itself been replaced by a metal one and, instead of lath and a masonry finish, sheetrock (gypsum sandwiched between paper) is attached directly to it. A variation of sheetrock called plasterboard (with or without

holes) is also widely used. With plasterboard, which has a specially treated surface, a coat of gypsum plaster mixed with sand is used as a base coat and the surface is finished with a mixture of gypsum or gauging plaster and slaked lime. The plasterboard is nailed directly to the skeletal structure, most often made of wood.

None of these walls has any structural significance—they do not support weight other than their own. Their purpose is to divide up space and retard the spread of fire.

The ability to retard fire is measured in terms of time. A wall is said to be half-hour, one-hour, etc. This means that the materials which make up the wall have undergone tests which have determined that these materials will retard a fire for the period of timed graded.

Building codes vary, but all set forth specific requirements with respect to wall fire-retardance. Generally, requirements for walls in public buildings are more stringent than those in multiple dwellings and private dwellings, but even in a private dwelling, for example, the wall which separates the garage from the rest of the house is ordinarily required to have a minimum half-hour rating.

Formerly, when a one-hour wall was required and a wooden skeleton used, the wood had to be chemically treated to resist the spread of fire, and each piece was so stamped. (Chemically treated lumber costs about twice as much as untreated lumber.) This requirement is rapidly disappearing with the use of advanced fire-retardant ingredients in the materials which are now used to cover the wooden skeleton.

The two types of walls which a carpenter will ordinarily construct today have either a wooden or metal skeleton. Sheetrock is normally used to cover the metal skeleton, either sheetrock or plasterboard with a wooden skeleton. I will detail the construction of both.

## Erecting a Half-Hour Wall (Wood Skeleton with Plasterboard)

The wall is made up of members, pieces that have various functions. The horizontal piece which forms the bottom is called the shoe or sole. The parallel piece at the ceiling is called the plate. The members which rise vertically between the shoe and plate are called studs. The shorter vertical pieces on each side of the doorway are called jacks. The short horizontal piece which extends between the jacks is called a header.

I locate the position of the wall to be erected by measuring from each end of an existing parallel wall; I mark, and pop a chalk line between the marks. I place an X on whatever side of the chalk line the new wall is to be positioned.

I measure along the chalk line from either intersecting wall and mark the center of the projected doorway. I intend to leave an opening in the skeletal structure into which I can later install a frame and door. This rough opening is abbreviated "r.o." The width of the r.o. is always 2 inches greater than the width of the door to be used. I intend to use a 28-inch door. (Standard doors begin at a width of 24 inches and increase in 2-inch multiples to 36 inches.) I therefore want to leave a 30-inch width r.o. I measure outward 15 inches from each side of the doorway's center mark, and mark.

I now get a 2 x 4 that will serve as the shoe. If the 2 x 4 is longer than the wall to be erected, I determine the distance between the intersecting walls by extending 1 x 2s and transfer this to the 2 x 4 and cut. If the 2 x 4 is shorter than the wall to be erected, I saw a second piece of 2 x 4 of sufficient length to reach the opposite intersecting wall.

I then place the 2 x 4 shoe at the chalk line and cover the X, an end butting the intersecting wall, and begin nailing the shoe at that end. I use #10 common nails spaced every 16 inches if the floor is wooden and #10 case-hardened wire-cut nails if the floor is concrete.

By starting the nailing at one end, I can shift the shoe continuously to align it along the chalk line, even if the 2 x 4 is warped, which is common.

I place a second length or lengths of 2 x 4 on top of the shoe to make an exact duplicate, which will serve as the plate. I tack (fasten temporarily, leaving heads of nails exposed for easy removal) the shoe and plate together to keep the plate from shifting while I am measuring and marking. Measuring from an intersecting wall, I mark the side of the shoe 16 inches in from the wall, then use a small adjustable square to extend the mark into a line across the shoe and plate. I place an X to the right of each. This indicates where the first stud will be placed.

The 16-inch module is standard and is the appropriate width between studs to which plasterboard will later be nailed.

Plate and shoe marked simultaneously at 16 inches for first stud

Plasterboard is manufactured in various widths. I will be using 32-inch. Since one end of the first piece of plasterboard will butt the intersecting wall, I want the other end to fall midway on the second stud. This will provide a nailing surface for both the first and second pieces of plasterboard, which will butt each other on the second stud. I therefore need to place the second stud 31-1/4 inches in from the intersecting wall. I mark the shoe and plate at 31-1/4 inches and place an X to the right.

From the 31-1/4-inch mark, I continue to measure and mark multiples of 16 inches until I have reached the opposite intersecting wall, placing an additional mark for a stud at the very end. Each successive piece of plasterboard from the 31-1/4-inch mark on will have both ends fall midway on a stud.

I now mark the r.o. width (previously measured and marked along the chalk line) on the plate and shoe. I place a J (for jack) toward the outside of each mark and then an X beside the J, also outward and toward the intersecting walls.

The purpose of marking the shoe and plate simultaneously is to eliminate the need of plumbing (making vertical) each individual stud. Since the stud marks are equidistant from an intersecting wall which is assumed to be plumb, each stud nailed at corresponding marks on the plate and shoe will also be plumb.

After marking the plate and shoe, I remove the plate and lay it parallel to the shoe at a distance roughly equal to the height of the ceiling. I turn it

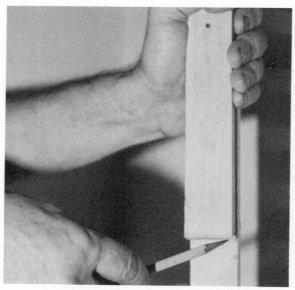

Measuring for stud length by marking overlap between two 1 × 2s, one end against ceiling, other end on shoe

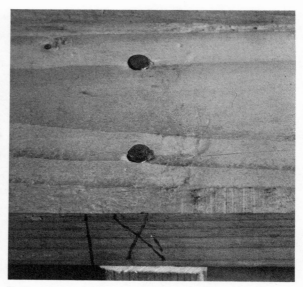

Nailing through back of plate into end of stud with two #16 common nails

on edge with my marks facing up. (On edge means placing the narrower 1-1/2-inch side on the floor.)

I determine the projected length of the studs by laying a 2 x 4 scrap flat on the shoe (representing the thickness of the plate) and extending two 1 x 2s so that one end rests on the scrap and the other end rests against the ceiling.

I lay the 1 x 2s on a 2 x 4 and mark the length. I total the Xs on the shoe to determine the number of studs I will need and cut them all 1/8 inch longer than the length indicated by the 1 x 2s. The purpose of cutting the studs a trifle longer than the actual distance between the shoe and plate is to create a wedge effect, thereby adding rigidity.

I nail each stud to the plate at the appropriate mark, covering the X by driving #16 common nails through the plate and into the ends of the studs. Two nails for each stud are sufficient.

I keep the bottom ends of the studs against the shoe for bracing during nailing. Since the shoe has already been nailed, it provides a convenient stop.

If the room isn't wide enough to assemble the wall on the floor, I raise the wall partially and assemble it from an angled position.

On either side of the marks that indicate the r.o. for the door, I have made J marks for jacks. The standard door height is 80 inches. The appropriate height of the standard r.o. is always 82 inches.

(Interior door framing only—exterior door framing is different.) Seven-foot doors are also available, and other heights can be custom made. The height of the r.o. will always be 2 inches more than the height of the door to be used.

Since the thickness of the shoe on which the end of the jack will rest is 1-1/2 inches and the r.o. height 82 inches, I cut two 2 x 4 jacks 80-1/2 inches. I then nail one jack to each stud that will be positioned on each side of the doorway, their lower ends flush. I then nail the attached studs' opposite ends to the plate.

The jacks are 30 inches apart. The header I want to cut will rest on their upper ends and butt the adjacent studs to which the jacks have been attached. I therefore cut the header to a length of 33 inches and install it by first nailing down through it into the jacks and then from the studs into its ends.

Occasionally, an exterior corner will be formed by intersecting walls. After the plasterboard has been attached, a metal strip called corner bead is installed over the exterior corner joint to make finishing the joint easier, cleaner, and to protect the corner against breaking when accidentally struck.

When purchasing a metal corner bead, its use with plasterboard should be specified. It will then extend 3/8 inch beyond the surface of the plasterboard, the thickness of the masonry bed coat to be applied later. The corner bead is sold in 8-foot and

Jack, stud, and header positions with location of nails

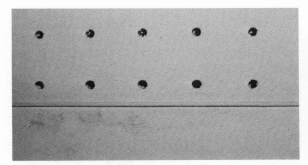

Plasterboard, with and without holes

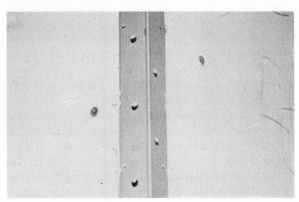

Corner bead on external corner of wall

Above the header is a space 33 inches wide between the two studs attached to the jacks. Along the plate within this area are marks for studs. I transfer these marks on the plate to the header by equidistant measurements from either of the studs. I cut and install 2 x 4s between the header and plate.

The wall is now assembled on the floor. Before I raise it onto the shoe and nail, I must establish the position that the plate will occupy on the ceiling. To do this, I select a straight piece of 2 x 4 and cut it about 1/2 inch shorter than the distance between the floor and ceiling. I place the 2 x 4 upright so that its 1-1/2-inch side is against the shoe and a foot or so from an intersecting wall. Against the 1-1/2-inch side of the upright 2 x 4, I place my 4-foot level.

Aligning plate to shoe with 2 × 4 and 4-foot level

(Many 4-foot levels are made of wood. I avoid these since they warp and are relatively unreliable. The one in the photo is made by the Sand Level and Toll Co. and is cast aluminum.)

I now shift the 2 x 4 till the bubble in the level is centered and place a mark on the ceiling that corresponds to the side of the shoe from which I have made the 2 x 4 plumb. I place an X beside the mark on the ceiling to indicate the side of the mark on which I will position the plate. I do the same with the 2 x 4 and level about a foot from the opposite end of the shoe and afterward snap a chalk line between the two marks.

It is preferable to establish the chalk line on the ceiling from the side of the shoe opposite the position of the wall, so that when the wall is raised the plate will be moving toward the chalk line. This makes positioning the plate easier than having to

10-foot lengths and is cut to size by snipping the sides with tin snips and hacksawing through the thicker center bead. To install, it is placed over the exterior corner and one nail is tacked through it at the top. A 4-foot level is then placed against the bead and it is shifted until plumb. It is then nailed every foot or so through each side along its entire length.

cross the chalk line and move the plate on till the chalk line reappears from under it.

I now grip the underside of the plate and with a helper (I will need two if the wall is more than 12 feet long) raise the wall, bracing the ends of the studs against the shoe to keep the wall from sliding forward. When the wall is about a third of the way up, we shift our grips so that one hand is on the plate and another on a stud. We continue to raise the wall after the plate is over our heads and arms by pushing on a stud.

When the wall is upright, some of the studs will be dangling and some will be resting on the shoe. I push the plate forward until it lies at the chalk line. If need be, I place a scrap of 2 x 4 against the plate and hammer the scrap to drive the plate to the chalk line. I align one end first, driving a #10 common nail through its underside into the ceiling. I proceed along the plate, driving it to the chalk line (and over the X) and nailing every 16 inches or so until it is installed.

I swing out the studs whose ends aren't on the shoe, place them on the shoe, then hammer them to their respective marks and over their respective Xs. I then toenail each stud to the shoe using #8 common nails, three to each stud.

I remove the nails which lie inside the r.o. from the shoe and with a six-point handsaw (6 teeth per inch) saw through the shoe adjacent to each jack, removing the piece that lies between them.

The tool I use to remove fully driven nails is called a cat's claw. The claw is placed at the nailhead, hammered into the wood under the head, then

Cat's claw positioned at nail to be removed

After being driven into wood surface, cat's claw pulled back under nailhead

pulled back. This raises the nail partially and permits its removal with a flat bar.

After the skeletal wall has been erected, the rough plumbing and wiring are installed. Electrical boxes are nailed to studs at desired locations, their forward edges extending beyond the edge of the studs at a distance equal to the projected thickness of the planned wall covering. Holes are then bored in the centers of each stud and the wire threaded through them to each box. Each wire is fastened to the studs with staples located 12 inches from each box. Later, as the wall covering is installed, each box is made accessible by removing an appropriate amount of wall covering.

The rough plumbing is also installed before the wall is covered and it is normal practice to extend water and drain nipples a few inches beyond the plane of the finished wall.

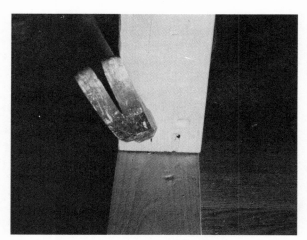

Bottom of stud being nailed to shoe

It has become a widespread practice to fill the spaces between studs (the bays) with insulation. This is supposed to reduce the transfer of sound from one side of the wall to the other. Unless heat transfer is a factor, this is a wasteful practice since the insulating material, usually fiberglass with foil backing, does very little to reduce sound transfer. If sound reduction is desired, a soundproofing material such as perforated Celotex will be much more effective.

Plasterboard is composed of gypsum between paper. It is one of the cheapest building products and is available in a variety of sizes for convenience in installation. Unlike sheetrock, its sides are untapered and its surface has been treated to give good adherence to the plaster with which it will be coated. I select sheets that are 16 by 32 inches since I find that this particular size is easiest for me to install alone.

BX cable in walls

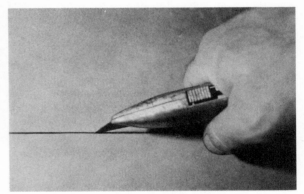

Plasterboard being cut with matte knife

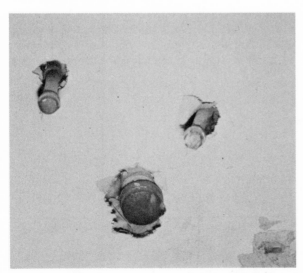

Rough plumbing after wall covering is installed and before fixture is placed and connected

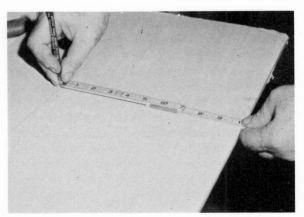

Quick marking for stud position or cutting

Having placed the second stud at 31-1/4 inches in from the wall, I begin by butting one side of the first plasterboard sheet against the nearest intersecting wall, placing the opposite side midway on the second stud. Its 32-inch dimension is laid horizontally. I use blue, ringed 1-1/2-inch lath nails and space them every 10 or 12 inches, driving them into the studs. I continue to install the plasterboard sheets horizontally along the bottom of the wall with the sides of each successive sheet located midway on a stud.

Since the length of the wall is not a multiple of 32 inches, I must cut the last plasterboard sheet to size to complete the row. To do this, I mark the projected cut on the front of the plasterboard, score the line with a sheetrock knife (essentially a razor blade with a handle), fold the sheet along the scored line, cut through the paper on the back of the sheet along the fold, and separate the cut portions. Plasterer's hatchets are often used to cut plasterboard, but I do not recommend them since they require sharpening often and a used razor blade costs little to replace when dull.

After the first course has been installed, I place a sheet of plasterboard above the first sheet I installed. The upper edge of the first sheet supports the weight of the new sheet. I lay the side of my arm against the new sheet to keep it against the wall. My left hand is free to place each nail while my right arm hammers it.

Plasterboard is sometimes installed so that the joints are "staggered" (meaning that the joints of successive rows are placed so as not to fall on the same stud). The assumption behind this is that if all the joints fall on the same studs a weaker wall will be created. There is little evidence that this is true, and I have never seen a wall that cracked because all the plasterboard joints were aligned.

I therefore install the second and all other courses of plasterboard sheets in exactly the same manner as the first until I approach the ceiling. Since the height of the ceiling is not a multiple of 16 inches (the height of each piece of plasterboard) I must cut all the sheets along the uppermost course so that their heights fit the gap between the course below and the ceiling. I cut the sheets and install them. Just as the shoe provided a nailing surface at the floor, the plate provides a nailing surface at the ceiling.

As portions of plasterboard enter the door r.o., I trim them off with the sheetrock knife, scoring them first on the back side using the jack as a reference, then bending each scored piece back and cutting through the crease.

In the area of the header, two cuts will have to be made to remove the portion of plasterboard that the lies within the r.o.

I cut the plasterboard along the underside of the header with a keyhole saw until I reach the jack. I then use the sheetrock knife to make the vertical cut along the jack and remove the unwanted portion.

A keyhole saw costs under $2. Steel tools dull very quickly when used on masonry materials and should be saved for other needs. This cheap saw can cut a great deal of plasterboard and sheetrock and has no other value.

The ends of the plasterboard around the r.o. will be hidden by the door frame and no special care need be taken to make them neat. However, none of the plasterboard should extend into the r.o. or it will interfere with the installation of the frame.

The functional ends of plumbing and wiring emerge beyond the plane of the skeletal wall and will have to be exposed as the plasterboard is installed. For example, when an electrical box lies in the projected position of a sheet of plasterboard, I spread powdered chalk on the outer edges of the box, place the plasterboard in the position it will be installed, and press it against the box. The chalk outline of the box is transferred to the back of the plasterboard. I punch a pilot hole in the center of the outline with a plasterer's hatchet, insert the end of the keyhole saw in the hole, and saw the outline.

Chopping a hole with plasterer's hatchet

Although the pictured hatchet is not as appropriate for line cuts as a sheetrock knife, it is an essential tool and useful for punching holes in plasterboard.

I make holes for plumbing lines and all electrical boxes in the same way. It is essential that the threaded holes in the electrical boxes be visible.

(I will detail the finishing of the r.o. for the door later in the chapter.)

## Erecting a One-Hour Wall (Metal Skeleton, Sheetrock)

For this wall I will be using a metal skeleton and fire-retardant sheetrock 5/8 inches thick called Type X. These combined with a few special minor items meet the requirements for a one-hour wall.

As with wood, the metal used for the skeleton can be purchased in lumber yards in various lengths and I select the most appropriate—stud lengths equal to or greater than the floor-to-ceiling height. The material used for the shoe and plate is different from the stud material, and is called "track."

Top of metal skeletal wall

Metal studs and back of sheetrock

Metal skeletal wall, bottom

I measure and mark for the metal shoe the same way I did for the wooden one.

I use a sabre saw with a metal-cutting blade to cut the shoe (a power hacksaw is better but much more expensive). I install the shoe with #8 common nails spaced every 16 inches. The metal is thin gauge and nails will drive through it easily. I omit the shoe along the 30-inch width of the r.o.

If the length of the wall is 12 feet or less, I select 4 x 12 sheetrock and install the sheets with the 12-foot side horizontal for easiest handling and a minimum of joints. If the wall is longer than 12 feet (the longest length of sheetrock available), I select a sheet the longest dimension of which is equal to or longer than the distance between the floor and ceiling. In this instance, since the ceiling height is 9 feet 6 inches and the length of the wall is almost 14 feet, I select 4 x 10 sheets and plan to install them with the 10-foot side vertical.

With this in mind, I mark the shoe 16 inches and 32 and 47-1/4 inches in from the intersecting wall. These indicate the positions for the first three studs. I place a mark at 47-1/4 inches for the same reason I marked 31-1/4 inches earlier—to have a surface for attachment of the second (adjacent) sheet by positioning the first sheet midway along a stud. The remaining studs are marked for placement every 16 inches as measured from the 47-1/4-inch mark.

I measure, mark, and cut the metal plate as I did the wooden one, establish its position on the ceiling in the same manner, and then attach it to the ceiling.

The method of attaching the plate depends on the material the ceiling is made of. If it is plaster

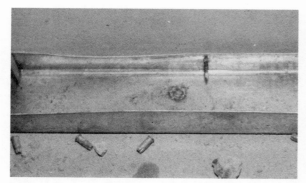

Rivet shot from gun securing shoe to concrete floor (same for plate)

over wood, as in ceilings in townhouses or tenements, #10 common nails driven into the ceiling joists through the plate will be satisfactory. If the ceiling is a masonry covering over concrete or structural tile, I use a riveting gun, which can be rented at a nominal cost.

The gun shoots bulletlike rivets that will secure the plate to the ceiling (or the shoe to a concrete floor). I space the rivets about 2 feet apart. Used carelessly, the gun can become a lethal weapon; one should take extreme care never to point it at anyone and to keep it out of the reach of children.

After the shoe and plate are installed, I use 1 x 2s to measure the distance between them; I cut studs 1/8 inch less than this distance. (Unlike wooden studs, metal studs cannot be cut an added 1/8 inch to permit wedging since they will crimp rather than bend.)

I install the metal studs (with the exception of the two studs at the door r.o.) by screwing through each side of the shoe and plate into the sides of the studs (two screws at the top and bottom of each.) I use self-tapping #6 Phillips-head sheet-metal screws 1/2 inch long, as shown in the photo.

Self-tapping screws used to attach sheetrock to metal studs

Screw through face of sheetrock and stud, view from back

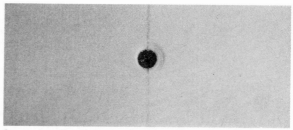

Screw head and depression around it on face of sheetrock

The end of the drill is equipped with a device which enables it to hold the screw. The screw is pressed moderately against the side of the shoe and the drill swiched on. The screw will make its own hole and a clutch in the drill will stop the driving action of the bit once the screw has secured both pieces. (This can be easily felt since the bit will no longer be exerting any force against the screw.)

The drill and gun can be rented at a nominal cost and the same store will usually carry screws and ammunition.

To frame the r.o. I cut two 82-inch jacks (from stud material) and attach them to studs with screws spaced every 2 feet or so. The bottoms of the jacks lie in the shoe.

I cut a header (from stud material) 36 inches—6 inches more than the 30-inch wide r.o. I place the header at the r.o. in the position it will occupy, both ends extending an equal amount beyond the jack. I mark the header at each end to correspond to the side of the studs facing the r.o.

Using the sabre saw, I cut off the *sides only* at each end of the header to the marks I have made. I now fold the center section up and attach the

Header installed above buck

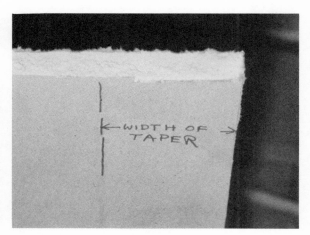

Taper on long sides of sheetrock

header to the studs, placing screws through the uplifted tabs at each end.

This completes the skeletal metal wall and I am ready to install the sheetrock. (If any wiring or plumbing will go on this wall, the roughing for it should now be done.)

When using sheetrock it is a good practice to select sizes that will produce the fewest number of joints, although this may result in wasting material. Since every joint will be covered later, the labor saved with fewer joints will more than justify the waste.

Standard sheetrock sizes are 4 by 8 feet, 4 by 10 feet, and 4 by 12 feet. Thicknesses range from 1/4 inch in multiples of 1/8 inch to 5/8 inch. Thicker and longer sheets are also manufactured but are not readily available.

I have selected 4 x 10 sheets and will install them with the 10-foot side vertical, since the ceiling height is 9 feet 6 inches. (Had the ceiling been 8 feet high, I would have installed the sheets horizontally, one 4-foot side resting on the other. This would place the seam at 4 feet, a convenient height to work, making installation a bit easier.)

The long sides of sheetrock are tapered as pictured. The 5/8-inch sheet thickness is evenly reduced to 1/2 inch or so at its very edge. When two sheets are installed butting one another, a V-shaped depression is created which, when filled later, will hide the seam.

The 4-foot sides of the sheets are not tapered. Joints between them are therefore more difficult to mask since any material placed on them will be above the plane of the surrounding area. It is

therefore a good practice to avoid joints on the 4-foot side wherever possible. It is also a good practice to place the cut end of a sheet against an intersecting wall when the tapered side has been removed.

The distance between the floor and ceiling is 9 feet 6 inches. However, neither the ceiling nor the floor is absolutely flat, creating a variation in height. If I were to cut all the sheetrock to a height of 9 feet 6 inches it would be too long in spots. Since I plan to finish the wall with baseboard that has a minimum height of 3/4 inch, any gap of 3/4 inch or smaller between the bottom of the sheetrock and the floor will be hidden. Knowing that any gap will be covered, and to avoid trying to position an overly long sheet, I remove 6-1/4 inches rather than 6 inches from all the sheets I intend to install. (The choice of removing an additional 1/4 inch from the nominal ceiling height rather than 1/2 inch or another figure is based on experience. If either floor or ceiling is severely undular, more should be removed. As much as a 3/4-inch gap between the bottom of the sheetrock and floor can be easily covered. If the gap will be greater than 3/4 inch, I create a second gap between the top of the sheetrock and the ceiling.)

If there are openings that must be made in the sheets to allow for electrical boxes or pipes, I now make them in the same way as described for plasterboard. I stand the first cut sheet against the framework where I have installed the stud at 47-1/4 inches. I place a scrap block of 2 x 4 on the floor a few inches from the sheet, lay a flat bar on it with its end under the sheet, and step on the other end of

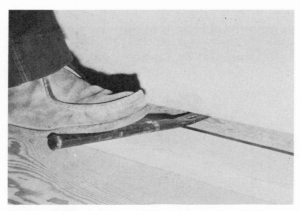

Flat bar over scrap and under sheetrock for lifting sheet while keeping hands free

the flat bar, which raises the sheet and butts it to the ceiling.

My hands are free and I attach the sheet to the metal studs with #6 1-inch Phillips-head sheet-metal screws by driving them with the drill through the sheetrock and into the stud. The screw will go into the sheetrock very quickly and easily but will suddenly encounter resistance as it strikes the metal stud. (The screw is self-tapping, which means it creates its own hole.) As soon as the resistance is overcome, the drill trigger should be released since the screw will be seated in the metal and turning it further will cause the screw to sink quickly too far below the surface of the sheet. The head of the screw should lie no deeper than 1/4 inch below the surface of the sheet.

After I have installed about six screws, I no longer need to keep the sheet elevated with the flat bar.

I install screws every 10 to 12 inches on all studs, jacks, and headers.

I cut excess sheetrock within the r.o. in the same manner as with plasterboard.

The pictured wall is what the completed installation looked like before finishing.

Typical joint between sheets of sheetrock before compound is applied

## Installing a Metal Frame and Door

The metal door frame which will be installed in the r.o. is called a buck. Pictured are two types. One, which is preassembled, is installed *before* the sheetrock is placed on the framework and may be used with either a wooden or metal skeletal wall. It is placed in position and the studs and jacks and header assembled around it. The buck has metal tabs with predrilled holes spot welded to its sides. It is secured by nailing through the predrilled holes into adjacent jacks or studs. The sheetrock is then cut to fit around the buck.

Assembled buck

Knocked-down buck

Factory-assembled buck secured to wall with nails through tabs

Mortise on buck's jamb for hinge leaf

Since the edge of the sheetrock must be butted against the edge of the preassembled buck, this requires the additional effort of fitting the sheets and applying joint compound and tape to hide the joint between the two. Sooner or later a crack will develop at this joint.

For these reasons I prefer to use unassembled or "knocked down" bucks, which are installed *after* the sheetrock is in place. With unassembled bucks there are no joints, no need for taping and compound, and no chance of cracks. The knocked-down buck requires additional effort to assemble and install, but it is still the preferable alternative.

The knocked-down buck is composed of three parts: two longer sides, called jambs, and a shorter one, the head.

When purchasing the knocked-down buck, two specifications must be stated in addition to the size: the thickness of the wall where the frame will be installed and the direction the door will swing.

The thickness of the wall I am building is 4-3/4 inches; the width of the stud is 3-1/2 inches and the thickness of two layers of 5/8-inch sheetrock (one sheet on each side of the studs) totals 1-1/4 inches.

One jamb has recessed portions for the hinge leaves, which are on the side where the door will be mounted. The other jamb has a recessed portion for the striker plate.

I install the buck by first slipping the head over the header and raising it as far as it will go. I slip one jamb over the jack with its hinge mortise on the same side as the room into which the door will swing, and the remaining jamb over the opposite jack with its striker-plate mortise on the same side.

Each jamb has two slots at the top, and the head has two corresponding prongs at each end. I slide the head down so that the prongs enter the slots. The tops of the jambs and the ends of the head have been mitered (cut at a 45-degree angle), and these should fit together as the head is lowered.

On the outer side of each jamb there is a slot an inch above the floor. I use an old wood chisel to remove a strip of sheetrock roughly 1 inch wide and 2 inches long beside each slot. This exposes the shoe. A metal strip with a hook at one end is provided with the buck. I place the hooked end of the metal strip into the slot. The strip's other end is flat and contains a predrilled hole. I lay this against the shoe. I place a 4-foot level against the jamb (hinge side) and plumb it. I then attach the strip to the shoe with a screw through the predrilled hole.

I plumb the opposite jamb and make sure that its distance from the first jamb is the same throughout their lengths. This should measure 1/8 to 3/16 inch greater than the width of the door. While door dimensions are reliable, the above clearance is necessary to assure that they will swing freely. If need be, small adjustments should be made by repositioning the loose jamb and head, which are then made stationary by placing a screw through the predrilled hole in the metal strip into the shoe (and through the jack behind it).

A one-hour wall requires a one-hour door. Any door rated for one hour has a permanently attached tag stating its rating.

The side of a one-hour door has mortises for hinge leaves that correspond to the mortises on the jamb; they contain threaded holes to receive machine screws. (The screws are part of the hinge purchase.)

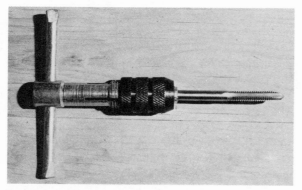

Tap and die to clean paint from threads

Quite often the threads will be clogged with primer paint. The paint is cleared away by screwing a tap and 3/16-inch die in the threads.

The bit will break if too much pressure is used; it is best to turn it counterclockwise when heavy resistance is felt before turning clockwise again.

The hinges used to mount the door are held together by a pin which is removed by pulling out the head with pliers. Each half of a hinge is called a leaf. The round extension on the leaf is called a knuckle. One knuckle has three holes, the other two. It makes no difference which is attached to the door or jamb so long as the corresponding leaf is used in the corresponding position. At the bottom of the three-holed knuckle is a small press-fitted piece called a plug or button. When the leaf is installed, the button (which prevents the pin from falling out) should always be on the underside of the knuckle. When the need to change the position of the button arises, it is removed by either twisting it with pliers or inserting a nail set through the knuckle and hammering out. The button is then hammered into the other end of the knuckle.

Because of its relatively heavy weight, three pairs of hinges are ordinarily used to mount a one-hour door. The pin is pulled from each pair of hinges and each leaf attached with machine screws into the three mortises on the jamb and three corresponding mortises on the door. The door is then placed on a scrap of wood to raise it enough for the top leaves to mesh. The pin is then inserted in the knuckle and the door shifted so that the remaining leaves also mesh.

If difficulty is encountered in getting the two remaining leaves to mesh, the door can be shifted as needed by using a flat bar with a block under it. (The misalignment of leaves is generally only slight.)

Two holes have also been bored in the door for installing the lock. (The lock is a key-in-knob type, almost universally used today.) The smaller hole is for the bolt half. The bolt is inserted with its flat end on the hinge side of the door and is attached with two machine screws. The knob half is then installed, also with two long machine screws. The striker plate is then installed on the jamb, again using two machine screws.

Occasionally minor adjustments are needed when the bolt doesn't quite fit into the hole of the striker plate or the gap between the door and frame is uneven and causes the door to stick. Adjustments to correct these conditions are made by loosening either of the metal strips which hold each jamb and shifting either of the jambs until the door operates properly, reattaching the metal strip in the new position.

For walls rated more than an hour there are special locks with longer-than-ordinary bolts or tongues. During a fire a door will contort and the added bolt length further serves to keep the door shut.

Wooden doors with various fire-retardant ratings are also available and may be substituted for metal-sheathed ones. They are filled with a gypsumlike material that will dull ordinary cutting tools, which makes it advisable to have the holes for the lock predrilled by the supplier.

## Installing a Wooden Frame and Door

Interior doors are manufactured in two styles, flush and panel. The flush are "hollow-core," the panel are "solid." A hollow-core door has a wooden frame around its perimeter, a horizontal piece at the standard height of a lock, and intermittent corrugated ribbons to which a veneer is glued. Interior doors are 1-3/8 inches thick in contrast to the 1-3/4-inch thickness of exterior doors. (Years ago interior doors were also 1-3/4-inch.) They are either 80 inches (customary) or 84 inches long. Other heights are custom made.

Lumber yards stock both flush and panel doors in widths beginning at 24 inches and continuing in 2-inch multiples to 36 inches. They are also manufactured in widths as narrow as 10 inches continuing in multiples of 2 inches up to 22 for use with such items as closets and cabinets. Doors wider than 36 inches are rarely used since they must be custom made and are expensive. When an opening is wider than 36 inches the usual practice is to use a pair of doors.

Luan, Philippine mahogany, is the cheapest and most frequently used veneer to cover the flush door, but birch, pine, and other woods are available if a "natural" finish is desired.

Panel doors are available in a variety of patterns, and lumber yards carry catalogues from which a choice can be made. Panel doors generally cost twice as much as flush doors, but their cost can be reduced if they are purchased from small companies that do not advertise extensively. A louvre-panel door generally costs the same as a standard-panel door.

Louvre blinds are often mistakenly referred to as doors. They are usually either 7/8 inch or 1-1/16 inches thick, shoddily made, and guaranteed to warp. A pair of 14-inch-wide blinds costs about the same as a 28-inch-wide louvre door, and the louvre door is much the better buy.

I have decided to install a 28-inch-wide flush door. I must now select and assemble the frame.

As with the metal buck and door, the dimensions of the r.o. for the wooden frame and door are 30 by 82 inches. The thickness of the wall is 4-3/4 inches. This thickness will probably vary slightly, and in order to avoid difficulties later, I purchase a door frame that is 4-7/8 inches wide. The additional 1/8 inch should be sufficient to overcome any variation in wall thickness.

The frame is sold "knocked down" or unassembled. There are twelve pieces, including, as before, two jambs and a head. There is also a "set" of casing, the wood which lies flat against the wall

around the perimeter of the door, consisting of six pieces, three on each side of the wall, and a "set" of door stop, consisting of three pieces.

The sides of the jambs and head are tapered and will be installed so that the widest part of the taper will be closest to the door. The purpose of the taper is to make it easier to nail the casing flat against the wall. The jambs also have a "dado" across their width, a U-shaped groove about an inch below each jamb's top, 3/4 inch wide and 3/8 inch deep. The head will be fitted into the dado and secured by nailing through the back of the jambs into the ends of the head.

The standard head for a 28-inch door is cut to a length of 28-3/4 inches so that when the frame is assembled the distance between the jambs will be 28 inches. This will ordinarily require that the door be planed, since it is also 28 inches. To avoid the needless work of planing a door to fit a frame, I order instead a head for a 30-inch door and cut the head down to a length of 28-15/16 inches. When the frame is assembled with a head of this length, the width between the jambs will be 28-3/16 inches. This leaves a 3/16-inch gap between the door and

Assembled frame and door prior to installation

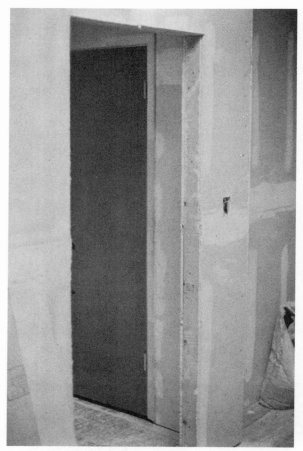

Rough opening for frame and door

Frame and door installed into rough opening

jamb on the lock side and eliminates the need to bevil or plane the door to avoid sticking. In addition, doors "move." They expand in hot and wet weather and contract in cold and dry weather. I have found that with the 3/16-inch gap, a door is unlikely to expand so much that it will stick, or contract so much as to be able to pass through the door stop. Nor is the gap so wide as to be unsightly.

To begin assembly of the frame, I stand in the room into which the door will swing and determine whether the hinges will be mounted on the left or right and mark this on the side of a jamb.

For convenience, I place a 2 x 8 on horses and lay the marked jamb on it. I measure 7 inches down from the bottom of the dado and place an X below the mark. I measure up 11 inches from the other end of the jamb and place an X above the mark.

I separate the leaves of the hinges by pulling the pins and place a leaf on the jamb at the mark made

7 inches below the dado and on the X. (I am using 3-by-3-inch hinges, an appropriate size for this hollow-core door. With heavier doors I use larger hinges, and with solid-core doors I place an additional hinge midway between the top and bottom ones.) The knuckle extends beyond the side of the jamb, the edge of the leaf is exactly on the side of the jamb. I trace the outline of the leaf and then repeat the process for the other leaf, which will be placed at the mark made at the jamb's other end.

I now wish to remove the wood within the outline to a depth equal to the thickness of the hinge (mortising). The most widespread way of doing this is to use a wood chisel, as now described.

I begin the mortise by scoring the outline of the leaf, holding a 1-1/4-inch chisel as pictured. The chisel's taper is facing toward the mortise; the flat back of its cutting edge lies at the inside of the pencil line. I maintain the vertical position of the

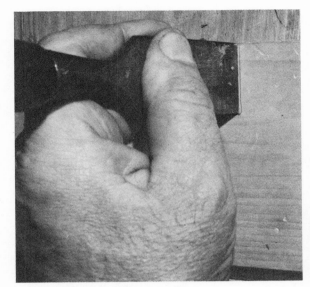

Position of chisel to begin mortise

Score marks across mortise after scoring outline of leaf

Removing chips

chisel while I hammer the handle. I hammer harder when scoring against the grain, lighter with the grain. In both instances the force of the hammering is what I estimate will be needed to drive the cutting edge of the chisel to a depth equal to the thickness of the leaf.

After scoring the outline, I place the chisel about 1/4 inch inside and parallel to the uppermost scored line going across the grain and I score a second line beneath it. I then continue in the same fashion until I have scored the entire area within the outline with lateral strokes 1/4 inch or so apart and

Smoothing surface of mortise, chisel taper is down

remove the partially cut chips by lifting upward with the chisel.

To make the surface in the mortise flat to receive the leaf, I turn the tapered end of the chisel down against the wood. Four fingers on the back of the chisel maintain pressure downward. My right hand guides the chisel as I make short jabbing strokes to smooth and flatten the mortise.

I place the leaf in the mortise and test its height in relation to the jamb with my forefinger. I want the leaf to be in the same plane as the jamb or slightly below. If the leaf is too high I will remove more wood with the jabbing stroke. If too much wood has accidentally been removed, I will raise the leaf by inserting a match cover below it before attachment.

If the outline hasn't been scored properly and the leaf extends a trifle beyond the side of the jamb, I tap the leaf forward until they are aligned. (The cut with the grain leaves a soft surface and the side of the leaf will bite into it, allowing this slight adjustment.)

If the long cut of the mortise has been made too far across the width of the jamb, I still position the leaf with its edge flush with the side of the jamb. A small gap will remain but will later be hidden by the door stop.

To fasten the leaf in the mortise, I place it in the proper position, then lay an awl across my left index finger (which steadies it) and press its point into the centers of the three predrilled holes in the leaf. (An awl is a pointed hand tool similar to an ice pick but with a thicker shaft.) I rotate the awl gently to enlarge the hole, then press down again moderately. I insert three screws into the three pilot holes and fasten with a Yankee screwdriver. No wax or drilling is necessary. The wood is pine and soft and the screws will not cause it to split.

After the leaves are attached to the jamb, I am ready to attach the leaves to the hollow-core door. I first note along its sides if it has been stamped, *hinge side*. Doors stamped this way have narrow rails on the hinge side which will not accommodate holes that must be made for the lock.

The jamb is still lying on the horses. I place the door on its side on top of the jamb so that the door's top end is 3/16 inch below the dado. I place marks on the hinge side of the door that correspond to the top and bottom of each hinge already fastened to the jamb. This will leave a gap of 3/16 inch between the top of the door and the bottom side of the frame's head after the frame has been assembled.

I continue the marks across the hinge side of the door with a T square. I mortise between the parallel lines with a wood chisel in the manner described for the jamb.

I install the leaves on the door after mortising and mesh them into the leaves on the jamb. I check to see whether a 3/16-inch gap exists between the top of the door and the bottom of the dado.

If some mistake has been made in positioning the leaves or if the gap is too large or small, I now make the necessary corrections by altering the position of the leaves on the door.

I remove the door and assemble the frame on the floor by nailing through the back of the jambs into the head, which is placed in the dado. I use two #6 common nails through each jamb.

I position the assembled frame with the leaves up. I now will install the casing, which will be nailed flat to the side of the jambs and head.

Clamshell and ogee are the two types of casing most widely used. The ogee is older and will be

Clamshell and ogee casing

Casing set back slightly from edge of jambs and head

Right-angle marks as reference for placement of casing

found in most apartments. Their cost is the same and selection is based on appearance.

No matter which type of casing is used, its bottom will be cut square and installed flush with the bottom of the jambs. The top of the casing will be mitered at a 45-degree angle. The head piece of casing will be mitered at each end.

The thinner side of the casing, as pictured, will not cover the whole edge of the jambs and head but will be nailed back slightly, rather than flush. I keep it back 1/8 inch, providing the maximum nailing surface. The casing is not nailed flush because any irregularity or imperfection in a flush alignment would be more noticeable.

At the joints between the head and jambs, I place right-angle marks 1/8 inch away from the inside corner.

I place a long length of casing in a miter box and, with an eight-point handsaw, cut an end square.

I place the length of casing on top of the left jamb, the squared end flush with the bottom of the jamb. (I am standing within the partially assembled frame which is resting on edge on the floor.) The thin edge of the casing is on the jamb. I place a mark on the upper end of the casing that corresponds to the right-angle mark on the jamb and head. I extend the mark lightly on a diagonal to indicate the direction of the miter.

If the miter box is new (they can be bought for as little as $2), I insert the saw in the diagonal grooves and make saw marks in the bed of the box.

I place the casing in the box and align the mark I have made on it with the saw mark. I want the mark on the casing to be barely visible after I have sawed it. The kerf of the saw (the gap caused by the flare of the saw's teeth) will be totally on the piece of casing I will not be using. After positioning the casing to accomplish this (the diagonal corresponds to the light pencil mark I made earlier), I hold the casing tight against the side of the miter box while I am sawing, making sure that the saw is vertical and not tilted.

I attach the sawed casing by nailing through its thinner side into the jamb below with #4 finishing nails spaced every 16 inches or so. I start at the miter and work down, maintaining the setback of 1/8 inch throughout the casing's length.

On the shorter head piece of casing I cut the same miter as on the jamb piece, butt it to the installed piece, mark the other end at the right-angle marks set back 1/8 inch, and cut an opposite miter in the uncut end. I nail this, also set back 1/8 inch.

I cut the same right miter for the top of the third piece, butt it to the miter at the right of the head, and mark its other end to correspond with the end of the jamb. I saw this in the miter box at a right angle and nail.

I place the partially assembled frame into the r.o. and push forward until the back of the casing lies flat against the wall. On the thick side of the casing, a foot or so from the top and bottom, I start two #10 finishing nails. (These are also on the hinge side of the frame.)

I place a 4-foot level against the jamb, shift the jamb until it is perfectly plumb, then finish driving the nails to secure both casing and jamb. (The #10 finishing nails will be going through the sheetrock and into the jack and stud behind it.)

I now mount the door on the secured jamb. I start two additional #10 finishing nails in the opposite casing and shift the jamb until I have a 3/16-inch gap between the jamb and door along the entire length. (This is best done by eye.) I then complete nailing to secure the opposite jamb.

I now do the intermediate nailing through the casing, spacing #10 finishing nails every 16 inches or so.

If there happens to be outward bulge anywhere along the jamb, I remove it by driving a shim (a tapered piece of cedar shingle) between the back of the jamb and the jack. I secure this position by driving a #10 common nail through the face of the jamb and into the jack. The nail should lie 1-3/4 inches from the hinge side so that it will later be covered by the door stop.

If the bulge is inward, I remove it by nailing through the jamb at the bulge and into the jack until the bulge is removed. I then drive a tapered piece of cedar shingle (1/2 inch at its thickest part) into the gap between the back of the jamb and jack and secure it with a #10 common nail. I then mark, cut and install the casing on the opposite side of the wall.

To install the lock I remove the door from the frame and lay it on horses with the hinge side up.

## Installing a Lock

The interior door lock most commonly used is the key-in-knob type as shown on the next page. It is necessary to bore two holes in the door to install it. The sizes of these holes are standard. The larger has a diameter of 2-1/8 inches, the smaller 7/8 inch.

The standard height for the knob is 36 inches above the floor. Although it will result in a slightly higher placement, I measure 36 inches up from the

Lock components

Brace and expansion bit

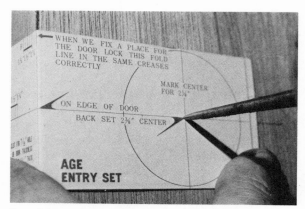

Template on door, awl marking center of hole

bottom of the *door* and mark. I use a T square to extend the mark several inches from the edge of the door.

I fold the paper template that comes with the lock so that the larger circle is flat on the face of the door and the smaller on its side. I align the horizontal line on the template with the 36 inch line I have drawn and, using an awl, pierce the template at the center dots of the circles. (There are two diameter lines in the smaller circle, and I use the one marked 1-3/8-inch. The other is for doors that are 1-3/4 inches thick.)

To bore the larger hole, I use a brace and Erwin expansion bit.

The chuck of the brace is opened by turning the forward ring counterclockwise. I insert the Erwin expansion bit between the jaws, slide it up as far as it will go, then tighten by turning the ring clockwise. The ratchet-control ring which is located directly above the right-angle turn of the brace

should be turned as far to the right as it will go.

The bit has a large screw at the back, which I loosen in order to insert a cutting knife. Two are supplied with the bit. I place the longer one into the notched slit and slide it forward until the distance between the threaded tip of the bit and the outer tip of the knife is 1-1/16 inches. (The cutter is ruled, but it is unreliable and I use a folding ruler.) I tighten the back screw which holds the cutter stationary.

I turn the brace and bit clockwise into a scrap of wood until I score a circle. To remove the brace and bit, I turn the ratchet-control ring counterclockwise all the way and turn the brace counterclockwise.

I measure the diameter of the hole. I want exactly 2-1/8 inches and may have to adjust the cutter again to obtain this.

I place the threaded tip of the bit into the hole made by the awl through the template. I have turned the ratchet ring clockwise as far as it will go. I keep the bit perpendicular as I turn the brace clockwise. When the cutter begins to score the veneer, I turn lightly and slowly and *watch the circle being scored*. Unless the bit is perpendicular, the circumference of the hole will be scored unevenly in depth. I can see this and make adjustments more easily than trying to eyeball the bit for verticality.

If the cut is uneven, I lean toward the shallower cuts on the circumference, which simultaneously raises the bit from the more deeply cut segments. Any tendency toward unevenness should be corrected while the cut is still shallow since it will be much more difficult to correct as the hole becomes deeper. After a depth of 1/4 inch or so has been attained, no further adjustments should be made.

I've never known anyone who couldn't determine unevenness by eye, but if one still has doubts, the depth at various points on the circumference can be checked with the brass extension of a folding ruler and compensation made.

When the depth of the hole has reached about 3/8 inch and a perpendicular course is established, I lay my left palm on top of the brace and increase downward pressure by leaning my chest on the back of my hand and adding the weight of my body.

When it becomes difficult to turn the brace in a complete circle, I employ the ratchet device by swinging the handle back and forth in a narrow arc directly in front of me. On the counterclockwise swing, the cutter remains stationary. On every clockwise swing, it moves forward and continues to cut in a circle. The handle is easiest to turn when it is close to the operator.

After the hole has been bored about halfway through, I begin to feel the underside of the door for the bit. As soon as the tip comes through the veneer, I turn the door over and continue boring the hole from the opposite side. If the hole is bored completely through only one side, the veneer will be splintered as the cutter comes through the bottom.

After the large hole has been bored, I place the door on edge on the floor with the awl hole up. I straddle the door and use my legs as clamps to keep it in an upright position. I place the tip of a 7/8-inch spade (speedbore) bit set in a 3/8-inch variable-speed Rockwell drill into the awl hole. (The Rockwell drill is modestly priced and much more useful than a single-speed type.) I press the trigger lightly producing a slow rpm and begin drilling, watching for differences in depth in the developing hole. I *do not* press down heavily on the drill and use only the minimum force necessary to maintain the drilling action. Variations in depth can be seen quickly in the hole since it is being bored more rapidly than with the brace, but for the same reason a slant can develop more quickly. As a means of control, I use short bursts until I have established a perpendicular hole. I then press the trigger back all the way for maximum rpm and continue to bore until the bit enters into the larger hole. I do not increase my light downward pressure. I can tell that I am pressing down too heavily when the rpm decreases substantially, creating an increasingly lower-pitched sound—from a whine to a groan.

I insert the bolt part of the lock into the 7/8-inch hole. The straight side of the bolt or tongue faces the hinges. I trace the outline of the rectangular plate on the side of the door, remove the bolt, then score the outline by tapping it with a 1/2-inch wood chisel to a depth I estimate to be the thickness of the plate. On the plate's long sides the scored line will be near the edge of the door and only very light tapping should be used (especially on flush doors) to avoid splintering the wood or separating the veneer.

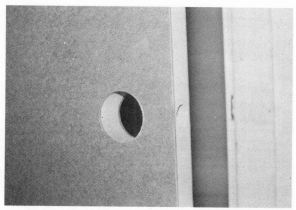

2-1/8-inch and 7/8-inch holes

Bolt being inserted into 7/8-inch hole

I mortise the outlined area with a 1/2-inch wood chisel to a depth slightly deeper than the thickness of the plate (1/16-inch is good). If the door should ever require planing, placing the metal below the surface of the wood will avoid the need of having to reset it deeper.

I reinsert the bolt and attach it to the door through the two holes in the plate with the two screws provided. These screws will probably have a

Knob half inserted from outside of room

Striker plate on jamb

Remaining half with holes in escutcheon plate inserted from inside of room

Phillips head rather than a slotted one. (The Phillips head has a cross which tapers down into the screw. Appropriate bits of various sizes are available for use in the Yankee screwdriver.)

I insert the knob half through the 2-1/8-inch hole. The blank escutcheon plate (the round piece of metal directly in front of the knob that hides the gap between the lock and the circumference of the hole) should be on the side opposite the hinges. (There are no screw holes in the blank plate.) This part of the lock has three metal extensions which are now inside the hole. The longest has a semicircular tapered end which slides through the semicircular opening at the rear of the installed bolt. The other two extensions are like small pipes with interior threads. One goes through a round hole near the center of the bolt and the other through the half hole at its very end.

The second knob is inserted from the opposite side of the door. Its escutcheon plate has two screw holes. I rotate the plate until the holes are aligned with the two interior threaded pipes of the installed

knob half. I insert two long machine screws through the holes in the plate and thread them into the pipes. I tighten the screws alternately to avoid misalignment until both knobs and plates are secured firmly against the door. I turn the knob to make sure that the bolt moves in and out freely.

If the lock is the bedroom or bathroom type, there will be a small hole in the center of the knob, which will be facing outside the room. If the key is lost or misplaced, a #6 finishing nail pushed through the hole will release the lock. Passage and closet locks ordinarily have no locking mechanism.

The pictured piece of metal is called a striker plate, and the bolt will strike it as the door is being closed. To install it, I first position the door so that the bolt is against the jamb, then I mark the bolt's top and bottom positions on the jamb, continuing this mark across part of the jamb with a T square.

I position the striker plate on the jamb so that its rectangular cutout (for the bolt) is centered between the two lines marking the top and bottom of the bolt. The side of the rectangle nearest the door should be exactly 3/4 inch in from the edge of the jamb.

I trace the outline of the striker plate and, with a 1/2-inch wood chisel, mortise to a depth equal to its thickness. I screw the plate to the jamb, then gouge out the rectangle where the bolt will be seated to the shape of the bolt. The gouge will be

**118**

straight nearest the door and tapered farther on. (Some manufacturers provide a metal box which lies under the striker plate to house the bolt, but it is rarely used.)

This completes the installation of the lock, and I am now ready to attach the door stops. They are milled in the same patterns as casing and are also sold in sets.

### Installing a Door Stop

I place a 7-foot length of stop in the miter box and trim an end to be square. This stop will be installed on the lock side of the door.

I stand the stop upright. I extend a T square, which I have placed against the underside of the head, and mark the same relative position on the stop. This is the distance between the floor and the underside of the head. I make a light diagonal line on the stop at this mark to indicate the direction of the miter.

I lay the stop on edge in the miter box and saw in the direction of the light line. A frequent error is to cut the stops with the miter going the wrong way. It is helpful to keep in mind that, since the sides are being mitered and not the face, the back of the stop, its flat side, is always longest. The mark I have made for length should barely remain after the cut, and I therefore position the stop so that the kerf of the saw will be on the piece not to be used.

Mitering door stop in miter box

I start five or six #4 finishing nails spaced 16 inches apart into the face of the stop. I close the door. I lay the stop against the jamb on the lock side and push forward *gently* until the bolt lies snugly against the back side of the rectangular metal cutout in the striker plate. I lightly tack in a

few of the nails, then open and shut the door to see whether it operates properly.

As the stop is being nailed, it has a tendency to shift further against the door. If this occurs, the door will not close unless it is slammed. On the other hand, if the stop is not snug and does not hold the bolt against the rectangular cutout, the door will rattle. To avoid either problem, I only lightly tack on the stop (leaving the nailheads exposed) to establish the proper position. After I have done this (removing the tacked nails to shift the stop as needed), I complete the nailing with the door open, which makes it easier to maintain the correct position of the stop.

I install the other two stops in the same manner. With their installation, finishing the r.o. is complete.

The method I have described wasn't used by my father and is not ordinarily used by other carpenters. Carpenters normally assemble the frame first, nail it into the opening, then make the door fit that opening by planing. I find this laborious and time-consuming—a carpenter who can complete two to three rough openings in a day is considered average. I have completed a great many rough openings using the method described and have taught it to hundreds of students and carpenters. Some students do as many as six openings per day; the average amount is about four.

## Repair and Renewal of Old Doors, Windows, and Hardware

In older structures (and in some newer ones) doors and windows which do not operate properly are a common problem. Restoring them to a functioning state usually involves less than a half hour's work (sometimes only minutes). And yet I know a woman who spent years getting herself locked in her bathroom because of a faulty lock. It took five minutes to repair. Her comment: "Is *that* all there was to it?"

## Repairing Sticking Doors

Doors that stick when shut or fail to close fully are a common problem. The operational failure may be caused by a loose hinge or by the bolt improperly hitting the striker plate, but it usually results from a build-up of successive layers of paint that must be removed.

If either of the leaves of the upper hinge has loosened from the jamb or door (there will be a much larger gap visible between the jamb and door at the top than at the bottom), I remove weight from the hinge by propping up the fully opened door with a wood scrap. I remove the loose leaf and fill the screw holes in the jamb or door with wooden kitchen matches (after breaking off their heads). I make pilot holes with an awl in the center of the matchsticks and replace the leaf.

If the upper leaf has not loosened (the gap between the door and jamb will be uniform along its entire length), I note the gap between the door and jamb on the lock side as I try to shut it. If the edge of the door hits the jamb at any point other than where the bolt hits the striker plate, I remove the excess paint in that area, using a spinner sander and 20-grit open-coat paper.

If the edge of the door (rather than the bolt) hits the striker plate as I try to shut the door and the amount of contact is 1/16 inch or less, I remove the excess wood from the door with a spinner sander and 20-grit open-coat paper, sanding at an angle that makes the leading edge of the door narrow enough to clear the striker plate.

If the amount of contact is greater than 1/16 inch, I first note how deep the lock has been mortised into the side of the door. If the lock is set 1/16 inch or so below the surface, I sand at an angle until I have made the wood flush with the lock plate. If the door still doesn't shut, I must remove the lock and mortise it more deeply.

The pictured lock is found in almost all interior doors of older structures. To remove it, I unscrew the set screw located at the forward end of the knob.

Set screw on knob

Two screws which hold mortise lock after knob and spindle are removed

I turn the knob counterclockwise and unscrew it from the spindle. (The interior of the knob's end and the exterior of the spindle are threaded. The set screw maintains the position of the knob after it has been threaded into position on the spindle.) Having removed the set screw and one knob, the second knob and spindle can be pulled out.

The rest of the lock, which is mortised into the side of the door, is held by two screws and I remove

Mortise lock

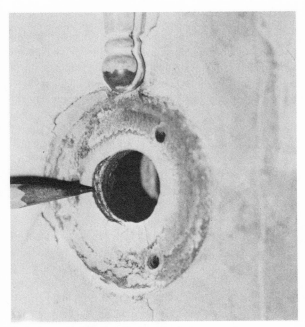

Hole for spindle, penciled arc to be removed

them. The lock itself, which is in one piece, can now also be removed.

The mortised area is made up of two sections, one to accommodate the plate around the bolt and one to accommodate the body of the lock. Using a 1/2-inch wood chisel, I remove 3/16 inch in depth from each section. The mortise that outlines the plate around the bolt needn't be touched; only the wood at the back of each section needs removal.

A hole to accommodate the spindle has been bored through the door. Using a sabre saw, I enlarge this hole at the circumference farthest from the side of the door. Toward the back of the lock is a square opening through which the spindle will be positioned. I remove enough wood for the spindle to be able to pass through that square opening, which will now be positioned 3/16 inch deeper into the door.

I reinsert the lock and attach it with two screws through the bolt plate. I push the knob and spindle through the square hole and thread the second knob onto the spindle, not tightening it excessively since this interferes with the bolt action. However, it should not be so loose as to permit the knob and lock assembly to rattle. I put back the set screw and tighten *hard*. This screw has a tendency to work loose; when it does, the knob turns without rotating the spindle, and the bolt will not move.

Having repositioned the lock deeper within the door, I am now able to continue sanding along the side of the door down to the bolt plate. This should eliminate the problem of the door sticking. If repositioning the lock has made part of the hole for the spindle visible, I fill the exposed part with plastic wood and sand it smooth.

When the sticking problem is not only at the lock or the immediate area around it, but has resulted from the entire door having swelled 3/16 inch or more (including layers of paint) along its entire side, sanding is no longer efficient. In this situation, I remove the lock and remove the excess width along the entire side of the door. I first remove the excess paint by sanding with the spinner; I then remove the excess wood with a power block plane as pictured and deepen the mortise for the lock.

A great deal of care must be exercised in using the power block plane, particularly when the guard has been removed as shown in the photo. (In this case I removed the guard because it made using the plane easier, but I strongly advise that the guard

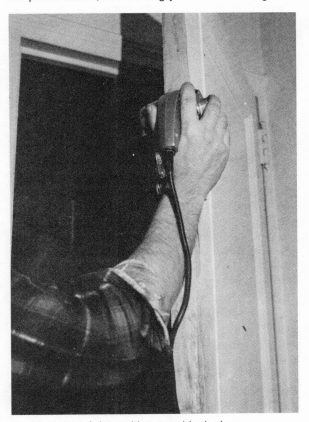

Planing edge of door with power-block plane

*not* be removed until the operator has become thoroughly familiar with the tool.) The left hand *must* be kept away from the tool. Only the right hand, as pictured, operates the plane.

I remove the door from the frame and pop a chalk line that is 3/16 inch back from the existing edge. I place the door on edge on the floor with the chalk mark up and straddle it, using my legs as a clamp to maintain it upright. I place the bed of the plane on the side of the door, making sure that the cutter is not against the wood so that it can spin freely when I turn on the switch.

I switch on the plane with my right hand and push it into the wood with light pressure. My downward pressure against the wood is only strong enough to keep the plane from bouncing up and down.

The cutter will remove 1/16 inch on each pass. I make three continuous passes over the side of the door, moving the plane from bottom to top. I check the cut against the chalk line on the face of the door to verify the amount of wood removed and to straighten bulges if they have occurred.

When replacing the door, I first mesh the upper leaves and tap in the pin, then mesh the lower ones and replace their pin. This is easier than trying to mesh top and bottom leaves simultaneously and maintain the mesh while inserting the pins.

## Repairing Doorknobs

Occasionally, when a knob is turned, it rotates uselessly on the spindle instead of actuating the bolt. This is caused by a loose set screw. The knob should be threaded to a snug position and the set screw tightened. If this doesn't solve the problem and the knob continues to turn without actuating the bolt, the set screw is probably worn or the spindle deformed so that they cannot tighten against one another.

To correct this, I remove the set screw and scratch a mark on the spindle to indicate its position. I remove the spindle and bore a hole in it 1/8 inch deep, using a drill bit the same size as the set screw. I replace the spindle, and screw the knob back to its original position so that the hole for the set screw is aligned with the hole in the spindle. I then tighten the set screw so that its end extends into the hole in the spindle; it should now actuate the bolt when the knob is turned.

## Repairing Locks

A bolt (or tongue) that remains stuck inside the lock may result either from dried paint or a broken spring within the lock. In either case, the lock must be removed. The two screws which attach the lock to the door are likely to be hidden by paint, and I scrape it away. Before trying to turn the screws, I hold the screwdriver at an angle and tap it along each screw's slot to chip away the paint that has dried there. I then remove the lock from the door.

The large screw in the case of the lock is removed, allowing the housing to come apart. When the knob is turned to retract the bolt, the spring in the photo stretches; when the knob is released, the spring returns to its original position, causing the bolt to extend. If I find the spring intact, I then know that the bolt has either become misaligned with the opening of the bolt plate through which it extends or has been "glued" by dried paint. If it is misaligned, I simply shift it to the proper position so that it doesn't make contact with the opening. If paint has caused it to stick, I scrape the paint away with a penknife.

However, if the spring is broken, I note where the break has occurred. If it is toward the middle of the spring, I must replace the spring. If the break is near either end (which is usually the case), I pull out the last coil before the break, form it into a hook at its end, and attach the hook to the post. This is done with needle-nosed pliers.

Cover of mortise lock removed (held by single screw); pencil points to post on which end of spring is attached

## Replacing a Front-Door Lock Cylinder or Installing a New Lock

The lock shown in the photo is widely used for the front doors of apartments. When moving into a new apartment there is often a desire to "change the locks." The lock itself needn't be changed, only the cylinder—that part into which the key fits and which controls the locking device. The entire procedure should take less than five minutes. Cylinders can be purchased in hardware stores and will fit any standard lock of the type shown. They may also be brought from the old apartment to the new one and exchanged.

To remove the cylinder, I first remove the four screws on the apartment side of the lock.

After removing the back of the lock, a metal plate becomes visible. I remove two long machine screws that go through predrilled holes in the plate and into two threaded holes in the back of the cylinder. The plate is now free to be removed, as are the cylinder and the brass ring around it.

I place the new cylinder and ring where the old cylinder and ring were located. The slot for the key is down. I place the plate in its former position and attach the two machine screws into the threaded holes in the back of the cylinder. This secures the cylinder and ring on the front of the door and the plate on the back of the door. Before I complete tightening the machine screws, I check the position of the ring and cylinder. The ring should fit flat against the door and cover the hole for the cylin-

Segal lock, screwdriver at one of four screws to be removed

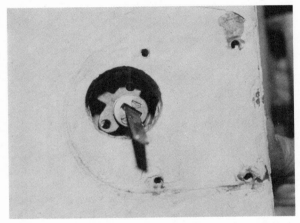

Cylinder viewed from inside apartment after plate is removed

Plate behind lock, screwdriver at one of two screws to be removed

Cylinder and ring viewed from outside apartment

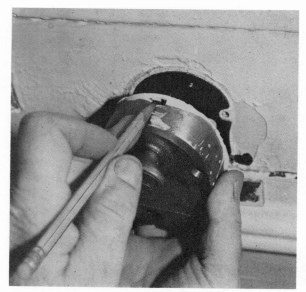

Arm which permits entry of cylinder extension

der. The cylinder should lie flat along the inner circumference of the ring. Both can be shifted as needed any time before the screws are completely tightened.

At the back of the cylinder is a long thin metal extension. At the back of the lock is a covered slot. The cover is moved away from the slot by pulling out a small arm at the side of the lock. The metal extension from the cylinder may now be inserted into the slot and the arm released. The back of the lock is reattached to the door with the four original screws, and this completes replacing the cylinder.

To install a complete lock of this type in an unbored door, I mark 46 inches up from the floor on the side of the door where I intend to install the lock and 1-3/8 inches in from the edge. Where the two marks cross, I bore a 1-3/8-inch diameter hole, using the Erwin expansion bit mentioned earlier. (The "metal" door is sheathed in soft metal; its interior is wood. The cutter will go through the metal sheath readily but it will dull appreciably.) As an alternative, I can bore this hole using a 1/2-inch drill and a 1-3/8-inch Greenlee spur bit.

In either case, before drilling the hole, it is good practice to punch a pilot hole through the metal with an awl. (A pilot hole should also be made with the awl before any screw is fastened.)

Once the 1-3/8-inch hole has been bored, I insert the ring and cylinder from the outside of the door,

position the plate on the back of the door (after removal of the back of the lock as shown in the photo), and attach the two with two long machine screws which go through the predrilled holes in the plate to the threaded holes in back of the cylinder. I then place the back of the lock over the plate, punch pilot holes into the door through the four predrilled holes in the back of the lock, and attach it to the door with the screws provided.

I place the bracket which holds the bolt on the casing and shift it so that the bolt can be raised and lowered freely through the holes.

I punch pilot holes for the screws with an awl and attach the bracket with the screws provided.

## Repairing Sticking Windows

In most older structures and in many new ones, the type of window installed is called "double-hung." As the name implies, there are two vertically movable units (called sash) which are hung independently of one another by means of a chain, pulley, and weight device hidden behind the jambs of the frame. In newer buildings the weights have been replaced with a spring or ratchet device.

The bottom sash is offset toward the inside of the apartment and the upper sash toward the outside. Both sashes operate between stops (or guides) which extend outward from the jambs to form a channel. Toward the inside of the apartment, the first set of stops (one on each side of the bottom sash) is usually milled to an ogee shape the same as door stops. At the back of the bottom sash is a 1/2-inch-thick strip of wood that is press-fitted into a vertical groove the entire length of the jamb. This center guide or stop serves both the bottom and upper sash and separates the two. An exterior molding on the outside of the window frame acts as the stop for the back of the upper sash.

Double-hung windows, though widely used, are poorly designed. The wood from which they are made is exposed continuously to the weather and subject to significant contraction and expansion. Moreover, paint not only fails to reduce this movement, but as successive layers are applied it further reduces the small initial tolerance necessary to make the windows operative. Paint is also often applied to both the sash and stops, which causes the window to "freeze" or become inoperative. Nevertheless, double-hung windows are in great

Flat bar for removing nailed window stop

Screwdriver at center guide

profusion everywhere and sashes that stick are a universal reality.

In most instances, only the upper sash will be inoperative, but I assume that the lower doesn't function either and I correct the condition as follows.

I first remove the two inner stops on the apartment side of the window (usually made of ogee door stop) by unscrewing them. If they are held by finishing nails, I insert a flat bar an inch or so from the bottom between the back of the stop and the jamb and pry them away.

When both inner stops are removed, I swing the lower sash into the room. Along each side of the sash is a groove in which the sash chain is housed. At the bottom of the groove is a hole in which the end of the chain is attached to the sash by either a coil or a nail. When the coil is lifted out of the hole or the nail removed (on both sides of the sash), the sash is completely free. (The other end of the chain is attached to a weight which will pull the chain through the pulley; I therefore temporarily knot the loose end of the chain to prevent this.)

I remove each middle guide by inserting a screwdriver in the joint between the guide and frame and prying outward from the groove in which it lies. I begin about an inch from the bottom and work upward. The guides are relatively thin, old, and tightly fitted and I must remove them gingerly to avoid breaking them. (If broken, they can be purchased at a lumber yard.) Once the center guides have been removed and the upper sash is free to swing into the room, I disengage the ends of the chains (knot them) and the upper sash is free.

Numerous coats of paint will be clearly defined along the sides of the sash. I use a spinner sander and 20-grit open-coat sandpaper to remove all the old paint. I then sand the bare wood with fine sandpaper to remove the scratches left by the rough paper and brush on a 50-50 mixture of Woodlife and linseed oil. Woodlife, pentachlorophenol, is a chemical preservative which helps to prevent rot and decrease the expansion and contraction of wood. The linseed oil fills the pores of the wood and helps to prevent the wood from absorbing moisture.

After the mixture has dried, I repaint the sash, solely for cosmetic reasons. Along the sides of the sash and the channel in which it will run I apply a film of clear grease before reinstallation.

If this procedure is followed, the sash will operate smoothly for at least several years.

## Repairing a Broken Sash Cord

A great many of the older double-hung windows operate on cord rather than chain. The cords break frequently, the chain rarely.

To install a new chain (nylon sash cord is available, but chain is still superior) I remove the guides and sash.

At the bottom of each jamb is a rectangular piece of wood which covers a corresponding hole cut out of the jamb. It is wedge-fit and held by a single screw. I remove the screw and the wood piece on the side of the broken cord so that the weight (a cylindrical piece of iron) located behind the jamb becomes visible. I remove the weight. It has a hole

# The Renovation Book

at the top through which the cord is tied. I untie the broken cord.

With wire-cutting pliers, I cut new sash chain to a length 10 inches longer than twice the height of the sash. I thread an end of the chain through the pulley mortised into the jamb near its top and lower the end to the pocket opening. I knot the end of the chain through the hole in the weight and place the weight back behind the jamb. I thread the other end of the chain on a coil (a concentric piece of heavy wire available wherever sash chain is sold) and place the coil in the hole on the side of the sash. I lay the chain in the groove on the side of the sash. Before reinstalling the stops, I raise and lower the sash to make sure that the weight doesn't hit the bottom of the frame when the sash is completely open. (If it does, I shorten the chain as needed by repositioning the coil on the chain.) Finally, I reinstall the rectangular jamb-hole cover and the stops.

## Repairing Sash Frames

The perimeter of the sash is composed of wooden pieces called stiles or rails and these stiles occasionally separate. This usually occurs at the joint between the bottom and side rails. I remove the sash and clean foreign material away from the loosened joint. I use the spinner sander and 20-grit open-coat paper to sand away all rotted wood. Unless the wood is in really sad shape, enough will remain after sanding to allow placement of epoxy glue in the joint. I am now ready to glue and clamp the joint.

As a rule (contact glue is an exception), glues require pressure to make a good bond and this in turn requires clamping. The pipe clamp is not the best of clamps (an I-bar clamp is superior), but it is adequate for the job as well as inexpensive and has a variety of other uses since it can be used with any length of 3/4-inch ordinary steel pipe.

The clamp has two movable parts; one operates on a threaded bolt with a handle to a span of 3 inches, the other over the entire length of the pipe. To operate the clamp, the pieces to be glued are placed in position; the leaves at the lower end of the clamp are then depressed and slid up the pipe against the side of one of the pieces. The handle of the second part of the clamp is rotated clockwise until the two pieces to be glued are pressed together tightly.

I place epoxy glue in the open joint of the sash, clamp it tightly, and let it sit for a couple of hours. After clamping, I fill the rotted spots that have been sanded away with plastic filler, allowing it to dry and then sanding it smooth. Plastic fillers adhere best when, as here, I am dealing with a movable piece. (Glazier's putty, exterior spackle, etc., are serviceable when filling something stationary.)

The bottom rail of the sash has an extension on each end (called a tenon) which fits into a corresponding slot (called a mortise) on the end of each side rail. As an added precaution against the joint separating, I nail two 1-inch brads at an angle through the side rail and into the bottom rail, driving the heads below the surface with a nail set. I then fill the holes with wood putty.

## Repairing a Broken Window Pane

I remove the sash and place it on a work table. Using a hammer, I knock out all the broken glass I can, then, with a screwdriver and hammer, I chip away all the old putty by driving the end of the screwdriver between the putty and the remaining glass.

When the putty and glass have been removed, small metal pieces will be visible protruding from the wood that had encompassed the glass. (They are called glazing points; the interior strips which divide the sash are called muntins.) I remove the points with a screwdriver or needle-nosed pliers.

I measure the opening in which I will be placing the new pane. Glass is sold in a variety of sizes and thicknesses. Single strength glass will be satisfactory for panes up to 30 inches square, while double strength should be used for most larger windows. I purchase the smallest standard size of glass that is larger than the opening I will fill.

The muntins and rails of the sash have rabbets (L-shaped cuts) on their sides to receive the glass. I place the glass in the opening so that two intersecting sides lie in the rabbet. The glass being larger than the opening, the other two sides will, of course, extend beyond the rabbet and they must be cut. I hold the glass cutter almost vertically and score the glass 1/8 inch smaller than the size of the opening. I use the sides of the rabbet which lie under the glass as a guide. After scoring the glass continuously from one side to the other, I grip the piece that will be waste between my thumb and forefinger and twist to snap it off. It should snap easily, but if it doesn't, I tap the underside of the glass along the scored line with the ball at the top of the cutter until a crack appears and then snap it off. I cut the excess off the remaining side in the same manner.

When scoring the glass, only *light* pressure need be exerted on the cutter. If I press down too hard, the glass will crack. If I use too little pressure, the cutting wheel will slide along the surface of the glass without scoring it. Unless I hear a scratching sound, the glass isn't being scored. (The scored line is also easily seen.) Before cutting glass for the first time, I suggest a practice try starting with very light pressure and increasing it a little at a time until scoring is achieved. (Dipping the cutting wheel into kerosene or turpentine will help.)

If the scored line is not continuous, jagged edges are likely to remain after the waste piece has been snapped off. If they are large enough to prevent the pane from fitting into the opening, I score the jagged excess again. The spaces between the teeth of the cutter differ to allow for different thicknesses of glass. I place the glass between the teeth and remove the jagged piece with an up and outward movement. It is not necessary to achieve a perfectly straight line without jagged edges, and only those pieces which prevent the glass from lying flat inside the rabbet need be removed.

I have been using single strength glass. Double strength, used for larger panes, is handled in the same way. Glass thicker than double strength, however, will not snap off in the way described. Instead, once the glass has been scored, the ball at the end of the cutter is tapped upward from the underside of the pane against the scored line until a crack develops. Afterwards the snapping can be done.

I place the cut pane into the opening and insert glazing points laterally into the adjacent wood so that a portion of the point lies flat and snugly over the glass. (The points are usually T-shaped and can be pushed into position by placing the head of a screwdriver against the raised portion of the T.) I place a point every 10 inches or so, with a minimum of two points on each side.

I place a band of glazier's putty about an inch wide and 1/2 thick over the perimeter of the glass and against the raised adjacent wood. Using a putty knife, I press the putty back against the wood until it extends only slightly beyond the rabbet below. I then turn the putty knife sideways and draw the knife from one corner of each side to the other, pressing down moderately and creating about a 45-degree putty slope between glass and wood. I smooth the surface of the putty by stroking it lightly with the putty knife and shape the corners into a miter with the tip of the knife.

## Mounting Objects on Masonry Walls and Ceilings

The pictured devices are those most often used to attach objects to masory walls and ceilings. All operate on the same principle (the plastic toggle fastener can be used in another way detailed later). A hole the same diameter as the "shield" is bored in the wall or ceiling. The shield is then fitted into the hole. The object to be mounted is placed in position and secured by a screw that goes through it into the shield. As the screw is tightened, the shield expands and presses against the circumference of the hole, creating an attachment. (Hooks

Glazing points

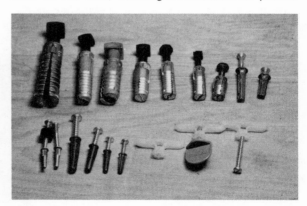

Various devices for fastening objects on masonry walls or ceilings

| SHIELD MATERIAL | SIZE | HOLE TO BORE | SCREW SIZE | TYPE |
|---|---|---|---|---|
| LEAD | 1/4 s | 1/4 x 1 | 1/4 x 1-1/2 | lag |
| LEAD | 1/4 l | 1/4 x 2 | 1/4 x 2 | (Same) |
| LEAD | 5/16 s | 5/16 x 1-1/2 | 5/16 x 1-1/2 | (Same) |
| LEAD | 5/16 l | 5/16 x 2 | (Same) | (Same) |
| LEAD | 3/8 s | 1/2 x 2 | (Same) | (Same) |
| LEAD | 3/8 l | 1/2 x 2-1/2 | (Same) | (Same) |
| LEAD | 1/2 s | 3/4 x 2-1/2 | (Same) | (Same) |
| LEAD | 1/2 l | 3/4 x 3-1/2 | (Same) | (Same) |
| LEAD plug | 1 x 6-8 | 1/4 x 1 | 1 x 6-8 | Wood |
| LEAD plug | 1-1/2 x 6-8 | 1/4 x 1-1/2 | 1-1/2 x 8 | (Same) |
| LEAD plug | 1 x 10-14 | 5/16 x 1 | 1 x 10 | (Same) |
| LEAD plug | 1-1/2 x 10-14 | 5/16 x 1-1/2 | 1-1/2 x 10 | (Same) |
| PLASTIC | 3/4 x 6-8 | 1/4 x 3/4 | 3/4 x 6 | Sheet Metal |
| PLASTIC | 7/8 x 6-8 | 5/16 x 7/8 | 3/4 x 8 | (Same) |
| PLASTIC | 1 x 10-12 | (Same) | (Same) | (Same) |
| PLASTIC | 1-1/2 x 12-16 | 3/8 x 1-3/8 | 1-1/2 x 12-16 | (Same) |
| PLASTIC (PEGBOARD) | 3/16 | 3/16 x 3/4 | 1-1/4 x 6 | (Same) |
| PLASTIC (TOGGLE) | 5/16 x 1-1/2 | (Same) | 1-1/2 x 6 | (Same) |
| PLASTIC (FOR DRYWALL) | 3/8 x 1-1/4 | (min.) hole | | |

and eyes may be substituted for screws if they are necessary to the installation.)

The table above sets forth the materials shields are made from, their sizes, and the screw that corresponds to each size. In the table, *s* means short, *l* long.

The lead devices are designed to be used in hard materials such as brick, concrete, and structural tile; *not* in plaster. Since a masonry wall is likely to have a 7/8-inch plaster and sand coat, the shorter lead shields when expanded will be pressing against a soft material which disintegrates easily. If the plaster is in good condition and the object to be mounted is light and stationary, a short lead shield will probably hold, although it is not the best arrangement. It is preferable to use a plastic rather than a lead shield when the required shield is less than 7/8 inch long. This is particularly true when the item to be mounted will not be stationary, creating stresses on it. For example, metal standards for bookshelves mounted directly on masonry walls appear stationary but are really not and short lead shields should not be used with them. As books are placed on or taken off the shelves, movement occurs, causing the shield to rub against the plaster covering the wall. Sooner or later (usually sooner) the hole becomes enlarged, the shield pulls out from its hole in the wall, and the standard comes down. With masonry, I personally avoid the use of lead shields entirely and use them only when the depth of the hole will be at least 1-1/4 inches; this guarantees that at least part of the shield will be expanding against material which is harder and firmer than gypsum plaster and sand.

When the object to be mounted, such as a manually operated can opener, will exert lateral pressure against the shield, it is advisable not to mount the object directly on the wall, thereby avoiding the lateral stresses completely.

Although I am discussing a can opener in this particular instance, the same method of installation can be used for a wide variety of other objects.

## Mounting a Can Opener

I cut a piece of 3/4-inch plywood 9 by 5 inches and place it against the wall so that its center will

Can opener fastened to 3/4-inch plywood being held by lead shields and lag screws

Drill bit being sharpened in bit-sharpening machine

correspond to where I want to locate the can opener.

On a diagonal 1-1/2 inches in from opposite corners, I bore two pilot holes through the plywood and slightly into the wall. I use a #8 finishing nail with its head clipped off as a bit since an ordinary drill bit will dull quickly when turning through masonry.

In the photograph is a bit-sharpening machine. It costs under $20; if a considerable amount of work is to be done, it will pay for itself by the number of bits it will resharpen. Complete instructions come with the machine and only a few seconds are required to resharpen a bit.

Using each pilot hole in the wall as a center reference, I bore a hole 1/4 inch in diameter and 2 inches deep. I use the impact drill with a 1/4-inch carbide-tipped bit. I wrap a piece of tape around the bit 2 inches from its end for use as depth reference.

It is important to hold the drill and bit firmly while boring the hole to avoid any drifting that might enlarge the diameter. Enlargement will also occur if the bit is warped. (If warpage is suspected, roll the bit on a flat surface; warpage will be verified by an uneven roll. A warped bit should be thrown away—it is too difficult to straighten.)

I tap a 1/4-by-2-inch lead shield into the hole so that its open end is flush with the surrounding plaster. If the hole has been inadvertently enlarged and the shield is loose, I cram slivers of wood between the shield and hole until the shield is tight. I keep the shield centered in the hole by driving the slivers (which act as wedges) on alternate sides around the circumference.

I place a 1/4-inch bit into the variable speed drill and, using the pilot holes in the plywood bored earlier as a center reference, bore two holes. (The easiest way to bore holes such as these is to place a scrap piece of wood underneath the plywood to receive the tip of the bit as it comes through.)

I slip washers on two 1/4-by-2-inch lag screws, insert them through the holes in the plywood and into the lag shields embedded in the wall.

I alternately tighten the screws with a ratchet wrench until the plywood is tight against the wall. The wrench is powerful and caution must be exercised to avoid tightening so hard that the lag screw is sheared. (If excessive resistance is felt while tightening the screw, the screw should be backed off for a turn, then tightened a bit, and thereafter tightened in this manner.)

I place the can opener on the plywood in the position I want it mounted, mark pilot holes with an awl, and use 3/4-by-6-inch wood screws to attach it.

With this arrangement, the pressure created by use of the can opener will be focused against the securely attached wood screws while movement against the lag shields will be minimized.

## Mounting a Shower Curtain Bar

The number of shower curtain bars that have fallen is evidence of the widespread misuse of lead plugs. Even though the plugs are holding a relatively light weight and the movement of the shower curtain creates minimal stress, the plugs frequently come loose. This occurs despite the fact that a mixture of special plaster called Keene (which is denser and stronger than ordinary mixtures) is often used on bathroom walls.

On the ends of each shower bar are flanges with predrilled holes. I temporarily prop up the bar with a length of wood and position the flanges. I mark pilot holes in the plaster with an awl, then drill these holes using the variable-speed drill with a 1/4-inch bit taped to drill to a depth of 1-1/8 inches. I insert a 1-by-10 plastic shield in each hole and attach the flange with a 1-by-10 sheet metal screw.

From time to time I have run out of plastic shields and have stuffed these holes with wooden kitchen matches instead. They work just as well as the plastic shield. If matches are used, their heads should be broken off first and an awl should be used to make a pilot hole for the wood screw in the wedged ends.

## Mounting Pegboard

Pegboard is available in a variety of sizes and colors and may be tempered or untempered. The untempered is not waterproof, the tempered is. The tempered may be "natural" or have a baked enamel finish. (The same material without holes is called Marlite and is extensively used as a wall covering in bathrooms, luncheonettes, etc.) Standard pegboard has holes 3/16 inch in diameter spaced 1 inch apart and will accommodate a variety of hooks and brackets. (It is also available with 1/4-inch

holes and correspondingly larger attachments for heavier objects.)

To install a 4-by-8-foot sheet of pegboard, I first draw a horizontal line on the wall where the pegboard will be mounted that corresponds to the projected location of the bottom side of the pegboard. I use a ruler and a carpenter's level to do this. I then tack a strip of wood (a cleat) along this line, leaving the nail heads exposed for easy removal later. (The cleat's purpose is to facilitate the handling and positioning of the pegboard during installation; it is removed afterward.) I place the sheet of pegboard on the cleat and shift it to the position I want. I draw a light line around the perimeter of the pegboard, then take the pegboard off the cleat.

If the core of the wall is gypsum block, I attach 1 x 2s, 1/4 inch inside the perimeter I have marked, by driving #10 common nails through each 1 x 2 at a downward angle of about 30 degrees. They will penetrate the plaster and go into the block. I space the nails 16 inches apart.

If the core of the wall is concrete, concrete block, brick, or structural tile, I follow the same procedure, using case-hardened nails instead. (These nails are processed in a hot cyanide bath which makes the metal stiffer and harder.) Case-hardened nails rarely bend and if pounded with excessive lateral force will snap in two. They come in a variety of types, the two most common being "twist" or "cut," either of which will work here.

To determine the composition of the core of a wall, try driving a common nail into it. If the core is gypsum block, the nail will enter it readily, but if it is one of the harder materials, the nail will bend.)

Having installed 1 x 2s around the marked perimeter I now measure along the vertical pieces, mark the midpoint of each, and nail another 1 x 2 horizontally between them, each end at the marks.

I position the sheet on the cleat so that its perimeter matches the outline I drew earlier and secure it to the 1 x 2s with 3/4-by-6 cadmium-plated screws. I space the screws every 2 feet or so. (Flanges or washers are sold for decorative effect and can be used under the heads of the screws to sit against the pegboard.)

There will now be a 3/4-inch gap between the pegboard and the wall (necessary for later placement of hooks, etc.) except at the perimeter and midpoint where the 1 x 2s have been nailed. I remove the cleat and the installation is complete.

Pegboard may also be mounted with hardware sold in "kits." These kits contain lead plugs, screws, and spacers. The spacers are 3/8-inch plastic pieces with predrilled holes through which the screw is inserted behind the sheet into the previously installed plug. They create a 3/8-inch void between the back of the pegboard and the wall, which permits hooks to be inserted in all the sheet's holes except those where the screws are located. The disadvantage of using 1 x 2s is that there are fewer holes available for use, but the sturdiness of the installation outweighs the advantage of using a kit.

## Suspending a Heavy Flower Pot from the Ceiling

The core of a ceiling in an apartment building will most likely be concrete or structural tile; a lead shield will work well in either.

Using the impact drill with a 1/2-inch carbide-tipped bit, I bore a hole in the ceiling to a depth of 2-1/2 inches where I want to suspend the flower pot. I insert a 3/8-Long shield into the hole and tap it in till the open end is flush with the ceiling. I now have the option of placing a 5/16-by-2-1/2-inch lag screw or an equivalent hook or eye into the shield. An eye is ordinarily best since it permits one easily to hang, remove, or change a pot if a hook is placed at the end of the wire or string holding it. The eye is screwed fully into the shield (a screwdriver inserted

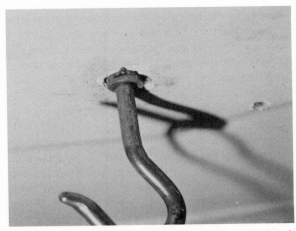

Lead shield in masonry ceiling with hook threaded into it

in the eye midpoint along its shaft will make turning easier) and the pot, on string or wire, is suspended from it.

Using this arrangement, I have suspended pots weighing up to 25 pounds. Manufacturers of lag shields suggest that a great deal more weight may be suspended from them, but the tests which determine their ability are usually made under ideal conditions. In practice, shields fail under much lighter stresses. Lag shields smaller than the one I have used will often support a hundred-pound weight, but instances of failure make use of the larger sizes a good practice.

## Mounting a Hammock

Ordinarily each end of a hammock will have a hook or eye attached to it. If the hammock does not have either, two metal eyes should be purchased. The thickness of the metal should be at least 3/16 inch. The ends of the hammock are then securely knotted to the eyes.

Because of body weight and movement, a significant amount of stress will be placed on the shields and I therefore prefer not to mount the hammock directly to them.

I mark the place on each wall where I intend to attach the hammock, making certain the marks are an equal distance from the floor and allowing sufficient space above the floor for the hammock to sag when occupied.

I cut two 6-by-4-inch pieces of 3/4-inch plywood. I center the pieces over the marks on the wall. Using a 1/8-inch bit in the variable-speed drill, I bore pilot holes through the wood and into the wall 1-1/2 inches in from diagonally opposite corners. I remove the plywood and, using the impact drill and a 3/4-inch carbide-tipped bit, bore a 3-1/4-inch-deep hole in each wall, using the pilot hole as a center reference. I insert a 1/2-by-3-1/4-inch lag shield into each hole and tap them down until the end of each is flush with the wall. I bore 3/4-inch holes in the plywood with a wood bit in the variable-speed drill, using the pilot holes as a center reference. I place washers on four 1/2-by-3-1/4-inch lag screws, push the screws through the holes of the plywood and into the shields. I tighten each screw alternately with the ratchet wrench until the plywood is firmly against the wall.

I draw diagonal lines on each piece of plywood to establish its center, bore a 3/16-inch pilot hole, then screw in the eyes. The hammock can now be hung.

## Installing Hanging Bookshelves

Two types of hanging bookshelves are commonly used: those which have already been assembled into a complete unit and those which are assembled through the use of individual metal strips and boards.

The unit bookshelves usually have a back of 1/4-inch plywood or Masonite. If they don't, it's a good idea to make the unit sturdier by providing one before attempting to hang it.

I draw a horizontal line on the wall, using a carpenter's level to mark the bottom of where I intend to mount the bookcase. I then tack a cleat along the line. (The top of the baseboard is often a convenient location and can serve as the cleat if this is where the bottom of the unit is desired.) I place the bookcase on the cleat and shift it left or right to the position I want. I drive #8 common nails at about a 30-degree angle through the backing and into the wall. (If the core of the wall is gypsum block, ordinary nails will do; if it's structural tile, etc., use case-hardened nails with a common head.) I place these nails an inch or so above the top of the second-highest shelf and space them every 16 inches or so. Placing the nails here keeps them out of sight when books are placed in the unit, and the bookcase will be held where stress is greatest. I drive additional nails an inch below the bottom of the second-lowest shelf. No other attachment is necessary.

The nails through the backing will support a weight many times greater than will ever be placed on the shelves. The downward angle at which they are driven will keep the unit from falling away from the wall. I have installed many bookcases and kitchen cabinets in exactly this manner and none has ever fallen or shown signs of working loose. This is the cheapest, easiest, and simplest way to attach any type of unit to any wall. (Of course, where wooden studs are behind the plaster—as in townhouses and tenements—the nails are driven directly into them.)

## Mounting Bookshelf Components

Hardware for adjustable individual bookshelves is available in two types.

One system uses posts which are extended between the floor and ceiling and tightened between the two. The second system uses standards which are mounted on a wall. Both systems use slots in which shelf or knife brackets are placed to support the wooden shelves.

To install a post-type system, I first determine the height between the floor and ceiling by extending the ends of two 1 x 2s between the floor and ceiling and marking the opposite end of one on the second. I then transfer this length to the posts I have purchased. (The post lengths should be the first size that is longer than the distance between floor and ceiling.)

Shelf standards and knife brackets

I remove the adjustable screw device at the end of each post, cut off the excess length with a hacksaw, and replace the device. (They usually slip on and off the post.) I place the posts at the locations desired, then raise the screw ends until the posts are slightly wedged. Using a carpenter's level, I plumb both posts in both directions and tighten.

The length of the shelf and the type of wood used will determine whether additional intermediate posts are necessary. If the wood is 3/4-inch pine or another "softwood," the weight of the books may cause it to sag if its unsupported span is 30 inches or more. (Sag distances vary considerably since wood cut at the center of a tree is denser than that cut from the outer part and will support more weight.) 3/4-inch hardwoods such as walnut, teak, or mahogany will take longer spans before sagging; 3-foot is average.

3/4-inch hardwoods will of course support longer spans before sagging, as will 1-1/2-inch stock. A shelving material often overlooked is 1-1/2-inch fir, a softwood. It is relatively cheap, will support spans up to 4 feet, and most lumber yards will not object if you select the best-looking boards since it is used as construction lumber and ordinarily not seen.

There are too many variables in wood to be precise; I have indicated the lower ranges. In general, I have found that I can't get away with a span greater than 4 feet.

If an additional post is necessary, I pop chalk lines on the floor and ceiling between the outer posts already installed and then install the additional post by locating it at the chalk line, equidistant from the outer posts.

These posts are manufactured by a variety of hardware companies and the brackets which fit into their slots are often *not* interchangeable. There is little difference in quality between the brands and I therefore shop for the cheapest.

Posts are superior to standards since they rest on the floor to carry weight. The wedge effect maintains them in an upright position, and they are quicker to install.

However, when using posts isn't appropriate, standards are the alternative. To install a standard-type system, I first draw vertical lines on the wall where I intend to mount the standards, using a carpenter's level. The outer standards may be placed anywhere from 1 inch to 1 foot in from each end of the shelf board. When part of the board extends beyond the shelf bracket, unsupported, a cantilever is created. The rule of thumb for cantilevers is one third out, two thirds in, so that a board 12 feet long might extend 4 feet beyond the bracket. However, this assumes an equal weight on both; to avoid any possibility of tipping, a shorter overhang distance is preferred.

I cut the standards to the desired lengths with a hacksaw, cutting from corresponding ends to allow for alignment of the slots of each standard; they will then be mounted with all cut ends either up or down.

I draw a horizontal line with a carpenter's level where I intend to locate the bottom of the standards. Where the line intersects the vertical lines drawn earlier, I place a standard and mark the intermittent screw holes with an awl. At each awl mark, I bore a 3/8-inch hole 1-1/4-inches deep using the impact drill.

To secure the standards to the wall, I have the option of using either a plastic shield or the device pictured, called a toggle fastener. The fastener is preferable with hollow walls such as sheetrock or plasterboard. (When using a toggle, a 5/16-inch hole is bored, the toggle is folded and inserted into the hole and tapped flush to it. A tool is provided to engage the toggle and spread out its folded ends at the back of the wall. The object is then installed and tightened to the wall with a 1-1/2-inch-by-6 sheet-metal screw.

Plastic toggle fastener, ends folded for insertion into hole

I place each standard along its vertical line, its cut end at the horizontal line, and screw a 1-1/2-inch-by-6 sheet-metal screw through each screw hole into the hole of the fastener. (Thicker screws in sizes up to #14 may also be used if the thinner screws do not bite adequately into the plastic. The minimum length remains 1-1/4 inches.)

A manufacturer asserts that in a solid wall this fastener will support 590 pounds. In practice, I'd hesitate to use it for weights greater than 100 pounds per fastener, and on townhouse or tenement walls I'd limit the load on each fastener to 50 pounds.

If the wall has a core of structural clay tile or concrete block, etc., lag shields and lag screws are used instead of the toggle fasteners. In this case, the holes in the standard must be reamed to allow for passage of the thicker lag screws. (A steel boring bit in the variable-speed drill the same thickness as the lag screw will enlarge the holes easily.)

Lag screw in enlarged hole of standard

After the standards have been installed, the knife or shelf brackets are inserted into the slots at equal heights. These brackets are tightened to the standards with the screw devices provided, or by matching the slots and cutouts.

## Mounting Shelves Made of Heavy Materials

The pictured marble shelf weighs about 250 pounds. Ordinarily its weight would be supported by a cabinet underneath, but in this instance a "floating" effect is desired.

Since its top surface is to be mounted 32 inches above the floor, convenient for someone to sit on, and will have various items resting on it as well, I allow for suspending a total weight of about 500 pounds.

The marble is 1-1/2 inches thick. I pop a horizontal chalk line 30-1/2 inches above the floor, thus allowing for the shelf's thickness.

I trim the marble to a length of 10 feet by using a masonry cutting blade in the portable electric saw.

I cut a piece of 3/4-inch plywood to a length of 9 feet, which will leave the marble extending beyond it 6 inches on each end. The width is 12 inches, appropriate for the 12-inch-by-12-inch shelf bracket I will be mounting on it. I attach the plywood to the wall at the horizontal line (centered on the projected location of the marble) with 1/2-by-3-inch lead shields and 1/2-by-3-1/4-inch lag screws, having first drilled 3/4-by-3-1/4-inch holes into the wall every 2 feet.

Pictured are the least expensive shelf brackets. Because of the rib pressed into their centers, they have greater rigidity than flat iron types of even greater thickness. I attach a bracket every 2 feet along the plywood with 3/4-inch-by-10 wood screws. The upper ends of the brackets are 3/4 inch below the upper edge of the plywood installed against the wall.

I cut another piece of plywood 9 feet long by 12 inches wide. The marble is 15 inches wide and I do not want the edge of the plywood to be visible after the marble is in place. I install the plywood on the brackets with 3/4-inch-by-8 wood screws.

I position the marble on the plywood so that its

Marble shelf

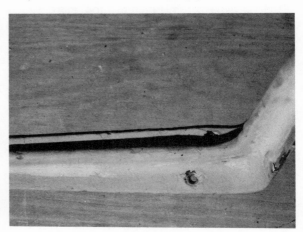

Shelf brackets

back rests against the wall and each end extends 6 inches beyond the plywood. To maintain the marble in that position, I bore two 1/4-inch-diameter holes in the underside of the marble to a depth of 3/4 inch, insert plastic shields, and fasten the marble to the plywood by driving 1-1/2-inch-by-6 sheet-metal screws through the plywood and into the shields in the marble.

The plywood shelf under the marble may be entirely unnecessary since the brackets are supporting the marble every 2 feet. However, marble is sometimes brittle and I can envision dropping a pot of food on the shelf and cracking it. "Faults," structural weaknesses, are common in marble and small impacts along them may cause marble to break. The added precaution of supporting the marble with plywood is a good practice.

## Repairing Furniture

A combination of temperature difference, moisture, and use will often cause the joints of a chair or other articles of furniture to come apart, particularly when the joint is simply a hole into which a dowel-like spoke has been press-fitted and glued. The wood expands and contracts, placing stress on the joint even when no one is sitting on the chair.

To repair such a joint, I roughen the surface of the spoke by running a rasp bit (placed in a variable-speed drill) intermittently over it about 1/2 inch along the portion that will be in the hole. I mix epoxy glue, spread it over the roughened area, and position the spoke in the hole. To avoid marring the wood, I place scraps of 1/4-inch plywood at both ends of a pipe clamp and tighten the clamp over the

Chair clamped after applying glue

joint. I wipe off excess glue and wait several hours before removing the clamp.

The clamp is made of ordinary 3/4-inch black iron pipe (galvanized pipe will do), threaded at one end. The clamping device consists of two parts. The part with the handle has a coupling attached which is threaded onto the pipe and remains stationary while the handle is cranking the flat metal collar up or down. At the opposite end of the pipe, a series of flat metal plates (poised on a spring located in the collar) is moved up or down by depressing the plates and sliding.

The pressure supplied by a clamp or strap (straps are convenient to use when dealing with rounded surfaces) always creates a stronger joint (except when using contact glue). In most cases, if pressure is not applied during the setting up time of the glue, the joint will have little or no strength.

Occasionally a chair spoke will be broken off where it enters the hole. To reconnect the pieces, I bore a 3/8-inch hole into the center of the spoke to a depth of about 3/4 inch, then bore a corresponding hole in the center of the broken piece which is lodged in the joint's hole. I roughen 1-1/2 inches on the end of a 3/8-inch dowel, cut the roughened end with a sabre saw, apply epoxy glue over the surface of the 1-1/2-inch piece of dowel, insert one end into the hole in the spoke and the other into the broken piece in the hole, and begin to tighten the clamp. I align the split ends, complete tightening the clamp, wipe off the excess glue, and allow several hours for the glue to set up before removing the clamp.

## Mounting an Air Conditioner in an External Wall

The optimum method of mounting an air conditioner is to recess it into an exterior wall underneath a window, as shown in the next photo. (When purchasing the unit, specify that this type of installation is being made, since the unit will differ slightly from those sold for window mounting.) Mounted in this manner, the unit will be relatively out of the way and will not interfere with operation of the sash or block out light. Its only disadvantage is that installation requires cutting a hole in the exterior wall, which involves a lot more time and effort than placing the unit in a window opening. It is placed underneath a window because a lintel (a metal

Air conditioner recessed into exterior masonry wall

header) is already in place above the window and no additional structural support will be required by the opening.

The dimensions of the r.o. will vary with the capacity of the unit and with varying manufacturers but each unit will have a specific r.o. (rough opening—the dimensions of the hole to be made which will accommodate the unit) which should be obtained at the time of purchase or located in the manufacturer's installation instructions. Before the r.o. is actually begun, provision must be made to keep debris from falling to the street while the opening is being made. To accomplish this I cut a piece of 3/4-inch plywood 1 foot wide to a length 1-1/2 inches shorter than the width of the sash located above the opening to be made. I nail a 1 x 3 to each of its sides, and another along its length. I leave one end open to be placed against the building. I then attach an additional 1 x 3 4 or 5 feet long to each side with one #8 common nail.

I now pop on the outside and inside of the wall chalk lines that correspond to the r.o. dimensions and locate them where I want to position the unit. (Since the unit is directly under the window and is relatively small, one can reach out easily to pop the lines on the exterior of the wall.) With a helper

holding one side, I place the shelf outside the building 6 inches below the bottom chalk line, its open side facing in. Since I have only placed one nail in each side arm, I am able to pivot them and temporarily nail the other ends into the window jambs.

I now add an additional #8 common nail to the ends of the 1 x 3s to make their attachment to the shelf more secure.

Most of the debris will be removed from inside the apartment and the little that falls outside will be caught by the shelf and its raised 1 x 3 sides.

I bore holes through the walls using a 3/4-inch carbide-tipped bit in the impact drill, which I locate in the corners of the r.o. I use a block-cutting cold chisel to score the interior surface plaster along the chalk lines.

After scoring the perimeter of the r.o., I use a plasterer's hatchet to remove the plaster within the perimeter and expose the lath behind it. Most walls will have furring strips—narrow strips of wood—on the back side of the brick wall with lath attached to them. If the lath is wood, I use a sabre saw and cheap rough-cutting wood blade to cut away both the lath and plaster within the r.o. I remove the portion of the furring strip that remains within the r.o. by scoring it first with the sabre saw, then cutting completely through it with a wood chisel.

The back of the interior brick wall should now be exposed. (There may be two or three courses of brick.) The corners of the r.o. are marked by the bored holes. The first brick to be removed will be the most difficult. To avoid disturbing brick outside the r.o., I remove the first one near the center by boring holes in its mortar joints, using the impact drill and a 1/2-inch carbide-tipped bit. (Standard thicknesses of mortar joints are 3/8 to 1/2 inch.) The mortar is much softer than the brick and the bit removes it easily. After most of the mortar has been cleared from around the brick, I whack it on a diagonal near one end, using a brick hammer and break off part of the brick.

I continue to remove mortar and pieces of brick in this manner until the first brick is removed.

I now work outward from the hole left by the removal of the first brick using a flat bar, which I drive into the mortar joints of adjacent bricks. I select those mortar joints opposite the hole which permit the brick to shift toward the hole when the flat bar is hammered into them. A brick will break or come loose fairly easily when there is a void on any of its sides, and I therefore continue to remove bricks adjacent to those already removed.

When I have enlarged the hole sufficiently to allow me to conveniently work on the course of bricks behind the interior one, I remove a center brick and repeat the dismantling process. (Some buildings will have three layers of brick, some two. The arrangements of the bricks will also vary, depending on whether an American, English, or Flemish bond, etc., was used. In any case, the procedure for removing them is essentially the same.) If the exterior wall has a double brick thickness, the bricks on the outside of the wall, particularly those directly under the window where very little weight rests on them, can be removed quite easily by working downward with the flat bar. While removing the exterior bricks, the shelf *must* be in place to catch debris.

After the hole has been cut, the perimeter will be ragged. I use the wide cold chisel to trim protrusions that extend into the r.o.

If a brick has come loose beyond the perimeter of the r.o., I remove it, knock off the old mortar with the brick hammer, soak it in water for a few minutes, then lay it back using as mortar a mixture of one part mortar cement and three parts mortar sand. I mix enough water to obtain a consistency of butter at room temperature. I use the same mortar to fill smaller holes beyond the perimeter after wetting the brick.

Different manufacturers have slightly different methods of installing the air conditioning unit, but in general all use a metal housing with an exterior flange which will cover the smaller ragged edges around the exterior of the r.o. A second flange will cover the r.o. ragged perimeter on the plaster wall. Each manufacturer will provide mounting instructions for the particular unit purchased.

## Mounting a Room Air Conditioner at the Top of a Window

The advantages of the arrangement in the photo are that the installation takes much less time than making an opening through an exterior wall and it permits the use of the lower sash. Its disadvantages are that it renders the upper sash inoperative and blocks light. It is also inconvenient in that it re-

Room air conditioner installed at top of window

quires one to climb up a ladder to switch on the unit or change the setting of the controls. (With such installations I install an outlet controlled by a switch located at a convenient height for turning on the machine.)

To make the installation, I first cut a piece of 3/4-inch exterior plywood to a width 4 inches greater than the height of the machine and to a length 1/4 inch less than the distance between the center guides of the sash.

Using a sabre saw, I then cut a rectangle from the center of the plywood piece that is 1/4 inch higher and wider than the housing of the machine.

To the back of the plywood (which will face the street), I bolt the metal frame on which the unit will rest. (It is available with purchase of the unit.)

I place the bottom angle-iron rails slightly above the bottom of the rectangular cutout so that the unit will slide and rest on them.

I cut two pieces of 2 x 2 to a length equal to the sides of the plywood and nail them with #10 common nails in the channel in which the upper sash moves. I have lowered the upper sash to do this. Both upper ends of the 2 x 2s are against the top of the frame.

I attach the plywood (and bolted metal frame) to the 2 x 2s with 1-1/2-inch-by-10 wood screws,

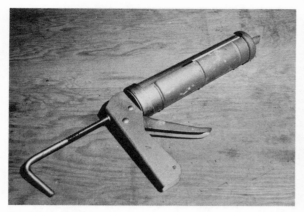

Caulking gun

Air conditioner and plexiglass installed at bottom of window

three on each side. The top of the plywood should butt against the divider strip at the top of the window frame.

On top of the upper rail of the sash, I lay a bead of butyl rubber or silicone caulking using the caulking gun pictured. (It costs under $1.)

I raise the sash so that it butts the bottom edge of the plywood and remove the excess caulking that is squeezed out.

To prevent the upper sash from moving, I nail a 1 x 2 in either channel so that its upper end butts the bottom of the sash.

I lay a bead of caulking on the plywood around the perimeter of the rectangular cutout and, with a helper, slide the unit into the opening until the flanges on it are tight against the plywood and caulking. I place two 3/4-inch-by-6 wood screws through the predrilled holes in the upper flange and into the plywood.

## Mounting a Room Air Conditioner at the Bottom of a Window

The advantages of this arrangement are that it is the quickest to install and it puts the unit's controls at a convenient height. Ordinarily its disadvantages are that it blocks light and renders the lower sash, and one used most often, inoperative. Both of these objections can be effectively reduced by using glass or plexiglass on each side of the unit (rather than the accordion panels provided) and by mounting a strip of wood to hold the unit rather than using the sash.

To make the pictured installation, I first cut two 2 x 2s to a length equal to the height of the unit and

nail them in the channel in which the lower sash operates. The bottom of each 2 x 2 should be butted to the top of the window sill.

I now nail a 2 x 2 across the window, each end resting on top of the 2 x 2s just installed, driving nails into each end and into the jambs of the window frame.

I measure the width of the unit's housing and install a vertical 2 x 2 between the horizontal 2 x 2 and the window sill, leaving an opening 1/4 inch wider than the width of the housing.

I slide the unit into the opening and attach the top flange to the horizontal 2 x 2 with two 3/4-inch-by-6 wood screws placed through the predrilled holes and into the horizontal 2 x 2.

I now have the option of filling the remaining opening with either glass or plexiglass. Personally, I prefer glass because plexiglass exposed to the weather quickly develops scratches and becomes murky and dirty-looking.

In either case, I cut and install 1/2-inch quarter round around the inside of the r.o. and flush with the inner sides of the 2 x 2s. (The flat sides of the quarter round are outward and against the 2 x 2 while the rounded portion remains exposed toward the room.)

I measure the height and width of the opening. If I am using plexiglass, I score it with a special knife designed to cut plexiglass, then snap it off. If I am using glass, I score it with a glass cutter. In both cases I cut the piece 1/4 inch smaller than the actual dimensions of the opening. I then lay a bead of caulking in the joint made between the quarter round and 2 x 2, insert the glass or plexiglass, and keep it in position with glazing points. (Two on the short sides and three on the long sides.) I place putty on the outside of the glass or plexiglass in the manner described on p. 127.

The bottom edge of most sashes has a groove while most window sills have a V-shaped piece of metal attached to them called weatherstripping. When the sash is lowered completely, the groove fits over the weatherstripping to prevent drafts. I purchase metal weatherstripping in a hardware store and cut it to length with a hacksaw. (The length is the width of the sash.) I place a bead of caulking on top of the horizontal 2 x 2 across the width of the window and install the weatherstripping on the caulking so that it is aligned with the groove in the bottom of the sash. I remove the excess caulking, lower the sash, and the installation is complete.

Of course the easiest way to install a unit into a lower sash opening is to simply lower the sash so that it is about 1/4 inch above the height of the housing, set the unit on the window sill, and push the unit forward until its flange is against the bottom rail of the sash. The sash is then lowered tightly against the top of the unit and is attached to the flange with wood screws placed through the predrilled holes in the flange. The accordion side panels are then extended out against the jambs. All sorts of small gaps are created by this installation and of course cause drafts and leaks. Caulking and felt weatherstripping will eliminate these but are unsightly.

# FLOORING

# 5

## Refinishing Wood Floors

Except in bathrooms and kitchens, most floors are surfaced with wood, usually 1 x 3 oak. Rather than replacing an old floor, it is often less work, less expensive, and more aesthetically appealing simply to refinish it.

People are often reluctant to use or keep wooden floors because they think that such floors require a great deal of maintenance. This misconception has arisen as a result of the institutionalization of the practice of using wax on them.

When this apartment was built, the floors were covered with one or two coats of thinned shellac and one or more coats of varnish. (This practice was widespread and continues even today, although polyurethanes often replace the shellac and varnish.)

The shellac sealed the wood and kept the more expensive varnish from seeping into it. The varnish had a shiny finish that many found displeasing, and around the turn of the century wax was placed over the varnish and buffed to dull its shine.

As a final covering over a wooden floor, I can think of nothing worse than wax. It requires constant maintenance and does not "protect" the floor. It simply dulls the shine of varnish and in the process retains all the dust and dirt that has settled on it and been ground into the floor.

The mythical protection afforded wood by a coat of wax is said to include protection against scratches, but anything that will scratch the varnish will also pierce the film of wax. Moreover, such scratches are easily treated.

A huge amount of wax and other materials are sold each year as protective coatings for wood, and this unfortunate practice has led to a huge expansion of sales of composition floor coverings (vinyl, tile, etc.) which are more expensive, inferior, much less durable, and *require even greater maintenance than properly finished wooden floors.*

Unless an aesthetic consideration is involved, or the use of a material such as quarry tile is projected, redoing an existing wooden floor should be

Standard 1 × 3 oak flooring

seriously considered without nursing the age-old misconceptions about maintaining it.

The core of the floor in this building is structural clay tile (it is reinforced concrete in modern structures) on which "sleepers" (lengths of wood on edge) have been laid. After the rough plumbing and wiring had been installed, the oak flooring was nailed to the sleepers. (In better older buildings, a subfloor made of 1 x 6 or 8 common pine was nailed to the sleepers and the oak then nailed to the subfloor and sleepers.)

Oak flooring is roughly 7/8 inch thick, and unless it has been thoroughly abused, removing 1/16 inch by sanding will result in a beautifully refinished floor of more than adequate strength. Occasionally, of course, there are patches deeply stained by grease and a few buckled or rotted boards, but replacing them involves much less work and expense than installing an entirely new floor. (I have never encountered an oak floor in such bad condition that renewing it wasn't the cheapest and best of all possible alternatives.)

In the final chapter, there are photographs of the finished floors in the apartment. I can't recall floors in worse condition than these formerly were. The lightest floors, maple, are in the kitchen, closets, and maid's rooms. The other floors are oak, one of which has been stained. All are seventy years old and proof of their own durability.

## Replacing Deeply Stained or Rotted Flooring

Due to water leakage over long periods around the radiators, the wood in these areas will occasionally be blackened. Chances are the stains extend deeply into the wood, but to avoid needless work, I check them out by sanding with the spinner to determine just how deep they actually go. If the stain is under a radiator or where no one will be walking, I sand the stain out if it doesn't extend more than 3/8 inch into the wood. I check out each stain in this manner. If the stain is located where there will be traffic, I do not sand deeper than 3/16 inch before replacing stained or damaged pieces.

To remove stained or damaged pieces, I set the depth of the portable saw (with combination blade) to 7/8 inch and, using the plunge-cut technique, cut through the center of the first piece to be removed along its entire length. (It is convenient to choose a board in the center of the area to be patched.) I drive a flat bar into the saw cut until its tip is at the bottom of the flooring. (If there is a subfloor, I engage the end of the flat bar into its side.) I place a scrap of wood on the floor against the back of the flat bar as a fulcrum and pry up on the damaged piece. Although the ends of floorboards are "matched" in a tongue and groove, they should slip out as the center of the ripped flooring is raised. If they don't, I make a plunge cut across the piece at its center. (When this is done one must be prepared for the possibility of hitting a flooring nail and having to resharpen the blade. A lengthier alternative is to score the piece with a wood chisel to weaken it so that the floorboard will break when the prying is done.) Once the piece breaks, it will come out easily, often leaving the flooring nails in the subfloor.

After I remove the initial piece of flooring, I place the scrap in the gap created; the scrap acts as a fulcrum to pry up the remaining pieces I want to remove. (If necessary, I turn the fulcrum on edge to get greater height, giving me more leverage.)

New flooring is sold by the board foot and is priced on the assumption that the size of each piece is a full 1 x 3. (Narrower and wider floorings, also available, are priced in the same way.) However, the actual width of a piece is 2-3/4 inches, and because each piece has a tongue which will be hidden in an adjacent groove, its actual exposed surface will be only 2-1/4 inches. When ordering flooring, the board feet purchased should be one-third greater in area than the square feet to be covered. This will also allow for waste.

If the total area to be covered with new flooring is 50 square feet or less, I use #7 flooring nails (sometimes referred to as horseshoe or cut nails) and nail them by hand with a 2-pound hammer. If a larger area is involved, a manually operated floor-nailing machine can be rented at a nominal cost. Special L-shaped nails in clips are used with the machine. One box will be enough for 1000 square feet.

The clips are first loaded into a slot at the back of the machine; its base is then laid on top of the board to be nailed with its slanted front on the tongue.

The machine's rocker arm is then struck forcibly with a rubber mallet. This drives the nail through the tongue into the sleeper or subfloor at the

Machine in position on flooring for nailing

Floor-nailing machine and hammer

Clip of nails being loaded into machine

proper angle, and the head of the nail will be embedded in the piece of flooring just above the tongue and hidden by the next board to be installed. The machine is then slid along the tongue to the next nailing position, which is usually 16 inches away.

If I am nailing by hand and the area to be covered has an adjoining wall, I butt the first piece of flooring against the wall at a right angle to the joists or sleepers, using a rubber mallet to avoid scarring the wood. If the area to be covered has no adjacent wall, I butt the first piece of flooring to the existing boards and nail the new piece with its groove over the tongue of the existing flooring. (If no mallet is handy to position the piece prior to nailing, I use a scrap of flooring against the piece to be installed.) Since the ends of the floorboards are matched, it is not necessary to support each joint underneath a new piece unless the tongue or groove of the adjoining old piece was damaged. If support is needed, I provide it by nailing a piece of 2 x 4 between sleepers so that it crosses beneath the end joint.

The flooring nail has a narrow and wide side; the wide side must be positioned parallel to the length of the floorboard or it will split the wood while it is being driven. I use a 2-pound hammer instead of an ordinary 16-ounce hammer since oak is hard and requires a good deal of force to drive a nail. If the nail turns while it is being driven, it should be removed and another started.

I nail the flooring to each sleeper. Sleepers are ordinarily spaced every 16 inches under the subfloor; occasionally they are 2 feet apart.

If the first new piece of flooring is to be installed against a wall, I position it with the groove against the wall, then cut the head off a #6 finishing nail with wire-cutting pliers and use it as a drill bit. (Ordinary drill bits heat up very quickly when boring through oak; a finishing nail works better. The head is cut off so that it will fit properly into the drill chuck.) I drill holes every 16 inches, 1/2 inch back from the groove side of the new piece, then face-nail through these holes with #8 finishing nails. (I also toenail the first piece with flooring nails.) The finishing nails will later be hidden by the baseboard. (If no baseboard at all is projected, I use a nail set to drive the nails below the surface of the oak and fill the holes with oak-colored wood putty before applying the finish to the flooring.)

To install the last piece of flooring, I split and remove the tongue and underside of the groove with a wood chisel or rip it off on a table saw. This will permit the last piece of flooring to sit flat between the next-to-last piece of flooring and the wall. I bore holes in the center of the piece that correspond to the positions of the sleepers beneath it, then attach the piece to the sleepers with #8 finishing nails.

When it is necessary to run gas or waste lines under a floor, I use the same procedure to remove the old flooring and cover with new.

Occasionally, particularly when flooring consists of relatively long lengths, two or more pieces will expand because of moisture and heat to form an inverted V which will not flatten for renailing. The condition can be corrected by removing one of the pieces in the manner described, removing the excess width with an electric plane or ripping with a table saw, splitting off the underside of the groove with a chisel, then face-nailing to reinstall. One can also set the portable saw blade depth to 7/8 inch and cut through the joint between the slanting boards along their entire length. This will remove 3/16 inch of wood, usually enough space to permit the two pieces of flooring to lie flat and be renailed. In making this cut, the blade will probably strike flooring nails, damaging its teeth, but the time saved compared to removing the buckle in the manner first described outweighs the loss of a blade or the cost of resharpening it. (Resharpening a blade after it has struck some nails involves filing the teeth along their original slants, a matter of twenty minutes.)

Occasionally one walks over flooring that "bounces." This results either from the flooring having worked itself loose from the sleepers or the sleepers having risen (even though the flooring is still securely attached to them). I determine which is the cause by stepping down on the patch in question. If each individual floorboard moves but doesn't cause the entire patch to lower, the sleeper is not at fault and the bounce can be removed by face-nailing each floorboard to the sleeper. If by stepping on an individual floorboard, the entire patch is lowered, the sleeper has risen. In this case, the flooring over the patch must be removed. After this is done in the manner already described, I clear away all debris under the exposed sleeper. I then spread plastic roof cement liberally (3/4 inch thick) over the core of the floor under the sleeper and press the sleeper down into the cement. I then toenail #8 case-hardened nails through the sides of the sleeper into the core of the floor and reinstall the flooring. The "cold tar" or plastic roof cement is a cheap way of keeping the sleeper "glued down" and is much better than simply toenailing, which has a tendency to work loose.

## Floor Sanding

The large machine in the photograph is a drum sander. It has a rubber-sheathed revolving drum over which sandpaper is attached; it is used to remove old finishes such as varnish or paint from old floors and to prepare their surfaces for a new finish. Because of its housing, the machine cannot sand adjacent to walls or in corners.

Drum sanders

Edger

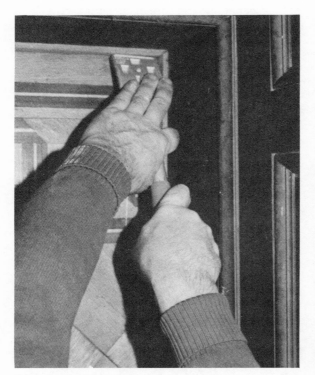

Hook scraper in corner

The smaller machine, the "edger," can reach areas that the drum sander cannot, except for a small patch in each corner. Like a spinner sander, the edger uses circular sandpaper discs but rotates at much higher speeds. The hook scraper, a hand tool, is used in those areas which are inaccessible to the drum sander and edger.

Sandpaper for use with these tools is available in two types, open- or closed-coat. The open-coat sandpapers are used for "rough work." Their purpose is to remove old material from the surface of the wood rather than to create a dense, smooth-finished surface. All sandpapers contain varying amounts of abrasive material impregnated in paper or cloth. In open-coat paper the abrasive material is impregnated only intermittently, thus creating gaps which reduce the possibility of old paint or varnish clogging the paper. Used for the same purpose, closed-coat paper will clog quickly and become useless, even though its abrasive material is unworn, while open-coat paper will be able to continue to remove material until the abrasive particles have lost their cutting ability.

Open-coat paper is manufactured in a variety of grits—grits being the hard material which actually does the sanding.

The 20-grit open-coat paper (20 particles per square inch) shown is neither the heaviest nor the lightest available but is generally the most appropriate size for removing varnish or paint from floors. If a floor has a significant covering of residual Mastic or similar material (glue that has been used for linoleum, etc.), a more "open" coat is needed since it has greater resistance to clogging.

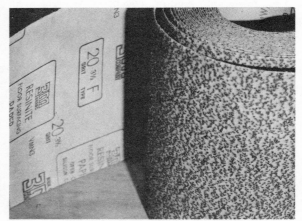

Roll of 20-grit open-coat sandpaper

The disadvantage of using a more open coat is that it will scratch the surface of the floor more deeply, which in turn will require more sanding later to remove the scratches. If the floor has been sanded in the not-too-distant past and has only a few coats of varnish or urethane, use of a less open coat is appropriate.

The sandpaper can be bought by the roll or in precut sheets that will fit the sander. A roll will ordinarily complete the initial sanding of about 7000 square feet of floor. One sheet, which costs about $1, will ordinarily complete a 10-by-10-foot room. While it is much cheaper to buy sandpaper by the roll (it can also be used with the edger and spinner sander), in most instances a lot will be left over. The size of the job will determine the economics of purchase.

Paint and hardware stores and companies that specialize in refinishing floors rent drum sanders and edgers by the day or week. Drum sanders are available in varying degrees of power for use with 120 or 240 volts. Of course a 240-volt drum sander requires the availability of 240 volts. Since the 240-volt machine is far superior, if three-wire service exists in the apartment or house, it is worth the effort to take a few minutes and provide a 240-volt source. (The procedure is detailed in the electrical section.)

When renting the machine, make sure that an old sheet of paper is on it so that it can be used as a model for cutting new sheets from the roll. The cutting is done from the smooth back side of the paper with tin snips or heavy shears. (A sheetrock knife will also do the job.)

Just below the right side of the wooden handle on the sander is a forked metal handle which controls the position of the drum. To raise the drum off the floor, the fork is squeezed together, pulled back and up, and released. To lower the drum, the fork is squeezed together, pushed forward and down, and released.

To fit a sheet of sandpaper onto the drum, I raise the drum off the floor. On each side are two square nutlike projections which control two metal bars in its interior. The drum has a slot across its width through which these bars can be seen. When viewed from an end, the bars have the shape of a marble cut in half. I turn the bars by turning the nutlike projections with wrenches supplied with the machine so that the bars' flat sides face each other, both inward toward the center of the drum.

I insert one end of the sheet of sandpaper with the abrasive side facing out into the slot as far as it will go, then rotate the drum so that the slot reappears. I smooth the paper on the drum by pulling it tight and then insert the remaining end in the slot by folding it (without creasing it) and wedging it against the end already in place. Both abrasive sides of each end are meshing within the slot. I am using 20-grit paper. I cut another strip of paper about an inch wide and press it down into the slot between the ends of the sheet already in place. The purpose of this additional strip is to bring the sheet tightly against the drum *before* I lock it into position. I am at the front of the machine and have wedged the additional strip below the surface of the drum. I place one wrench on the square nut at my right, the other on the nut at my left. I pull up on the right wrench and press down on the left simultaneously. This brings the rounded portion of both bars against the paper and tightens it against the drum.

Quite often, a great many sheets of paper will be torn in the first few seconds of use because the sandpaper has not been adequately tightened against the drum. Being loose, it flaps against the floor and is torn. The bars will remove some of the slack from the sheet as they are being tightened but if the paper has initially been placed too loosely on the drum, the nuts when tightened will be unable to remove all of the slack and the sheet will be locked in a loose condition. For this reason, the sheet must be hand-tightened in a snug position against the drum *before* locking. Sometimes the wedging strip of 20-grit paper will be too thick and a piece of closed-coat paper will work better—in general I have found that wedging two pieces of fine floor-sanding paper works best, but machines vary and a few minutes should be taken to determine the sander's particular characteristics.

The paper will also tear if exposed nails, tacks, etc., are above the surface of the floor. They must be pulled out or driven below the surface of the floor before sanding is begun.

If the floor has been painted, has numerous coats of varnish, or has a significant amount of Mastic, underlayment, or other unwanted material adhering to its surface, I operate the drum sander across the grain of the wood or on a diagonal. (Working on a diagonal has the added advantage of removing high spots in irregular flooring.) While it is a popular belief that sanding should never be done against the grain, the purpose of the first pass with the drum sander is to remove unwanted material, and sanding with the grain does this least effectively.

When the machine is in operation, a vacuum arrangement will be sucking the sanded material into a large bag. Before any work is done, I turn on the switch (with the drum off the floor) and note whether the bag inflates fully. If the bag has a tear or a hole, the sawdust will blow out through it. The tears are usually at the upper end of the bag where it is tied to a metal outlet spout. If the bag is retied below the tear any leakage will be stopped, and although the bag will have less capacity, it will nevertheless be sufficient since it is a good idea in any case to empty the bag before it is more than two-thirds full. A strip of electrician's tape will usually seal a hole.

During the first pass over the floor, when parts of the underlayment for linoleum or tile are being removed and relatively large pieces of material are being broken loose, these pieces will often clog the vacuum system. Whenever the machine is turned on and the bag doesn't inflate fully, I lay the machine on its side. Directly behind the drum is the inlet side of the vacuum. Using wire-cutting pliers, I clip off the hook and braided portion of a wire coathanger, straighten the remainder, form one end into a shallow hook, and insert it into the inlet, pulling out whatever material has accumulated. If necessary, the pipe leading to the bag can also be removed and the same wire can be used to remove material from the other end of the vacuum system.

Before starting the machine, I drape its cable over my shoulders and around the back of my neck and make sure that the drum is *off* the floor. *The single most common cause of a poor refinishing job is permitting the drum to rotate on the floor while the sander is in a stationary position.* The machine must be kept in *constant movement* while sanding is being done or a gouge will be made.

I position the machine in a corner of the room so that I can guide the sander toward the opposite corner comfortably. I switch it on and begin to push forward. *While it is moving, I lower the drum gently to the floor.* The drum is powerful, requiring no forward pressure to move it ahead; I only need guide it toward the opposite corner. If anything, I need a bit of back pressure to keep the sander from moving forward too rapidly. The pace should not be faster than a stroll. As the forward end of the machine approaches within two feet of the opposite corner, I seize the forked handle and (while the machine is still moving forward) raise the drum

from the floor. I turn the machine around and make a parallel pass adjacent to the first in the same manner. I continue this process on one side of the original diagonal, the length of each pass becoming smaller until it is no longer convenient. I then repeat the process on the opposite side of the original diagonal.

I now run the drum sander around the perimeter of the room, keeping the machine close to the wall. When sanding with the grain, wood is removed more slowly and I hold back lightly on the machine so that it goes forward more slowly. When I am sanding against the grain, I use no back pressure so that it goes relatively faster.

It is impossible to obtain a perfectly flat wooden floor with a drum sander, but an excellent job can be done if the machine is not used too much in any particular area. When it is necessary to make several passes over a spot because the surface covering is difficult to remove, the additional passes should be begun at least 3 or 4 feet before and continued 3 or 4 feet past the troublesome area. The purpose of this is to "feather" the depression—that is, to taper the floor down gradually to the troublesome area, then taper it up again into the same plane as the surrounding floor. This tapering is achieved by holding back more strongly on the machine where the material to be removed requires deeper penetration and holding back less strongly as the machine moves away from it. Tapering creates the appearance of a flat floor and eliminates any noticeable differences in height when walking over it.

The condition of the floor after the first sanding will determine what sort of paper to use in the second pass and in what direction to run the machine.

If the floor is still widely covered with material to be removed, I use the same 20-grit open-coat paper and run the machine on an opposite diagonal, intersecting the path of the first. This will flatten high spots and remove material more readily than if I repeat the direction of the first pass.

If a good part of the unwanted material has been removed, I use 20-grit paper and run the machine along the grain of the wood.

If most of the unwanted material has been removed, I use closed-coat paper proportionate to the amount of unwanted material that is left. This will range from 100-grit upward. (The greater the number of grits per square inch, the finer the sandpaper.) I run the machine on the diagonal opposite the first pass.

If only a few spots of unwanted material remain, I use a medium-grit closed-coat paper and run the machine along the grain of the wood.

The purpose of the second pass (which ordinarily will be done with closed-coat paper) is to expose all of the bare wood and remove all the scratches caused by the open-coat paper. Obviously, if a second pass with open-coat paper is necessary, this will not be achieved. The medium grit closed-coat paper is used only after all open-coat work has been completed. Inevitably, there will be places where scratches caused by the open-coat paper will not be sanded away by one closed-coat pass. These are eliminated by tapering, which should radiate out for at least several feet from the scratched area. Again, the machine must not be kept in one small area or a depression will occur rapidly.

I continue to use medium closed-coat paper and run the drum sander parallel to the grain until all bare wood is exposed and all scratches except the very shallowest have been removed.

If any high spots remain, I remove them by quickly sanding several feet away from the high spot, moving into and over the spot more slowly, then gradually increasing speed while moving away from the spot for several more feet. This is done in a series of overlapping parallel passes while controlling the speed of the machine by the amount of back pressure exerted against the steering handle. Here again, the results will be markedly inferior if the machine is allowed to linger over the high spot or if the pass doesn't include several feet before and after it.

Around the perimeter of the room a ribbon of unwanted material several inches wide remains to be removed. (A patch of a foot or so remains in the corners.) The edger, which is used to remove nearly all of this, turns at a much higher speed than the drum and revolves on a vertical rather than horizontal axis. Because of this, the sanding disc will produce a different surface on the wood even when the sandpaper used is identical to that on the drum. This becomes less noticeable the finer the paper, and the swirling arcs left by heavier grits will not be noticeable after finer grits are used. Because of this, and also because the amount of material to be removed by the edger is relatively small (one disc

should be sufficient to do a 10-by-10-foot room), I prefer to use closed-coat fine sandpaper on the first pass. While use of the longer-lasting heavier-grit paper will remove the material faster, it will also require at least one more pass with fine sandpaper so that the sanding done by the edger will have a surface similar to that done by the drum.

Precut discs for the edger can be bought, but it is much cheaper to cut them from the roll of paper used for the drum sander. (An old disc is used as a pattern.) The circular disc is cut with tin snips, then a 1-inch cross is slit into the center with a sheetrock knife and the loose flaps trimmed off. The edger is placed on its side and the center bolt and washer on the disc plate removed. (A wrench is supplied with the machine.) The disc is positioned over the hole and the washer and bolt tightened over it. Some people place an old disc behind the new one, slightly increasing the sanding ability of the edger.

The edger is on casters. The machine is switched on with the rear of the machine tilted back slightly—the disc up from the floor. A section of the front housing has a cutout so that the sanding disc is visible.

The edger is butted against the baseboard and slid back and forth along the floor while still in contact with the baseboard. If it is necessary to return to one place to remove material which remains after the initial pass, the edger is slid back and forth for several feet adjacent to the area even though the unwanted material covers only a few inches. These wide strokes avoid oversanding the one spot.

The machine *must* be kept flat on its casters, since any tilt will cause the circumference of the sanding disc to cut into the flooring (a gouge 1/4 inch deep can easily occur within a fraction of a second). The speed at which the edger is moved across the floor depends on what is being removed. The edger should never be kept in the same position, however, and sweeps should be made on the quicker rather than slower side even if this requires several more passes over a particular area.

Very often the joint between the baseboard and floor will be hidden by a piece of 3/4-inch quarter round. Despite the general practice of removing this, doing so is a waste of time and money. (The quarter round will probably split during removal and new pieces will have to be installed.)

If a quarter round is present, I use the edger to remove as much of the unwanted material beside it as I can. I go around the perimeter of the room and into the corners, continually sliding the edger in wide sweeps. Whatever unwanted material still remains on the floor, I remove with the hook scraper.

To use the hook scraper, my left hand is placed on top of the scraper behind the cutter to supply moderate downward pressure. My right hand is wrapped around the end of the handle and will pull the blade toward me. The scraping is done with the scraper pulled toward one, then lifted off the floor and reset. If it is slid forward on the floor, it dulls much more rapidly. Even with proper use, the scraper blade becomes dull quickly. In a 10-by-10-foot room, it will probably need to be resharpened three or four times. This is done in a few seconds by running a file on its beviled edge two or three times.

After all work with the edger and hook scraper has been completed, I place fine closed-coat paper on the drum sander. The finer the paper, the smoother and denser the final surface of the wood.

Sharpening hook scraper with mill bastard file

However, the finer the paper, the longer it will take to complete the preparation of the floor for finishing. A good surface can be obtained even with the coarsest fine paper and the selection of the grit should be made on the basis of how long one is prepared to spend to achieve a better-than-good quality.

I run the drum sander (with fine paper) along the grain of the flooring until the entire surface is smooth. This is minimal. I may leave it this way, make another pass with a new sheet of the same paper, or place an even finer paper on the drum for the additional pass. Personally, I make one additional pass using the same-grit fine sandpaper.

Sanding leaves sawdust. I use a vacuum cleaner to remove it from all surfaces (trim, baseboard, casing, etc.). A substantial amount of fine sawdust will remain even after vacuuming, and I remove it with a cloth dampened with denatured alcohol.

If there is a gap between pieces of flooring or a gouge in any piece, I make a paste of fine sawdust and clear epoxy glue and fill the gap or gouge while the paste is still wet. I press the paste into the gap and leave it higher than the surrounding area. Several hours later, after the paste has hardened, I sand the area with fine sandpaper in the edger.

This completes preparing the floor for refinishing. I must now tint the floor, or, if desired, leave the natural color. In either case a final polyurethane finish must also be applied. These steps are detailed on pp. 246–249 in the chapter on finishes.

## Composition Floors

Following World War II, synthetic floor coverings came into widespread use, and their popularity has continued. For the most part they are manufactured in 9-by-9 and 12-by-12-inch squares, but they are also available in large sheets and strips to simulate wood flooring.

These "tiles" are usually made of vinyl asbestos, synthetic rubber, or vinyl. The cheapest, vinyl asbestos, will also withstand wear and tear best. It has widespread home use in kitchens and bathrooms and is used commercially to cover the floors of luncheonettes, bus stations, etc. These tiles have so much surface porosity that after several days of ordinary use they accumulate a patina of grime. To forestall this, the cleaned surface is waxed and, once that is done, frequent and perpetual maintenance begins. Since wax retains dust and grime, a few hours after the vinyl asbestos has been cleaned and waxed it looks as if neither has been done for years.

Synthetic rubber tile has a denser surface than vinyl asbestos and therefore better resists the accumulation of surface dirt and stains. It is also more resilient and provides a more comfortable floor to walk on. I recently saw a rubber tile floor which I installed in a kitchen twenty years ago. It's still in reasonable shape, although it requires mopping two or three times a week to keep it fairly clean. (This floor has never been waxed.) Although the rubber tile is less porous than vinyl asbestos, it will stain and scrubbing is a part of its maintenance. In general, it costs about 25 percent more than vinyl asbestos and is available in a greater variety of patterns and colors.

Vinyl tile, the type on which wax is applied, is manufactured in a great variety of colors and patterns, is by far the most expensive of the three, and is by far the most impractical. I built a new house recently and the owner insisted on using a blue vinyl tile in one of the bathrooms. Even using extreme care during its installation, I was unable to avoid leaving several surface scratches. The tiles look very promising when still in the store in their boxes, but they require constant attention for even a reasonably clean appearance and are easily marred.

The only composition tile I can recommend using is the nonwaxing vinyl type. The surface of these tiles (or sheets) is dense enough to resist penetration of staining material and is also tough enough to withstand ordinary household use.

The cheapest method of installation for any composition tile is to place it directly on the existing floor. However, if the existing floor has an irregular surface, the tiles won't adhere well and the irregularities of the floor will turn up on the face of the tiles after a short time. Vinyl asbestos, which is much less pliable than the others, will adhere even less well and, if the irregularities are great, will not adhere at all. Even when it adheres well, vinyl asbestos tile is brittle—especially in cold weather—and will crack when it is walked on if there isn't continuous support directly below it.

## Underlayments for Composition Tile

The three kinds of underlayment used most often are Masonite (or other composition sheets), plywood, or 30-pound felt, a type of tar paper twice as heavy as ordinary tar paper. Which one to choose will depend on what the underlayment is going to cover and what sort of composition tile will be installed over it.

If the floor is concrete and has a reasonably smooth surface, felt, which is the cheapest, is also the most appropriate, since it will best resist rotting action.

If the concrete floor has holes or depressions, these can be filled satisfactorily by using either epoxy or latex concrete. These fillers can be feathered to very thin films and will still adhere. (The area to be filled should first be thoroughly cleaned and coated with Thoroughbond or another product which seals the surface of the concrete and provides a better surface for adhesion of the filler.)

To install 30-pound felt on a concrete floor, I spread plastic roof cement on the floor adjacent to a wall using a notched trowel. The width of the cement band should be about 38 inches and extend completely across the room. Cold tar or plastic roof cement is much cheaper than Mastic and works just as well in attaching the tar paper to the concrete. The trowel should be a cheap throwaway

Notched trowel

type, since the cement will be difficult to clean off it.

I lay the entire roll of 30-pound felt (50 feet) at one end of the plastic cement swath and roll it out for 5 or 6 feet. I stand on the felt and shift it with my feet so that its side lies against the wall, and I keep it in this position as I unroll it further. I continue across the entire swath in this manner, rolling out 5 or 6 feet at a time, shifting the paper with my feet as needed.

If a bubble develops in the paper and is difficult to work out, I slit the paper on the bubble, trim away the excess, and lay the slit parts back on the tar. No "perfect" fit is needed; a gap of even 1/4 inch between the sides of the cut doesn't matter. At the end of the swath, I cut the tar paper a few inches longer than necessary with a sheetrock knife, fold the excess against the wall and floor joint, then trim it along the crease, laying the trimmed end on the tar to complete covering the swath.

I walk over the length of installed paper and drag the side of my foot against its surface to insure contact between the bottom of the paper and the tar.

I cover the entire floor with tar paper in this manner, installing successive lengths adjacent to those previously installed.

With the felt glued to the concrete, any composition tile can be laid on it. In cementing the tile to the felt, it is best to use a waterproof Mastic, also applied with a notched trowel. (The purpose of the notched trowel is to leave the Mastic or plastic tar at a uniform height that will be the depth of the notches. This eliminates bulges or depressions caused by too much or too little Mastic in any particular area.)

Waterproof Mastic is several times more expensive than nonwaterproof, but it is a necessity: when the floor is mopped, water will seep down between the joints of tiles and dissolve the nonwaterproof Mastic, causing the tiles to lift. (Nonwaterproof Mastics make no mention of this fact on their labels and unsuspecting customers repeatedly purchase these "bargains.")

If composition tile is to be laid on a wood surface that has slightly uneven floorboards, 1/4-inch tempered Masonite will make an excellent underlayment. Sheets are available in the same sizes as plywood and 4-by-8-foot sheets are ordinarily convenient for handling and installation. Nontempered Masonite is cheaper than tempered but will deteriorate quickly in kitchens and bathrooms, where it will be subject to a good deal of water seepage.

To install the Masonite underlayment, I first remove the quarter round at the bottom of the baseboard, using a flat bar. The quarter round is inexpensive and I make no effort to save it.

I begin installing the Masonite in any corner, placing a full sheet with its length at a right angle to the flooring and its sides 1/4 to 1/2 inch away from both intersecting walls. The purpose of leaving this gap is to avoid trimming the sheet if the walls aren't exactly at a right angle. To nail the Masonite to the floor, I use 1-to-1 1/4-inch small-headed annular nails spaced every 10 inches or so.

I install sheets in a row until the distance to the opposite wall is shorter than the sheet. I measure the distance to the wall. I place four 2 x 4s on the flat on the floor, lay the sheet on top of them, pop a chalk line across the measured distance, set the depth of the power-saw blade to cut at 3/8 inch and cut the piece of Masonite so that the part I need will

have the kerf. This reduces its length by an additional 3/16 inch and provides an easy fit. After I install the first row, I begin another row adjacent to it, and repeat the process until the floorboards are completely covered by the Masonite.

At any doorway, I cut the Masonite so that it will lie halfway under the door when the door is closed. (This needn't be exact, since after the tile is installed, a saddle will be placed over it.)

If the composition tile is to be laid on a wood floor which is more than slightly uneven, plywood is a more appropriate underlayment than Masonite since it will better resist sagging between high spots. The thickness of the plywood used increases proportionately to the floor's unevenness, starting with 1/4 inch and continuing in multiples of 1/8 inch up to 3/4 inch. (It will usually be economical to sand away the highest spots and use 1/4-inch plywood.)

Exterior (as opposed to interior-grade) plywood should be used. The exterior-grade plywood has water-resistant glue between its plies. When I am installing plywood as an underlayment in a bathroom or kitchen or wherever water seepage is expected, I use marine plywood. This is a special type of plywood whose plies I have never known to separate after recurring contact with water.

Interior plywood, which does not employ waterproof glues, is significantly cheaper than exterior plywood and is adequate for use in rooms other than the kitchen or bathroom or wherever a significant amount of water seepage is not anticipated.

Both exterior and interior grades are available with only one side filled and sanded smooth, called "GIS"—(good on one side); this type should be purchased since it is cheaper.

I use annular nails to fasten the plywood to the flooring. In general, the length of nail used follows the formula "one third in, two thirds out"—in this case, one third of the length of the nail should be in the plywood and two thirds in the flooring to which it is being attached.

I lay the plywood in the manner described for the Masonite, first removing the quarter round and then starting in one corner with a full sheet and leaving a gap between the sides of the sheet and intersecting walls to avoid trimming if the walls are not at a right angle. When completing the first row of plywood sheets, I usually have an end left over and I use this end to start a new adjacent row.

This staggers the joints between rows and reduces unevenness in the surface of the plywood, thereby preventing the line of the joint from appearing on the surface of the tiles across its entire length.

(In houses with damp basements, it is advisable to install 15-pound felt under the plywood underlayment, which will act as a vapor barrier between the basement and floor above which the new tiles are being installed.)

## Installing Composition Tile

I vacuum the room and make certain that none of the nailheads are above the surface of the plywood or Masonite (no nails were used to install the felt). I pop chalk lines between the midpoints of opposite walls and divide the room into quadrants.

I spread Mastic on the back of a tile and place it at the intersection of the lines and in any of the quadrants. I repeat this with three additional tiles, placing each in a different quadrant. (I apply the Mastic to the back of the tiles rather than to the underlayment so that the Mastic will not obscure the lines and interfere with the initial alignment.) One corner of each of the tiles lies in the center of the room while the sides of each tile lie along a line that continues to the middle of a wall.

I now spread Mastic over an area of roughly 3 square feet within a quadrant and lay tiles within it. I align each new tile with those previously installed and avoid having to install a new tile *between* two already placed. I rub my palm over the top of the tiles to flatten them and to assure contact with the Mastic throughout.

I keep the lid on the Mastic can when it's not in use since its solvent evaporates quickly. I also limit the amount of Mastic I spread to the number of tiles I can install in a twenty-minute period to assure that it will be fully pliant when a tile is placed on it.

If I am installing vinyl asbestos (which becomes fairly brittle when a room is cold), I keep a propane torch going and pass the back of the tile across the flame to make it a little more flexible before laying it.

I am working outward from the center toward the corner, filling the first quadrant until the remaining border is less than the width or length of a tile. As I go along, I remove any excess Mastic squeezed up between the tiles by wiping with a rag dampened in turpentine. I use a putty knife to remove all the excess Mastic that lies around the border of full tiles. It is important to remove the excess Mastic that lies in the area where tiles will have to be cut since it will be some time before I do this and the Mastic will have dried. Once hard, it will have to be removed with the spinner, a needless operation.

I install the tiles in the remaining quadrants in the same manner, filling that quadrant in which the door lies last so that I can back my way out of the room.

The amount of time that must pass before the Mastic will secure the tiles and keep them from moving varies a great deal. If the room is hot and dry, a tile may be walked on in half an hour or so without shifting it. If the room is cold and damp, it may shift a bit even after twenty-four hours. In general, once I have installed all the full tiles, I prefer to wait overnight before walking on them. If I must walk on the newly installed tiles, I first lay a sheet of plywood over them, then check from time to time to see if any have shifted.

To cut the tiles for the perimeter of the room, I place a full tile directly over one already installed adjacent to a wall. I place a second tile on top of the loose one so that one side lies 1/8 to 1/4 inch away from the wall. Using the opposite side of the second tile as a guide, I score the loose tile under it with a sheetrock knife. I bend the loose tile along the scored line to separate it into two pieces. The piece that was visible while being scored will fit between the installed tile and the wall.

I *do not* want the cut tile to fit tightly against the wall since the quarter round will cover any gap and eliminates the need to be precise.)

I test the first piece of cut tile at various points along the wall and the wall opposite it. It should fit easily. If it does, I use the cut tile as a model. I count the number of cut tiles I will need to fill both borders along the walls and cut all of them. I then repeat this entire process for the two remaining opposite walls.

If the tiles are rubber or vinyl, I use a sheetrock knife to score the tile, then fold it at the scored line—which will complete the separation of the two pieces.

If the tiles are vinyl asbestos, I use a mechanical cutter, which can usually be inexpensively rented from the tile supplier.

The cut tiles are installed in the same manner as full ones. In each corner, a cut tile will have to be cut again to allow for the width of the gap of the intersecting wall.

If after all the tiles have been laid many are not lying flat, I go over the entire surface with a heavy roller.

Occasionally an odd tile will refuse to flatten. It can usually be made to conform by placing a damp cloth over it and passing a steam iron over the cloth and tile. If this doesn't work, I remove the tile, scrape away the Mastic, and install a new tile.

## Installing Other Types of Floor Coverings

Tiles with factory-placed adhesive on their backs are installed in exactly the same manner as those without the adhesive.

Tiles with hardwood surfaces are in wide use in new construction and have filtered into renovations despite their high cost. Their appearance is quite pleasing to many people and their factory finish will last several years with ordinary use. The wood, however, is usually 3/8 inch thick, and when the finish needs to be renewed serious problems are encountered since sanding will remove wood from a flooring that is already less than half the standard thickness (25/32 inch). For this reason I avoid the use of these tiles if a wooden surface is desired and purchase instead prefinished standard flooring that is competitively priced.

Vinyl strips that simulate wood flooring are manufactured and installed in the same manner as tiles. Their cost is often higher than standard wood flooring.

## Replacing Quarter Round

Use of 3/4-inch quarter round has become a widespread method of covering the joint between tile and baseboard. It is available in lumber yards in random lengths up to 16 feet. It should be painted or stained *before* it is installed to save a good deal of time and effort.

The pictured miter box costs $1; the saw is an ordinary eight-point—eight teeth to the inch. When a good deal of quarter round or other trim is to be installed, purchase of a more expensive manually operated miter tool should be considered. It operates with laterally cutting knives and is similar to a paper cutter. Thin slivers can be removed if neces-

3/4-inch quarter round being mitered in miter box

sary and it makes professional joints routine. However, the cheap miter box and eight-point saw make perfectly satisfactory joints. A variety of expensive metal miter boxes and "back" saws (ribbed on top for greater stiffness) are also available, but I have found them to be a total waste of time and money. The manual cutter is cheaper and does a better job, and the cheap box is adequate for most operations.

The joint at the intersection of two lengths of quarter round may either be mitered (made with two adjoining 45-degree cuts) or "coped."

To make a miter cut, I position the quarter round in the box with one flat side down and the other flat side against the side of the box. As I look at the box, the left miter is on my left and the right miter on my right.

To determine the lengths of quarter round needed, I extend two 1 x 2s from baseboard to baseboard on the opposite wall, transfer the length to the piece of quarter round to be cut, and make the necessary cuts. The quarter round is fairly flexible—especially over longer lengths—and when it is cut slightly long, the fit will be better. It is also essential that the saw be kept vertical during the cut or the joint will remain open. I nail each piece to the baseboard using #6 finishing nails spaced every 2 feet or so, which I countersink, fill with wood putty, and later touch up with paint or stain. I cut opposite miters to fit the installed pieces and use the right-angle cut in the box where I need to butt the quarter round.

Coping saw cutting mitered profile

Coped joint

To "cope" the joint instead of mitering it, I cut the ends of the first piece or pieces (that extend between opposite walls) at a right angle and install. I cut the ends of the pieces that intersect the installed quarter round as if there were a miter.

Using a coping saw, I cut along the profile of the miter as pictured, leaving a concave surface that corresponds to the convex surface of the quarter round already installed. I then nail the quarter round in the manner described above.

# MASONRY

6

## General Background

In older small buildings of most cities, the interior walls and ceilings have a wood core to which wood or metal lath has been attached. The lath is covered with a mixture of gypsum plaster, sand, and water on top of which a film composed of gypsum plaster, water, and slaked lime has been applied.

In larger structures, hollow structural clay tile, gypsum block, or concrete block forms the core of walls while reinforced concrete or structural tile forms the core of the ceiling. In some instances the plaster mixture is applied directly to the core material, while in others, particularly on exterior walls, the plaster is separated from the back of the wall by intermittent furring strips on which lath is attached and the plaster mixture applied.

In townhouses and tenements, the core of the ceiling is made of lengths of lumber whose ends rest on the brick side walls. These members are called joists and serve not only to support the floor but also provide a surface on which to attach the lath for the ceiling below.

In apartment buildings, a mixture of cement, sand, lime, and water (or gypsum plaster, sand, and water) is applied directly to the core and has come to be known as the scratch coat. Usually 3/8-inch thick, it gets its name from the fact that after the material has partially dried, horizontal indentions

Scratch, brown, and final coat applied directly to brick wall

are scratched on its surface so that the succeeding coat will have a greater and rougher surface area on which to adhere.

In townhouses and tenements, undressed (unplaned) wooden strips (wood lath) are nailed horizontally to studs leaving 3/8-inch gaps between each slat. The cementatious material is then pushed through the gaps, where it sags along the back side of the lath; after hardening it forms a "key" which prevents the material from falling off.

In apartment buildings the scratch coat is applied directly to the core of the wall or ceiling, which is first dampened. The cementatious material is held to the core by suction.

After a couple of days of drying, the scratch coat is again dampened and a second coat applied. This is the brown or bed coat. It is also 3/8 inch thick and is composed of a mixture of finely graded sand (1/8-inch maximum-sized granules) and cement or gypsum plaster, sand, asbestos fibers, and horsehair, which make the material easier to work with and also strengthen the bonding within its composition. The brown coat is allowed to dry for several days; it is then dampened and a final coat applied. This is 1/8 inch or so thick and made from a mixture of gypsum or gauging plaster and slaked lime.

On the whole these masonry walls and ceilings are long-lasting installations, and most of the work needed to keep them in repair has much more to do with the paint with which they are coated than with the structure of the wall itself.

## Repairing Shallow Cracks

In this photo the layer or layers of paint still adhere to the surface plaster. It is the plaster surface itself that has the crack. The crack pierces completely through the finish coat and extends slightly into the brown coat.

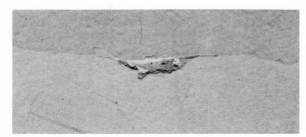

Shallow crack

To repair it, I lay the corner of a hook scraper so that it lies over the crack. My left hand is at the forward end and presses down moderately. My right hand is around the handle and will guide the scraper along the crack. I use enough pressure against the surface to cause removal of material to a depth of about 1/4 inch. The crack width that results will be slightly wider than the original crack.

To use the hook scraper properly, I pull it toward me, lift it, and reposition it rather than sliding it back and forth while continuously maintaining contact. This avoids prematurely dulling the cutting edge of the scraper. Nevertheless, after every 20 feet or so of enlarging cracks, it will become dull. To resharpen the scraper, I run a flat bastard file over the cutting edge along its original angle. Three or four passes will resharpen it.

The purpose of enlarging the crack is to provide enough surface for the filler material to adhere. The most common filler used for small areas is spackle, a plasterlike product available in any hardware store. It is fairly stable if stored in a place without excessive moisture. (If the spackle has hardened during storage, it should be discarded since its bonding strength will have diminished even though it can be made pliable again by mixing with water.)

Sponge, 3-inch spackiling knife and 16-inch rectangular trowel

I use the pictured tools for mixing and applying spackle.

In all masonry work, the difference between a quick and easy job and a hard and lengthy one will very often be determined by whether the proper proportions of material have been used and whether the resulting consistency is appropriate for the particular work being done. The mixes and consistencies I suggest have been derived through actual practice. In some cases they correspond to the manufacturer's recommendations and in others they don't. In both instances, quickness and ease are the determining criteria.

The same may be said with respect to the techniques used in applying the masonry material. Some are better than others, and those I suggest are the ones that I have found work best for me.

In general, the less water used when mixing masonry materials, the stronger the end product. The minimum amount of water that can be used is that amount which makes water completely available to all the dry material. From that point on, the amount of water to be added is determined by what the mixture will be used for. The maximum point is reached when water is running out the sides of the mix or collecting in hollows within it.

When spackle is mixed with water, it remains usable for about half an hour, and I therefore mix up only the amount I estimate I will use during that time. If this is difficult to estimate, I put half a cup of spackle in a flat plastic pan, add water (from a full measuring cup), and stir vigorously until I have arrived at a consistency of butter at room temperature. After I have applied this initial amount, I should be able to estimate what amount I will be needing and how long it will take to apply it, noting as well how much water I have used to obtain the necessary consistency. For future mixes, I place the water in the pan first and sprinkle in the spackle while mixing. This is better than adding the water to the spackle since it avoids lumping.

After mixing the spackle, I press the knife gently into the mix, which should yield with only slight resistance. If more than slight pressure is required to shape the mixture, more water should be added until greater pliability is achieved.

I hold the trowel face up in my left hand. I transfer the mixture from the pan to the trowel by sliding the knife under a fistful, lifting it, turning it over on top of the trowel, and wiping the knife clean by passing it down along the side of the trowel.

Before applying the spackle, I wet a sponge in a clean bucket of water and wash the crack to remove loose material and wet the surface. A dry surface will remove water from the mix and cause it to dry too rapidly, resulting in contraction and cracks. (Spackle ordinarily contracts during drying anyway, and creating a surface flush with those

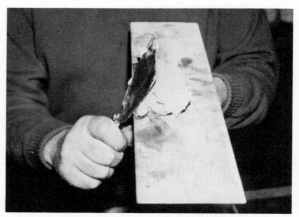

Spackling knife depositing compound on trowel

adjoining it often requires two or even three applications. However, where the area under repair is small, as here, the contraction is negligible and one pass will be sufficient if the crack has first been dampened.)

I remove spackle from the trowel by cutting vertically through a small portion at either end and sliding the knife along the trowel and off it. Continuing the movement, I turn the knife so that the spackle faces the crack and is parallel to it. I press the spackle into the crack and continue either above or below the filled area until less spackle is deposited in the crack than is needed to fill it. I turn the knife so that the blade is perpendicular to the crack, tilt it down at about a 30-degree angle, and, using moderate pressure, slide it over the area I have filled to remove any excess. I then slide the knife along the edge of the trowel, deposit the excess spackle, remix it into the remaining spackle, and repeat the entire process until the crack is filled. The optimum technique is one in which all these successive movements are continuous.

It is neither necessary nor desirable to ram the spackle into the enlarged crack—only gentle to moderate pressure is required. Too much pressure is not only a waste of energy, but also often causes the spackle to adhere to the knife rather than to the surface of the crack.

From time to time I run a wet sponge over the trowel before transferring spackle to it. I also intermittently dip the knife into the bucket of water. Keeping these tools wet makes handling the spackle easier and helps keep it in a more pliant state.

The surfaces adjoining the crack serve as my guide for filling. (Each side of the knife rests on these surfaces when removing excess spackle from the crack.) Inevitably, spackle clings to them. I remove the spackle when still wet by sliding the knife under it at about a 30-degree angle. When wet, the spackle can easily be removed by this simple motion; after it has dried, it will become more difficult.

Using a wet sponge to remove spackle from adjoining surfaces is not a good practice although it is widely used. It leaves streaks which will have to be wiped off before painting, and there is the risk of inadvertently marring the surface of the newly filled area as well.

During use, some spackle will become deposited along the edge on the handle side of the trowel. This should be scraped off while still wet *and discarded*. Spackle deposited here becomes dry and gritty fairly quickly, and even small amounts mixed into the good spackle will cause "streaking" (in which the hardened bits are dragged along the surface, causing scratches).

When the spackle is not being taken from the trowel, the trowel should be held in a horizontal position a few inches above the waist. When spackle is to be taken off the trowel, the end nearest the user should be lowered and the trowel moved against the approaching knife. If the trowel is kept in a horizontal position, it will be awkward to remove the spackle and the user's fingers will be drawn across the spackle on the trowel. The trowel is moved by rotating the wrist. If the entire mass of spackle slides down the trowel, the spackle is too wet and should be remixed. If the mixture is within the proper range of wetness, even with a maximum amount of water, it will sag rather than slide even with the trowel tilted as much as 45 degrees.

## Repairing Bulging Cracks

I remove all loose material with the hook scraper. Often, this kind of bulge will have been caused by paint lifting from the plaster surface even though the material below it is sound. I press my finger against the area to check. If no movement occurs, only the paint is bulging and nothing but that should be removed. If there is any movement of the material, whether I can see a crack or not, I remove whatever is loose. A bulge usually indicates a crack

in the brown coat. The final coat will rarely be cracked, while a crack in the scratch coat occurs a little more frequently.

I remove all remaining loose material from the area with a wet sponge, then mix the spackle. To fill this kind of crack I need a medium-thick spackle mixture. However, the consistency should not be so thick as to require more than gentle pressure to fill the area. If it is too thick, it will create bulges on the finished surface because the knife will simply slide over the spackle rather than depressing it into the same plane as the adjoining surfaces. The rippled effect seen on so many patches is often the result of the spackle being too thick and stiff when applied.

If the width of the area to be filled is less than 2 inches, I apply the spackle with moderate pressure into the deepest area first, then work outward toward each side. I position the knife so that its outer edges rest on the existing finished surface. While holding it at a steep downward angle and using moderate pressure, I pull the knife down over the spackle.

If there are still depressions, I apply more spackle and repeat the surface movement with the knife.

If there are streaks on the surface, I wait about ten minutes before filling them. This allows the surface of the spackle to become hard enough so that the addition of the small amount needed to fill the scratches will not create other scratches.

If the width of the area to be filled is more than 2 inches, I apply the spackle to the outer sides and work inward. After filling has been completed, I transfer the spackle to the knife from the trowel, wet and clean the trowel, and, with its sides resting on the existing finished surfaces, slide the trowel down and over the spackle at about a 60-degree angle.

There is little chance of filling a wide area with spackle and achieving a flat surface in one pass. Even when this has been done, the spackle will contract during drying and create a depression. There is no need therefore to waste time trying to achieve a perfectly flat surface on the first pass. Allow the spackle to harden partially and, while it is still wet, make a second pass with a mixture looser than that used on the first pass.

When the second coat of spackle is applied over the first, it will lose its pliancy very rapidly since water will be sucked out of the second mixture to a point where it becomes stiff almost immediately after being deposited. This rapid stiffening action should be delayed by the use of a very loose second-coat mixture, especially when the second coat is being used to fill a shallow area. The surface of the first coat can also be sprayed lightly with water to increase the delay. (Water atomizers used for plants are excellent for this purpose.) The idea is to lightly dampen the surface of the first coat; if the filled spackle is wetted rather than dampened, the bond will be weakened. In any case the mixture should never be so runny that water comes out of the sides or collects within it.

While spackle is quite easy to sand, this fact should not be used as rationale for leaving an irregular or marred surface, since the additional labor of sanding is time-consuming and needless. If only one small crack has been patched, the time it will take to sand it smooth and flat will of course be minimal, but chances are there will be a great many patched areas if a wall is being prepared for painting, and finishing these properly rather than sanding them will avoid a significant amount of needless work. However, if sanding should become necessary, using an orbital sander with emery paper is the best method.

A good deal of fine dust is created while sanding and the worker should wear a mask.

Orbital sander with emery paper for fine smoothing

## Patching Behind Flaked Paint

I remove all the loose paint by sliding the spackling knife along the finish coat and under the flaked areas. The areas formerly occupied by the paint are slightly below the remaining surface and these indentions would still be visible if paint were now applied. In standard paint jobs no attempt is made to fill the indentions, while in a good paint job they are filled.

The indentions vary in size and their size determines the technique used to fill them. The best consistency for the spackle is that of heavy cream.

To repair an indention the size of the knife or smaller, I lay the spackle in its center and, applying moderate pressure, draw the knife toward me at a very flat angle, almost parallel to the existing surface. *No matter what the result of the first pass, I leave it that way*, except if it has created a bulge higher than the surrounding area, in which case I remove the excess. I then make a first pass on the remaining half of the indention. When the spackle has hardened to a point where another pass will not alter it (this varies and may be as long as fifteen minutes), I make a second pass to fill in whatever spots were missed during the first. If any spots still remain to be filled, I will wait again and make a third pass.

The essential thing is to apply the spackle in a single pass at a time and resist the temptation of playing with it after that. If additional smoothing or filling is attempted while the spackle is still wet and movable, little improvement will be made and further marring will be likely. The best time to correct imperfections is *after* the spackle has become rigid, since only a single pass will be necessary and only the fresh spackle will be moved.

To repair an indention larger than the knife, I place the spackle along the left side (as I look at it) of the trowel. The open end of the handle is toward me. I deposit the spackle along the right side of the joint where the indention and adjoining surface meet and, working from right to left with the trowel at about a 60-degree angle, pull it across the area to be filled.

If the area is greater than 16 inches (the length of the trowel), I use the same technique, making sure that I maintain the same pressure across the width of the stroke. Since at all times one end of the trowel will be sliding on a finished surface, it will serve as a reference point for the other end, which I want to keep in the same plane.

If the area is very large, I will repeat this as many times as necessary but I fill *only* new areas. I do not pass over or disturb the spackle already applied. Again, I make only one pass, leave it, and remove only what is higher than the finished surfaces.

When applying spackle with the trowel, most of

the spackle will be scraped away if the trowel is held at too steep an angle. A second pass will be necessary. If the angle is too flat, "chattering" will result. The face of the trowel will hit only the high spots of the spackle, its path will be in intermittent rather than continuous contact, and the result will be a series of hills and valleys. Again, if chattering occurs, the entire area should be wiped clean with the trowel and another pass attempted. One develops a knack or a feel to determine the correct angle to hold the trowel, depending on the spackle's consistency and the particular surface to be covered. Some people learn this after only a few passes while others may take a great deal longer. Skill is involved in the use of a trowel and I know of no way of acquiring it except by actual practice, keeping in mind the sole objective—to make a smooth stroke maintaining continuous contact with the spackle and leaving behind a uniform deposit in plane with existing surfaces.

Filling indentions caused by the removal of loose paint is difficult and some negative results can be expected before the technique is learned. The following temporary step may be helpful in achieving the knack.

I apply loose spackle with the knife 2 or 3 inches inside the indented area and draw the knife back toward the periphery. I continue to do this around the entire periphery, thereby decreasing the size of the indented area. The applied spackle slants slightly outward toward the existing painted surface. I continue to apply the spackle in diminishing circles until the entire indention is filled.

The spackled surface will become a series of slight depressions and high spots that are in the same plane as the finished surface outside the indented area. I use the high spots to rest the knife on and fill the depressions.

This method takes considerably more time than making one pass over an area with a trowel, but until dexterity with the trowel is achieved, it offers the best alternative. Nevertheless, there is little chance of obtaining a smooth flat surface in plane with the surrounding area. Raised lines of spackle will remain where the knife made its initial contact and where the stroke ended. There will also be raised spots where new spackle was placed on that previously applied. The orbital sander with emery paper will smooth and flatten the surface. All sanding should be viewed as a temporary expedient,

however, and justifiable only until one has learned to achieve a good surface using the trowel alone.

## Repairing Narrow, Deep Holes

This kind of hole is encountered when the scratch coat has come loose from the lath, where an intersecting wall or cabinets have been removed from a wall, or where BX cable or electrical boxes have been newly installed. Spackle isn't used to fill these holes since it contracts too much, will require several passes, takes too long to harden, and is relatively expensive when substantial amounts are involved.

Type of hole that can be filled with one pass

Plaster of Paris is used as the filling material when an area is at least 3/8 inch deep and under 6 inches wide. It hardens in several minutes, during which time it can be molded easily into a smooth, flat surface. It forms a very strong bond when the masonry surface on which it is being applied is first washed free of loose material and dampened. Unlike spackle, it rarely develops cracks when large amounts are used in one area, and a smooth surface can easily be obtained by simple troweling.

Unfortunately, it hardens rapidly and, once hardened, becomes unusable. (While it can be softened with water before it is completely hard, this should not be attempted since its adhesive strength will be impaired.)

Retardants in powder form are available which, when mixed into plaster of Paris, extend its working life to fifteen or twenty minutes. I have found that these retardants are unnecessary even for the inexperienced person if the plaster is used only when appropriate and in a manner that corresponds to its quick-setting characteristic.

Speed is essential when using plaster of Paris, both in mixing and application. Only an amount which will be used within a few minutes should be prepared.

I wash the area to be filled with a sponge to remove all loose material and dampen its surface. I pour a cupful of water into a plastic container and sprinkle in an equal amount of plaster of Paris while stirring and mixing. I add more water or plaster as necessary to obtain a consistency similar to that of butter at room temperature.

I place the entire mixture on a trowel and, using moderate pressure, press it into the area to be filled, positioning the trowel parallel to the length of the indention. I then turn the trowel perpendicular to the indention's length so that each end rests on the adjoining finished wall, and I pull the trowel across the surface at about a 60-degree angle. Unlike spackle, which will often leave a marred surface because some of it will have adhered to the trowel, plaster has a stronger inner bond, and even though only a small portion of the sharply angled trowel will be making surface contact, the covering it leaves will usually be smooth and unbroken.

If foreign material is in the plaster of Paris or if it has streaked for any other reason, I wait until the plaster has hardened to make the second pass, moistening its surface before the pass is made. However, if after the first pass there are no depressions and only a surface roughness remains, I dampen the surface immediately and stroke it with a wet trowel to obtain smoothness.

When the area to be filled is less than 2 inches in width, such as the channel in which BX is buried, I remove loose material and dampen the surface first, then use the trowel to apply the plaster of Paris, preparing only a fistful at a time.

If a narrow (less than 6-inch), deep hole is located in a sheetrock or lath wall, usually found in tenements, townhouses, and newer buildings, a different technique is used. With sheetrock walls, the area behind the hole will be hollow except where the studs are located or if the lath has been broken. In either case, I first cram newspaper into the hole until it fits tightly in the hollow area behind the hole and provides backing. I then fill the hole with plaster of Paris, using the technique described earlier.

If the wooden (or metal) lath is secure behind the

hole, I first dampen the wood lath and surrounding masonry, then apply the plaster directly on the lath, using moderate pressure so that the plaster is pushed between the gaps of the lath.

## Repairing Wide, Deep Holes

This condition is encountered after a wall has been removed. There will be depressions in the ceiling and in intersecting walls corresponding to the area formerly occupied. (This section deals with repair of the walls; the ceiling is treated on page 164.) It is also encountered when masonry coverings of a ceiling or wall have fallen from the lath. When the area to be repaired is 6 inches or more in diameter and 3/8 inch deep or larger, neither spackle nor plaster of Paris should be used.

If the core of the wall is exposed, whether it is structural tile, gypsum block, concrete block, concrete, metal or wood lath, the steps taken for repair are essentially those taken when a new surface is being applied.

Nowadays, instead of applying the scratch and brown coats, a relatively inexpensive material called Structolite is used. It is purlited gypsum, a light and bulky material which adheres well to lath and masonry surfaces, remains usable for hours, and provides an excellent surface on which the finish film of plaster can be applied.

Since the areas to be repaired are relatively large, I estimate the amount of Structolite needed by filling a gallon can with the powdered Structolite and another gallon can with water. I then place the Structolite in a wheelbarrow or in a large plastic container, add water, and mix until I have obtained a consistency which retains its shape when I pass a trowel over its surface. I note how much water I have used in relation to the gallon of Structolite to obtain the correct consistency. After I have applied the mix to the area to be filled and observe how much has been covered, I am able to make an intelligent estimate as to how much Structolite I need to prepare.

Using a plasterer's hatchet, I chip away raised blobs of paint and plaster around the periphery of the area to be repaired. I wash out all loose material with a sponge and wet the surface.

I fill a wheelbarrow or mixing tub half full of Structolite, add water, and mix with a hoe until I have the correct consistency. If water collects in

Wheelbarrow and mixing hoe

one particular "secret" but in the cumulative effect of eliminating needless work in each of the steps.

The tool pictured is called a "hawk" and acts as a portable mortar board. I hold it in my left hand, a few inches above the waist. I transfer the mixed Structolite to the hawk with a 10-inch bricklayer's trowel.

I leave the pointed trowel in the wheelbarrow and use a 16-inch rectangular trowel for the application. If I am filling a wall area, I begin at the bottom and work upward.

The trowel is in my right hand, the open end of its handle to my right. To remove Structolite from the hawk onto the trowel, I tilt the hawk toward me, cut the side of the trowel into the mixture about 2 inches from its far end, and, with a forward and upward stroke, slide this portion off the hawk and on to the surface to be filled.

When working near the floor, I hold the hawk to the side of the area to be filled; once I have reached a height of 6 inches or so, I place the forward side of the hawk directly under the area I am filling. This reduces the distance the Structolite must travel between hawk and wall and also catches some falling loose material.

As the Structolite leaves the hawk, I rotate my wrist so that the bottom side of the trowel is tilted at about a 30-degree angle toward the wall. As I make contact, I maintain the same angle and continue with an upward movement. Each of these steps is joined into one continuous motion and my pressure throughout is light to moderate, *not heavy*.

Structolite is held to the wall by suction. Using excessive pressure while applying it will not increase its adhering power and will instead cause a loss of material by squeezing it out past the ends of the trowel. Excessive pressure will also pack the mixture prematurely, and "alligatoring" (a multiplicity of cracks in the dried mixture) will probably result.

If the pressure is too slight, the Structolite will not make sufficient contact with the block or lath and intermittent rather than continuous adhesion will be created.

Generally, the optimum pressure is equivalent to that which is needed to spread firm butter, but this is only a general guideline since varying amounts of water in the mixture and the varying surfaces on which it will be applied will require different pressures. In every instance, the objective is to secure

the mix or runs out of its sides, I add more Structolite until both conditions are eliminated. If the mix pulls apart when the trowel is passed over its surface, I add more water until this is corrected.

There are many ways of applying the Structolite; in every case the objective is a solid flat surface which adheres well to the structural material behind it and which has been placed at a depth of 1/8 inch or so below the existing surfaces to allow for the plaster finish. Again, it makes little difference in the final appearance how one gets the Structolite into the area to be patched, but there will be a huge difference in the amount of time it takes depending on the procedures followed. One common trait of professionalism in all the building trades is the development of simple procedures which lead to speed. It's not at all unusual for an uninstructed person to take twenty or thirty times as long to do the same job as a professional, using the same tools and materials. The difference lies not in any

Structolite on hawk

total initial contact with the surface on which the Structolite is being applied, compressing the material only slightly.

The Structolite I am placing on the wall core is very irregular, but I make no attempt to smooth it except for making a light pass with the trowel to flatten those peaks which are above the plane of the adjoining surfaces. I fill in low spots with new Structolite on succeeding applications by starting the stroke at each low point, always working upward. The stroke can be vertical or diagonal, whichever is required to fill or flatten. The total material I place in any given area should be thick enough to extend slightly above the existing finished surfaces.

I continue filling the patch until I have reached a point about halfway to the ceiling, or until about fifteen or twenty minutes has elapsed since the initial application at the base of the wall.

By this time the Structolite first applied will have become more firm, and I can now straighten its surface.

If the area being patched has a finished surface on both sides, I cut a 1 x 3 about 4 inches longer than the widest part of the patch. If the area has an intersecting wall on one side, I cut the piece 2 inches longer. In both cases, I want a straight 1 x 3 with no chips or gouges along its sides.

When both sides of the patch have finished surfaces, I place the 1 x 3 across the patch with its ends resting on the finished surfaces and begin to slide it back and forth and upward on a slight diagonal. This is called screeding. As I move the screed board upward, it removes Structolite that is

Screeding Structolite

higher than the finished surfaces. This will accumulate on top of the wide side of the 1 x 3 and, using the pointed trowel, I remove it from the board and use it to fill depressions that have now become easily discernible below the board. After filling, I lower the screed board and go over the filled area again.

If I encounter a sizable bulge, evidenced by the fact that the ends of the screed board are significantly higher than the existing surfaces, I do not attempt to remove all of it in one pass but go over it as many times as needed, removing small amounts on each pass until the bulge has been eliminated.

If the Structolite sags as I screed, I have not waited long enough for it to become firm, and I discontinue screeding and go on with the initial filling. The waiting time varies with the consistency of the mix and the surface to which it is being applied; watching for sag is a means of determining the proper time to begin screeding. By "sag" I mean that the flattened surface created by the passing screed board sinks of its own weight, making lumps. Screeding should be begun when the Structolite has become firm against its backing and while the outer layer is still slightly pliable. If the entire mass of Structolite shifts during screeding, not only will lumps be formed but the bond between the Structolite and the block or lath will be destroyed. *Only surface movement of the Structolite is desired.*

If there is an intersecting wall on one side of the patch, screeding is more difficult, since the board cannot be rested on two surfaces at both ends. I screed by eye while pressing one end of the board on the finished surface available. This requires steady pressure and an eye for flat, straight lines. If one is unsure about being able to do this by eye, one can as an alternative pop a vertical chalk line on the intersecting wall 2-1/2 inches out from the projected line of the finished corner. A 1 x 3 is then tacked to the wall at the line, its width extending outward from the line. While screeding, one end of the 1 x 3 screed board rests on the already-finished surface while the back edge of the opposite end is held against the 1 x 3 tacked to the intersecting wall.

Once screeding has been completed on the lower half of the patch, I apply filling to the remaining distance to the ceiling and screed it as soon as it has dried to a desirable consistency.

The surface of the Structolite after screeding is essentially flat but by no means smooth; there will be many slight indentions left by the screeding board as well as depressions and holes left inadvertently. These are not a problem. The function of screeding is to eliminate high and low ripples in the surface since the plaster film will follow any high or low spots in the Structolite's contour, producing a wavy finish. Attempting to compensate for a rippled surface while applying the finish plaster requires a great deal more effort than flattening the Structolite now.

Since it is very difficult to obtain a perfectly flat surface solely by screeding, a tool called a float is used after screeding has been completed.

The float pictured is similar to a trowel but has a wooden rather than a metal face. It is 18 inches long and can be used on patches with a diameter of up to 4 feet. A longer float, a darby, has two handles and is used for larger areas.

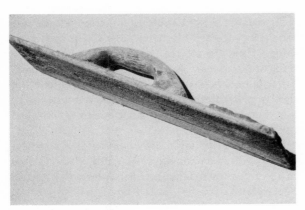

Wooden trowel or float

After all filling and screeding in an area have been finished and the Structolite is firm but still damp, I run the float over the area using broad semicircular motions and light-to-moderate pressure. If this causes the Structolite that lies 1/4 inch or so below the surface to shift, I stop at once since it is not yet firm enough to finish. If the surface Structolite has become hard and gritty and is difficult to shift and leaves scratches, I have waited too long, in which case I must *dampen the surface* to make it pliant by using an atomizer water sprayer or a wide brush.

The floating process flattens the irregular surface of the Structolite, packs its slightly, and brings the particles along the surface and slightly below it into closer contact with each other, creating a stronger and denser surface.

It is not only impossible to achieve a glasslike surface with floating, but also undesirable, since a smooth surface will not permit the finish plaster coat to adhere as well. All that is sought is a flat bed, the surface of which will be pitted and slightly irregular because of hard particles lodged within it. This rough surface, though flat, increases the bonding area for the plaster, and its irregularity fosters better adhesion.

The final step in preparing the bed is to depress the Structolite at its joint with the existing wall. I do this by tracing along the outer configuration with the end of a pointed trowel. A depth of 1/8 inch or so should be allowed for the final plaster coat. I will be ready to apply the final coat after allowing the Structolite to set up for twenty-four hours.

Wide, deep holes may also be encountered in "hollow" walls, those which have as their core either wood or metal studs. When the hole is greater than 6 inches in diameter (the maximum depth will ordinarily be 4 inches), the first step is to reinstall a material over the hole which will hold the masonry covering. Plasterboard is excellent for this. I place a ruler in the hole and extend it laterally until it encounters a stud. Noting the distance between the edge of the hole and the stud, I place a mark on the exterior surface of the wall which is 3/4 inch farther from the hole's edge than the measurement I have taken. With a carpenter's level I then draw a vertical line on the mark. I locate the stud on the opposite side of the hole, repeat the measurements, and draw a second vertical line. These lines correspond (roughly) to the centers of the studs which lie on each side of the hole. I place the level at the highest point of the hole and draw a horizontal line between the two vertical lines. I place the level at the lowest point of the hole and draw another horizontal line between the two vertical lines.

I score the vertical lines with a wood chisel, driving the cutting edge through the plaster and lath to the studs, and continue horizontally at each of the corners for 3/4 inch. I then bore a 3/8-inch hole anywhere along a horizontal line and, using a sabre saw with a cheap rough-cutting blade, I saw along each of the lines to remove the area I have marked, then cut a piece of plasterboard to fit the squared and enlarged hole and install it with lath nails spaced every 10 inches along each stud.

I now apply Structolite to the plasterboard as previously described and after allowing it to dry for a day, apply the finish plaster coat.

A viable alternative to Structolite in this and similar instances is a mixture of one part of gypsum plaster to three parts of finely graded sand, adding enough water to obtain a consistency of butter at room temperature.

## Repairing Narrow Ceiling Areas

The same types of cracks and holes encountered in walls can be expected in ceilings. The first step of course is to remove all loose material. In addition, large sections of plaster will frequently have come loose, particularly when the lath behind the plaster is wood. If sagging has occurred anywhere on the ceiling (this can happen without even cracking the surface of the plaster), the masonry covering must be removed. A simple test is to press the suspected spot; if movement occurs, it is loose. What appears as a small bulging area often turns out to be a large sagging section. I use the plasterer's hatchet to remove the visible defect, then work outward to remove *all* plaster that has separated from the lath.

When working on a ceiling, it is best to stand on a scaffolding of 2-inch-thick boards (spruce is preferable) placed on horses or ladder treads. (Horses are better. If additional height is necessary, 2 x 4s can be nailed to the horses.) To avoid having to stoop for materials, I also stand a concrete block or a milk crate on the boards and place the container of Structolite on top of it.

I arrange the scaffolding so that I can reach the entire area under repair without having to get off and rearrange its position.

After all loose material has been removed, I inspect the surfaces adjoining the patch. If, for example, the depression I am going to fill has been created by removal of a wall, the surfaces will be high and irregular due to successive layers of paint and poorly finished joints between the former wall and ceiling. These irregularities will interfere with the smoothing of the Structolite and I remove them by chipping with the plasterer's hatchet, striking at an angle toward the area to be filled.

Interior walls are roughly 6 inches thick and leave

a channel that wide when removed. Since the core of the wall will have extended to the core of the ceiling, structural tile, concrete, or lath, etc., will be visible and will provide a surface to which the Structolite will adhere.

I wash the area to be filled with a wet sponge and remove all loose material.

I mix Structolite to the butter-at-room-temperature consistency. I transfer the mix from the mixing container to the face of a 16-inch rectangular trowel using a 10-inch pointed trowel. Holding the trowel horizontally with the Structolite lying along its right side, I apply the mix to the center of the ceiling channel, tilt the left side of the trowel down by rotating my wrist, and, at an angle that will meet the existing surface, draw the trowel toward me and the left side of the channel. The pressure applied to the Structolite is slightly heavier than that used on walls. I repeat the process inversely for the right side of the channel, thereby creating an inverted V in the channel. I fill the V by laying Structolite in it parallel to the channel. I turn the trowel at a right angle to the channel and pull the trowel toward me to remove the excess. The ends of the trowel are sliding along the finished adjacent surfaces, which act as a depth guide. Throughout the trowel's movement I am exerting gentle upward pressure to pack the mixture and to insure total contact with the surface to which it will adhere.

If additional filling in the immediate area is necessary, I do it immediately. The straight-edge side of the trowel will serve as a sight level to indicate depressions.

I continue to fill and level the Structolite until the channel is completely finished. I then pack the entire surface by applying moderate pressure with the wooden-faced trowel. I then depress the edges of the patch with the tip of the pointed trowel.

When patching ceilings the Structolite will often fall as the trowel is removed. This will occur if *too much* pressure is being exerted to press the mixture against the surface of the backing. The pressure creates a bond between the Structolite and the trowel which is stronger than the bond to the backing and the Structolite is therefore pulled away. Of course, if too little pressure is applied, the Structolite will also fall. Even when the correct pressure is being applied, the Structolite may fall because its consistency is either too loose or too thick. It will also fall if the area hasn't been washed well and plaster dust remains over the surface. This will clog the pores of the backing and diminish the suction necessary for adherence.

Every motion made while patching a ceiling requires upward pressure, whether one is making initial contact or filling depressions. What pressure works best should be determined at the start by regarding the initial work area as a trial section.

If a portion of the Structolite sags but another part adheres, chances are that the consistency is a bit too thick or that it has not been thoroughly mixed. A bit more water and remixing will correct it.

If the Structolite develops cracks while drying, either too thick a mixture has been applied and it has dried too rapidly or it has not been mixed thoroughly enough. These cracks are usually not structural and can simply be filled when applying the finish plaster. However, if a large number of cracks continue through the Structolite to the backing—so that the area has become a series of small patches each held independently and separated from those adjoining—they are much less likely to retain their adherence and should be removed entirely and the patch refilled.

## Repairing Wide Ceiling Areas

If the area to be repaired has a diameter greater than 1 foot, the technique used is the same as that for patching large wall areas except that slightly heavier pressure is used to apply the Structolite. Also, the time available during which screeding may be done is much shorter than with walls since the effect of gravity is more pronounced. If screeding is undertaken prematurely, the back of the Structolite will be shifted, suction destroyed (or keys broken if the backing is lath), and the Structolite will fall. Similarly, if it is done too late, excessive pressure will be needed to float the surface which will in turn be transmitted to the back, diminishing its adherence and causing it to fall.

To determine if the time is proper, I run the screed board gently over a corner of the patch. If the Structolite pulls away from the finished adjoining surface leaving a gap greater than 1/16 inch, I am premature. If I can feel the Structolite beneath the surface shifting, I am also premature. If when I am moving the screed board back and forth over

the Structolite surface, large areas are moving simultaneously, I am premature. If I press my finger into the Structolite and more than 1/8 inch can be depressed without encountering significant resistance, I am also premature.

If, to flatten the surface, I must scrape rather than screed or need moderate-to-heavy pressure to move the surface material, I am late and should dampen the surface for better workability.

If I press my finger against the Structolite and encounter resistance immediately below the surface, the time is right. While screeding, the material around the periphery of the patch should not pull away from the adjoining surface more than a hair if at all. I should also be able to feel the firmness below the surface and only small areas on the surface should move.

While there is an optimum time in which to screed, I don't mean to suggest that there are only a couple of seconds in which to do it and failure to meet the time limit will result in disaster. In most situations one will have at least twenty minutes in which to work (often much longer) and this can be extended by dampening the surface.

Removing Structolite from hawk and onto trowel

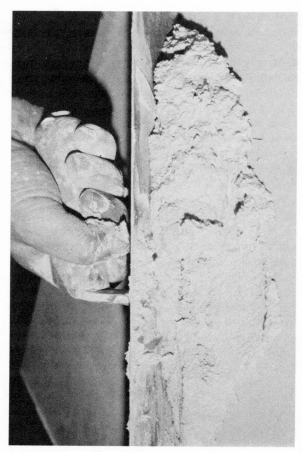

Applying Structolite to wall

Structolite before and after smoothing stroke

Edge of Structolite after application to wall

## Applying Masonry Coverings to New Walls

In the preceding chapter I detailed the construction of a new interior wall. An inner core was erected over which either plasterboard or sheetrock was then laid. I will now explain the final construction of such a wall, including application of the final masonry coat.

## Applying Gypsum Plaster and Sand Mixture on Plasterboard

If the interior wall has been constructed with plasterboard, the material I use to cover it is a mixture of one part gypsum plaster and three parts of finely graded sand, with enough water added to obtain a butter-at-room-temperature consistency.

A 3/8-inch thickness is optimum for the first or bed coat. To achieve this uniformly across the entire wall, "grounds" are first installed. In older structures 3/8-inch-thick wood strips were nailed over the lath or core along the bottom and top of the wall, and around the sides of rough openings for doorways and the like. They provided surfaces for the ends of the screeding board during the application of the bed coat and were left in the wall to be hidden later by the trim. The modern practices of omitting trim between ceiling and wall joints and using narrower baseboards, etc., have necessitated alteration of this arrangement.

I have found that the following arrangement is satisfactory.

I gather scraps of 3/8-inch sheetrock or plasterboard which are several inches wide and roughly 6 inches long. I tack them on top of the plasterboard along the bottom of the wall every 4 feet or so, then tack additional scraps in corresponding positions halfway up and at the top of the wall. These will serve as my grounds during screeding. I will remove them as soon as they have served their function and will fill the area they occupy.

For each square foot of surface to be covered, I will need approximately two pounds of gypsum plaster and six pounds of sand. A helper is essential since large amounts of material will have to be mixed and supplied continuously. The entire wall should be finished at one time since blending joints which have already hardened on a partially completed wall will require additional work. (If for any reason the wall is only partially finished before work is stopped, the edges of the material on the wall should be sloped to the plasterboard and left rough and irregular to obtain maximum adherence on the subsequent application.)

I thoroughly dry-mix the gypsum plaster and sand in the wheelbarrow and push the mixture toward the handle end. I then place water in the opposite end and draw the dry mix into the water a little at a time, using the mixing hoe. I continue to add water until the mixture has the consistency of butter at room temperature.

I stroke the surface of the mixture with a pointed trowel and depress it gently. If the mixture pulls apart instead of leaving a smooth unbroken swath, I add more water. If the mixture sags and doesn't retain its shape, I add more plaster and sand, sprinkling them in and mixing thoroughly.

I place a portion of the batch on the hawk, using the pointed trowel, and leave the trowel in the wheelbarrow. The amount should be what I can comfortably carry. I transfer the mixture from the hawk to the plasterboard with the rectangular trowel by sliding the trowel into the mixture along the surface of the hawk, then lifting the trowel. The side of the trowel should be tilted up toward the operator at a shallow angle while the nearest side of the hawk should be tilted down at a shallow angle. In the same movement and starting at the bottom of the wall, I lay the mixture against the plasterboard. The trowel is open to about a 30-degree angle. In laying the mixture against the wall with the trowel in this position, I depress the bottom side of the trowel to a point which I estimate to be 3/8 inch from the wall so that as I begin the stroke I will leave behind 3/8 inch of the mixture. I begin with an

upward stroke, pushing the mixture against the plasterboard with gentle, even pressure to maintain the same depth of deposit throughout. (If portions of the swath vary excessively in height, I depress the high spots by reversing the angle of the trowel and, using light pressure, bringing it back across the swath.) I apply the mixture until I have filled the area between four grounds, roughly 16 square feet. The main objective during placement of the mixture is to obtain at least 3/8-inch thickness throughout, and I am not particularly interested in the appearance of the surface although I remove obvious high spots and fill obvious depressions as I go along.

To screed the area, I place a straight 1 x 3 on edge, its ends on the grounds, and slide it back and forth on a slight diagonal, working from the bottom up. My strokes are short. As excess mixture accumulates on the wide side of the 1 x 3, I use it to fill depressions (which are apparent as gaps between the front edge of the 1 x 3 and the mixture) or return it to the wheelbarrow. If more than light pressure is necessary during screeding, the original mix is too thick and I must later add water and remix. For the moment, I spray water over the surface being screeded. I do not screed the edges of the applied mixture but leave them irregular to receive additional material.

I remove each ground surrounded by screeded material and fill the hole left while the mixture is still wet but firm.

Where necessary, I screed with only one end of the 1 x 3 placed on a ground and maintain the position of the other end by eye. Since the farthest point between grounds is only 4 feet, this will not be difficult. Later, surfaces already screeded and firm will be much closer and will provide an additional reference.

I continue to apply the mixture in batches, screeding intermittently while the surface is pliant and the material below partially stiff.

The amount of time it will take to apply the mixture and screed will of course vary with the skill of the worker. It is therefore a good practice to check screeded surfaces from time to time by troweling with the wooden trowel or darby. If the surface of the mixture is pliant and the material below it firm enough to prevent shift, troweling should be continued. The trowel is held flat and moved in wide circular patterns using light pressure. If the surface is gritty and requires more than light pressure to shift it, I have waited too long. I dampen it to make it more pliant and continue troweling. If some of the mixture remains on the trowel or if more than the surface shifts, I am premature.

I allow the bed coat to set for thirty-six hours or so before applying the finish coat.

## Applying the Final Plaster Coat

Whether the bed coat is Structolite or a mixture of gypsum plaster and sand and whether it covers a large patch or an entire wall, the material used for the final coat is a mixture of plaster and lime. It is a film with an average thickness of 1/8 inch and is held by suction.

To prepare the mixture, lime is first "slaked." A container is filled with water. The lime is sifted into the water and allowed to settle to the bottom. At least a few inches of water should completely cover the lime. Sprinkling in the lime insures that all particles come into contact with the water and avoids the formation of lumps. The lime is allowed to sit undisturbed for at least twenty-four hours. The slaked lime is now available for use as needed. It will remain stable for weeks if kept under water.

Two types of plaster may be mixed with lime. One, called gauging plaster, is finely ground and creates a dense smooth finish. The other, gypsum plaster, is less finely ground and if treated in exactly the same way as gauging plaster will result in a somewhat coarser though perfectly satisfactory finish. Gypsum plaster is slightly easier to work.

It should be kept in mind that the purpose of the final coat is to provide a smooth flat surface and *not* to fill depressions left in the undercoat. The optimum thickness of the plaster coat is about 1/8 inch and using it as a filler or trying to taper it down from high spots will lead to difficulties. Depressions should have been filled during application of the bed coat; if this hasn't been done, it's best to leave them untouched unless the variations are very marked. (If this is the case, I score the depression horizontally with the hook scraper, dampen, then fill with a mixture of gypsum plaster and sand.)

The most common proportion used for the final coat is two parts of slaked lime to five parts of plaster. However, this is not a cardinal rule and I have known plasterers to use equal parts of lime

and plaster. Personally, I get the best results by increasing the amount of lime in the two-to-five mixture. I suggest that before applying the final coat, you try several small batches with varying amounts of lime and use the mixture that works best. (This requires no extra effort since the mixture will be made in small batches anyway, even if the proportion is constant.)

The ordinary way in which a wall is viewed is from its front, and from this position the surface will appear flat. However, if the same wall is sighted along its entire length from one corner to another, it can be seen that the surface undulates. The undulations may be slight or quite pronounced, depending for the most part on how well the undercoat was applied. This is the reality of plaster walls; perfection should not be expected.

In addition to the tools already used, a corner trowel and a large brush for wetting the plaster finish will be needed for applying the final coat.

I remove a quart of slaked lime with the pointed trowel and place it on a 2-foot-square piece of Masonite or plywood. I slice through the lime, mash it down, and mix it thoroughly. This eliminates the hardness caused by packing and makes it more pliant. I push the lime out from the center of the scrap piece and form a ring of lime about 1-1/2 inches high and wide. The surface inside the ring is bare.

I place two quarts of gauging plaster in a plastic bucket.

I fill the circle with about 3/4 inch of water and begin to sprinkle the plaster into the water. Ideally, each particle of plaster should be surrounded by water, but since this is impractical, I sprinkle the plaster to avoid the formation of lumps. These will occur if an undispersed handful of plaster is dumped into the water. Wet plaster will then surround the clump of dry plaster and form a ball. (Putting water on dry plaster will also produce lumps.)

I remove plaster from the bucket until nearly all the water has been absorbed and then begin to mix the lime into the plaster by removing it from the inner portion of the ring. I add more water as needed, mixing continuously and sprinkling in more plaster until I have removed all of it from the bucket.

I want the consistency of heavy cream but do *not* want it so loose that water runs out the sides or collects anywhere. Ideally, I want the consistency to be at that point where the addition of any more water would cause it to lose its shape. If the mix is too loose and runs, I add a bit more lime and plaster. If it is too thick, I add a bit more water.

I use a pointed trowel for the mixing and act as quickly as I can.

I now have the option of introducing into the mixture a material called "retarder." This is a powder which will delay the time of hardening. (It can be introduced at any time during the mixing.) There are a variety of retarders on the market and the amount used depends on the brand. The working time of the mixture will probably be extended twice as long if retarder is added to it. I recommend its use, especially by those not experienced in plastering work.

I transfer the mixture to the hawk, using the pointed trowel. I transfer a portion from the hawk to the rectangular trowel by tilting the side of the hawk facing me down, pushing the side of the trowel into the mixture, and lifting. I want about two-thirds of the trowel to hold plaster. Most of it should be at the center and along the left side when the open end of the trowel handle is facing me. I begin at the bottom of the wall and transfer the plaster from the trowel to the bed coat with a long upward stroke. I am using light-to-moderate pressure and estimating the 1/8-inch thickness by eye.

Most mistakes will occur during this initial application of the plaster, and are usually due to incorrect positioning of the trowel during the stroke. The objective is to leave behind an even, continuous film 1/8 inch thick, which requires that the gap between the bottom side of the trowel and the bed coat also be 1/8 inch. If the trowel is held at too steep an angle, it will slice through the plaster during the stroke, make contact with the bed coat, and scrape away most of the plaster.

If the angle at which the trowel is held is too flat, it will deposit excess plaster.

The optimum angle at which to hold the trowel is about 30 degrees. It should be held with a steady, light, even pressure throughout the stroke.

After the initial upward stroke, I reverse the position of the trowel and return downward over the same swath to remove variations left by the first stroke and to even the surface. My pressure is a bit heavier on the second stroke than on the first.

On each succeeding application, I start a couple of inches in from where the last one ended. The end of the previous swath will have a thinner film since it was the last of the plaster on the trowel and the overlap builds this area up to the desired 1/8-inch thickness.

Intermittently, between applications of fresh plaster, I smooth the surface of the plaster already on the wall which has partially set up by wetting it with a brush and going over it with a wet trowel. I use moderate pressure and hold the trowel *almost* flat against the wall. If the trowel is held completely flat against the surface it will tend to pull up some of the plaster as a result of suction.

If the trowel is held at too wide an angle it will "chatter," making a series of connected jerks (rather than a smooth, even stroke) that will result in waviness unless the angle of the trowel is quickly reduced.

If the trowel "sticks" as it is being moved across the plaster, and the angle is correct, the plaster is a little too dry and should be moistened by flicking water across the area with the brush and troweled immediately.

The act of dampening the plaster surface and troweling is called glazing; its purpose is to pack the surface film and achieve a smooth, glasslike finish. It will also fill small nicks and gouges caused by accidental contacts of the trowel.

During application of the plaster there is a tendency to magnify every minor imperfection. A perfectly respectable job does not require a glass-perfect surface. While wetting and troweling can be continued for quite some time to produce increasingly better results, no more than three passes should be made over the same area, and one should ordinarily be sufficient. I have often seen students continue to glaze a wall that was already more than adequate only to end up with a worse surface.

I use the cornering trowel to apply plaster about 5 inches out from each corner and treat those areas the same way as the rest of the wall.

It is essential that the trowels be kept clean during the entire process, and this will require frequent removal of any hardened bits of plaster that accumulate on them. The film is very thin and even tiny particles of dried material will cause streaking and will interrupt the long and even strokes.

## Applying Joint Compound and Tape to Sheetrock

If sheetrock rather than plasterboard has been installed on the new wall (see pp. 105–108), then the seams between the sheets will be evident, as will be the indentions where nailheads or screws have been attached to the metal studs. There may also be gouges and small broken areas, particularly in the corners of each sheet, caused by dropping the ends rather than lowering them.

The material used to hide these areas is called "joint compound." Along seams between sheets and where the sheets intersect walls and ceilings, it is used in conjunction with a 2-inch-wide band of perforated paper called "tape." In indentions caused by screws or nails, the compound alone is used.

Tape, trowel and knife

Joint compound may be purchased ready-mixed or in a powder form which is mixed with water, allowed to rest for about twenty minutes, then used.

Personally, I much prefer the powder—which, incidentally, is cheaper. The prepared compound is more gummy, has a tendency to stick during a stroke, and responds less smoothly on the trowel than the powder. The powder is sold for use in three coats: two undercoats, gray in color, are first applied, and then a final coat, tan in color and called "topping."

### First Coat

If the ceiling has been covered with sheetrock, I want to work with my head a foot below it and I set

up scaffolding as described earlier. For working on walls, a 5-foot stepladder will be adequate.

The tools I will be using are a 16-inch trowel and a 3-inch semirigid Hyde spackling knife.

It is difficult to estimate the exact amount of joint compound that will be used on a job but one can make a rough guess of approximately 1/2 pound of compound for every 4 x 8 sheet. Once water is added, the mixture will remain usable for two or three days if kept covered with a cloth to prevent excessive evaporation. The cloth will also keep out foreign material, an essential precaution.

In a clean 2-gallon bucket, I mix the gray powdered compound with water, achieving a consistency of butter at room temperature. The volume of water is roughly equal to the volume of powder added. I mix a maximum of 5 pounds of compound at a time.

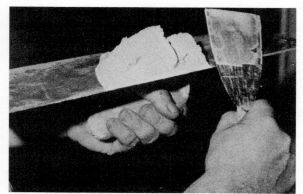

Compound deposited on trowel by knife

I transfer two fistfuls of compound to the right side of the trowel with the knife.

The long sides of the sheetrock (gyspum wallboard) have been tapered to form a V at their joints (the short sides are not tapered and will be dealt with later); this depression allows for the addition of the compound. However, the depth of this depression is only 1/8 inch or so directly at the joint and it diminishes after that so that 1-1/2 inches away from the joint it enters into the same plane as the rest of the sheet. When sealing these joints, only a very thin film of joint compound is to be applied at any one time. If thicker applications are made, the joint compound will take too long to dry—as much as a week in a cold and damp room—and will usually "alligator," reducing its adhesive strength significantly and making it look like dried mud. If an area requires filling to a depth

Joint compound laid over seam with trowel

of 5/16 inch or more, the sheetrock should be cut back to the studs and a new piece installed. (Depressions around nailheads or screws will rarely be larger than several inches in diameter and the use of joint compound alone will be satisfactory.)

I place the right side of the trowel against the bottom of the seam. The long side of the trowel is centered across the seam. Using moderate pressure to hold its edge against the sheetrock, I draw the trowel upward, holding it at about a 30-degree angle. I place additional compound on the trowel and continue up the seam in the same manner until I have filled the V along its entire length.

If the V is not completely filled with compound, I fill the bare areas with the knife, then pass the trowel over them to remove the excess. The ends of the trowel are resting beyond the depression and serve as depth guides.

If, when I first apply the compound, it does not retain its shape but sags, the mix is too loose and I add more compound.

If the compound pulls apart or lumps while troweling, either it has not been mixed thoroughly or not enough water has been added.

If, as the result of excessive hammering or mishandling, the joint has been chewed up, I first remove all loose material, then cover the broken areas with a thin coat of compound and allow it to dry before continuing to work on it. (If the room is hot and dry it will cure more quickly; if cold and damp, more slowly. Overnight is usually the minimum time to wait.) I am now ready to imbed the tape.

The tape I am going to apply is sold in various-length rolls, with or without perforations, and with an impression line at its center that will be used to fold it in half when it is placed in corners at intersecting walls. It is a treated paper to which the joint compound adheres well, and its presence diminishes the possibility of cracks developing.

I tear as many strips of tape as there are joints, making them an inch or two longer than the length of the joint. Starting at the top of a joint, I place an end of the tape on the compound so that it is centered over the seam, then, working downward, lay the tape against the compound using the knife to smooth it and to insure contact between the back of the tape and the surface of the compound. I fold the excess tape at the floor and tear it off.

I place a fistful of compound roughly centered on the right side of the trowel, hold the trowel at about a 15-degree angle and lay the compound over the tape at the top of the joint. Both ends of the trowel are beyond the V and I maintain moderate pressure as I draw the trowel down, leaving a film of compound over the top of the tape. I am not trying to cover the tape entirely at this point, only to insure an additional contact with compound along its back side, thereby imbedding it between two thin films. I continue in this manner until I have deposited a film of compound over the top of the tape along its entire length. I remove all excess compound that lies beyond the width of the V with the knife and deposit it on the trowel.

If, after troweling over the tape, any of it has lifted from the compound, I place additional compound on the spot and trowel it smooth.

If the film over the tape is uneven in thickness but none of it lies above the plane of the sheet, I leave it alone and fill the lower areas on the second coat.

Tape embedded, first coat

If the seam I am covering is on the ceiling, the procedure is the same except that while the tape is being imbedded into the compound, I hold its loose portion up with the trowel so that its weight doesn't pull the imbedded tape away from the compound.

Once the back of the tape has been completely imbedded in compound and the front partially covered so that no compound extends above the plane of the sheet, no further work should be done until the compound has dried. This will be evidenced by a change in color—from dark gray when wet to a light gray when dry.

Throughout the first application and those subsequent, fastidiousness is essential because of the thinness of the film. Bits of gypsum or hardened particles of compound must be kept from the working mix. This requires frequent scraping of the knife and trowel to discard hardened particles, covering the compound when it is not in use, and frequent washing of the tools with a sponge. If this seems too much of an effort, it should be weighed against the fact that its purpose is to avoid the need of sanding, a task that requires a great deal more work.

If there are any foreign particles in the mix (almost any particle will be visible, given the thinness of the film), the smooth long strokes that are essential for good results will be interrupted, and the continuous smoothness will be broken with raised lines at the point where the trowel is removed and the new stroke begun. Not only will the stroke have to be interrupted to remove the foreign particle, but the pressure used during the stroke will also have to be reestablished. (If the particle is not removed until after the compound has dried, the scratch it will leave as it is moved along within the compound will have to be filled.)

Whether screws or nails have been used to attach the sheetrock, the area around the heads should have been left indented. If the head of a screw or nail has been left above the surface, its position may only become apparent when compound is laid over the area and the click of the knife against the head is heard. The trowel and knife will have to be laid aside and the nailhead driven down with a hammer. This usually sprays compound over the person doing it. It is therefore good practice to make a quick check of all nail and screw placements and make certain that all nail or screw heads are below the surface of the sheet before filling is begun.

The compound used to fill the depressions around nail or screw heads should be thicker than that used for seams. If the surface of the compound pulls apart as the knife is drawn over it, the mixture should be thinned with water until this ceases.

I transfer the thicker compound to the side of the trowel by picking up a fistful with the knife, laying it on the trowel, then sliding the knife along the side of the trowel at its middle so that the compound tapers toward the center and is less likely to fall off. I remove a 1-inch strip of compound from the trowel by cutting into it with the knife, then sliding the knife forward and lifting. Using moderate pressure, I lay the compound over the indented area by

Nail indention

Filling nail indention, first stroke

Smoothing and removing excess compound, second stroke

holding the knife at about a 30-degree angle, then sliding it down and back in one stroke. I then raise the knife to about a 60-degree angle and scrape off the excess compound with a second stroke made at a right angle to the first. These are the only two strokes that should be made with each pass. The added depth of the mixture will cause significant contraction and three passes over the same area will usually be necessary.

Since each pass only takes a second or so, it is tempting to remain at the same indention and make certain it is filled. This should be avoided, since each needless second spent must be multiplied by every nail that has been used. It is significantly more effective to fill a particular spot on the next application, since it will be necessary to return to it two more times anyway, and the additional filling can then be done with no loss of time.

After filling over a dozen or so nailheads, the compound will accumulate toward the handle of the knife, making it awkward to use. I slide the knife

Paper folded in half for internal corner

against the side of the trowel to remove all of the compound, then pick it up again on the end of the knife. While filling indentions around nailheads, the amount of compound to carry on the knife should be around the size of a golf ball to begin with and, after practice, about twice as much.

I continue in this manner covering all nail and screw placement indentions with one coat. I will apply a second coat when they have dried.

The width of the tape is 2 inches. It is folded in half when used in the corners of intersecting sheetrock walls or in the joints between sheetrock walls and sheetrock ceilings. Joint compound of the same consistency as that used earlier with other seams is applied with the trowel to both surfaces in the corner. The width of each band should be a minimum of 1-1/4 inches. I tear a piece of folded tape to the length needed, then, starting at the ceiling, lay it on the compound, its creased center in the corner. I hold the top of the tape with a finger to keep it from moving, then, using moderate pressure, I flatten each side of the tape against the compound by drawing the knife held at a 30-degree angle over it. Excess compound is removed by placing one side of the knife in the corner, the other side against the surface of the sheetrock, and sliding the knife down with moderate pressure.

Unlike the thickness of the compound placed in the tapered joints, which is flush with the sheet, the tape and compound in the corners lie above the plane of the sheet. The thickness of tape and compound together should be about 1/16 inch.

## Second Coat

After the first coat has dried, the compound on the seams will be slightly below the surface of the sheets or, at most, flush with it. There may also be indentions not completely filled on the first application or resulting from substantial contraction because a large amount of compound was used. This is normal. If any compound that is higher than the sheet has inadvertently been allowed to dry, it should now be removed with emery paper on the orbital sander and the area wiped clean.

Any application of additional compound will raise the seam above the plane of the sheet. This is kept to a minimum and made less apparent by "feathering." In feathering, the compound is gradually thinned from its thickest point at the center of

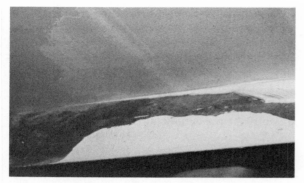

Second coat of joint compound over seam

the joint to its outer sides which will then blend into the sheet. Theoretically, this is an impossibility, since any additional compound will be above the sheet, but in practice the tapering of its sides can be so finely blended into the surface of the sheet that a coat of paint will hide it completely.

The following technique is standard. I mix the compound (gray undercoat) for the second coat to a consistency slightly thinner than butter at room temperature. (It requires less effort to trowel it.) I place a fistful of compound on the right side of the trowel and around the center. I start at the top of the seam. Holding the trowel at about a 45-degree angle and, maintaining moderate pressure, I draw the trowel down the seam until most of the compound is deposited on it.

I return to the top of the seam, hold the trowel at about a 60-degree angle and, using a bit more pressure than on the first stroke, draw the trowel down over the compound. The increased angle and pressure cause the compound to flatten into a band that lies 3 or 4 inches on each side of the seam. The objective of the first stroke is to place the compound on the seam in position for the second stroke, which will fill indentions and spread the compound into a band beyond the 3-inch width of the V. In addition, the second stroke should succeed in covering at least 90 percent of the tape. If I haven't succeeded in covering the tape completely in these two strokes, I leave the compound as is and complete the job on the third (final) application.

If correctional strokes are attempted while the compound is still wet, the result will almost invariably be worse than if it were left alone. One long, smooth, evenly pressured stroke should be the end of the second-coat application for the segment

over which it is made. If the result is pretty bad, fresh compound should be placed on the trowel and the stroke repeated with slightly heavier pressure. Trying to smooth out smudged or uneven areas with the bare trowel should be avoided.

The compound, which now extends in a band about 6 or 8 inches wide, will have irregular sides. In some places they may blend into the surface of the sheet, while in others they may form a raised line. These raised portions along the outer sides should not be thicker than a single layer of film and in those places where they are, the excess should be skimmed with the knife and removed.

I continue the second coat along the entire seam, starting several inches back from where I ended the previous stroke. A raised line will often occur at this overlap. I do not attempt removal of the raised line immediately, since any effort will most likely disturb the compound adjacent to it and create a worse condition. Instead, I wait until the compound has partially firmed, then remove the raised line with the knife.

As experience is gained in using the compound, it will be easier to maintain the same pressure along each entire stroke and the height of the overlap will gradually diminish. It will also become possible to remove the line with another stroke of compound once dexterity with the trowel has been achieved. However, until real familiarity is obtained, the best course is to leave the overlap alone after the smoothing stroke has been completed.

To apply the second coat over folded tape in a corner, I place compound an inch or so thick along the entire right side of the trowel. I hold the trowel in a vertical position and lay the right side in the corner. The left side of the trowel is open to about a 45-degree angle. (The amount of angle depends on the amount of compound on the trowel—I want only a small part of the compound to be deposited.)

I begin a horizontal stroke out from the corner, using light pressure, which I increase gradually while simultaneously opening the trowel so that at the completion of the stroke it is at a right angle to the wall and no compound is being deposited. The length of this lateral stroke is between 4 and 6 inches and its objective is to deposit a film which tapers from a high point in the corner and blends into the sheet 4 to 6 inches away.

Since a trowel is 16 inches long, the first pass allows me to cover (at most) 16 inches of the left side of the corner. I continue down the left side of the corner in a series of horizontal strokes, overlapping each about an inch or two until I have covered the entire left side. I apply enough compound on each stroke to cover at least 90 percent of the paper.

Unless each stroke is applied with equal pressure, an overlap line will occur—the greater the difference in pressure, the higher the line. If one feels comfortable with the trowel, these overlap lines can be removed by centering the trowel over them and stroking outward horizontally with light-to-moderate pressure.

If this creates additional lines at the top and bottom of the trowel, no further troweling should be done. After the compound has firmed (I wait twenty minutes or so) the overlap lines can be smoothed by light scraping with the edge of the knife.

The right side of the corner is covered by placing an inch-thick band of compound along the left side of the trowel and repeating the series of lateral strokes. (The top edge of the left side of the trowel must be clean or compound will press into the compound already applied and mar it as the trowel is laid in the corner). If marring does occur along the center of the corner, I wait for the compound to firm a bit, then remove any compound that lies above the surrounding surface, leaving the spots created to be filled by the final coat.

If after the left side of the corner has been covered difficulty is encountered in placing the trowel on the right side, both hands should be used to steady the trowel during initial placement.

If most of the paper remains visible after a stroke, I am applying too much pressure at the beginning of the stroke.

If the width of the deposit after each stroke is not 4 to 6 inches, I am opening the trowel too quickly.

The amount of compound deposited on each stroke should be just enough to hide the paper. If thicker amounts are being left, I am holding the trowel at too flat an angle or my initial pressure is too light.

I allow the second coat to dry (at least overnight) before applying the third or final coat.

## Final Coat

I mix the tan topping to a consistency of butter that is barely able to retain its shape in room temperature—it should not be so loose that it slides off the trowel or permits water to accumulate within it.

I place half a fistful of compound on the right side of the trowel and around the center. I position one end of the trowel's right side on the center of the seam and the other end on bare sheetrock. I draw the trowel at a 60-degree angle toward me with moderate pressure and continue the stroke for as long as my arm will reach. This will deposit the topping in a band roughly 8 inches wide from the center of the seam. I repeat this stroke on the opposite side of the seam, overlapping the center of the seam by an inch or so.

The purpose of these two strokes is to fill all remaining indentions and nicks, etc., as well as the coarser surface of the undercoat and to complete and broaden the tapers that extend from the center of the seam. Since the tapers have already been formed by the previous applications, I simply follow them outward until the outer ends of the trowel are in contact with the bare surface of the sheetrock so that the compound deposited at that point will blend into its surface.

The final coat requires the least amount of compound and I therefore carry smaller amounts on the trowel. The steeper angle of the trowel causes smaller amounts to be deposited.

One complete stroke of maximum length delivered with moderate pressure should complete each segment. If small areas which need to be touched up remain, I wait until the topping has firmed, then remove whatever lies above the surface; when the topping has completely dried, I fill any indentions.

The third coat of topping is applied in corners in exactly the same manner as was the second coat; it is also touched up in the same way. I use compound on my forefinger to fill or smooth any troublesome spot along the center of a corner.

When the topping has dried completely, ordinarily after a day, I sand any high spots I may have missed with the orbital sander and emery paper. Little if any sanding should be necessary.

## How to Butt the Sides Smoothly

Sheetrock is not manufactured with a taper on its 4-foot sides. Since the surface where the 4-foot sides butt is in the same plane as the rest of the sheet, the addition of tape and compound over the seam will place its height above the surrounding area, even on the first coat. Moreover, the 4-foot ends are not covered with paper as are the longer sides, and with only slight abuse in handling and installation, gypsum falls out. Ordinary nailing along these ends also tends to create a chewed-up seam, and these are the most difficult to cover satisfactorily.

To mask these seams, I first remove all loose material and nail any loose fragments. Compound will not "glue" chewed-up material together, and any piece that cannot be secured by nailing should be removed before the compound is applied.

I prepare a thicker than ordinary consistency of undercoat and fill the holes along the seam, depositing a maximum thickness of 1/8 inch on each application. If necessary, I make several applications (waiting for the previous ones to dry) to fill the holes. In those areas which have diameters equivalent to indentions around nailheads, I deposit 3/16 inch or so on each application. My objective is to fill and even out the chewed-up areas of the joint without rising above the plane of the sheet (I add the compound in layers to avoid alligatoring), leaving a flat bed for the tape. (I repair the joints during intervals in the normal course of work.)

After the compound used for preliminary filling has dried, I prepare a mixture of gray undercoat of butter-at-room-temperature consistency. I apply the undercoat over the seams and imbed the tape into it in the same manner as at the tapered seams. I cover the tape with a light coat of compound. The entire band of compound should be about 3 inches wide and, allowing for the thickness of the paper and the two layers of compound, one below and one above the tape, its total thickness should be 1/16 inch or less. I allow the first coat to dry.

The consistency of the second coat should be looser than the first, though not as loose as the topping. I place a fistful of compound on the right side of the trowel and around its center. I position the inner edge of the compound about 4 inches from the center of the seam and, applying moderate pressure at a 45-degree angle, draw the trowel along the left side of the seam. The compound is flattened into a band 6 to 8 inches wide measured from its edge to the center of the seam. The moderate pressure should result in a thickness sufficient to cover most of the paper. Since I have had one end of the trowel on bare sheetrock and

the other end on the previously applied tape and compound, a wide taper will result, its high point on the seam, its low point along the bare sheetrock. I position the compound on the left side of the trowel and repeat the stroke on the opposite side of the seam. I treat raised overlap lines, indentions, nicks, etc., in the same manner as I treated them during application of the second coat along the seams at the tapered sides.

The final coat is also applied in exactly the same manner, except that the coat here will be much wider.

In general, the wider the taper, the better the result will look since the difference in height between the center of the seam and its outer sides will have been distributed over a wider area. This width can be as much as 16 inches—the length of the trowel—but the difference in appearance between a joint that has been tapered over 16 inches rather than 10 inches is so minimal as to be hardly worth the additional effort. However, due to the lack of a depression on the 4-foot sides of sheetrock, a wide band of compound is a necessity.

## Additional Information

Occasionally a bubble will form under the tape where insufficient contact has been made with the bed of compound. Of course this should have been corrected immediately by lifting the paper and applying fresh compound under it, but such errors sometimes go unnoticed until the compound has dried. To remove a bubble, I cut out all the loose tape with a sheetrock knife and fill the area as I would an indention around a nailhead.

A professional should tape and apply joint compound to a 1200-square-foot "sheetrock" house in three days; I have seen a man working on stilts do it in two.

When one begins to use joint compound, it is important to understand that the flat wall or ceiling on which it is being applied must be considered a tool. The surface of the sheetrock is a frame of reference throughout the process, whether a knife or trowel is being used. The initial tendency to concentrate solely on moving the compound must give way to moving the compound while *feeling the flat surface below it*. It is the flat surface which permits the trowel to be held with steady pressure throughout the stroke, and steady pressure is essential if one is to avoid waviness.

The optimum angle of the trowel during the smoothing stroke is not an absolute and will vary with the consistency of the joint compound. When first beginning, students find it helpful to mix joint compound to the same consistency each time and to maintain the consistency through the intermittent addition of water and remixing. (Compound which has been placed on the wall and then removed as excess will lose some of its water in the process and become thicker.) Once the consistency is constant, it will be easier to determine the optimum angle to hold the trowel for that specific consistency.

Joint compound works well in a relatively wide range of consistencies. Each person has a different "touch" in the sense that each will apply it naturally with varying degrees of pressure. It is well worth the time for each person to experiment on a seam in order to find the consistency and trowel angle which works easiest and best.

As greater experience is achieved, the feel of the compound as it is transferred from the knife to the trowel and from the trowel to the sheetrock will cause the worker to adjust the trowel to the proper angle. Here again, to achieve this end, keeping the proportion of water to compound constant is helpful.

Nor can I overemphasize the importance of keeping the compound meticulously clean. This requires very little effort, especially when compared to the time and effort that will have to be spent in dealing with foreign matter in the compound.

Among the tempting rationales that should be resisted are: "It doesn't matter, I can always sand it later"; "If I lay a thick covering of compound here, it will save me the job of coming back to it"; "If I go over the seam now while it is still wet, I can correct what I didn't do on the first stroke"; "If I smooth the raised overlap line now, it will mean less sanding later. . . ." An incorrect technique repeated a great many times results in an inordinate amount of wasted time and effort.

## Installing Ceramic Tile (General Information)

Ceramic tile is one of the oldest and most universally used construction materials. Fashioned from baked clay, it is extraordinarily durable. (The tiles placed in the Baths of Caracalla in Rome are still intact after several centuries of exposure.) In the United States, tile is a rarity in structures more than one hundred years old. Introduced here from Europe at that time, its use has been limited for the most part to bathrooms and kitchens. (While in Central and South America tiles are often used as ceiling coverings, we install plaster and simulated plaster finishes, creating a permanent maintenance problem that benefits only the paint industry.)

Ceramic tile has seen limited use in the United States because of the unnecessarily high costs that have been charged for its purchase and installation. With the introduction of organic adhesives (Mastic), a totally inexperienced person can now install tile much more quickly than a professional using masonry methods. As a result, the cost of installation has been dramatically reduced. The cost of the tiles, however, remains an anomaly, since the retail price for a square foot of the same tile would be 60¢ in the United States while less

6-inch quarry-tile floor

Vitreous mosaic-tile floor

Glazed 6-inch quarry-tile floor

than 5¢ in Mexico. As long as this excessive materials cost continues, it will limit the expanded use of tile. This is particularly regrettable since the increased use of tile would eliminate the use of many inferior building materials and substantially reduce the cosmetic-maintenance bill Americans pay every year.

Tiles are manufactured from a variety of clays and in a variety of finishes depending upon their use. On bathroom walls, for example, glazed non-vitreous tile is primarily used. The face of the tile is coated with a "glaze" and then baked in a kiln to create a permanent, fairly impenetrable surface. Colors applied to the tile prior to baking are also made permanent by the glazing process.

Wall tiles are manufactured in a variety of shapes and sizes. The most common is a square 4-1/4 inches on each side and 3/16 to 1/4 inch thick. The tile usually has two small extensions on opposite sides so that when the tile is butted to others, a gap between them will be created which will later be filled by "grout" (a finely ground cement). The conservatism of the tile industry is again evidenced by its manufacture of tiles that still require the use of grout. Certainly some type of tongue-and-groove arrangement could be developed that, when used with a sealer liquid, could create a much better installation.

On bathroom floors, vitreous mosaic tile, either clay or porcelain, is used most often. The clay used in floor tiles has smaller particles than that used in wall tiles, creating a denser tile. Floor tiles are also fired at a higher temperature than wall tiles but they are not ordinarily glazed. Color is obtained through the use of dyes. Like porcelain, the color goes through the entire tile so that even after a great deal of use, its integrity remains.

The porcelain tile is even denser than the clay (lowering its absorption rate), and its hexagonal shape has become the trademark of old bathroom floors.

Another type of floor tile which has come into widespread use in kitchens, restaurants, etc., is called quarry tile (the name may be misleading since the tiles are not cut from a quarry). Its thickness varies between 3/8 and 3/4 inch and it is manufactured in a variety of shapes, most commonly square or hexagonal. It may or may not have coloring other than its natural tone, wears very well even with heavy traffic, and has a low water-absorbency rate.

Packinghouse tiles are also used on floors, although for the most part their use has been limited to industrial installations where heavy loads are anticipated. They have begun to be used residentially for outdoor terraces and similar construction. Their colors vary only with the color of the clay used, and they are between 1-1/4 and 1-1/2 inches thick.

Whatever the type, there are two methods of installing ceramic tile: masonry or Mastic. I will detail both.

The surface on which the tile is to be installed is called backing; it should be flat or its irregularities will cause an irregular tile surface, poor adhesion, and the cracking of the more uneven tiles. Backing can be provided by exterior or marine plywood, tempered Masonite, sheetrock, flexboard (sheet asbestos), plaster, or concrete. The Mastic will adhere well to paint over plaster—provided, of course, that the bond between the paint and plaster is secure and that the plaster itself is well bonded.

In many older structures where linoleum and underlayment have been placed on a concrete floor, the adherence may still be sufficiently strong, despite appearances, to install quarry tile directly over the linoleum with good results.

The use of GIS (good on one side) plywood as an underlayment for either wall or floor tile will provide the necessary flat surface. Plywood is easy to cut and fit, needs no additional work at the joints, and is relatively stable. However, it is expensive and is sometimes manufactured with inferior glues which allow the plies to separate when exposed to moisture. If plywood is to be used beneath bathroom floor tile, only marine plywood should be purchased since the regular presence of water on the floor would tend to rot other grades of plywood. Exterior plywood holds up well in other areas. Interior plywood, which is cheapest, does not.

Tempered Masonite reacts better to moisture than plywood but is more flexible. If a floor or wall is very irregular, it will not be nearly as good in producing a stiff unyielding surface and will require evening the surface (furring) before installation to reduce the spans.

Flexboard, the most expensive backing, is by far the best material since it is the most impervious to moisture. However, it is difficult to install, since it is brittle and will easily crack under stress unless supported continuously. It is also hard to nail; sheets thicker than 3/16 inch require the drilling of pilot holes before nailing. Flexboard should be cut to fit with a masonry blade in a power saw—and since this produces asbestos dust, it must be done outdoors.

Sheetrock of course can be used only as backing on walls (or ceilings). It is far cheaper than any of the other materials and is the easiest to work with. On the negative side, its seams (no tape necessary if used for backing) and nail holes will have to be filled and it will deteriorate when subjected to moisture.

Tiles installed with Mastic on old plaster wall

## Installing Tile Directly on Plaster Wall

The glazed nonvitreous tiles in the photograph are Mexican. Like a great many tiles, they are *not* uniform in size. This means that all the larger tiles will have to be cut down to the size of the smallest (which is quite an undertaking) or that the spaces allowed between the tiles will have to be made larger. The latter is the obvious choice.

Having only a limited number of these tiles, the owners decide to economize by extending the tile partially below the butcher block rather than to the floor.

Using a 4-foot level, I tack a straight piece of 1 x 3 horizontally across the position of the bottoms of the last row of tiles. This is necessary to keep the tiles from slipping down before they have fully adhered.

Two types of Mastic are available, one for walls and one for floors. Each is available in 1-gallon containers and each gallon should be sufficient to cover about 125 square feet. During use, the lid should be kept on the container since the solvent will evaporate rapidly and leave the mixture too thick and gummy to use. It is also highly flammable.

In order to spread the Mastic uniformly and to avoid lumps or thinly covered areas, I use a cheap notched trowel and apply moderate pressure against the wall as I spread the Mastic. Because of the high volatility of the solvent, I will coat an area that I can place tile on within five minutes.

I remove all the tiles I will use from their containers and select and stack the smallest ones beside me. I cut small scraps (1 inch square or so) of 1/4-inch plywood to use as spacers between the tiles. Given the variations in tile size, 1/4 inch is the smallest gap I will need to avoid trimming the larger tiles. I mark the center of the area I will cover on the 1 x 3 cleat. I apply the Mastic in that area and press the first tile against the Mastic, its bottom resting on the cleat and one side placed 1/8 inch away from the center mark. I place a 1/4-inch spacer against the centered side and butt another tile to it, its bottom side also resting on the cleat. I complete the bottom row of tiles in the same manner, using only the smallest tiles.

I trowel on another swath of Mastic above the first row and lay the second row (course), using two 1/4-inch spacers between the bottom of the second course of tiles and the top of the first. At each end of the row, I use the smallest tiles.

I align the tiles of the second course vertically by splitting their excess width between gaps on each side. I do this by eye.

I begin the third course with a small tile at each end (with 1/4 inch spacers under them) and pop a line above the *tops* of the tiles. I lay the tops of the tiles of the third course along the chalk line. 1/4-inch spacers will be too thick for the larger tiles and I use thinner scraps made of folded cardboard.

In this same manner, I complete the entire area. I keep the tiles in vertical alignment by eye, shifting the wider ones so that their excess width lies in the gaps for grout. I maintain horizontal alignment by alternately spacing the tiles on 1/4-inch scraps, then aligning their tops on the next course by popping a line between shorter tiles at each end.

I allow the tile to set up overnight. I remove the spacers the next day.

I am now ready to apply the grout. It is ordinarily a white powder. Powdered pigments can be mixed into the grout to obtain a variety of colors. Most paint or hardware stores carry both grout and pigments in stock and if a particular color is desired, the amount of pigment to be used in the mixture will be specified. (They dry to a slightly lighter shade than the mixture when wet.)

A premixed grout with a vinyl additive is also available. This grout is slightly superior to the powdered grout and much more expensive. Unless I anticipate a good deal of water exposure, I use the cheaper powder. In this instance I used the vinyl grout at the insistence of the owner. I mixed a tan pigment into the grout by stirring them together in a plastic bucket.

Using a 3-inch spackling knife, I apply the grout to the face of the pictured rubber float, two fistfuls at a time. I pass the float over the surface of the tiles with moderate pressure. Using the corners and sides of the float, I push grout on the surface of the tiles into the gaps between them and press it down. I remain in the area and completely fill all the gaps between tiles before moving on to a new one.

After fifteen minutes, I return to the area where I first applied the grout and wash it with a large sponge, rinsing it often to remove the excess.

I repeat this an hour later. The next day a film of dried grout will remain on the surface of the tiles. It will come off easily by wiping with a cloth.

Rubber float and sponge

Tiles installed on plywood backing

## Cutting Tile

The tiles in the photo have been installed on a 3/4-inch plywood backing. The plaster wall behind the backing was in such bad condition that it would have taken a lot longer to repair the wall than simply to place plywood over it. The core of the wall is gypsum block, and ordinary #10 common nails driven into it hold the plywood securely. The 3/4-inch thick backing is unnecessary; in this case I used it because scraps were available. 3/8-inch or 1/4-inch plywood would be adequate.

The pictured tile cutter costs under $12. If more than 100 square feet of tile is to be installed, the tool will pay for itself in time saved. Otherwise an ordinary glass cutter and straightedge will be more economical. The tile cutter is essentially a glass cutter mounted on an arm which slides on a rigid bar. The metal plate on the right is adjusted by loosening a wing nut and serves as a fence when

Tile to be scored and cut on tile cutter

more than one tile is to be cut to the same dimension.

To cut a tile, the following sequence is recommended:

1. Place a pencil mark on the edge of the tile face at the desired cut. The mark can be on either side and needn't be continued across the tile.

2. Lift the cutter's handle and slide it completely back.

3. Place the tile on the rubber bed with the pencil mark aligned at the V on the ruled scale. (If more than one tile is to be cut to the same dimension, loosen the wing nut and slide the fence so that it butts the tile, then tighten the wing nut and place all successive tiles at the fence.)

4. Pull up the handle so that the cutting wheel lies on the mark and hold the tile stationary with the left hand.

5. With only enough force to create a scratching sound, push the handle forward across the face of the tile to score it. If no scratching sound is heard, try again with more downward pressure. If the tile still isn't scored, as evidenced by the scratching sound (the line will also be visible), the cutting wheel is probably dull and should be replaced.

6. Lower the handle, slide it back so that the butterfly-shaped piece behind the wheel is centered over the tile, then raise and swing the handle quickly so that the butterfly strikes the tile, breaking it.

A metal bar directly under the scored line assists in the impact action. If the tile doesn't break, examine the scored line on its face. It needn't or shouldn't be deep, but if it is intermittent, it should

be rescored. If it still doesn't break after rescoring, place the tile in the left hand and tap on its back with a hammer which is centered over the scored line. Increase the force of the taps until the tile breaks. Occasionally a tile will break at an undesired place. Try to recut the pieces for use elsewhere, but such losses must be expected. On an average, 1 percent of the tile will be lost in this way.

If a glass cutter is being used, the tile is scored as if it were glass; it is then tapped on the back side with the hammer centered along the scored line (see p. 126 for glass cutting).

## Installing Tile on Bathroom Walls

The first step is to install the backing on which the tile will be mounted. Earlier in this chapter I discussed those materials suitable for use as tile backing on floors and walls. In the carpentry chapter I detail how this material is to be cut and installed. In bathrooms, a few additional details must be dealt with before the tiling is actually begun.

Tile installed around rough plumbing over bathtub

One is the area directly above the tub. An old and continuing practice involves the use of grout to fill the joint between the bottom of the wall tiles and the tub. This has led to a traditional eyesore since it usually crumbles, falls out, and stains. Despite the fact there is a lip on the tub which rises above the exposed finished surface, water is sloshed out through this deteriorated joint to cause rotting in the bathroom wall and floor and in the ceiling of the room below.

This can be avoided by the use of a product called tub mold, a narrow strip of chrome steel prebent to conform to the contour of the tub. It is available in different sizes and shapes to conform to each particular tub.

Before it is installed (over the backing), a heavy bead of butyl or silicone caulking is laid in the joint between the tub and backing. The metal molding has a thin extension at its top which is then nailed through the backing into "cats" (pieces of 2 x 4 installed horizontally between studs) previously installed around the tub during framing of the wall. (The molding should be held tightly against the caulking while being nailed.) Later, when the tile is installed, the bottom side of each tile will rest directly on top of the molding and hide the thin strip which has been nailed.) With the tub mold installed, there will be no discoloration, leaking, or any other problem at the joint.

Traditionally, the tile used in many bathrooms is installed only to a height of 5 feet and only in the tub area. The height was established partly in reference to the height of an average person but also as a means of reducing labor costs. Since average heights have gone up considerably and since labor costs have gone down with the introduction of Mastics, consideration should be given to completely covering the bathroom walls and floors with tile. Also, since savings in materials costs—especially in an area as small as a bathroom—are minimal, it is less expensive in the long run to tile completely if the cost and maintenance of substitute materials are taken into account. The maintenance of materials cheaper than tile will quickly eat up an initial savings, and any material as viable as tile will cost as much and probably more.

Before the wall tile is installed, one must choose the type of baseboard tile to be used. In general, most baseboard tiles have an interior radius at their bottom which is about 1/4 inch thick. This corresponds to the thickness of vitreous mosaic floor tile, but does not correspond to the dimension of the wall tile even though the baseboard tile may be obtained in the same colors. The use of the baseboard tiles may be eliminated completely by using pieces called coves. These have a square back and concave front, and each edge is the thickness of the tile to which it will butt, one thickness for the wall and another for the floor. A cove installation will include pieces for inside and outside corners at intersecting walls. The vertical joints at intersecting walls can be treated with the same coves stacked over the corner (laid end to end one on top of the other from floor to ceiling), and coves are available with concave or convex exteriors to suit interior or exterior corners.

Coves take longer to install than regular baseboard tiles. In addition, because each piece is relatively small, it is more difficult to align coves, especially when they extend from wall to wall and floor to ceiling. For these reasons, I do not recommend their use.

One will also have to decide how to treat the joint between the walls and ceiling. This can be done by simply continuing the tile to the ceiling and allowing for a grouted joint or, as I prefer, closing the joint with a strip of teak or similar hardwood suited for use in the presence of high humidity.

To install the tiles, I first pop a level chalk line on the bathroom walls at the height of the baseboard tiles I have selected. Most floors are uneven and I align the tops of the tiles with the chalk line (rather than their bottoms with the floor) so that I will begin the first course with a uniform level height. Instead of applying the Mastic to the wall, I apply it to the back of each baseboard tile, using a notched trowel so that the Mastic will not obscure the chalk line. I start with the corner baseboard tiles, those that have surface projections at a right angle that corresponds to the intersecting walls. I align the top of each tile with the chalk line and, if necessary, place a shim (a folded piece of cardboard) on the floor under the tile if a gap exists between it and the floor to keep it from sliding down until the mastic has set up. After installing all corner baseboard tiles, including those in any exterior corners, I begin to fill in between the installed tiles, aligning the top of each new tile with the chalk line. Baseboard tiles do not have built-in spacers and I install each by eye, leaving a gap between them (for later grouting)

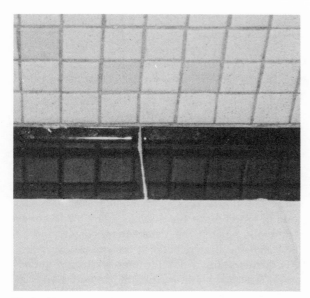

Typical baseboard tile

about the thickness of a paper match. I continue to fill the baseboard row until I am obliged to cut a tile to fit between a corner tile and one previously installed.

Since baseboard tile has a cove along its bottom, it is difficult to score completely with an ordinary tile cutter. It should be done in two steps—scoring along the flat surface, then over the coved portion. If the latter proves awkward, a glass cutter can be used to score the cove area. When scored baseboard tile is broken, it will often be irregular around the cove.

The irregularity can be removed by clamping the jaws of the tool pictured (called nippers) over the portion to be removed and squeezing the handles, clipping it off. (The nippers have "blips" on the inside of its handles to keep the jaws from shutting completely and deforming the cutting edges.) Nippers are modestly priced and will pay for themselves in labor saved. (They are essential for use with mosaic tiles but useless with quarry or packinghouse tiles.)

If using the cutter and nippers does not achieve the desired break, a more time-consuming but surer alternative is available.

I mark the back of the baseboard tile for cutting. I then place a masonry blade in the power saw and turn it upside down as shown. I raise and maintain the guard in an upright position by wedging a sliver of wood between the guard and inside the housing.

Nippers on cove of baseboard tile

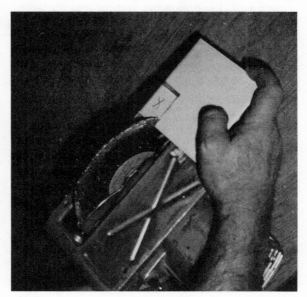

Tile being sawed with masonry blade on circular saw

**183**

While depressing the trigger with my left hand, I guide the tile through the blade with my right and cut through the cove. I then score the flat portion that remains with the tile cutter and break.

The gap between tiles to allow for grout should be 1/16 inch. Therefore, when cutting a tile to fit between two others, it should be 1/8 inch narrower than the distance between the two tiles already installed. Occasionally when tiles are broken there remains a ragged edge along the break that is greater than 1/16 inch but too small to remove with the nippers. When this occurs I remove the ragged edge by pressing the tile *lightly* against the side of the masonry blade, but caution must be exercised since masonry blades have little lateral strength and may shatter if the tile is pressed against them too strongly.

I finish installing each baseboard course by laying the cut pieces.

I am now ready to install the wall tile. I will work on one wall at a time and start in a corner. I pop a chalk line between the floor and ceiling that lies 4-3/8 inches in from the intersecting wall. I spread mastic on the backs of 4-1/4-by-4-1/4-inch wall tiles and lay them on the wall in a vertical row, the side farthest from the intersecting wall aligned with the chalk line. I have established the chalk line 1/8 inch greater than the dimension of the tile to allow for variations in the intersecting wall. This gap will later be covered by the tiles installed on the intersecting wall. I continue the vertical row for ten or twelve tiles.

I select a straight length of 1 x 3 (a few inches shorter than the floor to ceiling distance), place it vertically alongside the row of tiles in the corner and mark along its side the top of each tile in the vertical row. I will use these marks as a height reference at various points on all the walls and will shift later-placed tiles slightly to maintain rows at the same height as the tiles I have just installed.

I now spread Mastic on a 2-by-2-foot area of wall adjacent to the vertical row of tiles and press tiles into the Mastic. I lay them in horizontal rows, working outward from the intersecting wall, the first row on the baseboard tiles, then each succeeding row on top of the one previously installed. (It is more efficient to install tiles in a 2-foot patch than to shift position to fill a horizontal row all the way across the wall. No tiles should be extended beyond those installed on the row below in order to

avoid having to install a tile *between* two tiles already in position.

I remain in the same area and install tiles until the vertical row first installed extends to a point that is less than 4-1/4 inches from the ceiling. I mark the tops of the additional tiles on the side of the 1 x 3.

I now continue in the same manner and install tiles across the entire wall until the width of the gap between the last vertical row of installed tile and the opposite intersecting wall is less than the width of a tile. I use the spacer extensions on each tile to leave uniform gaps for grouting by simply butting each new tile to those previously installed. From time to time I place the 1 x 3 beside a tile to check its height against the established corresponding height of the tile installed at the corner. By doing this frequently and shifting tiles slightly if necessary, I maintain a uniform height. I maintain vertical alignment by eye.

While working, I keep eight or ten tiles stacked in my left hand. I clasp each along the outer edges with my right hand, lay the tile into the Mastic with moderate pressure, and slide it so that it butts against the tiles below and beside it. (The closer the tile is initially placed beside those previously installed the better, since the sliding motion should be kept to a minimum to maintain a uniform height of the Mastic.)

To complete the less-than-tile-width gap on the opposite intersecting wall, I need to cut a tile to complete each horizontal row. I measure the gap at the bottom, center, and top. Ordinarily it should not vary more than 1/8 inch. If this is the case, I set the fence on the tile cutter to cut a hair narrower than the smallest width I have measured, count the number of tiles I will need, cut them all at the same time and install them.

A gap still exists on the wall between the uppermost course of tiles and the ceiling. I nail a 1-inch-wide strip of 1/4-inch plywood on the wall and butting the ceiling. I now cut and install the last horizontal row of tile so that the upper sides of the tile lie 1/4 inch below the bottom side of the plywood. After grouting, I will nail a 1/4-by-1-1/2-inch strip of teak or other hardwood on top of the plywood band, its lower side covering the gap and the tops of the highest course of tile.

I am now ready to apply tile on the intersecting wall. I begin by popping a vertical chalk line 4-3/8 inches from the face of the previously installed tile at the corner. I install a vertical row of tiles, aligning the side farthest from the corner with the chalk line. I check the tiles' horizontal alignment intermittently with the marked 1 x 3 and shift as needed.

If after butting a tile to an intersecting tile, the side farthest from the corner will lie beyond the chalk line, I remove an equivalent amount from the side that lies in the corner (using the masonry blade and power saw). Occasionally the gap between tiles on intersecting walls will be greater than 1/16 inch but it will rarely be noticeable after filling with grout.

I install tiles on the remaining walls in the same manner. However, there are areas where special treatment will be necessary, such as under the wash basin where three pipes (two water lines 1/2 inch in diameter and a waste line 1-1/2 inches in diameter) emerge from the wall.

Tile is laid until the pipes interfere. If a pipe is going to intersect the outer edge of one or more tiles I mark the position of the pipe on the back side of each tile and cut out the part to be removed using the masonry blade and power saw. It is not necessary to cut a circular area which conforms to the shape of the pipe. Instead the outer dimension of the pipe should be squared for easier removal. An escutcheon plate will be placed over the pipe and will hide the gaps between the cut tile and the pipe's outer diameter. This technique will work in all situations except when the pipe lies entirely within one tile and does not extend to any of its sides.

Typical rough plumbing for basin

When the pipe lies entirely within a tile, I have two alternatives. First, I can mark the position of the pipe on the back of the tile. Using a 1/4-inch-diameter carbide-tipped bit in the variable-speed drill (set towards slower rpm), I bore a series of holes along the circumference of the circle, spacing the holes as close to one another as I can manage. I bore additional holes within the circle, removing as much material as I can. By boring from the back of the tile I reduce the possibility of damaging the glaze on its front. I then remove the remaining material within the circle by striking small pieces at an angle with the sharp end of an upholsterer's hammer, aiming each blow toward the center of the circle. (A felt-lined clamp can be purchased to hold the tile firmly while this is being done, reducing the chance of cracking the entire tile.)

An alternative method which is quicker but trickier to execute is to mark the position of the pipe in the form of a square on the back of the tile. The masonry blade and power saw are turned upside down and the tile is then lowered into the spinning blade along the marked lines until the blade emerges on the front of the tile and cuts out the area. The diameter of the blade will be much greater than the area to be removed and saw marks will be left on the back of the tile beyond the marked lines. They will be deepest near the area removed and shallowest toward the edges of the tile. (Masonry blades quickly shrink in diameter when used and in this instance the smaller the blade, the better the results.) The score marks will weaken the tile and additional Mastic should be used to install it. But given its location under the sink, it is not likely to be exposed to any shattering impact.

The pipes above the tub and at the toilet are dealt with in the same manner.

Whether tub mold is used or not, the tiles which lie above each corner of the tub will have to be cut in an arc to conform to the shape of the mold or the tub. I mark the position of the arc on the back of the tile, shaping the curve by eye. (A lengthier alternative is to cut a piece of paper to the size of a tile, place it at the corner of the tub, then scissor out the arc. The paper is then laid on the tile and the arc traced on its back.) Once again, I turn the power saw and masonry blade upside down and move the tile into the blade until the blade reaches the marked line of the arc. (The blade is perpendicular to the arc, cutting through the portion to be discarded.) This removes a width within the arc of about 1/8 inch. I make a series of parallel cuts adjacent to the first, each cut ending at another point along the arc. Thin lengths of tile will still be attached in the areas between cuts. I remove these with the nippers, cutting off successive small lengths to avoid the stress that might break the tile if bigger bites were taken. I trim and smooth the ragged edges along the arc by gently passing the arc over the spinning blade. Only very slight resistance should be felt against this lateral movement.

It is common practice to recess a number of fixtures into the bathroom walls. These usually include a toilet-paper holder, a soap and toothbrush holder above the basin, a soap holder with grab bar above the tub, and a medicine chest. These fixtures, made of ceramic or metal, require a rough opening. Their sizes vary.

A typical r.o. for a medicine chest is 14 by 18 inches. (The depth will vary. Standard hollow-wall framing with 2 x 4s will always offer adequate space. In a solid wall a 4-inch chest is recessed 2-1/2 inches into the wall while the remaining 1-1/2-inches is allowed to extend past its plane.) The hole for the r.o. should be cut before the tile is installed. A vertical piece of 2 x 4 should be placed on each side of the r.o. so that the medicine chest can be secured to it by placing screws in the predrilled holes along its sides. The tiles are then laid to the edge of the r.o. It is not necessary to be exact—a 1/4-inch gap between the tiles and edges of the r.o. is acceptable. (The tiles should not extend *into* the r.o. at any point.) The medicine chest has a flange that will fit over the gap on the perimeter of the r.o.

A typical r.o. for a metal toilet-paper holder is 5-1/4 inches square. (It is 2-1/2 inches deep.) If the wall is hollow, the hole is cut first and the tiles then installed to within 1/8 inch of its edges, since the lip of the holder is narrow. After the tile is in place and grouted, the holder is then installed by use of a metal bracket which is attached to the back of the holder with two machine screws. The bracket is larger than the opening and must be inserted into the r.o. on a diagonal, first one end, then the other. The screws are then tightened, drawing the bracket against the back of the wall while tightening the lip against the tiles. (If the bracket isn't available, a wooden cat should be placed in position during

framing the wall to receive two wood screws placed through the predrilled holes in the face of the holder.)

If the wall is hollow and the fixture ceramic, the fixture may be attached directly on top of the backing, using Mastic. The tile is then cut to fit around the fixture, allowing a gap for grout.

A more secure installation (for use, for example, with a ceramic soap holder and grab bar) can be achieved by cutting a hole in the backing the size of the r.o. and filling the hole with newspaper until it is wedged securely. (A depth of 1-1/2 inches or so should be left between the newspaper and the wall.) I mix a fistful of plaster of Paris, lay it on the back of the fixture, then immediately place the fixture into the opening and press firmly against the wall. It should be kept in that position *without movement* for at least a minute and, if possible, longer. Care should be taken *not to shift the fixture as the pressure is eased.* The paper backing will cause the plaster to spread on the rear of the wall while it is also bonding to the back of the fixture. This forms a large key which holds the fixture after drying. Any excess plaster squeezed out around the lip of the fixture is scraped away carefully without moving the fixture. (This should be done within five minutes of installation, while the plaster is still a bit plastic.) In making this type of installation it is preferable to buy ceramic fixtures in which there are holes in the back to create a more secure bond with the plaster of Paris.

With the fixture in place, tiles are installed around it, leaving gaps for grout.

(It should be noted that some ceramic fixtures are designed to lie over the tile rather than flat on the backing. If this is desired, it should be specified at the time of purchase.)

During the application of the tile, some Mastic will inadvertently get on the tile faces. This should be removed *before* the Mastic has dried by wiping it off with a gasoline-soaked rag. (Turpentine will also do.) The solvent is used for cleaning purposes only and should not be used to thin partially dried Mastic to make it "reusable."

Having installed all of the baseboard and wall tiles, including those around pipes and fixtures, I allow the tile to set overnight.

The material used to fill the gaps around tile is a finely ground cement called grout. A variety of organic and epoxy grouts that are immune to most chemicals are also manufactured, but unless some special situation requires their use, they should be avoided since they are expensive and their special characteristics aren't commonly necessary.

The gaps the grout will be used to fill are very narrow. To insure that the gaps are adequately packed, it is best to prepare a mix that has a consistency similar to that of heavy cream which still pours.

I spread the grout over the face of the tiles with a rubber-faced trowel, working it into the joints with small circular motions and pressing down firmly with the sides of the trowel at the corners and over the gaps. I allow the grout to set for twenty to thirty minutes, then wash off the excess with a large sponge rinsed very often. I repeat this half an hour later. Toward the end of the day, I go over the tiles again with a wet rag to remove any grout that still remains. The next morning the tiles will be covered with a white film which I remove by wiping with a dry cloth.

It is important to remove the excess grout before it has dried; removing dried grout is difficult and laborious.

Most wall tiles have a slight radius along their edges which has a tendency to create wide and irregular joints. If necessary, their appearance can be improved through tooling with a sharp wood chisel.

## Installing a Quarry-Tile Kitchen Floor

Quarry tile is manufactured in a variety of shapes and sizes. Its standard thickness is about 1/2 inch, although thicker and thinner tiles are available. The thicker the tile, the better its load-bearing qualities, but for kitchen use 1/2-inch tile is more than sufficient. Due to its great density and low water-absorption rate, quarry tile is very resistant to wear. It is not impervious to stains, but most liquids can be mopped up without a trace. Its colors will not fade. Quarry tiles are usually the color of the clay used. However, only small amounts of color are ordinarily added and their range is limited to black, buff, and similar shades. Colors vary within the same batch and uniformity should not be expected.

It should be kept in mind that the tiles will not necessarily be exactly the same size, particularly if they are hexagonal. I allow for this inherent variation by widening the grout joints between tiles to

1/4-inch, although this will require the use of a good deal more grout. Using narrower joints will require the trimming of individual tiles, a procedure to be avoided. If the tiles are checked for uniformity in size before their installation and are found to be consistent, a smaller joint can be used, but in no case should it be narrower than 1/8 inch.

To begin the kitchen installation, I first remove all the tiles from their containers and stack them beside the door. I check them for uniformity and remove those that are significantly larger or smaller than the norm. I will use these tiles along the perimeter, where I anticipate cutting will be needed.

Having installed one of the underlayments previously discussed, I divide the kitchen into quadrants by popping chalk lines between the centers of opposite walls.

I place Mastic on the back of the first tile and lay it 1/8 inch away from the intersection of the chalk lines at the center of the room. In the same manner I lay three more tiles, each in a different quadrant and each 1/8 inch from the chalk lines.

I place a swath of Mastic along one of the chalk lines bordering the quadrant farthest from the door, keeping the Mastic about 1 inch from the chalk line so that the line remains visible, then lay a row of tiles, each tile aligned with the first and 1/8 inch from the chalk line. I continue to lay tiles in the same row until the distance between the last tile and the wall is smaller than the width of a tile. I remove the excess Mastic between the last tile and the wall with a cheap 3-inch putty knife. I return the excess Mastic to its container, replace the lid, and wipe the putty knife clean with a solvent (gasoline or turpentine) saturated rag.

I install three additional rows in the same manner, each row beginning with a different tile at the center of the room and each row in a different quadrant. I now have four rows, each lying on one side of a chalk line. I now install four additional rows, each on the opposite side of the chalk line. I place each new tile 1/8 inch away from the chalk line and in line with a corresponding tile on the opposite side of the chalk line. The gap between the two tiles is 1/4 inch, a distance small enough to permit placement by eye.

Having established a double row of tiles which intersects at the center of the room in the shape of a cross, I am now ready to fill the quadrant farthest from the door, using the already-installed tiles as a reference. If the kitchen is not unusually large and care is taken to place the initial rows accurately, the balance of the tile can be laid by eye (checking alignment intermittently with a straightedge) and a wall will be reached before any cumulative misalignment of tiles can lead to negative results.

If the width or length of the kitchen is more than 15 feet and the tiles used are under 6 inches square, a row of tiles may become misaligned if placement is being done by eye. To avoid this, I pop chalk guidelines every other row and align the newly placed tiles 1/8 inch away from the lines in the same manner as the first rows installed.

To fill a quadrant, I spread Mastic over a 2-foot-square area and lay tiles adjacent to those already installed. I carry a 1/4-inch scrap of plywood about 6 inches long and an inch wide and use it as a guide to keep a uniform gap of 1/4 inch between tiles. When placing the tile only moderate pressure need be applied and the initial placement should be as close to the final position as possible to avoid excessive shifting. I continue to apply Mastic to adjoining areas and lay tiles until the gap between the last tile and the wall is smaller than a tile. I then fill the remaining three quadrants, completing the quadrant nearest the door last, working myself out from its center toward the door. This avoids the risk of stepping on tiles before they have adhered properly.

Before terminating work in each quadrant, I check the position of the tiles for uniformity. If any have shifted or were placed inaccurately, I shift them as needed. I also remove Mastic on the face of the tiles or around their perimeter. In addition, I measure the gaps between the last tiles and the walls. The gap along opposite walls should be about the same. I will therefore cut the tiles for opposite walls at the smallest measurement taken. I count the number of tiles along two intersecting walls. I will cut double the number of tiles that are placed along each wall since the cut tiles will fit along the opposite wall as well.

I set the fence on the tile cutter to cut a hair narrower than the smallest measurement taken for two opposite walls and cut double the number of tiles placed along one wall. I repeat this for the tiles that will be placed along the opposite two walls.

This arrangement will work when the joint be-tween the wall and the tiles along the perimeter will be covered by baseboard tile or 3/4-inch quarter round. If neither of these is projected, I remove an additional 1/8 inch from the border tiles to allow for grouting the joint at the wall.

It is difficult to estimate the length of time it will take for the Mastic to set and hold tiles securely. It varies with different brands, different temperatures, and like factors. It can be an hour under good drying conditions or twenty-four hours under bad. Ordinarily I wait overnight before returning to the floor and installing the cut tile. If this isn't feasible and I wish to install the cut tiles immediately, I place plywood sheets over the installed tile and lay the cut tile while standing on them. If the area in which I am placing the cut tiles is 2 inches or less, I apply Mastic to the back of the tile before laying it. If it is larger than 2 inches, I apply the Mastic to the underlayment before laying the tile. In each corner, I cut the already-cut tile again to allow for the gap along the intersecting wall. After installing all the cut tile and removing the plywood sheets, I check the position of all the tiles to see if any have been shifted and misaligned. I align those which have shifted, then, before grouting, allow the tile to sit overnight.

The next day I prepare a mixture of grout and water, using 5 pounds of grout at a time. To this I add 20 percent (by volume) mortar sand. While grout used directly out of the bag works well enough between the wall-tile joints, it will rapidly disintegrate in the joints of a floor unless strengthened by the addition of sand. (There is some sand already present in the grout, but it has very small particles which tend to disintegrate when walked on. The addition of larger particles of sand will roughen the grout's texture, but the additional strength it provides is necessary.)

I mix the grout, sand, and water in a plastic bucket, to a consistency of butter which barely retains its shape. This consistency is very important, since the quarry-tile floor is a permanent installation whose weakest part will be the grouted joint. A much looser mixture would pack the joints more fully and easily but would result in a weaker bond. A thicker consistency would strengthen the bond but packing would be more difficult and not nearly as full. The consistency I have chosen is a compromise between the two and the bond should last a lifetime.

If the grout is to be colored, the powdered pigment is mixed in at this time.

I dump the entire mixture in the corner diagonally opposite the doorway and move it over the joints and tiles with the rubber float while maintaining a firm downward pressure. I use the corner and side of the trowel to depress grout into the gaps and push the mound of remaining grout to new areas. However, I remain in the same area until *all* of the joints are packed and completely full. (If I leave some joints only partially full and return later to complete them, the bond between the two applications will be weak; if too much time has elapsed between applications, the result will be two thin layers of grout in the same joint. The upper layer will disintegrate with ordinary use or come away as scale.)

I proceed in the same manner—in patches—and grout the entire floor.

Although I have been pushing the excess grout into new areas, a significant amount still remains on the face of the tiles. I want to remove this before it has dried without disturbing the grout in the joints. I wait about three quarters of an hour and then wash off the grout from the face of the tiles with a wet sponge. I then wait another hour and wash the tile faces again. I use a putty knife to scrape off grout which is difficult to remove from the face of the tiles, but wherever possible I continue to use the sponge, which I rinse very often. Excess grout along the tiles' edges must of course be removed with the knife.

The floor can be used the following day.

Quarry tiles are not glazed, and although they are highly resistant to absorption they are by no means impervious. A number of products are marketed as sealers which supposedly coat the surface and "seal it" in a manner similar to glazing.

I have used several of these products to seal quarry-tile floors and the results have been abysmal. One discolored in a couple of days and peeled off, another peeled and flaked within a month, and all showed signs of abrasion within a short period of time under normal use. I strongly recommend that all sealers be ignored and quarry tile be left as is.

I also strongly recommend that wax and other floor products not be used on the tile.

Most unsightly stains that develop will be extremely shallow because of the high density of the tile and its low absorption rate. Many stains can be sanded out easily using emery cloth on the spinner sander, and since the color goes all the way through the tile, the result will be satisfactory.

## Installing a Porcelain-Tile Bathroom Floor (Masonry Bed)

Porcelain tile is vitreous, which means that because of its density it absorbs very little moisture and is highly resistant to staining. It is unglazed and its colors result from the addition of stains and oxides. Normally it is only manufactured in small sizes and it is referred to as mosaic tile for that reason. To ease its installation, backing is placed on either the front or back of the individual tiles, joining them together in a sheet, usually 1 foot square. The front backing consists of paper with a water-soluble glue that is easily removed by wetting. Backing on the back is a mesh that leaves more than enough surface for the tile to adhere and therefore doesn't require removal.

Porcelain tile floor

189

Mosaic tile in sheet, mesh backing on back

Cut tile and tile to be cut with nippers

The tile shown on p. 189 is a familiar sight in bathrooms of older structures. In other colors, shapes, and sizes, porcelain is widely used in newer construction as well.

To install a similar floor in an older structure, one must first deal with the bathroom's existing floor. If a substantial renovation is being undertaken, the old floor and bathroom fixtures are removed to expose the floor joists and a new subfloor composed of 1 x 6 common pine (or plywood) is nailed on top of them. After the rough plumbing has been finished, a masonry bed is placed on the subfloor and the tile is installed.

It is not always necessary, however, to remove the existing floor.

If the existing floor is made of tile, new tile can be applied directly over it if the bed of the old tile is sound. The soundness of the bed can be determined by visual inspection of its surface. If the cementatious material has not powdered, flaked, or scaled, if it doesn't have structural cracks and doesn't move when walked on, it needn't be re-

moved. Even in very old bathrooms, it is rare to find a structurally defective bed. Epoxy or latex concrete is then applied to fill any holes caused by missing old tiles, the floor is scrubbed to remove dirt, Mastic is applied to the surface of the old tile, and the new tile installed. A better result will be achieved if the toilet is removed first and reinstalled after the new tile has been grouted. (This isn't essential, however. If the toilet isn't removed temporarily, the new tile is cut to fit the contour of the base, allowing a gap for grout.)

If the old floor is wood covered by linoleum or composition tiles (often found in townhouses, tenements, suburban houses) and the linoleum or composition tiles are securely attached, the new tile can be laid directly over it, again using Mastic as the adhesive.

However, if the surface covering of the old bathroom floor is loose, it should all be removed. The existing floor is then covered with marine plywood or tempered Masonite and the new tile is laid on the new underlayment with Mastic.

I am installing a porcelain-tile floor on a masonry bed. Before I installed the bed I covered the subfloor with 15-pound felt (tar paper) to prevent water from being drawn out of the masonry bed and weakening it.

To install the tile I prepare a mixture of 1 part lime, 10 parts cement, and 30 parts sand. I dry-mix this thoroughly with a hoe. The bed I intend to lay will be about 1-1/4 inches thick. As a rule of thumb, for every 10 square feet of floor area in the bathroom, I will need one quarter bag of cement and three quarters bag of sand, using the proportions given. (Sand is sold by the yard, which is 27 cubic feet, and a bag of sand is 1/27 of a cubic yard. A bag of cement equals 1 cubic foot.)

I move all the dry mixture to the back of the wheelbarrow, add water to the front, and begin to mix. I continue to add water, mixing small batches until I have wetted the entire mix. The consistency I want is much thicker than that ordinarily used and is called a "dry" mix. The term is misleading since all of the material must be completely wetted. This heavier consistency will resist deformation much more readily than a looser one and the work of laying the tile floor will go a lot more quickly and easily. The optimum consistency utilizes the least amount of water necessary to wet the mixture completely but enough to keep the mix from pulling apart when a trowel is stroked over its surface. When the mixture is depressed forcefully with a trowel, little if any water should be squeezed out of it.

I dump half of the mixture in the wheelbarrow onto the floor near the corner farthest from the bathroom door. I spread the mix across the floor with a long wooden trowel. I will be making two applications; on this first, I want a thickness of about 3/4 inch. I therefore keep the bed slightly higher and screed the excess.

Screeding, as explained earlier in the chapter, is stroking a straight piece of wood across the surface of the wet mass to achieve a flat surface at the desired height.

Most bathroom areas are fairly small and screeding by eye will not be too difficult. However, chalk lines can be popped on the walls at heights of 3/4 and 1-1/4 inch to act as references for the first and second applications.

It is not desirable to achieve a smooth surface during the initial application. The objective is a firm bed that is essentially flat with a rough surface. The long wooden trowel will achieve this.

Before I begin laying the floor or when the first application is a few inches from the door, I tack a cleat 1-1/4 inches high across the width of the doorway. Its ends butt the door jambs on each side and its forward edge lies midway under the closed position of the door. The cleat provides a form for the concrete and establishes where it will end.

After the initial bed has been laid, I wait ten or fifteen minutes and place scraps of plywood large enough to walk on over the concrete. (I don't want to cover the floor and use only enough to provide access to all parts of the bathroom.) I begin the next procedure when my weight on the plywood will not depress the bed more than 1/4 inch or so.

While the bed is still wet and capable of supporting my weight, I place wire lath (or metal reinforcing mesh) over its entire surface. Since I will be placing concrete over it that is only 1/2 inch thick, all the lath should lie flat on the surface or slightly below it.

In the same manner as the first application, I lay a second layer of concrete over the wire lath to bring the thickness of the entire bed to 1-1/4 inches. The surface of the second layer must be flat and regular (not smooth) and troweling with the wooden float will provide this after screeding has been done. The

wooden float is laid against the surface with light downward pressure and moved in wide semicircular strokes. Material loosened from high spots is shifted to depressions and worked into the mixture with the same circular motions. Since bathrooms are ordinarily small, it may be awkward to use a long trowel, but best results will be obtained if the longest one possible is used.

When the second application is still wet and holds my weight while I am standing on a piece of plywood, I apply a thin film of adhesive by using a preparation called "neet," a cement product which is the masonry equivalent of Mastic. As an alternative I can use a product called Dryest which is also applied in a thin layer to act as an adhesive. (Amounts needed will of course depend on the square-foot area involved; average requirements are printed on the package.)

Starting in the corner farthest from the door, I spread the neet in a film about 1/6 inch thick over about a 3-foot-square area. I work from a crouch on a piece of plywood. I place a sheet of tile in the corner so that its sides lie parallel to the intersecting walls and 1/16 inch from them (to allow for grout). I avoid shifting individual tiles. If necessary, I move an entire row, using the side of a metal trowel as an alignment reference. The backing will not keep the tiles in alignment and any sort of pressure against an individual tile will move it. When the sheet is in position, I place a 2 x 4 block on it and pound down gently.

It is not necessary to pound the tiles with great force, only enough to imbed them securely. I continue to lay sheets, pounding each area covered to achieve a flat surface which I test by running my fingers over it.

As the tile is being pounded, concrete from the bed is being forced upward in the gaps between the tiles. This will serve as grout. Excess concrete is removed after each patch of tile has been installed.

I remove strips or individual tiles as needed by cutting the plastic backing with a sheetrock knife.

I cut individual tiles as needed with the nippers described earlier.

The tile in the bathroom will form a joint with the flooring in the next room. The usual practice is to cover this joint with a metal saddle which is placed on top of the tile and the flooring of the adjacent room where they meet. If there is a difference in height between the two, a saddle can be purchased

Chrome saddle

Vitreous tile floor on masonry bed cut around toilet waste line

which allows for it. If I am using a metal saddle I therefore continue installing tile until it butts the cleat in the doorway.

After the floor is dry, I measure the difference in height (if any) between the tile and the floor of the adjoining room. I purchase a saddle that has a bend that corresponds to the difference in height. I cut it to length with a metal-cutting blade in the sabre saw and install it over the joint between the tile and adjoining floor with screws through the predrilled holes.

As an alternative arrangement, I can use a marble saddle in the photograph. Here the floorings from both rooms butt the saddle, the width of which is identical to the wall. The outer edge of the saddle will butt the inner edge of the cleat.

A marble saddle is usually 1/2 inch or more thick, a thickness greater than the tile. I therefore have the option of placing the saddle at various heights in relation to the tile. My preference is to install it 1/4 inch higher than the tile since the additional height will serve to keep water from being sloshed into the adjoining room without creating a tripping hazard. I therefore remove about 1/4 inch of concrete in the area where the saddle will be installed, smooth the bed, apply a film of neet, and install the saddle with its far side butting the cleat.

I then continue to install tiles to the saddle, leaving a 1/16-inch gap to allow for grout.

The floor can be walked on after a day and is ready for ordinary use after three or four days.

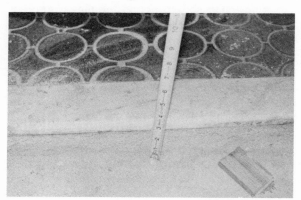

Marble saddle on concrete bed

# KITCHEN CABINETS AND COUNTERS

**7**

## General Information

Kitchen renovations are common. In fact, most renovation dollars are spent in the kitchen, and for the reader who wishes to do his own work, the kitchen area provides the greatest savings. The kitchen in the photographs is a typical example. Despite inflated prices, the cost of *all* materials, including those used in masonry, plumbing, electrical, hardware, and cabinetry work was under $600. None of it was junk. Most was medium-priced and of good quality and several items, such as brass water lines and a Corion countertop, were quite expensive. Except for two stainless steel sinks, the fixtures (stove, refrigerator, etc.) were not new and are not included in the materials cost. If a commercial contractor had done the same job, his bill would have been $7000 to $8000 for materials and labor. This incredible gap between the materials cost and the price of the entire job is a common feature of commercial construction work and it has prompted me to build all of my own kitchens, whether in new homes or renovations, rather than subcontract any of the work.

East side of cabinets

In building the kitchen to be described, I was assisted by two inexperienced young men. At no time did they encounter anything too difficult for them to execute and for the most part all they needed was information. This experience affirmed

**193**

South side of cabinets (north side is the same)

West side of island

once again what I have come to believe from a good many prior experiences—all the work needed to renovate a kitchen is well within the capacity of inexperienced people.

Whenever practicable, I prefer to build the cabinets and counter as independent units and then install them. This wasn't feasible in the kitchen photographed because when the wall that divided the kitchen from the pantry was removed, two pipes that had been imbedded in that wall were left standing. One was a hot water riser, the other a drain. Both pipes rose through the floor and continued through the ceiling and both were located within the counter area. Relocating these pipes would of course have been possible, but several factors relating to the building management made it impractical. I was left with two alternatives: to build independent units with U-shaped cutouts to accommodate the pipes, then fill in the area after they were installed; or to build the cabinets in place

and work around the pipes. I chose the latter since it involved less work and provided equal quality.

A large variety of materials is available with which to construct cabinets and counters. Cabinet wood may be pine, teak, walnut, plastic-sheathed plywood, plain plywood, veneered plywood, textured plywood, birch, oak, or a number of South American woods such as sedgua or ramon (walnutlike and a good deal less expensive) or Hawaiian woods such as koa. Counters can be fashioned from Formica, tile, butcher-block wood (maple), and solid plastics, among other materials. When choosing materials, keep in mind that the total amount used will be relatively small and that the difference in cost between excellent and poor materials will amount to very little. Since the kitchen will be subjected to a great deal of wear, shoddy materials may cause all sorts of maintenance problems which will rapidly eat away any initial savings.

In designing the kitchen, I strongly recommend avoiding the use of paint. It is no more than a cosmetic (a poor one at that) and it carries with it the perpetual effort and expense of maintenance, undertaken solely to keep up the appearance of the paint rather than for protection of the material under it. The headache of repainting can be avoided by omitting paint entirely. There are satisfactory alternatives and I will detail some of these in the chapter on finishes.

The techniques used to build the kitchen in the photographs are applicable to a large variety of other kitchens using materials other than the ones suggested here. The kitchen design and materials selected happened to suit the people for whom the kitchen was being built and I will be comparing their choices with other options (indicating how the latter can be installed) as I go along.

*Before* work is begun, I strongly recommend that a sketch be drawn which includes everything that will be built or installed in the new kitchen. It is also wise to buy and have on hand *all* of the materials and appliances that will be needed.

## Basic Cabinetry Procedures

The chapter on carpentry contains a section on basic woodworking procedures. All of these will be used in the kitchen. Additional procedures and tools will be used, including a router, a tool which I will use extensively.

Front of router

This particular router is electrically operated and has a shaft speed of about 22,000 rpm. At the base of the shaft is a chuck which holds the "bit." The bit is the shaped piece of metal which actually does the cutting. A large variety of differently shaped bits are manufactured for use with the router and the cut made depends upon the particular shape of the bit, although one bit can often be used for more than one kind of cut. The bits are made of steel or steel with carbide-steel tips. The carbide-tipped ones will provide a cleaner cut over a longer period of time and work well with materials other than wood, such as plastic. They are reground when dull. They are significantly more expensive than plain steel bits, but their longevity and versatility are worth the expense. I avoid the plain steel types.

The router is manufactured by the Stanley Co. (Model H 260 A, 9 amps) and is rated at 1-1/2 horsepower. The rating is misleading and academic since it is arrived at while the machine is spinning freely, whereas the user is interested in how it will perform while in use—that is, how much the bit will slow down when going through teak, oak, etc.; how well the bushings or bearings will stand up; and so on. The machine costs around $65 and is in the lower-price range of the Stanley line. It is adequate for light professional work. I have found no better or worse performance in equivalent routers manufactured by other companies. If a router is to be purchased for heavier and more exacting use I would choose among the more expensive and powerful models, which may be as much as four or five times as expensive as the cheaper ones. If

Chuck opened with wrench

this isn't possible, the model in the photo or its equivalent from another manufacturer will be adequate. I would avoid purchasing any model that is smaller and cheaper.

To install a bit in the router, the hexagonal nut directly above the chuck is turned counterclockwise until the jaws in the chuck are loose. The bit is then inserted fully between the jaws and the nut turned clockwise until tight. (A wrench is supplied with the router.)

To raise the bit after it has been tightened in the chuck, the arm at the top of the base and on the back of the machine is turned counterclockwise till loose. A large yellow ring at the top of the base is graduated into 1/64-of-an-inch marks and further subdivided into marks equaling 1/256 of an inch. As this ring is turned clockwise, it will lower the

Shank of bit inserted into chuck

Locking arm loosened to raise or lower router table for shallower or deeper cuts

Bit tightened in chuck with wrench, switch in locked position

base so that less of the bit extends below it to allow for shallower cuts. The amount the bit has been raised or lowered can be precisely determined by noting how much the ring has been moved past a stationary arrow located at the front of the base. If the ring is turned clockwise from one 1/64 mark to the next, the bit will cut 1/64 inch less deep than it would have in its former position.

To lower the bit and cut more deeply, the locking arm is loosened, the ring is turned counterclockwise, the base is pushed up tight against the raised ring, and the locking arm is then tightened to maintain the base in position.

In practice, I approximate the needed depth of the bit by eye and make a test cut into a scrap of wood. I measure the depth of the cut with the brass extension of a folding ruler and then raise or lower the bit the amount required by turning the ring. I always make a second test cut to verify whether I have in fact the depth I want.

Near the top of the back of the machine is a yellow switch with On and Off positions marked beneath it. A third position is indicated by an arrow pointing up on the switch itself. When the switch is depressed first and raised, it will pop forward into a

Graduated ring

Measuring depth of test cut

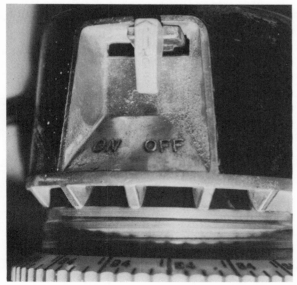

Switch in lock position

slot above the Off position. This locks the shaft, a convenience when changing bits since the hex nut above the chuck can be turned solely with the wrench.

Before moving the switch laterally to the On position, *care must be taken to make sure that the bit is not resting on or against any material and that it can ROTATE FREELY.* The precaution I take is to rest no more than 1 inch of the base on the material I want to cut. When first using the tool, I would take the added precaution of looking at the bit to make sure it is free. The router develops full rpm very rapidly once it is turned on.

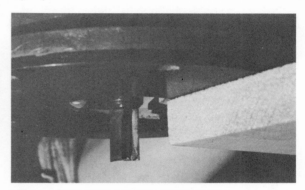

Bit away from wood prior to starting router

The router should be able to cut from any direction with equal results. The base should always be flat on the work; it makes no difference whether the back or front is placed facing the operator, anywhere in between, or shifted during a cut.

Usually the worker will be pushing the router forward or pulling it back. When cutting parallel to the grain less stress will be placed on the bit than when cutting across the grain, and of course the deeper the cut, the greater the stress. Cutting should therefore be slightly faster when it is being done with the grain and slightly slower across the grain. The speed at which the user pushes or pulls the router to make the cut is an important part of using the machine properly.

After starting the machine and allowing the bit to reach maximum speed freely, the bit will slow down as it is pushed forward into the wood. If you continue to push it forward more rapidly and with greater force, it will slow down even more, and you may soon smell overheated insulation on the armature and will probably blow a fuse. Excessive speed also reduces the rpm of the bit below its proper level, causing the cut to be chewed up (chunks of wood are ripped out rather than cut out) and reducing the life of the machine considerably.

However, if you cut too slowly, you are likely to make the bit heat up excessively, diminishing its sharpness.

When the bit spins freely, it creates a characteristic high-pitched whine. The pitch of the whine will lower somewhat as the bit begins to cut and the speed of the shaft is reduced, but this change in sound should not be dramatic. There is a specific range of proper working speed and the whine that corresponds to it can be heard when the bit is first entering the wood. Maintaining that same sound is the best way to assure that the bit is being moved through the cut at its optimum speed. One should cut as quickly as possible without placing undue strain on the motor as evidenced by a flatter-pitched sound. The cut will become visible as the router is moved forward; if the cut is not clean (its surface smooth and the edges straight), chances are that the router is being pushed along with excessive force and speed.

The router is not a dangerous tool but can easily become one if attention wanders while it is being used. A bit which turns at 22,000 rpm deserves the concentration of the user. I've found that the most dangerous moment is immediately after a cut has been made. There is a tendency to relax while switching off the machine and lifting it from the work. There is no guard around the spinning bit, which will continue to rotate for a short time after the machine has been turned off. It is at this moment, while the operator is looking at the cut and the bit is still spinning, that a collision between the bit and the operator is most likely. The left hand seems to be the part of the body most likely to make contact with the still-spinning bit. An absolutely safe procedure is to *switch off the machine and allow it to remain on the work until the bit has stopped.* If this precaution and the others I have mentioned are observed, no apprehension need be felt in using the router.

Often a fence (or guide) will be used with a router to obtain cuts of exact length or width. The surest way to avoid having to retrim any cut is through accurate measuring, marking, and placement of the fence. A carpenter's pencil doesn't work well because of its line's bulk. An ordinary #2 pencil with a sharp point will produce a thinner line and

will create less confusion about where to place things. Right from the first cut, it would be wise to establish a pattern for yourself in relation to your marking. Mine is to cover the pencil lines with the fence to the point where they are barely visible. In trimming, the lines are then almost removed. Whenever marking, I allow for this fact. As long as some pattern is established—whether the pencil line is to be entirely removed, left completely, halved, or whatever—greater accuracy will result. One of the excellent features of the router is the fact that the actual cutting is almost automatic and involves no skill at all. The accuracy of the cut depends solely on the user's accuracy in measuring and marking the wood and placing the fence.

## Constructing the Cabinet Base for the Counter

The cabinets are to be built as an "island," accessible from all four sides. On the north side, the width of the aisle between the countertop and wall will be 28 inches. The width of the west aisle will be 36 inches. The washing machine and dryer face into this aisle and the greater width is for convenience when operating these machines. The remaining sides face open areas.

To end up with aisles of the dimensions given, it will be necessary to begin the bottom of the cabinets at a greater distance from the walls to allow for the "kick" space (the setback at the very bottom), the thickness of the face of the cabinets, and the amount the countertop will extend beyond the finished face of the cabinets.

Completed 28-inch aisle

Completed 36-inch aisle

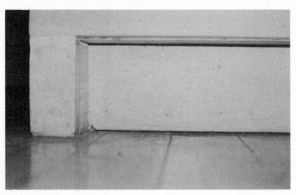

Kick space

There are no standard dimensions for kick space, but 3-1/2 inches in both depth and height is commonly allowed.

The face of the cabinets will vary in thickness, depending on the material used. In this instance I will be using 3/4-inch white pine.

Similarly, there is no standard dimension for the projection of the countertop beyond the face of the cabinets. I am using a 1-1/2-inch projection, which is common, but any distance between 3/4 inch and 2 inches can also be used. If the projection is less than 3/4 inch, the joint between the bottom of the countertop and the face of the cabinets will become noticeable and may require additional work. A small projection also appears disproportionate to the cabinets' bulk. If more than a 2-inch projection is used, the depth of the counter must be increased proportionately to allow enough space within the area of the cabinets for installation of the sink. In this case, the larger projection also places the user farther away from the faucets and will dig into his body.

The three setback dimensions I am using total 5-3/4 inches (3-1/2, 3/4, 1-1/2). To obtain aisles of 28 and 36 inches, it is therefore necessary to place the kick 5-3/4 inches back from the desired width of the aisle. In this instance, the distances from the two walls will be 33-3/4 inches and 41-3/4 inches.

Using these last two dimensions, I measure out from each wall at two points and pop chalk lines between the marks.

On the sides where there is no kick, I reduce the total amount of setback by 3-1/2 inches to only 2-1/4 inches, which represents the projection of the countertop and the thickness of the pine facing of the cabinets.

The dimensions of the completed island will be 9 feet along the east and west sides and 6 feet along the north and south.

My first step is to pop chalk lines on the floor which will outline the perimeter of the island area, each line set back the appropriate distance from the overall 9-by-6-foot dimension. I use the two previously marked chalk lines and opposite walls to position the north and west sides of the cabinet.

The washer and dryer are contained within the area of the island, and obviously no cabinets will be built where they are located. However, for the sake of appearance, they will be placed between two walls which will rise to the height of the countertop. Each of these appliances is 27 inches wide (total, 54 inches).

I pop two additional chalk lines 54-1/4 inches apart to mark where the outer sides of each machine will be placed. The extra 1/4 inch will allow placement of the appliances after the short walls are built and will facilitate their removal for maintenance.

I have already installed the rough plumbing and wiring for the appliances (see p. 62); these lie approximately 36 inches back from where the front of the appliances in their final position will be located. I intend to erect a short wall behind the back of the appliances for the purpose of stabilizing the cabinets and providing a surface on which to secure the pipes, wires, and outlets.

2 × 4 kick on edge along chalk line

I cut 2 x 4s to the lengths needed to form the perimeter by first placing them beside and inside the chalk lines and marking. This eliminates measuring each piece needed and avoids the possibility of ruler error. (I use this marking technique whenever possible since I am not cutting a 2 x 4 to conform to the measurement of a ruler but to members already installed to chalk lines previously measured and marked.)

To cut the 2 x 4s I use a 40-tooth carbide-tipped blade in the portable power saw in conjunction with a protractor as discussed in basic carpentry procedures (p. 93).

Because the floors in most older structures are rarely level, I lay on edge the cut pieces of 2 x 4s, (2-inch side on the floor) on the inner side of the chalk lines before I install them. I use a 4-foot carpenter's level to determine the highest point along the perimeter and shim up as needed with pieces of cedar shingles to bring low points level. (When ordering wood for the cabinets some "shim" shingles should also be obtained. These are the cheapest kind and they are handy for a variety of uses.)

I tack the shims into position, then toenail the 2 x 4s on edge around the entire perimeter. I use #8 common nails, which I drive downward at an angle through the backs of the 2 x 4s into the wooden floors.

I nail scraps of 2 x 4 every 30 inches or so on the flat behind the 2 x 4s on edge, then drive #10 finishing nails through the front of the kick and into the scraps.

If the floor is concrete, I use lead shields and lag screws to fasten 1 x 2 scraps into the floor, then nail the kick to these. The kick should be secured every 30 inches or so.

I change the carbide blade in the power saw to a plywood blade (sometimes called a miter), which I will use from now on since its narrow kerf produces fine cuts and lends itself to greater accuracy than other blades.

The standard overall depth of cabinets and countertops is between 24 and 25-1/2 inches. While this is not an absolute, if the depth of the counter is less than 24 inches, difficulties will be encountered when installing the sink since the clips used to attach the sink to the counter may not fit the limited space.

The owners prefer a counter with greater-than-normal depth and since the Corion countertop purchased came in a width of 30 inches, that dimension is chosen. Since the counter will project 5-3/4 inches beyond the kick, the back of the cabinet will be 24-1/4 inches from the front of the kick. I therefore pop a chalk line 24-1/4 inches from the front of the kick. I cut and install 2 x 4s along the inner side of the chalk line.

The o.o. dimension of the 2 x 4s installed is 24-1/4 inches. On top of them, I want to install a 3/4-inch plywood base for the cabinets—extending it 3-1/2 inches for the east and west sides, where a kick is projected. This will require ripping the plywood to a width of 27-3/4 inches. I lay a 4 x 8 sheet of 3/4-inch GIS interior plywood on top of four 2 x 4s lying flat on the floor, pop a chalk line at 27-3/4 inches, and rip with the bad side up.

I measure 3-1/2 inches back from the factory edge of the plywood at each end and mark. I lay the ripped piece on top of the installed 2 x 4s, align the 3-1/2-inch marks with the outer edge of the 2 x 4, and attach with #8 ringed nails spaced every foot or so. I keep the factory edge of the plywood at the

Plywood base of cabinet extending 3-1/2 inches beyond kick

front of the cabinet and the ripped cut at the back, where irregularities will not show.

Since the cabinet is longer than the 4 x 8 sheet of plywood, I cut additional pieces to cover the remaining 2 x 4 outline, omitting the 3-1/2-inch extension where no kick is projected (the north and south sides).

The span of the plywood (its unsupported distance) is roughly 24 inches. Although 3/4-inch plywood will ordinarily bend under a person's weight over such a span, no such weight is likely to be placed on the floor of a kitchen cabinet. If for some reason a weight greater than 150 pounds is anticipated, an additional 2 x 4 should be placed midway between the outer 2 x 4s and parallel to them before the plywood is installed.

I have chosen the 3/4-inch thickness mainly because I will be attaching the face pieces of the cabinets to the edges of the plywood and the 3/4-inch thickness is the minimum necessary to fasten pieces adequately. I have used both 5/8-inch and 1/2-inch-thick plywood, but nailing into the edges of material so thin is difficult and often causes the plies to separate.

I have chosen GIS plywood because there is no reason for the down side to be finished and it is cheaper. Similarly, I have chosen interior rather than exterior plywood for reasons of economy since I do not anticipate enough wetting to cause plies to separate.

## Constructing Cabinet Framework

Once the level platform has been installed with plywood extending 3-1/2 inches beyond the kick

while remaining flush elsewhere, the skeleton or framework of the cabinets can be started. It will be made entirely of 1 x 2s, the actual size of which is 3/4 by 1-1/2 inches. Two 1 x 2s glued and nailed together are far stronger than a single 2 x 2 and will be more than sufficient to bear any weight likely to be placed on the countertop.

(Working with 1 x 2s requires techniques particular to them, and the reader is advised to read the entire section first before starting the framework.)

The most widely used wood for 1 x 2s is either pine or spruce. Often, the spruce will be poor grade—warped and twisted—and totally unsuitable for cabinets, although lumber yards will charge the same amount for it as pine. Common pine should therefore be used for the framework. Less wastage and easier fabrication will result if it is purchased in 10-foot lengths.

Throughout the construction of the framework—before nailing pieces together or to the plywood—I will be spreading casein glue over areas to be joined. A cheap 1-inch-wide brush will be handy for this and can be kept serviceable by washing it with water while the glue is still wet.

I will be using #6 ring nails, which have thread-like rings over their shanks and which hold much better than their smooth-shanked counterparts. (Galvanized finishing nails have a rough surface and, while not as good as ring or annular nails, would be adequate. Ordinary steel nails should be avoided since they hold least well.)

The standard height of a countertop is 36 inches from the finished floor. The washer and dryer are this height, and the dishwasher was manufactured with this height in mind. (The dishwasher was

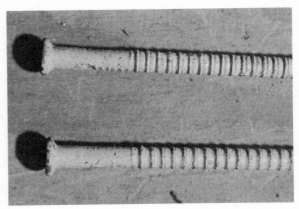

Ring nails

Division of 9-foot east side

brought from a previous apartment where it had been used as a portable. We had to convert it for under-the-counter use. This took half a day. Such additional labor can be avoided if an under-the-counter dishwasher is initially purchased.) Other counter heights may be constructed for the convenience of taller or shorter people, but the appliances will not vary from the standard.

The photograph shows how the cabinet area is divided. Behind each piece on the face are 1 x 2 pieces of framework to which the face piece has been attached. To establish the position of the framework pieces, I mark off the vertical division of the front of the cabinets on the forward edge of the plywood base. I begin this at the point that corresponds to the center of the sink. Sinks vary in width; this one is 33 inches. The width of the cabinet opening below the sink will be equal to the sink's width plus an additional 2 inches on both sides. I intend to close off this area with side panels and do not want them to extend into this dimension.

I therefore measure outward 18-1/2 inches to the left from the center of the sink as I face it and mark this on the plywood. I place a 1 x 2 scrap beside this mark, still working outward, and make an additional mark that is 1-1/2 inches away from the first. This is the position the vertical 1 x 2 will occupy.

I measure outward 18-1/2 inches to the right from the center of the sink and, in the same manner, establish the position of the vertical 1 x 2.

The dishwasher is to be located to the right of the sink compartment. It is 24 inches wide. Still working outward, I measure off 24-1/4 inches, then use a

1 x 2 as a spacer to mark 1-1/2 inches for the vertical position of another stile. The additional 1/4 inch will ease installation of the dishwasher and allow it to be pulled out for maintenance.

Still working outward from the right, I mark the corner and end of the plywood base to receive an additional 1 x 2.

The area remaining to the left of the sink compartment will be used for a cupboard and drawers. There is no standard width for either, but for the sake of appearance the owners have decided to divide the space equally. I therefore place marks for a 1 x 2 at the corner and end of the plywood base on the left side of the sink. I find the center distance between the inner sides of the 1 x 2 in the corner and the 1 x 2 on the left side of the sink compartment, then mark for a 1 x 2 to be centered between them. I have now divided the front edge of the plywood base with 1-1/2-inch marks indicating compartment positions for a cupboard, drawers, sink area, and dishwasher.

I continue around the outer perimeter of the island and mark off vertical positions for other enclosures in the same manner. This will depend on each person's own needs.

(I have been working on the east side of the cabinet. To avoid repetition, I will limit further instructions to this side.)

The top of the plywood base is 4-1/4 inches off the floor (3-1/2 inches for the 2 x 4 on edge and 3/4 inch for the thickness of the plywood).

The Corion from which the countertop will be made is 3/4 inch thick. Since I want the countertop to be 36 inches off the floor, I will have to cut the vertical lengths of the framework 31 inches long. This will bring the height of the framework to 35-1/4 inches; when the Corion is installed over it, the top of the Corion will be 36 inches off the floor.

I count all the marks I have made that indicate vertical 1 x 2s and cut an equal number 31 inches long, using a table saw if possible. If one isn't available, a portable power saw used with a protractor will be satisfactory.

I cut an end of a 10-foot length of 1 x 2 square, place it lengthwise on top of the plywood base (with the squared end flush to the end of the plywood) and mark the opposite end at the other end of the base. I cut it to that length and tack it to the plywood so that its side and ends are flush with the edge and ends of the plywood. I transfer the

Marking divisions on 1 × 2 and plywood edge simultaneously

1-1/2-inch gap at top of vertical stiles for lap joint

Assembly of 1 × 2s at corner, top

Completed joint, two ends of horizontal stiles, and two ends of vertical stiles

Toenailing bottom of vertical stiles to corner of plywood base

marks on the edge of the plywood to the 3/4-inch side of the 1 x 2.

After applying glue to the 31-inch pieces, I nail them to the long 1 x 2 piece at each side of the marks.

I cut as many 29-1/2-inch 1 x 2 pieces as I have

31-inch pieces and glue and nail them together as shown in the photo.

I am nailing on the floor, where it is more convenient. With a helper, I now place the partially

Temporary brace for framework

assembled framework on top of the plywood, shift the bottoms of the vertical 1 x 2s so that they are approximately aligned with the marks on the edge of the base, and toenail through the ends of the vertical pieces into the plywood.

I use three nails, one on each side except the front; while driving the toenails, I hammer the end into alignment with the marks.

I stabilize the wobbly, partially assembled framework by temporarily tacking diagonal braces that extend down from the corner pieces to the 2 x 4 kick pieces on the intersecting sides.

I cut and assemble a duplicate skeletal framework for the back of the cabinet and install it in the same manner. (Its length will of course be shorter, but its interior vertical pieces should correspond to the vertical pieces in front; only the corners will be different.)

There are no compartmental divisions along the north and south sides of the cabinet; I construct their framework in a similar manner but space the vertical members every 16 inches.

In order to stabilize the entire framework, I nail the intersecting ends in the corners together. This nailing is made easier by clamping a scrap of 1 x 2 1-1/2 inches below the top and resting the horizontal 1 x 2 on top of the scrap during nailing.

C clamps will be useful during the assembly, not only in this instance but whenever an excessive amount of bouncing about will be encountered as pieces are being nailed. The clamped scrap is positioned to provide backing for the piece being installed.

After installing the partial framework along the

C clamp holding scrap under horizontal stile as nailing aid

inner and outer perimeters of the cabinet, with vertical stiles dividing the compartments, I attach horizontal 1 x 2s on edge between the long outer and inner skeletons; they are placed flush with the tops of the long horizontal members and only where there are vertical stiles. Their purpose is to stabilize the cabinet in the corners and along the interior sections. They also serve to support the countertop. I omit them from areas where there are no vertical stiles since their placement (such as in the sink or dishwasher area) would interfere with the installation of fixtures. I will also be using the tops of these horizontal pieces as a nailing surface for the upper ends of the plywood panels which will separate the sink compartment.

The compartment to be occupied by the drawers is defined by vertical pieces on each of its sides. I

Horizontal stile held by furniture clamp as aid in nailing

must now decide whether or not to use hardware to facilitate the gliding of the drawers. If I choose to use hardware, I select types which employ plastic rollers. Of these, the ones which are top-mounted are least expensive and work best—the side-mounted ones are the most expensive and work worst. Each brand (I have found no difference among them) will have instructions on how to modify the drawer opening to use them.

To construct the assembly on which the drawers will glide, I cut four pieces of 1 x 2 to a length of 31 inches. These will be installed in a vertical position, and their length will place them in the same plane as the rest of the framework. I place a sheet of 3/4-inch plywood on horses to serve as a work table.

The owners want four drawers with heights of 6, 4, 8, and 10 inches from top to bottom, in that order. Such heights are arbitrary and can of course be changed to suit the user. However, installing both a 4-inch and 10-inch drawer is practical.

The top of each drawer will be below a horizontal

stile. I intend to finish the face of the cabinets with a 1 x 3 (3/4-by-2-1/2-inch actual measurement) stile which will lie with its upper edge against the bottom of the countertop. Since it will extend 2-1/2 inches down from that point, I begin my measurement 2-1/2 inches down from what will become the upper end of the 31-inch piece. Since I am allowing 6 inches for the first drawer r.o., I mark 8-1/2 inches down from the end I will use for the top and place an X below to indicate the side of the mark to place the runner. (The runner is the piece of wood on which the bottom sides of the drawer will glide.) I allow 1-1/2 inches for a horizontal stile to be installed later and make my next mark at 7-1/2 inches which allows for the 6-inch height of the second drawer r.o. I then mark 9-1/2 inches for the 8-inch drawer and 11-1/2 inches for the bottom drawer. I place all four 31-inch-long pieces side by side with their ends flush and, using a framing square, continue my marks across the face of each one.

The purpose of these marks is to establish not only the position of the runners, but the horizontal stiles as well. Since the marks are equidistant and the plywood base is level, each runner will also be level when the 31-inch-long pieces are placed in an upright position. Also, by marking all four 31-inch pieces simultaneously, not only will each runner be level, but it will also be level with the corresponding runner on the opposite side of the drawer.

The depth of the cabinet (determined earlier ) is 27-1/4 inches o.o. This has been reduced by two thicknesses of 1 x 2 at the front and back (the top of the framework) so that the i.d. measurement is now 3 inches less or 24-1/4 inches. I cut eight pieces of 1 x 2 24-1/4 inches long to serve as runners, two on each side of four drawers.

I nail the runners on edge to the 31-inch pieces (next photo). I place each runner at the mark and on the X previously made. I nail through the back of each 31-inch piece and into the side of each 24-1/4-inch runner. I use #8 galvanized finishing nails. I set the vertical 31-inch pieces 5 inches back from both ends of each runner to increase the support for the runners (rather than attaching the runners at their ends). I now have two skeletal assemblies, mirror images, with each runner secured on two vertical pieces.

I position one of the assemblies at one of the vertical stiles previously installed to mark a side of

Drawer runner nailed to upright

Finished rough openings for drawers

the drawer compartment. I want the full 1-1/2-inch width of the runners to extend into the drawer r.o. I nail the bottom end of each 31-inch vertical piece into the plywood base and the upper end into the horizontal crosspiece previously installed between the two long horizontal rails at the top of the front and back of the cabinet framework. All of the runners face inward. I install the remaining assembly on the opposite side of the compartment, all the runners facing inward and its full 1-1/2-inch width in the r.o.

I now measure and cut a 1 x 2 to fit horizontally between the original vertical pieces that delineated the drawer compartment. I start at the bottom of the first drawer and install the cut piece horizontally so that its upper edge lies a hair below the top of both runners. I nail through the horizontal piece into the ends of each runner. (This will complete the first r.o. since the long 1 x 2 horizontal rail is already in place in the framework of the cabinet.) I install three more horizontal pieces of 1 x 2 in the same relative position as the first, each slightly below the tops of the runners and each nailed through its surface into the ends of the runners. Installing

these horizontal pieces between the vertical pieces completes the r.o. for the drawers. I have placed the horizontal pieces slightly below the surface of the runners so that the bottoms of the drawers will not strike them and interfere with smooth opening and closing; only the bottoms of the sides of the drawers will make contact with the runners.

The drawers will be gliding on the runners but they must also be kept from sliding laterally when pulled out or pushed shut. A simple way to do this is to install a 1 x 2 on edge centered across the width of the r.o. with its bottom edge extending into the r.o. for half an inch. I cut four pieces of 1 x 2, each 24-1/4 inches long (the i.d. of the cabinet), to act as guides and prevent lateral movement of the drawers. Each will be installed at the top of a r.o. and serve the drawer below it.

Guide extending down 1/2 inch into each rough opening for drawers

I mark the centers of each of the horizontal pieces across each drawer's r.o. at the front of the cabinet. I measure the distance between a vertical stile at the side of the r.o. and the center of the r.o. I measure and mark this same distance on the corresponding vertical stile in the framework at the back of the cabinet. I install a vertical stile 31 inches long that is 3/8 inch from the center marks I have made. Along this vertical stile, I make marks which correspond to the heights of the tops of each horizontal piece of each rough opening. I mark 1/2 inch up from the bottom edge of each end of each guide.

I attach the front end of the guide by nailing through the horizontal piece into it. It is centered over the center mark and extends 1/2 inch down into the r.o. of the drawer. I attach the back end of the guide by nailing through it into the side of the newly installed vertical 1 x 2. This centers it automatically in line with the center of the guide at the front since I have offset the vertical piece 3/8 inch, half of its thickness. I align it with the height at the front of the guide by nailing it 1/2 inch below the marks made to correspond to the lower edge of each horizontal piece at the front of the cabinet. I use two nails at each end to keep the guide from twisting.

To close off the drawer compartment from the areas on each of its sides, I cut 1/4-inch plywood to fit, and install it over the outer sides of the drawer framework.

To close off the remaining open side area under the sink, I nail a 1 x 2 on the flat to the plywood and install another on edge between the front and back at the top of the cabinet. Both of these pieces—which will serve as cleats—are aligned with each other and with the vertical pieces at the front and back, which delineate the sink compartment. I cut 1/4-inch plywood to cover the opening, then bore a 3/4-inch hole 2-1/2 inches diagonally below the upper corner which will be at the back of the cabinet to allow for the dishwasher drain. I then nail the plywood to the cleats. This completes the side panels for the sink compartment since the panel on the opposite side has already been installed in connection with the drawer assembly.

This also completes the work I need to do within the interior of the sink cabinet, and I am now ready to install its back. During the course of installing the rough plumbing, I brought a 2-inch drain and two 1/2-inch water lines into the cabinet area directly below the sink. I now apply powdered chalk to the pipe ends, cut a piece of 1/4-inch plywood to fit the back of the cabinet, and place it in the position it will occupy against the powdered chalk ends. This transfers the positions of the pipes to the plywood and I cut out the necessary holes with a sabre saw. I then insert the plywood into the opening below the sink and push it forward until it rests against the framework at the back of the cabinet and around the pipes. I nail it to the framework. I install similar 1/4-inch plywood panels to the remaining framework at the back of the cabinet.

The framework should now be rigid and the temporary braces tacked on earlier can be removed. Except for the plywood panels, none of the material used so far will ordinarily be visible when the cabinets are completed. From this point on, however, everything used will remain visible and a different technique is called for. Before finishing the cabinets is undertaken, it's a good idea to check the framework and make any corrections needed. To that end I shall now discuss some of the factors involved in building the framework not covered earlier.

### Additional Information on Building Framework

A number of the 1 x 2s purchased to build the framework are bound to be warped. The worst of these, a small percentage, should be used only in short lengths. The warpage in others will be removed as pieces are nailed to each other. Most warpage takes the form of a curve visible when a 1 x 2 is sighted down its length by lifting an end (when placed on edge the curve becomes a high spot and is referred to as a crown). To use two warped pieces, they are first laid flat against each other, crowns in opposite directions. They are nailed together, starting at one end while holding them aligned manually as long as possible. They are then turned on edge and the higher one is driven down by toenailing to bring them into alignment.

Throughout the building of the framework, particularly when it is still rickety, nailing a new piece may become a chore since it will bounce about while the nail is being driven, threatening its exact placement. Nails should therefore be started through the piece *before* it is brought to the position it will occupy. If during final nailing the piece is shifted from the position it will occupy and this distance is 1/4 inch or so, it can be driven back to its correct location with an additional nail or two.

For installing some pieces, a furniture clamp rather than the C clamp mentioned earlier will be more appropriate.

should be placed on the bottom of the edge that will be closest to the blade so that when the 1 x 2 is pushed forward to make contact, the teeth will first cut at the point of the mark. The first cuts should only be nicks until it is certain that the piece is properly positioned. Since the nicks will be on the back side of the piece, the piece can be shifted to incur as many as necessary in order to get the exact length without marring the front surface.

The table saw is also useful for ripping, particularly large sheets such as a 4-by-8-foot sheet of plywood. It is best to do this with a helper. The helper, stationed at the back of the saw, has only one responsibility—to lift the cut pieces as they are being fed through the blade. *Nothing else.* The helper is simply taking the weight off the cut pieces so that the sheet is not being raised on the operator's end. The operator positions the fence, lays the forward end of the sheet on the table, and positions its side against the fence. His left hand, which is placed at the corner farthest from the blade, holds the sheet level with the saw's table and exerts

Rockwell 10-inch tilting arbor table saw

Cutting 1 × 2 on table saw, mark is at bottom of forward edge

A good deal of ripping and cutting to length will be required. It is done best with a table saw.

The pictured table saw is a 10-inch Rockwell model with a tilting arbor. It is relatively light and powerful and costs about $250. Like a good many other table saws, it is equipped with a totally inadequate fence which needs frequent adjustment. The machine's vibrations also cause the blade to lower. Despite these characteristics, this model works well and is the best I have encountered within its price range.

When a piece is being cut to length, the mark

lateral pressure so that the opposite side of the sheet maintains contact with the fence throughout the cut. The right thumb lies on the back edge of the sheet and supplies the forward pressure necessary to push the sheet through the blade. As the cut nears completion the thumb is checked is to make certain it is not in the path of the blade. If the piece being ripped is 4 inches or less, a 1 x 2 scrap is used to push the back edge of the sheet through the blade, when less than 6 inches remain to be ripped.

Trimming 1 × 2 with power-block plane

When the framework has been assembled there are likely to be places where ends of pieces aren't flush.

The tool pictured is a Porter Cable Model 167 electric block plane. The protruding ends can easily be trimmed with it. It will remove 1/16 inch on each pass. It is light and powerful and requires only one hand during use. Trimming should not be done from one end alone since this will splinter the wood at the far end. Before trimming is completed, the plane should be positioned at the opposite end and the partial cut completed.

Like the router, the cutting bit rotates at great speed and similar precautions should be taken. (In the photo I have removed the guard. I don't recommend this until the user has acquired a good deal of experience.)

An inferior but adequate alternative to the block plane, the spinner sander can also be used with a coarse closed-coat paper to remove small amounts of excessive material.

From time to time during the assembly of the framework, the 4-foot level should be used to check for plumb and level. Variations may develop because a piece is slightly out of position, too long, etc. If the work is check frequently, discrepancies, when they occur, can be removed easily before additional pieces have been installed.

## Installing the Face of the Cabinets

With the framework completed, its front is now ready to be covered with the final material, relatively narrow stationary strips called rails or stiles.

Larger pieces for doors and drawer fronts will also be used.

If a hardwood is selected, 1/4-, 3/8-, or 1/2-inch-thick stock will suffice (of course, the thinner the wood, the cheaper it will be). With a hardwood face, I attach the stile by using casein glue and clamping, thereby completely avoiding the use of nails. (Twenty minutes to a half hour should be allowed for clamping time.) This is more time-consuming than gluing and nailing but it does eliminate the scarring that results from nail placement.

Idaho white-pine paneling, 1 × 8, tongue and groove, V-jointed.

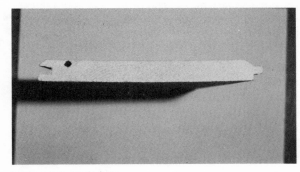

Idaho pine, end view

The pictured Idaho white pine was the wood selected by the owners. It is not as soft as redwood or as hard as teak. Its medium hardness resists scarring and nicking moderately, and it will stand up to ordinary kitchen wear. It is widely used for wall paneling and is frequently mill-designed in 1 x 8 dimensions with a tapered V and tongue and groove along each of its sides. I will use these boards for the face paneling and doors. For the stiles I use square-edge white pine stock, which is modestly priced. I have used a great deal of this wood and its condition on delivery is generally excellent. The knots are small and tight, warpage is minimal, and there are few nicks and gouges. For inexpensive wood, it is the best buy I know.

I will be installing the pine stiles by placing glue on their backs (also on the corresponding framework pieces) and by using 1-1/4-inch-long ring nails with very small heads.

These particular nails are not in wide circulation and may be difficult to find. They hold very well and leave a minimal scar. They are also available in various colors to match the particular wood being used. I do not countersink and fill them, since this tends to make them more noticeable than if the heads were flush with the wood.

Exactness in stile length and tightness at the joints are essential prerequisites for producing good results. I will therefore be installing the stiles by making frequent references to the steel framing square and 4-foot level, removing any errors that may have crept in during the framework assembly.

To achieve exactness in length, a table saw will do well. Used with a 40-toothed carbide-tipped blade, the cuts will be clean. If need be, the miter gauge can be adjusted to the steel square to produce square ends. (The procedure is detailed in the literature that accompanies all table saws purchased.)

If the portable saw with a plywood blade is used, the results will not be as good, although they will be satisfactory.

The best results can be obtained by using the portable saw to make cuts slightly longer than needed, then trimming off the excess with a router. This technique requires substantially more time than using the portable alone or the table saw, but a quality equal to professional furniture-making can be achieved.

Building these cabinets, I will use all three methods but concentrate on the router.

To begin, I stand a length (8-foot) of 1 x 8 white-pine paneling at the northeast corner and on the 6-foot (north) side of the framework. I draw a line across its back that is flush with the top of the framework. I rough-cut slightly above this line with the portable saw. I measure down exactly 2-3/4 inches from the first line, which is the height of the

Squared line at end and parallel line set back 2-3/4 inches

Level clamped along 2-3/4-inch line as fence

cabinet, draw a parallel line, and clamp my small level at the second line.

The side of the level will act as a straightedge (fence) for use in conjunction with the router. A dry 3/4-inch piece of wood 3 inches wide and selected

1/2-inch carbide trimming bit in router

Router being pushed into work

for straightness (teak is good) can be used instead. I am using the level since it does have a straight edge and is ordinarily on hand.

The carbide-tipped bit in the router is 1/2 inch in diameter; its shape can be used for making grooves 1/2 inch wide and up to 3/4 inch in depth.

It can also be used for trimming ends and I am using it for that purpose now, trimming the end of the 1 x 8 down to the first line.

The diameter of the router base is exactly 6 inches. The bit is located in the exact center of this circle. Since the diameter of the bit is 1/2 inch, it will be cutting half of this amount (1/4 inch) from the center of the circle, and the same amount 2-3/4 inch in from the circumference of the base.

I lower the bit so that it extends fully below the table. Since I will be trimming material 3/4 inch thick, I will need nearly all of the cutting surface of the bit.

I place an inch or so of the router base on the paneling and switch on the machine. The circumference of the base is securely against the side of the level. I ease the router forward, making only light contact with the wood. I increase my forward pressure and push the router ahead until it is about three quarters of the way across the board. My pressure is also sideways, to maintain constant contact with the level. I move the router laterally an inch or so away from the level (still keeping the base flat on the wood), push it forward beyond the opposite end of the board, then bring it back into the cut by pulling the machine toward me.

If I were to continue the cut by pushing the router through the opposite side, as the bit went through it would most likely tear away some of the wood.

When I no longer feel (or hear) any resistance caused by the cutter making contact with the wood, I move the router laterally an inch or so away from the level and switch off the machine. The base remains on the wood until the bit stops turning completely. I can hear this. I lift the router and the cut is complete.

When installing tongue-and-groove paneling, the tongue of each board is left exposed for toenailing and is then covered by the groove of the next board. I therefore need to retain the tongue on this first piece. However, if I leave the groove on the first piece to be installed, the tapered half of the V beside it will remain visible and form an anomalous joint. I want to remove this taper and achieve a flush joint with the back of the stile that will later be installed in the same corner and on the east side of the cabinet. To remove the half-taper (and of course the groove), I measure back 2-3/4 inches from the edge of the taper at the top and bottom of the board, then clamp the 4-foot level at these marks.

I place the base of the router on only an inch or so of the wood, so that when I switch it on the bit will rotate freely. The base butts the level securely. I ease the router forward until it begins to cut, then, increasing my forward pressure, push the router ahead until I have trimmed away all but a few inches. I then reverse the router position and come into the wood from the other end, pulling it toward me until the trimming is completed.

Because I am trimming off a hollow groove for the most part, the power of the bit will have a tendency to rip off chunks and mar the surface. To avoid this, I move the router along more slowly than if I were trimming solid wood. (If the wood were solid, I would remove most of it in a rough cut with the portable saw.)

If the router is allowed to drift away from contact with the level at any point during trimming, some of the desired trim will not be removed. To correct this, I slide the router over the same area again, making certain that the base and level are in continuous contact. The level, acting as a fence, will not permit the bit to cut into the material that will be used.

I align the trimmed side of the paneling so that it is flush with the front of the framework and tack it, having first placed casein glue on its back. I position the level against the side of the board and shift it to plumb. I face-nail the piece an inch below the top and an inch above the bottom, with two nails.

Finished northeast corner, lower assembly

Ordinarily I would cut the bottom of this first piece to the shape of the kick, but the owner preferred to have it this way.

To begin the east side of the cabinet, I select a 10-foot 1 x 2 with at least one good side and rough-cut it 1/4 inch or so longer than the overall length of the front (east side) of the cabinet.

Plywood scrap to support base while trimming 1 × 2s

Since the 1 x 2 is narrow, the 6-inch base of the router will rock on the surface during the cut. To eliminate this, I nail a scrap of plywood to my plywood work table on horses. The scrap should be about 6 inches wide and 3 feet long. I position it 1-1/2 inches in from the side closest to me (where I will be working) and extend it 2 inches or so beyond the intersecting side.

Using this arrangement, I provide an adequately wide surface on which the router base can be moved, which also allows me to make a cut completely across the 1 x 2 without changing the position of the router. The side of the plywood scrap will butt the far side of the 1 x 2 being trimmed and will eliminate the tearing which would otherwise occur if the cut was made completely from one side.

I use a T square to make a right-angle line across the 1 x 2 a hair from an end. I measure back 2-3/4 inches from the line, draw a parallel line, place the 1 x 2 beside the scrap of plywood nailed to the top of the work table, then clamp the level at the second line and to the work table.

The arrangement pictured is that used for all the cuts from now on.

I trim an end of the 1 x 2 (now squared) and tack it at one end to the plywood base of the cabinet. I want the tacked end to be flush with the outer surface of the board installed at the corner on the north side. I raise the opposite end so that its bottom edge lies at the bottom of the plywood base and mark it to correspond to the outer side of the vertical piece of the framework, which delineates the end of the sink compartment and the beginning of the dishwasher compartment. I rough-cut slightly beyond the mark and trim to the mark with the router as previously described.

After applying glue to the front edge of the plywood base at the northeast corner and the back of the 1 x 2, I nail the 1 x 2 to the edge of the plywood base, positioning the bottom edge of the 1 x 2 flush with the bottom side of the base. I space nails every foot or so, raising or lowering the 1 x 2 as needed to align its bottom with the bottom of the plywood. I do this by feeling with the forefinger of my left hand while nailing with my right. Whenever I encounter an upright framework member, I drive an additional nail through the 1 x 2 into it, which strengthens the framework and additionally secures the 1 x 2.

I select a 1 x 3 with at least one good side, mark, cut, and trim it in exactly the same manner as the 1 x 2 except that I install the 1 x 3 with its top edge aligned with the top of the framework. I also tack the 1 x 3 in place before nailing and place a level on it, adjusting the 1 x 3 so that it is perfectly level. If necessary to achieve level, I place the top edge of the 1 x 3 above the framework to avoid trimming the framework. I glue and nail the 1 x 3 in the same manner as the 1 x 2.

1 × 2 finish stile nailed to edge of plywood base

1 × 3 finish horizontal stile installed at top

I rough-cut a 1 x 2 1/4 inch longer than the i.d. between the lower side of the 1 x 3 and upper side of the 1 x 2, the 1 x 3 running horizontally at the top of the cabinet and the 1 x 2 running horizontally at the bottom of the cabinet. I trim one end square with the router and place the trimmed end on the horizontal 1 x 2 at the northeast corner. I place at the top of the vertically positioned 1 x 2 a mark that corresponds to the bottom edge of the 1 x 3 since it is to fit between the two horizontal pieces. Since the piece is too long and cannot fit between the two horizontal stiles, it must be held at an angle; its marked length will therefore be slightly longer than the actual i.d. This slightly additional length will make for a tighter joint and is desirable.

I draw a squared line across the piece on the mark and trim it with the router.

To place the piece vertically between the horizontal stiles, I lay a tip of the end on the 1 x 2 at the bottom, apply moderate upward pressure on the 1 x 3, and slip the top end under it. Once the tips of the vertical piece are between the horizontal stiles, I lay a scrap of wood on the piece and tap it into the correct position with a hammer.

1 × 3 and corner stile, end view

During the placement of this vertical piece, the horizontal stiles may easily become marred, particularly if the piece has been cut too long. If it is too long and is wedged into position with excessive force, it will simply raise the 1 x 3 or lower the 1 x 2 (the horizontal stiles), creating a curve at either locale. Excessive force should *never* be used to cram a piece into position. If moderate upward pressure against the 1 x 3 does not create enough space to permit installation of the vertical stile, it should be retrimmed. (One of the excellent features of a router is that it permits trimming away very small amounts from an end and leaving a smooth clean surface.)

After installing the vertical stile in the northeast corner on the east side, I install a vertical stile on top of the vertical framework piece that separates the sink and dishwasher compartments. Before completing the nailing (two nails an inch from the top and bottom and one midway on its length), I check it for verticality with the level and shift if necessary. I am not attempting to align the stile perfectly with the framework piece behind it but to position it vertically, which will also form a square with the horizontal stiles already leveled. (I check the joint between the vertical and horizontal stiles with the framing square and shift when needed.)

Each of the compartments that lies between the vertical stiles just installed is demarcated by vertical pieces in the framework. I place the 4-foot level beside each of these, plumb the level, and place light pencil marks on the 1 x 2 and 1 x 3 horizontal stiles to indicate the plumb positions of the new stiles to be cut and installed over them. I cut and install the vertical stiles as previously described. (I cut the vertical stile which will divide the sink compartment but do not install it at this time, waiting until after the plumbing has been completed before doing so. I have also omitted this piece from the framework for the same reason—to allow enough space under the counter to do the plumbing work without being too cramped.)

The horizontal stiles which fit between the vertical ones are now installed in the same manner— marking the position of each with the level and checking them with the square.

## Installing Cabinet Doors

The batten door in the photograph is made from a number of individual boards which are glued and screwed together by using 1 x 3 pine pieces called battens across their backs. The boards are the same 1 x 8 white-pine paneling used to cover the north and south sides of the cabinet.

In this kind of installation the doors are made larger than the opening defined by the stiles. The stiles will therefore serve as door stops and will eliminate the need for additional work to keep the doors from swinging into the opening.

Since the wood is 3/4 inch thick, the doors when shut will lie 3/4 inch out from the stiles if no further work is done to them. Because this protrusion is considered by some to be too "heavy" in appear-

Front of door

Upper batten

ance, the four sides of the door are often tapered from front to back to reduce their apparent thickness. In the doors in the photos, I have reduced the visible thickness to 3/8 inch by making a cut known as a "rabbet" on the backs of the doors around their perimeters.

Back of cabinet door

3/4-inch offset doors that appear flush

3/4-inch offset hinge mounted on stile and back of door

Lower batten

When a door is in a different plane from the stiles, it is called "offset." Standard offset hinges are manufactured which allow for this difference. Since the rabbet is 3/8 inch, I will use 3/8-inch offset hinges. Had the rabbet not been made, I would have used 3/4-inch offset hinges.

When the face of the door lies in the same plane as the stiles, it is called "flush." The installation of a flush door requires greater effort since its perimeter cannot touch the stiles at any point (to avoid sticking) and the gap between the door and stiles must be kept uniformly narrow to avoid unsightly appearance. Its hinges will also have to be mortised. Unless there is an overriding aesthetic reason for keeping the doors in the same plane as the stiles, the additional work of such an installation should be avoided.

Doors can also be installed so that they appear to be flush but are actually offset their full thickness, usually 3/4 inch. In this instance, the door covers all the stiles completely. Special hinges for this purpose are available.

In choosing the type of installation to be made (all are possible at this point), the determining factors should be the appearance desired and the amount of work one is willing to undertake. The differences in cost will be small.

### Making 3/8-inch Offset Batten Doors

I measure the height and width of the door opening. The 1 x 8 boards actually have only 7-1/4 inches of surface showing after their installation. I select as many pieces as will be needed to cover the width of the opening, allowing an additional 1/2 inch for a 1/4-inch overlap of the stiles on each side. I will want to remove the groove on the end piece on the side where the hinges will be mounted and will most likely have to rip the end piece on the opposite side to obtain the total width. For the sake of appearance and to leave a wide enough surface on which to attach two screws, I will rip both outside pieces to obtain strips on both sides that are at least 2 inches wide.

If a second door is to be installed beside the first to form a pair, I take into account the fact that the second door will also have its outside pieces ripped for width and I try to find a pleasing balanced arrangement.

The length of each piece will also have to be 1/2 inch greater than the height of the opening, allowing for the 1/4-inch overlap of the horizontal stiles at the top and bottom. Since I will be trimming these ends with a router, I allow an additional 1/4 inch and rough-cut each piece 3/4 inch longer than the height of the opening.

I select the two pieces of paneling that I will use on the outermost sides of the door. I remove the groove of the piece on which the hinges will be mounted and the tongue and V of the piece on the opposite side by ripping them roughly with the portable saw, then trimming with the router.

A quick and accurate way to rough-cut with the portable saw is to tack the ends of the piece to be ripped to the work table and position the power saw with the side of the left forefinger against the side of the wood as it is being ripped. It is maintained in the same position throughout the cut, acting as a fence. (With practice, the quality of rips can be made to almost equal those obtained with a table saw. In this instance, since the ripping is to be rough, the blade should be positioned to cut 1/8

3/8-inch rabbeting bit cutting at 3/8-inch depth

inch or so more than the required width to allow for later trimming with the router.

The carbide-tipped bit in the photo is designed to make the rabbet cut. The width of its cutting part is 3/8 inch. Directly below it, attached to the shaft, is a metal ring. The circumference of the ring is set back exactly 3/8 inch from the outermost tip of the cutter. When the ring (which acts as a fence) is held against the side of the wood, the bit will automatically cut 3/8 inch laterally.

The bit must be adjusted so that it will also cut to a depth of 3/8 inch. I do this by first setting the depth of the bit by eye, making a test cut in a scrap, measuring the depth of the cut, then raising or lowering the bit as needed by using the graduated ring. I make a second test cut to be sure I am cutting at a depth of 3/8 inch.

I placed a ripped end piece of paneling face down since I want the rabbet on the back of the door and use C clamps to hold it steady on the work table.

Using the router in the same manner I did the trimming bit, I cut the rabbet along the entire length of the side I have ripped (the outermost side of the door), sliding the ring below the cutter against the edge of the wood.

The ring will have a tendency to move laterally away from the wood, particularly if a knot is encountered. As a result, the lateral part of the rabbet will no longer be a straight line and its 3/8-inch width will be reduced. When this occurs, the router is simply shifted back so that the ring butts the wood and the router is again passed over the partially cut rabbet. In no case will the cut be greater than 3/8 inch in width, since the ring will not permit it.

Sometimes a knot may have fallen out or a gouge may exist along the side of a board to be rabbeted. If the side is not made straight before rabbeting is begun, the roller will follow the contour of the side and the resulting rabbet cut will follow the gouge. It is therefore necessary to examine the side of the wood being rabbeted and fill and sand smooth any depressions before any rabbeting is done. If a light-powered router is used, unnecessary strain may be placed on the machine if the entire rabbet is cut on one pass. If this occurs, as evidenced by excessive heat and/or a decrease in the speed of the bit accompanied by a change in sound, the ring should be brought only partway to the edge of the wood and the rabbet only partially cut, completing it on successive passes.

I make the same rabbet on the other side piece of the door.

I have cut these vertical rabbets now, since after the door has been assembled the battens will obstruct the path of the router.

I now lay all the pieces needed for the door face-down on the work table, the rabbeted sides outermost. I align the tops, using the side of the framing square as a straightedge and draw a line slightly below their ends, which I square with the outer rabbeted sides.

I measure, mark, and draw a parallel line 2-3/4 inches below the first line.

I select a straight 1 x 3 piece of pine and cut two pieces 2-1/2 inches shorter than the width of the door. I mark 1-1/4 inches in from each outer side along the second parallel line. One batten will lie between these two marks and along the 2-3/4-inch line.

I brush casein glue on one batten and the wood on which it will be placed and lay it in position. I will be attaching the batten and pieces of paneling with wood screws. The total thickness of the batten and paneling is 1-1/2 inches. Obviously I do not want the tip of the screw to come through the face of the door, yet I want a length that will adequately tie the two together. A screw length of 1-1/4 inches is best, since—for appearance's sake and to prevent snagging—I want the head of the screw slightly below the surface of the batten.

Screws are manufactured in varying thicknesses and are numbered in relation to the thickness of the straight unthreaded portion of the shank. (The second part of the number is the length of the screw.) I will use a #8 1-1/4-inch screw. (The lower the number, the thinner the screw.) The screws should also be rust-resistant and in this case are cadmium-plated, the cheapest of this type.

I use C clamps to hold the batten to the paneling after shifting it to its marked position and drill pilot holes through the batten and partially into the paneling below. I use a 5/64-inch bit to make a pilot hole appropriate for the screw I have selected and wind tape 1 inch above its tip as a depth reference.

Table for Pilot Holes

| SCREW DIAMETER | PILOT HOLE FOR PINE* |
|---|---|
| 2 | 1/32 |
| 4 | 3/64 |
| 6 | 1/16 |
| 8 | 5/64 |
| 10 | 3/32 |
| 12 | 3/32 |

*For hardwood, add 1/64 inch to pilot-hole diameter.

I drive the screws with a Yankee screwdriver and attach the batten to the paneling.

I measure down from the topmost line across the ends of the paneling and mark the other end at a distance which equals the height of the door opening plus the 1/2-inch overlap. I draw a squared line parallel to this 2-3/4 inches above it, mark 1-1/4 inches in from both sides along the second line and position the second batten between the marks and at the second line. I attach the second batten as I did the first.

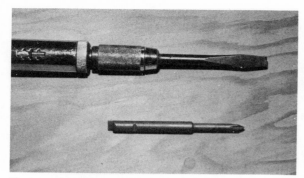

Yankee screwdriver and Phillips-head bit

3/8-inch offset hinge installed in 3/8-inch rabbet

Using the side of the batten as a fence and the 1/2-inch-diameter trimming bit, I trim the top and bottom of the door with the router.

Using the rabbeting bit in the router, I cut a 3/8-inch rabbet at the top and bottom. With rabbets already cut along the sides, this completes the 3/8-inch rabbet around the entire perimeter.

As long as the router base is kept flat on the wood while rabbeting, it will cut to the same 3/8-inch depth throughout, never deeper. The surface should therefore be kept free of chips or bits of material on which the router base may come to sit, causing a shallower cut. (If the cut is not deep enough in spots within a small area, the excess is removed with a wood chisel. If the area is large, another pass with the router is in order.)

## Hanging Cabinet Doors

The door has a rabbeted perimeter 3/8 inch wide while each of its sides has been cut to overlap the stiles by only 1/4 inch. When the door is centered exactly into the opening, there will therefore be a 1/8-inch gap at the back of the door between the inner line of the rabbet and the stiles. This "play" or tolerance allows the door to be shifted so that it can be hung level and plumb without any uncut portion of the back of the door striking the stiles, preventing full closure.

Shown are 3/8-inch self-closing offset cabinet hinges. When the door is moved less than 45 degrees from the stile, a spring within the hinge will close the door and keep it shut. This will eliminate the need for installing prong or magnetic devices to keep the door closed.

Hinges may be installed at any height, though they are most effective when located a short dis-

tance from the top and bottom of the door. When installed, they will help prevent warpage in the area where they are set. I usually place them 2 inches up from the bottom and 2 inches down from the top.

I mark these distances on the hinge side of the back of the door, placing an X below the top mark and an X above the bottom mark to indicate where the hinges will be placed in relation to the mark. I place the hinge on the top X, its offset portion lying in the rabbet and, using the screws provided with the hinge, attach the hinge to the back of the door without mortising. The screws are 5/8 inch long and pilot holes made with an awl will be sufficient. I simply press the awl point down into the center of the hole in the hinge, using my left index finger to stabilize it for better aim, then enlarge the hole by gently rotating the shaft.

I attach the other hinge in the same manner.

Level in position for marking tops of doors 1/4 inch above openings

Top of door 1/4 inch above opening

Maintaining position of door with knee while freeing hands to install hinge

I place the door into the opening and, using a level, shift the door so that its top is level and the inner side of the rabbet is clear of the stiles. I hold the door in this position by pressing it against the stiles with my knee. This frees my hands to make pilot holes with the awl and to screw the remaining portion of the hinge to the stile. (The hinge is made in one piece—there is no pin which when pulled will separate it into leaves.) I install the top screw for the upper hinge first and the top screw for the lower hinge next. Once they are in place, I am no longer obliged to keep the door in position with my knee, and I drive in the remaining screws.

I place the 4-foot level on top of the closed door and mark a light line across adjacent door openings to serve as a reference for aligning the tops of all the remaining doors.

Small circular pieces of felt with glue on their backs are provided with the hinges and are attached to the back of the door in the rabbet opposite the hinges for the purpose of muffling closing noises. They will undoubtedly fall off after a short while.

All the remaining doors are assembled and installed in exactly the same manner, their tops aligned with the top of the first one installed.

## Making Drawers

For the sake of economy, the drawers will be made from scraps of 3/4-inch white pine. Ordinarily, a 1/2-inch stock would be used for the sides and back. This stock is made from clear wood only (no knots) and, although it is not as thick, costs much more than the 3/4-inch white pine.

The heights of the openings left for the drawers are all even numbers—6, 4, 8, 10 inches. Since the width of a 1 x 6 is actually 5-1/2 inches, the 1 x 6 stock can be used for the sides and back of the drawer without the necessity of ripping 1 x 4, 1 x 8, 1 x 10 for the other drawers, since each opening is 1/2 inch higher than its corresponding standard stock. The 1/2-inch difference will not decrease the available space in the drawer since things can be

Completed drawer

placed in it higher than its sides without obstructing its movement. It is also a good practice to keep the height of a drawer below that of its opening to discourage cramming, since the sides are ordinarily used as references and objects are kept below them.

For the top (6-inch) drawer, I cut a 1 x 6 to a length that is 1/4 inch less than the width of the opening. This will be the back piece and it is the o.o. dimension of the width of the drawer. When the drawer is pulled out or pushed in, it will have a slight amount of lateral play, and I do not want this play to cause the sides of the drawer to strike the stiles. When I install the drawer, I intend to position it so that this 1/4-inch gap is divided into a 1/8-inch clearing on both sides.

Theoretically I can make the drawers 27-1/4 inches deep, but in practice great depth is more of a liability than an asset since pulling out a very long drawer to get something placed at the back of it is cumbersome. Anything longer than 18 inches becomes increasingly counterproductive. The owner has wisely chosen an 18-inch depth.

Since I intend to make a rabbet joint at the back corners, I must deduct 3/8 inch in length to allow for this. I therefore cut the sides of the drawer to a length of 17-5/8 inches. When assembled, the side will extend to the face of the stiles.

The front of the drawer, like the cabinet doors, will extend 1/4 inch beyond the opening on all four sides. I therefore rip and trim a piece for the front (or face) that is 1/2 inch greater in width and height than the opening.

I cut a 3/8-inch rabbet along the vertical sides of the back piece in the same way I did for the doors. When assembled, these rabbets will be toward the inside of the drawer.

I cut 3/8-inch rabbets along each vertical end of the two side pieces. These rabbets will also face the inside of the drawer.

Before I assemble the back and sides, I want to make some provision for the bottom of the drawer. The material used most often is 1/4-inch plywood. However, tempered Masonite (1/4-inch) is more attractive and easier to keep clean; I choose it.

Two methods are commonly used to attach the drawer bottom. One is to rabbet the bottoms of the sides and back to a depth of 3/8 inch, the back of the face to a depth of 5/8 inch (to keep it in the same plane), and then nail the bottom within the rabbet from the underside. Since the material for the bottom of the drawer is 1/4 inch thick and the depth of the rabbet is 3/8 inch after the bottom has been nailed in place, the sides and back of the drawer will extend 1/8 inch below the bottom. The back corners are then sanded a trifle so they will not make contact with the runners and only the bottom edges of the sides of the drawer will glide on the runners.

A superior but more time-consuming assembly method is to cut grooves 1/2 inch above the bottoms of the sides and back to a depth of 3/8 inch and install the bottom of the drawer within them.

The bit pictured is designed to cut a 1/4-inch-wide groove to any desired depth using the router. In this case I will use a 3/8-inch depth, which is more than adequate to support the drawer bottom when its sides rest inside the groove.

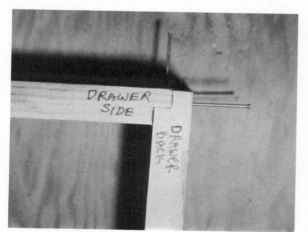

3/8-inch rabbeted joint at back and side of drawer

1/4-inch bit and 1/4-inch groove it produces

I establish a 3/8-inch depth with the pictured bit. I am going to cut the groove 3/8 inch above and parallel to the bottoms of the sides and back. Since the diameter of the bit is 1/4 inch, it will be cutting at a point 2-7/8 inches from the fence. (The radius of the base is 3 inches; deducting the radius of the bit [1/8 inch], I arrive at the distance at which the bit will be cutting.) Since I want the groove to lie 3/8 inch above the bottom of the sides and back, I add 3/8 inch to 2-7/8 inches for a total of 3-1/4 inches. If I draw a line that is 3-1/4 inches up from each bottom and parallel to it and clamp a fence along the line, I will be cutting a 1/4-inch groove which lies 3/8 inch above the bottoms of the sides and back and also parallel to them. I cut these grooves into the sides and back.

Establishing fence line for cutting groove in side piece of drawer

Fence clamped, groove cut for Masonite bottom

Much greater care is needed while cutting grooves than when trimming. In trimming, if a portion is missed because the router base has drifted from the fence, the excess can be trimmed off with another pass. When making a groove, if the bit is allowed to wander from the fence, the line of

the groove will be broken and the entire groove will be misplaced. It is therefore essential that *continuous contact* be maintained between the router base and the clamped piece being used as a fence. To insure that no wandering takes place, I direct my attention to the contact being made between the router base and fence. It is not necessary to look at the groove being cut; doing so is precisely what causes most wandering errors.

Furthermore, I alter the standard procedure of completing the cut from the opposite side. Instead, I take the additional time to clamp a scrap at the far side of the piece to be grooved and cut the groove completely in one pass from one end to the other. Since there is a greater possibility of error when first entering the cut then when cutting is already in progress, avoiding the second entry reduces the chances of error.

I assemble the sides and back, first applying glue to each joint surface, then nailing with #6 annular nails. The rabbet permits me to nail from two opposite directions for a stronger joint. I place a nail an inch from the top and the bottom on one side and nail at midpoint from the intersecting side in both joints. During the assembly, keep in mind that the rabbeted joints must be placed so that the *back piece is the full drawer width*. It has been cut to allow a 1/8-inch gap on each side as it passes through the stiles. If the side pieces are positioned so that they extend the width of the back, the drawer will be too wide to fit into the opening.

I measure the i.d. width of the drawer at the back piece. (The i.d. width between the grooves is 3/4 inch greater.) I cut a piece of Masonite 1/4 inch less

Sides and back assembled, grooves cut

Masonite slipped into grooves in sides and back

I draw a vertical line at the center of the front piece. I divide the i.d. distance of the back piece, measure outward from the center line these equal amounts, and draw two additional vertical lines on the front piece. These lines correspond to the interior width of the drawer at its back, and when the front ends of the sides are attached to the front piece, they will lie in a corresponding position. I draw a parallel line 2-3/4 inches inward from one of the lines and clamp a fence along it; using the 1/2-inch trimming bit in the router set to a depth of 3/8 inch, I remove all the wood that lies between the outer line and the edge of the front piece of the drawer. I repeat this on the opposite side.

The vertical cuts made along the sides of the front piece will permit the attachment of the front ends of the drawer's sides. (I make the attachment after all necessary cuts have been made on the back of the drawer front.)

I now want to remove wood along the bottom of the front piece to permit attachment of the forward

Marking back of drawer face for vertical rabbet along side

wide than the total width of the back and the grooves so that no binding will occur when I install the bottom. 1/4 inch of the Masonite will still lie within the grooves, which is sufficient support. I cut the Masonite 3/4 inch longer than the i.d. length of the sides. 3/8 inch of this excess will lie inside the groove in the back piece (there is no possibility of binding here). The other 3/8 inch will extend past the sides at the front of the drawer and will later be attached to the back of the drawer face. I brush glue in the grooves and along three edges of the Masonite and insert it into the grooves. (I omit the glue along the front edge for the time being.)

I take the piece I have cut for the face of the drawer and turn it on its back. (The front will not be worked on. After cutting and trimming the face to size, all subsequent cuts are on the back.) I want to make cuts around its perimeter which will permit the drawer when shut to lie 3/8 inch beyond the plane of the stiles. I also want to make cuts along the sides and bottom which will create a rabbet joint that is square to the back of the door. On the bottom, the cut must also allow for the Masonite to be attached and maintain its plane as established by the grooves in which it lies.

end of the Masonite. Since the Masonite extends 3/8 inch, I will cut to a depth of 3/8 inch. The top of the cut which I will make along the bottom of the front piece will be the height of the top surface of the Masonite. This is 5/8 inch above the bottom edge of the drawer. To this I must add 1/4 inch, which I have allowed for the overlap. I therefore draw a line parallel to the bottom of the front piece at a distance of 7/8 inch. I place a second line parallel to the first at a distance of 2-3/4 inches. I clamp a fence along the second line and, with the trimming bit set at a depth of 3/8 inch, remove all

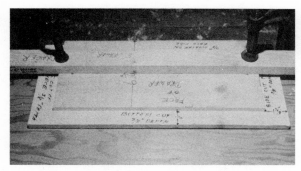

Fence clamped for bottom rabbet on back of drawer face

Notch at top of drawer back to fit guide

the wood which lies between the bottom line and the bottom of the front piece.

Along the top of the front piece, I make a simple 3/8-inch rabbet to extend down to the tops of the drawer's sides.

I brush glue on the ends of the side pieces and attach them to the vertical side cuts on the front piece using three #6 annular nails, one an inch from the top and bottom and a third centered between them. I attach the front end of the Masonite to the underside of the bottom cut by nailing through the underside of the Masonite with 1-inch-long #6 annular nails.

I place the back of the drawer in the opening. The previously installed upper guide prevents it from entering. I shift the drawer so that a 1/8-inch gap exists between the outer sides of the drawer and the stiles. I mark the position of the guide on the top edge of the back piece. I remove the drawer and cut a U-shaped notch in the back piece which corresponds to that portion of the guide which extends into the opening. I want the notch to be a hair wider and deeper than the guide, enough so

Masonite nailed to underside of rabbet on back of drawer face

that the drawer doesn't stick but not so large that it swings too much laterally as it is moved, defeating the purpose of the guide. I hope to leave a 1/32-inch gap on each side. This rather small tolerance is hard to achieve with an ordinary hand saw or sabre saw. I therefore cut the notch along the sides with a hacksaw to the desired depth, then use a wood chisel across the notch to complete the removal of the piece. If one is apprehensive about doing this, the notch can initially be cut slightly smaller than needed and the excess removed with a knife.

To keep the drawer from being inadvertently pulled out completely, I install on top of the back piece two screws which extend 1/4 inch above the upper stile at the front. When the drawer is pulled, the screws will keep it from coming completely out. The drawer can still be removed by pulling it to the screws, then lifting the front end until the tops of the screws clear the bottom of the stile.

Only the bottoms of the sides should make contact with the runners. I therefore sand a bit off the bottoms of the back corners so that they are a trifle above the runners.

I spread paste wax on the runners and the bottom edges of the sides and work it in with a few pulls and pushes.

I draw two diagonal lines from opposite corners on the drawer's face. These should be light for easy removal. I bore a 1/8-inch-diameter hole where the diagonal lines intersect. I place a knob with a threaded metal extension attached to it into the hole and attach it from the back with a nut. (Another type of knob is simply screwed to the face.) The drawer installation is now complete.

**223**

## Finishing the 6-foot Sides of the Cabinets

I start at the north side, where I have already installed a piece of paneling in the corner which enabled me to begin finishing the east side. The V and groove of this piece was ripped and trimmed off one side but the tongue was left on the other side. If a shoe mold is to be used at the bottom, all the paneling should be cut at the same time and about 1/4 inch shorter than the actual length needed. The top of each piece is then installed flush with the top of the framework and the 1/4-inch gap left at the bottom where it will later be hidden by the molding. Since I am not using a shoe mold, I place each 1 x 8 piece in the position it will occupy and mark its back where it meets the top of the cabinet framework. I cut them all with the portable saw in conjunction with the protractor. The floorboards are irregular; I must therefore measure and cut each piece individually.

After cutting each piece to length, I tap its groove into the tongue of the previously installed board, then toenail it at the top and bottom to drive it forward and create a tighter joint between the tongue and groove of the two pieces. To strengthen the framework and reduce the chances of warpage, I place an additional #8 galvanized finishing nail through the face an inch or so from the top and bottom and centered across the width. (The panel length here is less than 3 feet; when lengths longer than 4 feet are being installed, the span must be shortened. This is done by placing a horizontal member called a "cat" between the pieces in the framework to permit intermediary toenailing and the drawing in or out of warped boards.)

I continue marking, cutting, and nailing pieces until the last piece is to be installed. It is ripped to remove the tongue and V so that it will lie flush with the framework of the intersecting side. After this installation, the side is complete. (The width of the last piece will be the distance between the end of the tongue of the previously installed board and the intersecting corner.)

## Installing a Corion Countertop, Splash, and Shelf

There is probably no surface in a dwelling which receives as much and as varied use as the kitchen

Corion countertop

countertop. In choosing a material for this surface, durability and ease of maintenance are the primary considerations.

For a long time, Formica (a trade name—similar laminates are manufactured under different names) has preempted the field. Oak, stainless steel, porcelain tile, and maple butcher block have also seen use, but laminated countertops are still by far the most common. A number of plastic products have entered the field and one of these, Corion, was chosen for this kitchen. The photo shows its appearance one year after installation.

No "sealer" or other finishing product has been used on it and it has stood up extremely well. Formica requires a 3/4-inch plywood base beneath it; Corion does not. If the expense of the base is deducted, Corion costs a little more than twice the amount of a Formica installation.

Before beginning to work on the countertop, I first install several pieces of 1 x 2 within the framework and around each pipe that will be brought through the Corion. The pieces are installed in the same plane as the top of the framework and around each pipe to form a square. These will support the ends of the Corion which will be left after the pieces to allow for the pipes have been removed. It will also support those pieces of Corion that are reinstalled around the pipe area.

Since the depth of the countertop and the width of the Corion are both 30 inches, I do not need to trim. However, since the finished length is to be 9 feet, 1 foot of sheet length will have to be removed. To do this, I draw a squared line (for the router fence) 14-3/4 inches from one end and parallel to it I draw another at 12 inches. I place the Corion sheet on 2 x 4 blocks on the floor so that after the cut is made, *both* pieces of Corion will be supported. (The 1-foot piece to be removed is heavy and, if unsupported, will break before the cut is completed.) I also want the Corion raised off the floor high enough so that the cutting blade will not hit anything below.

I intend to make a rough initial cut with a masonry blade, then follow by trimming with the router. I try a number of test cuts using different saws and blades and discover that a hollow-ground rough-cutting blade in the sabre saw works best.

Hollow-ground blades are expensive but essential since the cheaper types cut very poorly, heat up quickly, and become dull rapidly.

The sabre saw has two speeds. The higher speed works better here. I make the rough cut along the 12-inch line, allowing as little excess as possible for later trimming. I clamp a fence along the 14-3/4-inch line and trim the rough cut with a 1/2-inch trimming bit in the router. This leaves an edge equal in smoothness and straightness to those factory-cut.

I locate and mark the position of any pipe which will rise through the Corion by placing the trimmed sheet on the partially completed cabinets and shift-

Masonry blade in circular saw cutting Corion, view from bottom

Sabre saw cutting Corion, rough cut

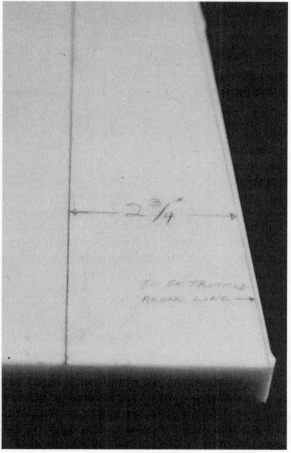

Corion marked for trimming with router after rough cut

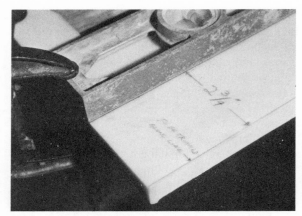

Fence clamped along 2-3/4-inch line

Trimming Corion with 1/2-inch carbide-tipped bit

ing it until it extends exactly 1-1/2 inches over the sides and equidistantly along the entire front. I place a steel framing square with its tongue along the back edge of the Corion and the arm butting one side of the pipe and draw a line down the arm. I repeat this on the opposite side of the pipe, giving me two parallel lines which are equal in width to the outside diameter of the pipe. I then measure how far the edge of the Corion extends beyond the cabinet face, deduct 1-1/2 inches from that amount, and measure that distance in along the parallel lines and draw a squared line across them to denote the depth of the cut. (The back edge of the Corion is butting the pipe, which prevents its proper placement.) If 1-1/2-inch pipe is handy, I stand an end between the parallel lines and at the line across them (toward the rear) and draw the outline of the pipe on the Corion. If there is no pipe handy, I set a compass to the outside diameter of

the pipe and draw the half circle. Again, the drawn circle must be toward the rear and at the cross line between the parallel lines. I then cut the drawn piece from the Corion. Using the sabre saw, I saw on top of the lines, thereby making the slot slightly larger than my measurements and avoiding any possibility of binding when the Corion is shifted into its proper place. (The pipe will later be covered by rope the thickness of which will hide any resulting gap and there is no need to attempt a perfect fit.)

A slot the width of the pipe's outside diameter remains at the rear of the Corion; I will later fill it with a piece of Corion. It will be supported by the 1 x 2 pieces installed in the framework around the pipe. The piece of Corion I have just sawed out is too narrow to use here since its width has been reduced by the kerf of two cuts along its sides. My procedure for measuring, marking, cutting, and installing the new piece will be exactly the same as that used to remove the old.

I now make provision for attaching the countertop to the cabinets below it. Rubber cement, which can be used to fasten Corion to itself or to wood, is available in tubes the same size and shape as caulking tubes and fit into ordinary caulking guns.

Neoprene cartridge in caulking gun, structural adhesive

The tube has a tapered plastic tip which is sealed to prevent the solvent from evaporating. I turn the handle of the gun so that the ridges along it face up and pull it back as far as it will go. Using a sheetrock knife, I cut an inch or so off the tube's tip, slicing it at an angle so that when rubber cement exudes from the end it will have a thickness of roughly 1/2 inch. I turn the handle so that the ridges face down and the long side of the angled cut I have made at the tip faces up. I squeeze the trigger—which pushes the handle forward, forcing its lower end into the tube. The lower end has a disc the size and shape of the interior diameter of the tube which pushes the rubber cement out. (If excessive force is needed, this means that some of the cement has probably dried in the tip and I insert a common nail into it and pierce the dried material.)

I lay a bead of rubber cement along the tops of all of the framework pieces, place the Corion in position, then place any heavy objects handy on top of the Corion to exert clamping pressure and maintain the Corion in position until the rubber cement has set (at least several hours). The resulting adhesion is excellent.

## Cutting the Hole for the Sink

Ordinarily it is more convenient to cut the hole for the sink before the splash is installed since the splash will only be a few inches from the back of the sink and may make cutting awkward. I follow the same practice here, although it doesn't matter since the counter is deeper than normal.

I turn the sink upside down on the Corion and position it. Its center dimension is given on the plan or should at least have been determined before the rough plumbing was installed. It may be located wherever wanted, but the nearer it is to the front edge, the more convenient it will be. However, it must be at least an inch beyond the inner side of the framework to allow for the sink's installation with clips.

After I position the sink, I trace its outline. I then draw a parallel outline 3/8 inch smaller than the first. Before cutting, I prop up the Corion to be sawed with 2 x 4s which extend to the base of the cabinet. The purpose of these "legs" is to prevent the Corion from breaking of its own considerable weight before the cut is completed. Using a carbide-tipped bit, I bore a 3/8-inch hole so that its circumference lies along the inside edge of the *smaller* outline. Starting at the hole, I then cut on the line of the *smaller* outline, using a rough-cutting hollow-ground blade in the sabre saw, and remove the piece.

(The sink is now ready to be attached to the countertop and the rough plumbing completed. This is detailed in the chapter on plumbing.)

3/4-inch radius bit and edge it produces

The edges of Corion are sharp. To decrease the possibility of injury caused by accidental contact with them, their sharpness is removed. (Only those edges exposed to traffic need be treated.) This is usually done by "rounding over." The sharp square edge is shaped into an arc by use of a radius bit and router.

The bit pictured has a 3/4-inch radius which when employed fully produces the edge shown. A wheel directly below the cutting surface acts as a guide and slides along the uncut edge of the Corion to maintain a uniform lateral distance throughout the cut. By raising the bit to different heights, the edge of the Corion can be shaped into different designs. Similar bits are available which will produce smaller arcs (down to a 1/8-inch radius) along the edge of the Corion. The bits are expensive. As an alternative, the sharp square edge can be rounded over into an arc by using fine sandpaper and the spinner sander.

## Making the Splash

The splash is that part of the counter which lies at a right angle to it at the back edge. It does not have to be made of the same material as the countertop but it should have the same endurance qualities.

There is no standard height for the splash and it is often, as here, determined on the basis of appearance. However, to prevent water from sloshing down the back of the cabinet, a minimum height of 4 inches is advisable. I cut it to height and length by rough-cutting with the sabre saw, then trimming it with the router.

Corion splash installed

Duplex receptacle recessed into splash

(Two outlet boxes like the one shown were installed as part of the rough wiring; their installation is detailed in the chapter on wiring.)

I place powdered chalk on the front edges of the electrical boxes, place the splash in the position it will occupy, and push it against the boxes. This transfers the chalk outline of the boxes to the back of the splash. I bore a hole within each outline and cut out the outlined area with a sabre saw, placing the blade directly over the lines so that the outlines will be slightly larger than the boxes, which will enable me to make minor adjustments in the position of the splash if necessary.

I lay a bead of white rubber cement along the back edge of the countertop, then place the splash on edge over the boxes and on the bead of cement. I place a pipe clamp at each end of the splash and a third at the center. The clamps lie between the top of the splash and the underside of the countertop. I tighten each clamp just enough to keep it upright

but loose enough to shift the splash a trifle. I place the framing square with one side on the countertop and the other on the splash and shift the top of the splash as needed (the bottom lies at the edge of the countertop) so that it is aligned into a right angle with the countertop. (Both surfaces butt the sides of the square continuously.) I then clamp the splash down fully.

The joint made by rubber cement and clamping will be more than sufficient to hold the splash. However, difficulty may be encountered in maintaining the splash at a right angle as the clamps are being tightened, since it will tend to slide in the still-wet rubber cement. If this occurs, the splash must first be positioned at a right angle by sandwiching it between 2 x 4s that are clamped to the countertop. I then place additional clamps on the splash and tighten it down into the cement.

I have used white rubber cement since the Corion is white and the cement residue in the joint will be less noticeable. If white rubber cement is not available, I use ordinary buff-colored rubber cement and place it at the middle and back of the joint; I then add white epoxy glue at the front (exposed) portion of the joint.

## The Shelf

A shelf is to be installed on top of the splash. I cut it to the length and width needed by rough-cutting with the sabre saw and trimming with the router. One side of the shelf will be supported by the splash. To provide support for the other side, I cut a 2 x 4 the length of the shelf. I cut two additional 2 x 4s which are the same length as the distance between the floor and top of the splash and nail these two on the flat to the ends of the 2 x 4 which is the length of the shelf. I stand up the assembled three pieces. The horizontal 2 x 4 will be used to support the far side of the shelf but must be set back 2 inches from the edge of the shelf so that it will not be noticeable. The Corion is strong enough to be unsupported that amount. I therefore mark the floor 2 inches back from the projected position of the shelf and, using #8 common nails, toenail the upright 2 x 4s to the floor at the marked position. To further stabilize the upright position of the assembled 2 x 4s, I cut and nail 2 x 4s between the vertical members of the cabinet framework and each of the upright pieces. I locate these horizontal

Corion shelf installed

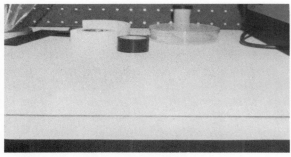

Formica countertop with 3/4-inch lip

5/4 × 2 Formica lip

pieces near the top of the cabinet, since I have already nailed the uprights to the floor. I lay a bead of white rubber cement along the top edge of the splash and the horizontal 2 x 4 and position the shelf on both. I lay several 5-gallon paint containers on the shelf as an alternative to clamping during the time the joints are setting up.

## Installing Formica Countertops

A Formica countertop can be placed on the same cabinets. However, its framework will be built somewhat differently, since the material used for the face stiles will also form the skeleton. This is possible since a 3/4-inch sheet of plywood must lie continuously under the Formica.

I build the kick, the plywood base, and the framework at the back and sides of the cabinet in the same way as before. Since I will have a second sheet of plywood at the top of the cabinet that is exactly the same size as the plywood at the base, I use the vertical face stiles as supports by nailing them to the edges of the plywood at the top and bottom. I then fill in the horizontal pieces between them. I cut, trim, and fit the Formica after its counter plywood base has been installed.

I build these Formica countertops elsewhere in the apartment. After the cabinet is built and before the Formica work begins, I add a strip of wood called the "lip" along the top edges, using a 5/4 x 2. (The lip can be smaller or larger or omitted entirely, depending upon the appearance desired.)

I rip a strip of Formica roughly 1/4 inch greater than the length and height of the already installed lip. If a table saw is used, the finished surface should be facing up during the cut, and if the portable saw is used, the finished surface should be facing down. In both instances, a plywood blade should be used since the laminate will chip along the cut if the blade's teeth are widely spaced. Even with the plywood blade, some chipping will occur, but the purposely greater dimensions allow for this. This strip of Formica will lie on the 2-inch side of the lip (its face).

I spread contact glue with a cheap brush on the back of the Formica and on the 2-inch face of the lip. I allow the glue to set until it is no longer sticky to the touch. (The time varies—twenty minutes or so is usually sufficient.)

I hold the forward end of the strip with my right hand and the rest in my left. I place the tip of the forward end in position at the end of the lip. By feeling with my right middle finger, I align the factory edge of the Formica with the bottom of the lip. Only the very tip of the Formica is in contact with the lip. When the tip is positioned, I begin to lay more of the strip against the wood, keeping the factory edge aligned with the bottom of the lip with my middle finger. I continue to place the strip in this manner until it is entirely against the lip.

The carbide-tipped bit in the router is designed to trim Formica and leave a square edge. (Another type leaves a very small radius or arc for a "rounded over" effect.) A guide at its lower end directly beneath the cutting edge automatically prevents the cutter from cutting beyond the edge of the wood. I place the router base flat against the 2-inch side of the lip, the bit above the ragged edge of the Formica which lies above the top of the plywood counter. I start the machine, lower the bit into the Formica, and move laterally along the ragged edge with the guide resting on the top surface of the plywood. The bit then cuts the Formica into a straight line that is flush with the top of the plywood.

Groove and plastic edging for lip

and let dry at least two coats of contact glue before positioning the Formica.

As a further alternative to facing the lip with Formica, a flexible plastic strip may be used. Available in different widths and colors, it is easily installed.

A groove 1/2 inch deep and 1/16 inch wide is cut into the edges where the strip is to be installed, using the router and a splining bit. The depth is controlled automatically by a guide and the width is constant since the thickness of the cutting edge is 1/16 inch. Before making the groove, the bit is adjusted so that it will cut along dead center. The router is then pushed around the perimeter with its base flat on the material being grooved and the guide butting against the edge.

(The material in the photo is "chipboard"—chips of wood pressed and glued together to form sheets. It is a satisfactory plywood substitute for cabinet work.)

The back of the plastic strip has a wedge-shaped piece which is pressed into the groove. No glue is needed. The excess can be cut off with a hacksaw or a metal-cutting blade in the sabre saw.

Formica trimming bit, straight cut

I trim the excess length in the same manner.

I rough-cut Formica to cover the countertop, leaving 1/4 inch or so of excess beyond the plywood surface. After gluing with contact glue (no clamps necessary), I trim the edges with the router bit guide butting the already installed strip of Formica on the lip.

The procedure for installing the Formica countertop is exactly the same when the edge of the plywood is used for the lip. However, since the edge of the plywood is porous, it is best to apply

## Building Wall Cabinets above Counters

The pictured cabinet is mounted on a kitchen wall. While it is not above a counter, this type of cabinet can be used in such a locale, its top located the standard height of 7 feet above the finished floor. The techniques used to build this cabinet are the same used to build those of all sizes over a counter. I will now detail them.

Wall-mounted cabinet

The cabinet is 12 inches deep, 4 feet wide, and its overall height is 24 inches. (Cabinets used above the counter are usually closer to 30 inches in height. Given the height of 7 feet for the top, the splash for a standard-size cabinet would therefore be 18 inches high. This can be modified by building a larger cabinet, but the lower the cabinet comes to the countertop, the more cramped the space will be for washing dishes, etc. If the splash area is 18 inches high, it can be divided by building a 6-inch splash and leaving a foot of wall visible above it.)

Using the table saw or portable saw with a protractor, I cut two pieces of 1 x 12 common pine to a length of 24 inches. These are the side pieces.

I measure down 11-5/8 inches from an end, mark, and place an X below it. My mark is on the edge of the wood. Since I plan to divide the cabinet at midpoint with a shelf 3/4 inch thick, by marking in this way the shelf will be positioned exactly at center. I keep the ends of both side pieces flush and, with a T square, draw a line across the edges of both boards at the mark. I have placed the lines on the edges for easy reference when nailing the center shelf. I measure and place the same marks on the opposite edges of the side pieces.

I cut three 1 x 12s (the top, bottom, and shelf) to a length of 46-1/2 inches. With the thicknesses of the side pieces, the overall width of the cabinet will be 4 feet, as planned.

I place a 46-1/2-inch length on edge on the floor with one end butting the wall. I nail a side piece at a right angle to the opposite end using 3 sixpenny ring nails. I nail a second 46-1/2-inch piece to the other end of the side piece.

I stand the three pieces up with the side piece flat on the floor and nail the second side piece to the other ends of the 46-1/2-inch pieces.

1 x 12s will often vary in width. I keep all variations to the back of the cabinet, keeping the front flush. I also watch for the best surfaces of each piece, placing the good side of the bottom and middle horizontal pieces up and the good side of the top horizontal piece down. Since the outside of the sides will be visible, I place their best surfaces toward the outside.

I place the center horizontal shelf in position, using the marks I have made on the edges as a reference, and nail. I turn the partially assembled cabinet upside down and nail the other end of the middle horizontal piece. I have now assembled the sides and three horizontal pieces.

I turn the cabinet to lie face down on edge. If the widths of the boards vary more than 3/16 inch, I remove the excess with the electric block plane. The edges at the back will be hidden and I do not spend time bringing them into perfect alignment, removing excess width only over the 3/16-inch tolerance.

Using the portable saw, I rough-cut a 4-foot piece of 1/4-inch plywood (or Masonite) 24-1/4 inches wide. I place the plywood, good side down, on the back of the cabinet. I tack a blue lath nail (smooth shank) through the plywood and into the edge of the pine. I align the 4-foot edge of the pine with the 4-foot side of the plywood, pushing the pine in or out as needed so that both are flush, and nail from one corner to the other.

I shift a 2-foot side of the cabinet so that its edge is aligned with the 2-foot factory edge of the plywood and nail.

This will bring the cabinet into square since it is aligned with the square plywood sheet.

I nail the remainder of the perimeter and trim away the excess plywood with the portable saw. I check the center shelf board to see that it is lying straight and shift it if necessary. I pop a chalk line across the back of the plywood, using the nails previously installed in the sides as a center reference and nail through the plywood on the chalk line into the center of the back edge of the middle horizontal shelf.

The plywood back, in addition to its use as a square reference, securely ties all the individual 1 x 12s into a whole unit. The nails driven through it spaced every 8 to 10 inches also serve to prevent the shelves from sagging when weight is placed on them. (If the width of the shelf is 6 inches or less, no support will be needed at the front of the shelf. If the shelf is wider than 6 inches, sagging will begin in proportion to the width. It is therefore advisable to use vertical stiles at the front of the shelf when the width is greater than 6 inches.)

The face stiles and doors are installed in the manner detailed for cabinets under the counter.

To mount the cabinet on the wall, I drive four #10 common nails through the plywood and into the masonry core of the wall. I locate them 1 inch above the middle shelf, where they will not be noticeable, and drive them at a downward angle of about 45 degrees.

To facilitate mounting the cabinet, especially if I am working alone, I draw a level horizontal line with the 4-foot level at the proposed height of the bottom of the cabinet. I tack a cleat at and below this line, place the cabinet on the cleat during installation, and afterward remove the cleat.

The pictured cabinet took me an hour and a half to build, using the techniques I have detailed. Cabinets twice as large take about twenty minutes longer.

When there are no obstructing pipes (as there were here), I use the same technique for constructing cabinets both above and *below* the counter. If the cabinets will lie within intersecting walls I modify my procedure by omitting the installation of the stiles until I have installed the cabinets, building them 1/2 inch less than the distance between the intersecting walls. I then butt the stiles against the walls at each end to cover the gap.

# FINISHES

**8**

## Paint

As I have continually pointed out, the material most often used to cover and finish surfaces—paint—is also the worst. A poor cosmetic, it deteriorates rapidly and must be redone every few years. In many cities the application of multiple paint coats has been institutionalized by mandatory provisions in rent laws that require periodic repainting. This attempt by lawmakers to require maintenance of a fresh appearance in the interior of dwellings has had the effect of discouraging manufacturers from improving their product, since they know that periodic repainting required by law insures continuing sales. This built-in obsolescence has evolved to the point that the consumer no longer even questions the fact that in two or three years he or she will be obliged to repaint a freshly painted surface to maintain its appearance.

Advertising assertions of one-coat, long-lasting paints are simply that—advertising assertions. In every single instance that I have used paint to cover a surface, I have never been able to use only one coat and have often been dissatisfied with the appearance of two. Moreover, the paints I have used include well-advertised brand names (outrageously priced) as well as cheaper, unadvertised products. Like aspirin, I have found no difference between them.

Before paint is applied to *any* surface, I therefore suggest that alternatives be considered. The most obvious is to remove the existing paint, leaving the surface in its natural state or treating it with another finishing material.

## Removing Paint from Wooden Cabinets

The seventy-year-old cabinets (see next page) are covered with a least a dozen coats of oil-based paint so thick that the doors no longer close. Irregularities caused by flaking paint have marred the surface so much that even a fresh coat of paint will look old before it has dried. The glass panels, also covered by multiple paint layers, might as well be cardboard.

Old, freshly painted cabinets

Stripped kitchen cabinet, new glass

Stripped kitchen cabinet and counter

This photo shows the same cabinets stripped of paint. (Once the paint has been removed, the doors operated perfectly without need of planing.) The cost of removing the paint was about double the cost of repainting. Stated another way, the cabinets were stripped at a cost equivalent to two repaintings. Done a year ago, they show almost no sign of use. Chances are they will remain in excellent condition without further treatment for the next fifteen years, and considering the number of repaintings that would have been required during the same period, the initial cost of paint removal will be more than justified.

They are made of fir, a wood used for many kitchen cabinets in older apartments and townhouses. Occasionally a more expensive hardwood will have been used, but rarely will a cabinet have been made from a type or grade of wood so poor that it deserves to be hidden. What wood lies under the paint can easily be determined by removing a patch from the back of a door using a hook scraper or similar tool.

The method I use to remove the entire paint surface is called "burning." For some inexplicable reason, use of this excellent technique has been limited to professionals, while laymen have been steered to "paint-remover" solvents, the use of which is relatively costly, messy, and a great deal more time-consuming.

A propane torch can be purchased at a modest price in a hardware store. The propane is carried in the cylindrical tank, which can be replaced when empty. The torch has a variety of uses, including soldering copper joints. The tip which concentrates the flame in one spot is not the best pattern for removing paint, but I suggest its use until familiarity with the "burning" technique has been acquired. Later, a "fan" tip can be used which spreads the flame over a larger area, permitting more efficient paint removal.

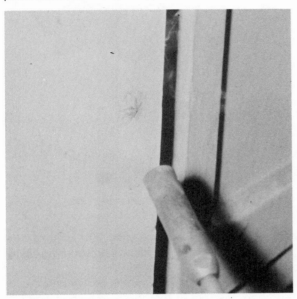

Propane torch flame directed at paint to be removed

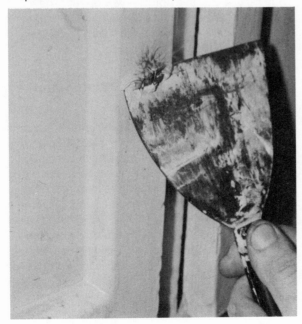

Scraping blistered paint

The torch is lit by turning the valve above the tank counterclockwise until the gas is heard escaping *slowly.* (If too much gas escapes it will blow out the match rather than ignite. It is even better to use a flint "sparker" instead of a match.) A match is lit or a spark is made to ignite the propane, then the valve is used to adjust the flame. For removing paint I want a flame with a relatively wide outer portion.

I hold the torch in my left hand and a 3-inch spackling knife in my right. I direct the flame against the paint. After a very brief interval, the paint will begin to blister. As soon as this happens I move the flame to an adjacent area, keeping part of it on the blister so that successive layers of paint under the blister will also loosen. The total time required to loosen *all* layers of paint will be very brief. As I begin moving the flame away from the blister to the adjacent area, I move the knife to the blistered area and scrape away the loose paint by sliding the knife along the wood below it. The movement of the flame and the removal of the loosened paint should become continuous; as the flame is being moved steadily over an area at a speed proportionate to the number of coats, the knife should be following behind it removing the loosened paint.

If the flame is permitted to remain on an area for too long the paint may ignite, but the fire will be limited to the area touched by the torch and a flash fire over the entire surface *will not* suddenly develop. The burning paint can easily be snuffed out by blotting with a rag.

The wood below the paint may char, but only on its surface. After the paint has been removed, the surface charring can be sanded with 100-grit paper on the spinner sander. The marks left by the spinner sander are then removed using the orbital sander with fine emery cloth.

To protect the floor from blobs of hot or burning paint, it's a good idea to cover the area where stripping is being done with a piece of flexboard or any other nonflammable product.

It is also necessary to have on hand a scrap piece of nonflammable material on which the knife can deposit the paint removed. The paint becomes hard and brittle within a second or two after removal and will come off the knife relatively easily.

One of the best features of removing paint with a torch is that *all* layers of paint are removed simulta-

Stripped cabinets after paint removal by burning and before light sanding

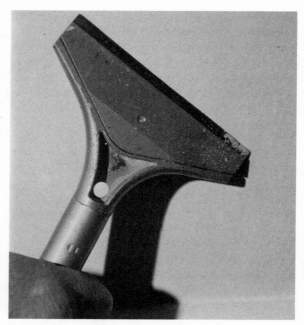

Paint scraper for removing paint from glass

neously, exposing the wood surface completely. Moreover, it makes little difference whether there are three coats or thirteen, since the time required for the latter is only slightly longer than the former.

The exposed wooden surface may have an oily film over it caused by oil in the paint, but it can easily be removed by using fine emery cloth on the orbital sander. Since sanding the surface of the wood will ordinarily be undertaken to achieve a uniform appearance, no additional work is really created by surface charring or the oil deposit.

When other than flat surfaces are encountered, the sides and corners of the spackling knife can be used for removing the paint. Of course, any metal tool that fits the shape of the area being scraped will do. If for any reason it isn't feasible to use the flame in a particular area, the hook scraper or sander can be used as an alternative.

Particular attention must be paid to the flame as it approaches glass panels, since its heat can crack them. Since the torch cannot be used over the painted glass and other methods of paint removal are at best tedious, purchasing new glass should be considered. The old glass can be removed easily by removing the stops around it at the back of the door. The stops are usually attached with brads (small nails) and the same pieces can be used again after the new glass is installed. The cost of new glass is far less than the labor involved in scraping the paint.

If removing the paint from the old glass is decided upon, the tool in the photo—which is simply a wide razor blade in a holder—works well. The blade should be held at about a 30-degree angle against the glass while it is slid forward with short jabbing strokes against the painted surface.

## Applying Wood Finishes (Watco and Satin Polyurethane)

After all paint has been removed from the cabinets and their surfaces have been sanded (sanding should take relatively little time, proving once again that the wood is in excellent condition), the wood will be porous and susceptible to finger marks, stains, dirt, etc. Although not used on the cabinets shown in the photos, my choice to finish the wood is a product called Watco. It is a liquid natural oil with hardeners in it that is applied with a brush then rubbed with a rag. If clear Watco is used, the color of the wood is only slightly darkened. In addition to a clear finish, Watco is available in a variety of stains which permit the grain of the wood to remain visible beneath a protective coat while reducing the contrast between different-colored woods. I have used a single coat with satisfactory results, but two coats are preferable.

The drying time varies, but if one allows the Watco to dry overnight, that should be sufficient. When Watco dries, it leaves a hard surface that stands up well. The surface will be neither glossy or matte, but roughly equivalent to the sheen obtained with satin varnishes or very much like the non-glossy furniture finishes widely used today. Despite its excellence (it is widely used as a furniture finish though not under its trade name), it suffers from a limited distribution and may be difficult to find.

Watco is durable, quickly and easily applied, somewhat overpriced, and an excellent finish for kitchen cabinets (as well as furniture).

As an alternative, one can use a satin polyure-thane as a finish on kitchen cabinets. The plastic film it leaves is tough and durable. It dries to the touch in three hours under average weather condi-tions and a second coat can be applied after six hours, eliminating the need for light sanding be-tween coats which the manufacturers recommend. However, if the first coat is allowed to set up for twenty-four hours or more, light sanding will be-come necessary to insure adhesion of the second coat to the surface of the first.

Polyurethanes manufactured by different compa-nies range widely in cost, but I have never found a difference in quality between them and therefore purchase the cheapest.

Polyurethane is more difficult to handle than Watco. Since it is clear and brushed on, drips and runs are easily formed and difficult to see. Bubbles also form easily and, if allowed to remain, leave a noticeable white-edged ring after drying and punc-ture. Any polyurethane lying on the wood under the bubble will remain wet since it is not exposed to air, and the dried material of the bubble, when punc-tured, will be trapped by the still-wet polyurethane and cause a smudge. (Since Watco is spread with a rag, it neither runs nor forms bubbles.) Additional-ly, the drying period during which polyurethane may pick up and hold dust and dirt blown on its surface is relatively long, and any impregnated foreign material will have to be removed with steel wool. If drips which occur as the polyurethane is being applied are not removed, they will form a crust and remain plastic in their interior. Such spots will have to be removed by sanding and the

area recoated. To avoid these difficulties, I apply polyurethane as follows.

I remove the lid from the can and knock holes in the rim with an awl to permit the urethane that will accumulate there to drain back into the can.

I use a 2-inch-wide nylon sash brush which has an angled rather than straight end. This allows easier access into corners. I dip the brush into the polyurethane to a depth no greater than 1-1/2 inches; then, as I raise it, wipe off the polyurethane on the side of the brush closest to myself by sliding it along the rim of the can. The 1-1/2-inch depth corresponds to the maximum amount I want to carry on the brush during any one application. If I dip it more deeply, the polyurethane will run toward the handle of the brush after a few dozen strokes.

Using *light* pressure, I lay the polyurethane-filled side of the brush on the surface of the wood and, maintaining the same *light* pressure, stroke down-ward from the point of application, then upward past that point for an equal distance. On each succeeding stroke I overlap the end of the previous one by a couple of inches. My pressure throughout each stroke is only that necessary to spread the liquid into a film.

If excess pressure is applied to the brush, the polyurethane will be squeezed out along its sides, thus creating a source of runs. The polyurethane will also be pressed into the ∙ipper part of the bristles and will drip as the brush is being moved from the can to the wood.

*Polyurethane is particularly susceptible to bub-ble formation and leisurely application is a must.*

When viewed directly, runs and drips are difficult to see. Before I finish brushing an area, and before it has dried, I view the surface from the side, where any irregularities are more apparent, and brush out any imperfections.

I wipe the brush clean with a rag soaked in mineral spirits *before* the polyurethane liquid builds up and reaches the handle. If more polyure-thane is to be applied the following day, I store the brush overnight in a can filled with mineral spirits covering the entire bristle area. I suspend the brush by placing wires through the hole on its handle and hanging them on the circumference of the can which I cover with a rag. If no further application of polyurethane is planned, I wash the brush thor-oughly in mineral spirits, removing *all* polyurethane in the bristles. (Unless this tedious chore is done thoroughly, the brush might as well be thrown away.)

I have finished kitchen cabinets using a variety of shellacs and varnishes, mixtures of linseed oil and turpentine, and by applying clear lacquers in conjunction with heat. I recommend that all such finishes be avoided and that the choice be confined to Watco or polyurethane.

## Refinishing Painted Doors

The interior doors of older dwellings will ordinarily be made of clear (few or insignificant knots) and attractive wood. On the East Coast fir and pine are commonly found, while on the West Coast redwood is widely used. Generally, these doors are paneled. Their perimeters are usually made of 1-3/4-by-5-3/4-inch stock, while the area within the perimeter is divided in a variety of ways. When the paint is removed, it will usually reveal wood that is in excellent condition. The door is most conveniently worked on if it is removed from its hinges and placed on horses. Paint will have often "glued" the pin. To loosen it, I drive the end of a screwdriver into the joint between the pin and knuckle near the top of the hinge.

When the pin has been loosened, the screwdriver end is placed under the flange of the pin and driven upward.

The bulk of the door has a flat surface, and burning the paint off is relatively easy. Sanding, too, is easy since the wide flat surfaces can be done with a belt sander, first using medium (80-grit), then fine (120- or even 200-grit and up for very fine work) paper.

The thinner material used for the panels may or may not be the same wood used for the framework.

Belt sander on door

Before one decides to refinish all interior doors "naturally" by removing all of the paint from every door, it's a good idea to remove a patch of paint from a panel and the framework of each door and check to make certain the wood is uniform. If it isn't, staining may become necessary. (Since it was nearly universal practice to select the same style and wood for each door and to maintain it throughout, one door will probably be made of the same wood as all the rest.)

Since hardware on older doors is often solid brass, removing paint from it should also be undertaken. Soaking the hardware in paint remover will usually offer the easiest method for paint removal.

The frames around interior doors are also usually made of wood. The jambs and head are commonly clear pine, while the casing may be any one of a dozen other kinds of wood. The contrast between the two woods is not likely to be great since all are relatively light-colored.

The paint is removed from the frame and door by burning. Light sanding with 200-grit closed-coat paper in the orbital sander should then be done to remove oil from the surface. Once all the wood has been exposed, undesired sharp contrasts in color can be reduced by applying Watco to which an appropriate factory-mixed stain has been added. The stained Watco is brushed on lightly and wiped off quickly with a rag when the contrast is to be reduced slightly and laid on more heavily and wiped off less quickly for greater reduction. If there is no contrast, or if the existing contrast is found to be pleasing, clear Watco can be applied.

As an alternative to Watco, a coat of stain followed by two coats of polyurethane can be applied. This arrangement offers a much greater variety of color shading, since individual stains are available in many more colors than those mixed with Watco. (At the time of purchase it is essential to specify that polyurethane is to be applied over the stain so that a type of stain compatible with polyurethane is supplied.)

## Finishing Walls

About twenty years ago I renovated a building for a group of doctors. I covered all the plaster walls with a white wallpaperlike material the surface of which is protected with a clear plastic film. (It is very similar in texture to lightweight oil cloth.) The group recently tired of the appearance and contracted for another renovation. The plastic-coated sheets were still in almost as good a condition as when I first hung them. They had never been painted and were only wiped off with a soapy cloth from time to time as a part of normal cleaning and to scrub out dirty scuff marks. Given the traffic in the clinic, periodic repainting would have been required every two years. The added cost of the original installation was more than justified by the money and effort saved in eliminating continued repainting and repair.

In the past twenty years a variety of "wallpapers" have been introduced, a great many of which have protective coatings that stand up adequately to hard household use. These include clothlike papers which are almost identical in appearance to white painted walls and which never flake, chalk, alligator, or require recovering.

The price of these durable, washable "wallpapers" (they are not truly papers but are sold in rolls and installed in the same manner as wallpaper) is still such that if a medium-quality product is purchased, the same proportion in savings that existed twenty years ago can still be realized—the initial cost of installation will be recovered within four years (two repaintings).

The use of wallpaper over plaster walls is by no means a new idea. It is standard in England and Ireland, and the homes of those countries are replete with the gaudy rococo flowered patterns often selected. In many New England homes the wall surface was papered after a 3/8-inch-thick coat of gypsum plaster and sand was first applied. Today papers are available in a huge variety of patterns and solid colors, including several shades of white, and before a wall is painted serious consideration should be given to using wallpapering as an alternative.

Whether paint or paper is chosen, before either is applied to a wall or ceiling, the raw plaster surface (or any allied product such as spackle used to repair an old wall) must first be sealed. This is done by applying a film of either shellac or "size" over the raw surface, preventing it from interacting with the wallpaper paste or paint.

If paint is applied directly over a raw plaster surface, the plaster will show through it when it has dried and a dozen coats will not hide the raw areas. If wallpaper is applied directly over a raw plaster surface, the water in the paste will be withdrawn by the plaster and very poor adhesion will result. By applying a film of sealer to the raw surface such situations are avoided.

It is best to apply the shellac or size in two coats. If shellac is used, the first coat should be thinned with 10 to 15 percent denatured alcohol (also used to clean the brush or roller) and the second coat with 5 percent denatured alcohol. The first coat will dry *to the touch* in about twenty minutes under ordinary weather conditions, but *it is probably not completely dry and a minimum of two hours should be allowed before applying the second coat.* A minimum of two hours should also be allowed for the second coat to dry, and if the shellac is being applied in cold and damp weather, it may not dry for several days.

If paint is applied over shellac which has not dried thoroughly, the paint (particularly if it is latex-based) will develop a multiplicity of cracks and the cracks will appear in each successive coat.

Size is cheaper than shellac and, although not as good, it is satisfactory. Both can be applied with either a roller or brush. I prefer to use a wide 4-inch brush since the sealers have a strong tendency to "run" and are easier to control with a brush.

## Hanging Wallpaper

While thicknesses of wallpapers vary, all are relatively thin and will reveal imperfections in the wall. The smoothness of the wall and the absence of foreign particles will determine to a great extent the quality of the result.

I am using a plain white vinyl paper. If the room is larger than 10 feet square, I am able to set up a 3/4-inch 4 x 8 sheet of plywood on horses to use as a work table within it. If smaller, I use the nearest adjacent room that is large enough to accommodate the work table.

I use ordinary wheat paste to hang thin paper or cloth, vinyl paste if they are thick. One pound of paste will be enough for 150 square feet of surface. I place 12 pints of water in a clean plastic bucket and gradually sift the powdered paste into it, stirring continuously with a mixing bit in the variable-speed drill. I keep stirring until all lumps have disappeared.

Wallpaper tool kits are available for under $2. They contain a circular cutter which, although new,

Mixing bit in variable-speed drill

Brush for applying paste and brush for smoothing paper

will have to be filed (using a flat bastard file) and honed with a carborundum stone in order to make it sharp enough to cut. (Triangle cutters made in England work much better but are hard to find.) The kit also contains a roller and two brushes.

The long-handled brush is used to spread the paste, while the other is used to smooth out bubbles and wrinkles after the paper is on the wall.

Papers are sold in rolls of different widths and lengths. Cost is determined by the square footage contained in a particular roll so that no savings can be expected from purchasing longer or wider rolls. The wider rolls are a little more difficult to handle but involve less work because they create fewer seams. The rolls are protected by an additional strip along the edges called selvage. Selvage should not be trimmed when using the technique I will now detail.

I measure the total width of the walls and divide this total by the width of the roll being used to arrive at the number of pieces needed.

I measure the height the paper will occupy and cut all the pieces about 3 inches longer so they will extend above and below this height when I first place each sheet on the wall.

Using the 4-foot level as a straightedge, I cut the paper to length with a sheetrock knife, measuring the first sheet with a ruler and then using it as a model for the rest. I cut all the pieces I will need.

I measure out from a corner a distance that is 1/2 inch less than the width of the roll and, with the 4-foot level, draw a plumb vertical line at this mark between the top and bottom of the wall.

I place the smoothing brush in my back pocket and the circular cutter in my nail apron. I place a length of paper face-down on the work table, one end a few inches from the edge. I brush paste on the back surface about halfway down the length, then bring the pasted end back over itself (without creasing the paper) so that both pasted surfaces lie against each other and the end is about a third of the way down the entire length of the sheet. I pull the opposite end up on the table (it will hang over the edge if its length is more than 8 feet), complete brushing on the paste, and fold this end toward the center—bringing it close to the end already there but not over it.

I use a 5-foot stepladder and bring the folded sheet to the corner where it is to be installed. I separate one end from the rest of the sheet and place the top of the sheet against the wall so that an inch or so lies on the ceiling.

I keep both palms pressed against the sheet and wall and slide the sheet laterally until its edge is aligned with the plumb vertical line. I align the sheet and press it to the wall only above the bottom fold.

I now shift the opposite side towards the corner by pressing down gently with my palms and sliding the sheet.

With the sheetrock knife, I slit the paper in the corner along the inch or so that lies on the ceiling. This will permit the paper in the corner to be folded without wrinkling.

I remove the smoothing brush from my back pocket after I have smoothed most of the bubbles and wrinkles by shifting the paper with my hands. I wipe the brush over the paper, working outward from its center, and create a crease along the corner by jabbing the brush into the corner over the paper.

I unfold the lower portion, continue to align its edge with the plumb line, and complete pasting the rest of the sheet in the same manner as I did the upper portion.

The objective in this first step is to establish an initial length of paper with a side that is aligned vertically. I also want the ends of the paper to extend above the wall and ceiling joint and below the baseboard. I also want the paper to come around the corner by 1/2 inch at most (if it is more than this it becomes increasingly difficult to make it lie flat), since I will end the papering in this corner with another sheet and will need a small strip of paper beneath it.

Finally, I want all the paper to make smooth and flat contact with the wall. To achieve this, I first remove the larger bubbles and wrinkles by sliding the paper outward from them with my hands until they are almost gone, then brushing outward in three directions, maintaining the alignment along the drawn line. I apply only light pressure with the brush and cover the entire surface of the sheet in order to insure continuous contact between the sheet, paste, and wall. Even after all the bubbles have been removed, the sheet will not be perfectly flat because of the still-wet paste. This irregularity will disappear as the paste dries.

If at any time I inadvertently crease the paper and a sharp wrinkle results, I lift the sheet from the wall far enough to pull it gently away from the crease, then reposition it. If at any time a series of wrinkles or large bubbles appears, I lift the paper away from the wall in the troublesome area, reposition the edge along the vertical line, then work the sheet toward the corner by gradually pressing the sheet against the wall and eliminating most, if not all, of the bubbles and wrinkles. (While hanging the first sheet, one quickly learns at what point there are too many bubbles and wrinkles to be removed with the brush and when lifting and repositioning the sheet become necessary. In general, if a bubble is more than several inches in diameter or a wrinkle more than several inches long, they are best removed by repositioning the sheet.)

Once the sheet has been installed properly, its ends must be trimmed. I jab the brush into the joint between the wall and ceiling to crease the paper into a distinct line. I then lay my left hand on the paper near the joint to keep it from shifting and roll the circular cutter along the folded paper over the joint. I repeat this at the bottom of the sheet to remove the excess along the baseboard. If the cutting disc has not been keenly sharpened, the paper will bunch up and the cut will only be partial and ragged. (If it becomes too difficult to trim the ends of the sheet with the cutting disc, a sheetrock knife with a new razor blade should be used instead.)

I paste and fold the second sheet of paper in the same way as the first. I place it on the wall so that one side laps over the previously installed length by 2 or 3 inches. I initially position the sheet by sliding it along the wall with my palms, then complete the application with the brush, stroking outward from the center in all four directions to remove small bubbles and wrinkles and to insure continuous contact between the sheet, paste, and wall.

When positioning the second sheet, I use the edge of the first as a plumb reference. I do this by eye, keeping the overlap equidistant all the way down the sheet. The first sheet creates a visible bulge under the overlap and its edge is all the reference I need.

I place the 4-foot level with its side anywhere on top of the overlap and, using the sheetrock knife, cut through *both sheets* for their entire length. I remove the cut strip from the top sheet, then lift its edge and remove the cut strip from the sheet below. I then place the edge of the second sheet back against the wall. Both edges should butt perfectly since they were cut simultaneously.

I roll the roller over the joint between the two pieces of paper to flatten them and squeeze out any excess paste at their edges.

The cut down the overlap can be done by eye and even if done irregularly, the joint will match. I use the straightedge since I find it just as quick and more convenient.

I install successive sheets along the wall in the same manner until the distance to the corner is less than the width of a sheet. If the distance remaining will create an overlap on the intersecting wall greater than 1/2 inch, it will be very difficult to go around the corner and keep the sheet flat on both walls. If the distance is less than 6 inches or so, I place the sheet with 1/2-inch on the intersecting wall and the balance as an overlap on the last previously installed sheet. I then trim off the excess in the same way as with two ordinary adjoining sheets. If the excess is greater than 6 inches, I do not paste it entirely so that when it is trimmed along the overlap, the surplus piece will be available for use elsewhere.

I paper the remaining walls in the same manner as the first until I need one last sheet to complete the room.

I then measure the distance between the corner and the previously installed sheet. I fold the last sheet in half without making a sharp crease and align the sides. Using the 4-foot level as a straight-edge, I cut the sheet 3 or so inches wider than the measured distance. I apply paste and place the sheet on the wall so that the trimmed side lies in the corner over the 1/2-inch lap made around the corner by the first sheet. I align the trimmed side at the corner joint and cut the excess from the other side in the same manner as any other overlap.

I check all the walls. If a bubble has been left inadvertently, I remove it by slitting with a razor blade, placing fresh paste on the back of the slit paper, then sliding the paper back into place. Since the slit paper is slightly larger than the area it will occupy, each side of the slit should be slid together rather than simply pressed back. I then roll the roller over the slit sides. The papering is completed.

## Painting Rooms

If alternatives have been considered and painting chosen, the surface on which the paint is to be applied must first be prepared. All patches—whether plaster of Paris, spackle, or gypsum plaster and lime—and all new plaster walls must be "sized." Sizing is the act of sealing raw cementatious surfaces with a film to keep the cementatious material from interacting with the paint while providing a satisfactory surface to which the paint can adhere. Shellac or one of many sizing products may be used. Sizing products can be applied with either a roller or sponge mop while a brush is ordinarily used with shellac. At least two coats of size should be applied, allowing several hours for drying between coats and before applying paint. Sizing is cheaper than shellac and a gallon will ordinarily cover about 600 square feet of wall area.

Shellac is about 30 percent more expensive than sizing, but if applied carefully will seal the wall with one coat. It should be thinned with 10 percent denatured alcohol if one coat is projected (15 percent, then 5 percent if two coats will be used) and applied with a brush since thinned shellac runs badly and is less easy to control with a roller or mop. A gallon of shellac when thinned will cover about 500 square feet of wall area.

Although shellac dries to the touch within twenty minutes or so, several hours should be allowed for thorough drying under ordinary climatic conditions before the paint is applied or it will cause the paint to alligator. Such cracks cannot be covered by additional coats of paint. (If this condition is encountered or comes about inadvertently, the alligatored area should be allowed to sit for at least a week, then covered with a 15 percent alcohol-thinned coat of shellac. After allowing it to dry for several more days, new paint should then be applied. This will ordinarily correct the condition. Latex paint is much more susceptible to alligatoring than oil-based paint and the latter should be used in repainting to correct earlier deficiencies.

Paint is essentially a mixture of pigment and vehicle. The vehicle is the liquid substance which carries the pigment and allows it to be spread; the pigment material provides the color. Paint type is usually designated by the vehicle—oil or latex, for example; sometimes, as with red lead, it may be designated by the pigment.

Today most paints use either a latex or an oil vehicle. Latex can be applied directly out of the can without thinning, and water can be used to clean brushes or rollers. Oil-base paints often require thinning with turpentine or mineral spirits, which must also be used for cleaning the applicators. Latex paint has increased in popularity since World War II because it has a shorter drying time than oil-base paint and because it uses water as a solvent. Both latex and oil-base paints have various additives, each of which is designed for a particular purpose, and my choice of paint is dependent upon the particular surface to be covered. When choosing a paint, it should be kept in mind that its price has no relation to its quality. A brand-name paint does not guarantee better quality than a "no-name" paint which is sold at a quarter of the price. I therefore choose the cheapest-priced paint, making certain only that it is the paint type suitable for the job I intend it for. Before the paint is purchased, its consistency should be checked by opening the can. With latex paint, the thicker the consistency, the better it will cover. If the paint moves freely within the can and sloshes about, chances are that it is too diluted and it should not be purchased. With oil-base paint, the separated oil should be at least half an inch deep. After mixing, the consistency should be at least as thick as heavy cream.

I use latex paint for all ceilings, where traffic isn't a problem, since it is the easiest to apply. I apply at least two coats even if I am using white paint to cover a ceiling that is already white.

I use latex paint for all walls except those in the kitchen and bathroom, where a good deal of moisture and traffic can be expected. For those areas I use alkyd paint which is more durable, especially in humid conditions, and which derives its name from the synthetic resins of which it is made. Latex and alkyd paint are available in flat, semi-gloss, and gloss. In general, the greater the sheen, the more durable the paint. I choose which to use on the basis of the amount of use to which a room or wall is likely to be subjected. However, the relative difference in strength between a flat and high-gloss finish is not so great as to preclude a choice based solely on aesthetics. In either case a minimum of two coats should be applied. No undercoat is necessary, and the same paint can be used for both coats. While latex and alkyd paint are quick-drying, at least several hours should be allowed between coats.

In a room where extraordinary use is anticipated, such as a child's room, I use an enamel paint for all walls and woodwork. Enamel paints have varnish vehicles and are much tougher and easier to keep clean than other types. Their exterior surface resists penetration of stain-forming materials and is a good deal more "washable" than other paints. They are available in flat, semi-gloss, and gloss finishes—and again, the greater the sheen, the greater proportion of varnish and the greater the strength of the enamel. However, the relative difference in strength between a flat and gloss is not so great as to preclude the use of flat enamel when extraordinary wear is anticipated.

I use alkyd paint for bathroom and kitchen walls because it produces a relatively tough film and is better resistant than the other paints around humid conditions.

The techniques used to apply latex, oil, and alkyd paints are quite similar—I will indicate the few small differences as they arise.

## Painting a Room with Latex Paint

If feasible, I first remove all furniture from the room. If not, I remove as much as necessary to allow access to all surfaces that will be painted. I cover the remaining furniture and floor with a layer of plastic sheets, then place drop cloths on top of it.

It is substantially more economical to buy paint in 5-gallon containers than in smaller ones. (A gallon of latex paint will ordinarily cover about 400 square feet on the first coat and about 600 square feet on the second.) I purchase 5 gallons, then transfer paint from the 5-gallon container to a gallon can, filling it to within a few inches of the top.

I place a 6-foot aluminum stepladder in a corner with the paint can on its shelf. I stand on a tread so that my head is a few inches below the ceiling. I intend to paint along the joint between the wall and ceiling first, and the more horizontal the surface to be painted is to my eye level, the easier the work will be.

I intend to paint a band a few inches wide at all joints of intersecting walls and ceilings and along the baseboard, since these are areas where roller access is poor. I use a 2-inch-wide nylon brush, which is small enough to manipulate easily but large enough to paint a sufficiently wide band.

I dip it into the paint no deeper than 1-1/2 inches. A greater depth becomes counterproductive, since the additional paint will soon wind up over my hand and the handle. As I raise the brush, I slide the side closest to me against the rim of the can to remove excess paint, thus preventing future drips and runs.

I lay the paint-filled side of the brush against the wall and ceiling joint about 8 or 10 inches in from the corner. The side of the brush, not its tip, is placed against the surface of the joint. Using gentle pressure, I stroke the brush to the corner, then return over the swath and continue past the starting point another 8 to 10 inches before returning to the starting point.

On each subsequent application, I overlap the end of the previous stroke by a couple of inches, since the amount of paint at the end of a stroke is likely to provide insufficient cover. At no time should more than gentle pressure be used to spread the paint. Obviously the paint can be extended further than the 16 to 20 inches I achieve on each stroke, but this so reduces the thickness of the film as to defeat its purpose—to cover the surface. (This is particularly true with latex paints, which when "stretched" lose their ability to cover much more rapidly than oil-base paints.)

I continue around the room painting all surfaces that the roller will not be able to reach.

I then half-fill the roller tray with paint. The roller I use with latex paint is 1/4-inch mohair 9 inches long. (A long-haired roller should be used with oil or alkyd paints.) I attach a 4-foot extension pole to its handle.

I dip the roller into the front of the tray, keeping its arm above paint level, then roll it over the ridges at the back to distribute the paint evenly and remove any excess.

If the paint is not distributed evenly over the roller, bare spots will be left on the surface, requiring additional passes. The paint needed for these passes must come either from adjoining surfaces, which will thin the paint layer over the entire area, or the roller will have to be redipped. In either case additional work will be created.

However, if too much paint is allowed to remain on the roller, it will drip off as the roller is swung toward the surface and will drop off during the pass. In addition, the layer of paint applied will be too thick and will have to be rolled out over a greater distance. Again, this will create needless additional work.

I begin at the ceiling, laying the paint-dipped roller against it lightly. I roll it forward about 3 feet, then backward about 6 feet. I then reposition the roller on the same spot where I first made contact and repeat the same-length stroke at a right angle to the first to form a cross, maintaining the same light pressure throughout. I apply the paint in the same pattern across the entire ceiling, filling one patch at a time and overlaping it several inches with an adjacent patch. I remain in one area until it is awkward for me to reach a new one, then shift the tray and reposition myself.

If I press too hard on the roller, paint will be squeezed toward its sides and two lines of thick paint will remain behind which will have to be rolled flat.

If the roller slides rather than rolls along the surface, I have allowed too much paint to adhere to it. The mohair covering of the roller should be barely visible before the roller leaves the tray. If the thickness of the paint hides the mohair, additional rolling on the ridges of the tray is needed to remove

the excess to a point where the mohair is again visible.

Since this is the first coat, I do not expect a uniformly shaded ceiling. However, the disparity between the light and darker areas should not be too obvious and I can keep it to a minimum by using light uniform pressure throughout the application.

The objective of the first coat is *not* to hide the surface beneath it completely, and an inordinate amount of time can be wasted trying to achieve this. The first coat should entirely cover the ceiling and reduce by about 75 percent the visibility of the surface beneath it. The second coat will hide it completely.

The pace at which the roller is rolled over the ceiling must be *leisurely*. If it is done too quickly, paint will be sprayed over the worker and bubbles will form in the paint, requiring additional rolling.

Inevitably, paint will accumulate on the ends and sides of the roller and should be wiped off with a rag before they begin to drip. Streaking will also occur as lines of relatively thick paint trail behind the roller. Judgment must be used to determine whether the streaks are thick enough to be visible after the second coat. If they are, they should be rolled out lightly while still wet.

If the ceiling is sheetrock and shellac hasn't been used to seal the joint compound, it will take several additional passes over the joint compound to completely hide it. (Oil-base paint will not hide the joint compound at all.) It is therefore best to seal all joint compound using two thinned coats of shellac *before* any paint is applied.

If the ceiling is plaster and neither shellac nor sizing has been used to seal it, the plaster will continue to "bleed" (show through) despite an indefinite number of coats. It too must be sealed by two coats of size or two thinned coats of shellac before paint is applied.

If wooden moldings with knots (or any other wooden surface) are being painted, the knots will continue to show through and must therefore first be sealed with two thinned coats of shellac. (Unsealed knots appear as brown rings in the paint.)

Although latex paints are advertised to dry within an hour or less, they are only dry to the touch. Unless there is an immediate need to apply the second coat, I prefer to do it on the following day. Otherwise, I wait a minimum of three hours.

Before applying the second coat, I cover any area where paint has been rolled out too thinly, then cover it again after applying the second coat.

Once the ceiling has been completed, the walls will be painted in the same manner. Vertical strokes will be used, however, since a horizontal or diagonal stroke is awkward. I complete each vertical stroke with an upward pass and overlap the previous swath by a few inches. Before painting the walls, the window sashes, frame, and trim are painted.

I use alkyd semi-gloss paint for the windows because it produces a tougher and more washable film than latex paint and better resists the effects of moisture.

Alkyd paints are oil-base and thinned with turpentine. A gallon will cover about 350 square feet on the first coat and about 25 percent more on succeeding coats. At least twenty-four hours should be allowed for drying between coats.

To paint a window, I first free both sashes. Using a hook scraper, I remove all loose material from the muntins, sashes, frame, sill, etc. I vacuum the area and go over it with a dry rag. This is the minimum amount of preparation that should be undertaken. If one is willing to spend a couple of hours on each window, all old paint should be removed until the wood is exposed, using the spinner sander or the hook scraper in areas that the sander can't reach.

I mount the paint tray on a ladder tread so that it will be about waist-high while painting lower areas and place it on the ladder shelf when working on areas above my height.

I dip a 2-inch sash brush into the paint to a depth of no more than an inch, since I intend to cover a relatively small area on each application. As I raise the brush, I slide the side which will not lie against the wood along the side of the pan to remove the paint. I lay the side of the brush with paint on it against an upper muntin, the tip angled in the corner.

I press the brush lightly against the wood, positioning the paint-filled side at the joint between the wood and glass and draw the brush down the side of the muntin. Since the bristles of a sash brush are cut at an angle, the longest ones will more readily reach into corners than those of conventional brushes.

Angled end of sash brush

Sash brush at corner of muntin

**245**

"Cutting-in"—painting a straight line along the joint between the wood and glass—takes a little practice, but the time spent learning it will be much less than that wasted by applying masking tape or similar devices on the glass along the joint. If paint inadvertently gets on the glass, it can be wiped off easily while still wet with a thin rag drawn tightly around the end of a 1-inch spackling knife.

If the paint is allowed to dry, it can be scraped off with a razor blade in a holder. If part of a dried blob butts aginst the muntin, a razor cut should be made at the joint so that a ragged edge will not be left when the blob is scraped from the glass.

When first positioning the sash brush, the end carrying paint will be relatively unstable. It is therefore advisable, especially when learning to "cut in," to lean against an unpainted adjacent surface and hold the right wrist with the left hand to stabilize the end of the brush and improve its aim. It is also advisable to initially place the brush a small distance away from the joint. Once the brush is making contact with a surface, its movement is much more easily controlled and it can then be shifted to the joint without hitting the glass. As familiarity with cutting in is acquired, both these steps can be discarded.

The painting sequence I follow is to do the uppermost areas of the window first so that spills and drips can be seen and removed as lower surfaces are encountered. It is also more convenient to paint areas of greatest depth first, then work back. When the reverse is done, the painter no longer has a surface to lean on and must avoid already-painted areas while stretching to paint those of greater depth.

Following this premise, I paint the upper muntins first, then the lower ones. I follow with the sides of the sash, the guides, stops, casing, and finally the window sill.

Since I have freed the sash, I take care not to paint the stops and guides along with the sash, but keep the paint separate from each to avoid freezing the window again after the paint has dried. Unless both sashes operate fully, the lower part of the upper sash will not be possible to paint.

A minimum of two coats (and often a third) will be needed over the windows, since this is usually the first place paint deterioration sets in. (This can be delayed if the outsides of the window are reputtied.)

## Finishing Floors

The steps which are necessary to prepare a wooden floor for refinishing have been detailed in the chapter on Flooring (see pp. 140–153). After they have been completed I am left with a finely sanded smooth surface. The room has been vacuumed to remove all sawdust and the floor mopped with a rag dampened in denatured alcohol to pick up smaller particles left after vacuuming. I am now ready to apply the finish.

During the application of the finish, windows should be shut to keep foreign material from blowing in and lodging on the wet surface.

If there are gaps between or gouges within pieces of flooring, I fill them with a paste made up of fine sawdust and clear epoxy glue. If I intend to stain the floor, I tint the paste with the stain while it is being mixed. I leave the paste higher than the surrounding area, allow several hours for it to dry, then sand it with fine sandpaper on the edger. (If plastic wood or similar products are used as a filler, they will also have to be stained when wet; once the filler has dried, it will not accept the stain.)

The lighter floors are maple and oak without any stain. The darker floor is oak that was tinted with a

Natural 1 × 3 oak refinished with three coats of polyurethane

Oak tinted with walnut stain and covered with three coats of polyurethane

1 × 3 maple, natural, covered with three coats of polyurethane

walnut oil stain. (A gallon of stain will cover approximately 750 square feet of flooring and should be compatible with polyurethane, which will be used for the final finish.)

Test patches are first made to establish the tint desired. I brush the stain on the floor with a cheap 3-inch-wide brush, then immediately wipe it off with a rag. If the result isn't dark enough, I make several other applications, allowing the stain to remain for successively longer periods on each before wiping it off until the desired shade is achieved. (The floor tint becomes darker the longer the stain is allowed to remain.)

Most stains will dry to the touch within a few hours, but the stain should be allowed to dry at least overnight or to the point where none of it will come off when rubbed briskly with a rag.

As an alternative to using stains, products such as Firzite can be used to give the floor a white translucent appearance. It too is applied by brushing and wiping. Since the grain of the wood is more dense than the wood around it and will absorb less of the Firzite, the grain will stand out more and will appear relatively darker than the area around it. A mixture of white oil-base paint and turpentine in equal amounts can be used as a cheap alternative to Firzite.

## Applying Polyurethane with a Roller

Polyurethane can be applied with a 4-inch varnish brush or a short-haired roller. The brush will generally give better results but the roller is much quicker. I use both, the roller (attached to an extension pole) for the main spreading and the brush for removing spatters and drips as well as for reaching areas where it is awkward to use the roller.

I pour the thinned polyurethane in a paint pan to a level that is just below the metal arm at the side of the roller so that the polyurethane will not get on the arm and drip on the floor as I move the roller from the pan to the work area. For the same reason, after dipping the roller I roll it lightly over the ridges at the back of the pan. Unwanted drips of the clear liquid can be easily missed and stepped on.

I start at the corner farthest from the exit and gently swing the roller from the pan to the floor. The liquid is heavy, and if I swing the roller quickly some will fly off at the moment of acceleration and more will be released upon the sudden stop. I therefore use a *leisurely* motion when transferring the polyurethane from the pan to the floor.

I start each stroke about 3 feet from where I intend to end the swath, pushing the roller forward 3 feet, then returning over the swath for a distance of 6 feet, then retracing the last 3 feet back to the starting point. I stroke *with the grain* throughout the entire application.

I roll the roller over the floor using only *light* pressure, a trifle more than that created by the weight of the roller. "Heavy" pressure is a frequent cause of a bad job. When coupled with excessive speed, bubbles become entrapped in the liquid. When they dry and are punctured by normal use, a whitish ring will be left around their edges. There will also be no adhesion between the polyurethane and the floor. A slow, deliberate stroke is mandatory.

If drops of polyurethane are allowed to "dry," the upper surface of the drop will form a crust but the polyurethane within it will remain plastic. When the drop is later walked on the crust will be broken and the semiliquid polyurethane smeared. For this reason, after I complete each patch of floor, I check the surface for drops and roll them out before moving on.

After selecting the stain desired, I apply it to the floor with the cheap 3-inch-wide brush and wipe it off with a rag. The time I allow before wiping it off has been determined on a test patch. I allow the stain to dry fully before proceeding further.

Polyurethane is used to finish all the floors. On the first coat a gallon will cover approximately 350 square feet, on the second 600 square feet, and on the third slightly more.

In purchasing the polyurethane, avoid brand names. Shop around. One manufacturer's product may cost half as much as another's and yet there will be no difference in quality between the two. I have used a great many manufacturers' polyurethane products and have never found a higher-priced product to be superior.

All floors will be given three coats of polyurethane. The life of the floor will be substantially increased with three coats and can be expected to last from seven to ten years.

To increase the penetrative strength of the polyurethane, the first coat is thinned by adding a pint of turpentine to each gallon. It is omitted on successive coats.

I also check the dry floor area between the pan and the patch I have just completed. If there are drops or drips I brush them out. When I position myself to apply the polyurethane, I remain in the same spot until I have finished the patch and dealt with all drips, drops, etc. I thereby avoid grinding my socks into any irregularities as I walk from one position to the next. ((Working without shoes on is an optional precaution against smudges and scuff marks.)

I always stroke with the grain, not because it is necessary but because I can more readily see where I have ended an application and need to begin another. The lines of the floorboards also provide a ready reference for the inch or so of side overlap that I need to make. (Several inches of overlap are necessary at the ends since less polyurethane is laid in those areas.)

It is both unnecessary and undesirable to run the roller over a swath more than one time. One pass with light pressure is sufficient and will leave a proper thickness of film.

As I apply the polyurethane in patches and move farther into the room, some of the polyurethane will begin to dry. After a short while the dry polyurethane will not look uniform because the wood's porosity varies. This is especially true during the first coat. There will also be flat spots without a sheen which appear to lack polyurethane when in fact they do not. (If doubt exists, touch them.) There is no need to go over these areas again.

If the application is being made in cold and wet weather, a minimum of twenty-four hours should be allowed for the polyurethane to dry before the second coat is begun. If the weather is hot and dry, the drying time may be as short as a few hours, but I would still allow it to set at least overnight. To determine the condition of the polyurethane, I pierce the dry-to-the-touch coat with an awl and note if any stickiness remains on the tip.

In any weather, the time needed for drying can be substantially reduced if the temperature in the room is increased.

When the polyurethane has dried, its texture will have a slight but definite roughness as a result of dust and the nap of the wood (small wood fibers that have been drawn erect). Ordinary use will wear away a good deal of this, but it may also cause entry of liquids under the protective surface which will lead to premature erosion. If only one coat is used, the floor will last a couple of years before it evidences significant signs of wear.

If more than one coat is to be applied, most manufacturers recommend fine sanding between coats to insure the bond and to remove any foreign material lodge in the surface of the first coat. When I first began using polyurethane, I undertook fine sanding between coats and obtained the desired result. However, since it meant additional work, I began omitting sanding between coats a good many years ago and I have still obtained the same results. By cleaning the surface of the floor meticulously before applying the first coat and by keeping it clean throughout the application, I discovered that foreign particles became a negligible factor and that sanding could be dispensed with.

However, when sanding between coats is omitted, *it is essential that the polyurethane applied not be allowed to dry for more than twenty-four hours before the succeeding coat is applied.* However, since twenty four hours is too much a variable depending on temperature, humidity, air circulation, etc., I have adopted a standard procedure and apply the second coat twelve hours or so after the first. This has worked under a variety of climatic conditions and with a great many applications. I usually complete the first coat in the early evening, then apply the second coat the following morning.

After twelve hours the floor is not dry enough for heavy use but is dry enough to be walked on. It is also wet enough to bond with the second coat.

If sanding is to be done between coats, I use a steel-wool pad on a rotary buffer which removes the nap and dust and also faintly scars the surface. This scarring is necessary to promote bonding between coats when twenty-four hours or more have elapsed between the coats. If the sanding is omitted, the succeeding coat will hold only intermittently. In places where it has not bonded, the polyurethane will peel away in strips. (The same thing will happen if oil or grease, etc., is accidentally dropped on the floor and not removed.)

The third coat should be applied identically to the second.

Additional coats will be counterproductive.

*No wax or any other "floor product" should be placed on top of the polyurethane.* It needs no maintenance other than dry or damp dust-mopping. It will resist staining by household materials, and spills which have been allowed to dry will usually come away with soap and water. If a material isn't soluble in soap and water, a rag dampened in turpentine will usually remove it, wiping lightly.

Although polyurethane provides a hard and durable surface, it will scratch if something sharp and hard is dragged over it. Scratch marks can be masked by rubbing them with a rag dampened in lemon oil.

Polyurethane, as the final finish for a wood floor, is an excellent material and far superior to any other alternative.

# INDEX

[*Note:* Page numbers in boldface (**138**) refer to locations of photographs.]

# Index

# Index

# Index

# Index

# Index

# Index